Peter Baumgartner | Tina Gruber-Muecke | Richard Sickinger (Editors)

PURSUIT OF PATTERN LANGUAGES FOR SOCIETAL CHANGE

Designing Lively Scenarios
in Various Fields

Editors: Peter Baumgartner, Tina Gruber-Muecke, Richard Sickinger

Book Design, Page Layout and Editorial Staff: Ingrid Muthsam, Wolfgang Rauter

www.purplsoc.org

info@purplsoc.org

Creative Commons Licence CC-BY-ND

creativecommons.org/licenses/by-nd/4.0

Edition Donau-Universität Krems

ISBN Paperback: 978-3-903150-14-0

ISBN eBook: 978-3-903150-15-7

Printed on demand in many countries. Distributed by tredition

Krems, August 2017, 2nd Edition

Every effort has been made to make this book as complete and as accurate as possible, but no warranty or fitness is implied. The information provided ist on an „as is" basis. The authors and the editors/publishers shall have neither liability nor responsibility to any person or entity with respect to any loss or damages arising from the information contained in this book. Responsibility for the information, licencing and views set out in their articles lies entirely with the authors.

Foreword

by Peter Baumgartner, Tina Gruber-Muecke, Richard Sickinger

Introduction: Pattern Languages for Societal Change

This book focuses on the pattern approach established by the Austrian-born Christopher Alexander, architect, mathematician, and philosopher, and collects selected papers on work presented at, or related to the PURPLSOC World Conference held at Danube University Krems, July 3 – 5, 2015. PURPLSOC is the acronym for "In Pursuit of Pattern Languages for Societal Change", a series of (roughly) biennial conferences on patterns in and with disparate fields such as architecture, design, media, arts, IT, management, pedagogy, social activism, social innovation and diverse grassroots movements. PURPLSOC has its origins in the PUARL Conferences held at the University of Oregon in Portland in 2009, 2011, and 2013 (in cooperation with ARUS), and is organized as the 'World Conference on Pattern Languages' at Danube University Krems in Austria in the summer of 2015. Both PUARL and PURPLSOC are organized in a biennial structure, therefore the whole Conference Series has reached a new level of interdisciplinary involvement and a new international format and organization. PURPLSOC is run by a Steering Committee with the help of a larger Advisory Board, which appraises and evaluates the submitted contributions for oral presentation at the Conference and for the inclusion of papers in this book (http://www.purplsoc.org/committee/). Its aim is to substantiate the broad applicability and richness of pattern related work in all fields, and, by sharing best practice examples from outside the scientific community, to further raise awareness of Christopher Alexander`s approach within the wider public. Both conferences contribute to strengthening the pattern movement at Danube University Krems where we hope to establish a university wide interdisciplinary center for Pattern Research in the near future.

The remainder of this foreword is structured as follows. In the following section, we provide a brief review of prior research on pattern languages (PL) in a global context. This review provides a starting point for PURPLSOC readers interested in the topic and wishing to study it in greater depth. We then introduce the papers included in the conference proceedings and summarize briefly how each relates to and extends the existing literature; we also offer broad conclusions based on the collection of papers as a whole. Next, we provide suggestions for future research in this area. Finally, we reflect on the process of the conference proceedings with an outlook toward encouraging and guiding potential future authors of papers on patterns and pattern languages.

Review on Prior Research on Pattern Languages

This section aims to provide the reader with a review of selected prior research on pattern and pattern languages in a global context, with a particular emphasis on the historical development.

Christopher Alexander's interest in patterns and pattern languages originates in his book "Notes on the synthesis of form" (1964) which aims at developing an analytical design process based on mathematics and deductive logic. In the preface of the paperback edition (1971) Alexander distances himself from this idea but remains fascinated by the power of the diagram, or pattern, which he defines as "an abstract pattern of physical relationships which resolves a small system of interacting and conflicting forces, and is independent of all other forces, and of all other possible diagrams". Developing this central idea leads to his renowned book „A Pattern Language" (Alexander, 1977) in which Alexander subsequently defines 253 invariant spatial patterns associated with the stability of human-environmental systems in both towns and buildings. Each pattern sits at the center of a network of associated patterns forming a unique pattern language. For Alexander this creates "a fundamental view of the world. It says that when you build a thing you cannot merely build that thing in isolation, but must also repair the world around it, and within it, so that the larger world at that one place becomes more coherent, and more whole; and the thing which you make takes its place in the web of nature, as you make it." (Alexander, 1977) In "The Timeless Way of Building" (Alexander, 1979), a philosophical introduction and examination of the pattern language concept, Alexander introduces the concept of the „quality without a name" or "being alive" as the central quality of built environment. Ten years after the book was published, Alexander's idea of pattern language for architecture (Pattern Language 1.0) was adopted in the field of software design (Beck & Cunningham, 1987; Gamma, et al., 1995) (Pattern Language 2.0). Since the 1990s, an increasing number of fields pertaining to human action have adopted the methods of pattern language (Pattern Language 3.0) (Coplien & Harrison, 2004; Manns & Rising, 2005; Manns & Rising, 2015; Hoover & Oshineye, 2009). Pattern Writing Techniques have emerged as a research field (e.g. elements of pattern writing for software design, social relationships, and other fields) (Iba, 2014). For Alexander developing and implementing patterns and pattern languages does not only relate to conveying information and solutions but goes further: "However, that is not all that pattern languages are supposed to do: The pattern language that we began creating in the 1970s had other essential features. First, it has a moral component. Second, it has the aim of creating coherence, morphological coherence in the things which are made with it. And third, it is generative: it allows people to create coherence, morally sound objects, and encourages and enables this process because of its emphasis on the coherence of the created whole." (Alexander, 1999). Building on his work on patterns and pattern language Alexander went on to develop a morphogenetic understanding of the formation of the built environment in his four-volume work "The Nature of Order: An Essay on the Art of Building and the Nature of the Universe" (Alexander, 2003).

Papers in the Conference Proceedings

We turn now to the 13 papers accepted for the Conference Proceedings. In each case, we provide a brief synopsis of the paper, together with comments on the linkage and contribution of the paper to the literature discussed above. Concerning the contents of this book, we are proud to remark that the selected papers cover a broad range of topics, including

1. the study of the work of Noam Chomsky, Christopher Alexander and Heinrich Lausberg in the context of framing educational patterns, as in the paper by Aspalter and Bauer.

2. an approach to easing the labor-intensive application of abstract patterns to concrete use cases, as in the paper by Falkenthal et al.

3. pattern language generations and the proposal for a 4th generation pattern language, as in the paper by Finidori et al.

4. the use of pattern language for learning from recurrent design patterns of nature derived from diverse living examples found in great repositories of natural design patterns, as in the paper by Henshaw.

5. a pattern language for dementia which consists of 40 patterns, categorized into three different groups: words for those living with dementia, words for caring families, and words for everyone., as in the paper by Iba et al.

6. a set of 24 behavioral properties that capture "wholeness" in a lively human activity, found through the investigation of pattern languages of human action, as in the paper by Iba et al.

7. an overview of the frontiers of pattern languages, based on the studies of Takashi Iba over the past 10 years, as in the paper by Iba.

8. a cooking language, a new approach to cooking, derived from the idea of pattern languages, as in the paper by Isaku et al.

9. the study of patterns and societal change, developing the theoretical relation between potential attributes of changemakers and Alexander's concept of liveliness with pedagogical approaches, as in the paper by Nakamura and Iba.

10. a pattern language for coastal communities for surviving an earthquake with an accompanying tsunami, as in the paper by Neis and Wright.

11. the possibility of implementing Alexander's System A, of generating beauty and life in the world, at the large scale of a city, as in the paper by Porta et al.

12. the contention that the relationship between Alexander's System A and System B can be understood as complementary, and not as a contradiction, demonstrated through the case of Unrecognized Bedouin Villages that are located in the Negev drylands of Israel, as in the paper by Rosner-Manor and Rofè.

13. the utilization of a key attribute of patterns, combined with storytelling, to ensure emotional engagement and therefore a high rate of implementation of patterns, as in the paper by Sickinger.

Some broad conclusions can be proposed based on the research contributions of the papers in this book and the prior literature.

» Each paper in the conference proceedings shows that consequences emerge from a complex set of processes over a significant period of time, involving a wide range of actors and institutions.

» Pattern languages do not have a simple deterministic impact on development. Like other instances of pattern languages being applied to complex social issues, outcomes are not only determined by technology. Social influences are crucially important to the trajectory of any technology-based project.

» The mutual influence between pattern languages and social processes can result in solutions that work relatively well.

» Applying Pattern languages to social change requires an understanding of local meanings, existing work practices, and institutional contexts, as well as a willingness to engage with the dynamics of socio-technical change over time.

Future Research Directions

We hope that the papers included in this book will help to point the way forward to future research efforts on pattern languages that will be both rigorous and relevant to the most pressing concerns related to societal change. Our foremost interest in the area of future research is the rapid expansion of research on pattern languages and societal change. In this section, we provide some additional dimensions for expanding future work, discuss theoretical and methodological issues and identify qualified literature for research in developing countries.

Dimensions for Expansion

We want to outline some dimensions for the possible expansion of the research provided in this book.

First, future research is needed to provide a wider geographical spread. As a second dimension it would also be good to see more research on the institutional context. An example for this could be educational institutions or nongovernmental institutions as they both are challenged with searches for educational problems for our society. A third dimension of expansion concerns the study of pattern culture and language development. Fourthly work in the area of pattern communication is needed to ensure the use and implementation of pattern languages. Fifthly the developments of pattern renewal processes are important to ensure that patterns are being improved and are up to date.

Topics for Future Work

It is impossible in this short introductory paper to provide a detailed preview of potential future research topics, since the scope of such work is very wide indeed. Instead, we will mention a few important areas for future work which have been somewhat neglected to date. Further research is needed in this domain to better understand notions of culture, and to investigate the role of patterns in society in a wider variety of regional and national contexts.

Within the educational context, on topic could be learning patterns, but also patterns of identifying non-formal and informal learning. Within the artistic context, topics could be a pattern language for films based on costumes, settings and music in films. Within the organizational context, topics could be collaboration patterns, presentation patterns and change making patterns. An interesting question could also be to analyse organisations with regard to growth and identify underlying patterns of growth

Theoretical and Methodological Issues

We welcome the theoretical diversity which reflects the enormous variety of the topics being studied in terms of research issue, level of analysis, sectoral context, and cultural location. We would suggest, however, that there is a need for more studies to be explicitly critical, in the academic sense of that term, and to draw on appropriate critical theories to support research objectives.

With respect to methodology, much of the current literature on pattern languages uses case studies and broadly interpretive research methods. We would also like to see more action research studies and works on the methodology of pattern mining. There are surprisingly few reported in the literature on pattern languages for societal change. Action research would appear to be particularly relevant in contexts where resources are scarce, when it can be argued that outside researchers should not only go away with data for their academic papers, but should also aim to make a contribution in the research setting itself.

Connection to Other Literature

The field of pattern languages has always drawn on literature from other related fields, for example economics and organization studies. We would like to see synergies between patterns, pattern languages, and other research fields better developed in the future.

Acknowledgments

We end this introductory paper with some reflections on the process of editing the book. We believe that the selected papers are immensely important for the corresponding areas of interests and that they will be frequently quoted and consulted in the years to come. The editors would like to thank all the authors who have submitted their precious manuscripts to this conference and to ask for their understanding for our possible mistakes. Moreover, we would like to thank George Platts as the game master of the PURPLSOC 2015 conference as well as the whole audience for their active participation, great enthusiasm and spirit.

Our thanks also go to the many anonymous reviewers, who have worked so devotedly under our severe constraints. We would also like to thank all the reviewers, too many to mention by name, who responded to our requests for reviews in a professional and timely way. This book bears the name of the editors, but hidden referees would merit, in many cases, to be credited as well for so many freely given suggestions, generous improvements and detailed corrections.

We would like to thank the Department of Interactive Media and Educational Technologies at Danube University Krems for the administrative support, and in particular Ingrid Muthsam and Wolfgang Rauter who handled the high volumes of work associated with the conference proceedings.

Dear reader, we hope you enjoy this book.

Peter Baumgartner
peter.baumgartner@donau-uni.ac.at

Tina Gruber-Muecke
tina.gruber-muecke@donau-uni.ac.at

Richard Sickinger
richard.sickinger@donau-uni.ac.at

References

Alexander, C. (1964). Notes on the synthesis of form. Cambridge: Harvard University Press.

Alexander, C., Ishikawa, S., & Silverstein, M. (1977). A pattern language: towns, buildings, construction. New York: Oxford University Press.

Alexander, C. (1979) The Timeless Way of Building, Oxford University Press.

Alexander, C. (1999). The Origins of Pattern Theory: The Future of the Theory, and the Generation of a Living World. IEEE Software, 16(5), 71–82. doi:10.1109/52.795104. Lecture at the 1996 ACM Conference on Object-Oriented Programs, Systems, Languages and Applications (OOPSLA)

Alexander, C. (2003). The nature of order: an essay on the art of building and the nature of the universe (Vols. 1–4). Berkeley, California: Center for Environmental Structure.

Beck, K. and Cunningham, W. (1987) 'Using Pattern Languages for Object-oriented Programs', OOPSLA-87 Workshop on the Specification and Design for Object-Oriented Programming.

Coplien, J. (1999) "A Pattern Language for Writers' Workshops," in Harrison, N., Foote, B., Rohnert, H. (eds), Pattern Languages of Program Design 4, Addison-Welsey Professional.

Coplien, J.O., Harrison, N.B. (2004) Organizational Patterns of Agile Software Development, Prentice Hall.

DeLano, D.E. (1998) 'Patterns mining,' in Rising, L. (Ed.): The Patterns Handbook: Techniques, Strategies, and Applications, Cambridge University Press.

Gamma, E., Helm, R., Johnson, R. and Vlissides, J. (1994) Design Patterns: Elements of Reusable Object-Oriented Software, Addison-Wesley.

Hoover, D. and Oshineye, A. (2009) Apprenticeship Patterns: Guidance for the Aspiring Software Craftsman, O'Reilly Media.

Iba, T., (2014) A Journey on the Way to Pattern Writing: Designing the Pattern Writing Sheet. PLoP 2014 proceedings.

Manns, M.L. and Rising, L. (2005), Fearless Change: Patterns for Introducing New Ideas, Addison-Wesley.

Manns, M.L. and Rising, L. (2015) More Fearless Change: Strategies for Making Your Ideas Happen, Addison-Wesley Professional.

Contents

From Noam Chomsky and Christopher Alexander to Heinrich Lausberg: Rhetorical Framing for Pattern Analysis — 22
Aspalter, Christian | Bauer, Reinhard

Leveraging Pattern Applications via Pattern Refinement — 38
Falkenthal, Michael | Barzen, Johanna | Breitenbücher, Uwe | Fehling, Christoph | Leymann, Frank | Hadjakos, Aristotelis | Hentschel, Frank | Schulze, Heizo

Towards a Fourth Generation Pattern Language: Patterns as Epistemic Threads for Systemic Orientation — 62
Finidori, Helene | Borghini, Sayfan G. | Henfrey, Thomas

Guiding Patterns of Naturally Occurring Design: Elements — 88
Henshaw, Jessie Lydia

Words for a Journey: A Pattern Language for Living Well with Dementia — 152
Iba, Takashi | Kaneko, Tomoki | Kamada, Arisa | Tamaki, Nao | Okada, Makoto

The Fundamental Behavioral Properties — 178
Iba, Takashi | Kimura, Norihiko | Akado, Yuma | Honda, Takuya

Pattern Language 3.0 and Fundamental Behavioral Properties — 200
Iba, Takashi

The Cooking Language: Applying the Theory of Patterns into Cooking
Isaku, Taichi | Kubonaga, Emi | Iba, Takashi

234

Fostering Changemakers with Change Making Patterns: A Conceptual Framework for Social Change and Its Educational Applications
Nakamura, Sumire | Iba, Takashi

250

Survival Pattern Language: A Wayfinding Escape Pattern Language for Surviving an Earthquake with an Accompanying Tsunami
Neis, Hajo | Wright, Perrin

270

The Production of Cities: Christopher Alexander and the problem of "System A" at large scale
Porta, Sergio | Rofè, Yodan | Vidoli, Mariapia

296

Combining systems A and B: Creating a Pattern Language for the Unrecognized Bedouin Villages in the Negev, Israel
Rosner-Manor, Yaara | Rofè, Yodan

326

Patterns that Emotionally Engage - The Application of Storytelling for the Implementation of Pattern Languages
Sickinger, Richard

354

About the Authors

Yuma Akado is a student who belongs to the Faculty of Policy Management in Keio University. While she studies under professor Takashi Iba on Pattern Languages of human activities, she has been creating patterns, and organizing workshops. She is one of the members from Generative Beauty Project, which conducted pattern-mining workshops in Japan, Korea, and the US, aiming to open up, and involve more people into the process of creating pattern languages. She has also created Cooking Patterns, a pattern language on cooking.

Christian ASPALTER is professor at the University College of Teacher Education in Vienna (PHW) and lecturer in teaching methodology at the University of Vienna, Austria. He is Head of the 'Centre for Didactics of Text- and Information Literacies' and project leader of the national reading plan ÖRLP ('Austrian Reading Framework'). His current work focuses on topics related to reading and writing in a digital context, information literacy, general didactics and rhetoric pattern analysis.

Johanna BARZEN studied media science, musicology and phonetics at the University of Cologne and gained first practical experience while working for some major television channels like WDR and RTL. Next to this she studied costume design at the ifs (international film school Cologne) and worked in several film productions in the costume department in different roles. Currently she is Ph.D. student at the University of Cologne and research staff member at the Institute of Architecture of Application Systems (IAAS) at the University of Stuttgart doing research on vestimentary communication in films.

Reinhard BAUER graduated in Romance Studies and German. After a one-year period as a foreign language assistant in Spain, he worked as a language teacher in secondary vocational education, contributed to various Spanish textbooks and lectured on the Didactics of Spanish as a Foreign Language at the University of Vienna. He completed a postgraduate Master's degree in eEducation at Danube University Krems, where he worked as a staff member researching e portfolios and educational patterns. He received his PhD from Alpen-Adria Universität Klagenfurt in 2014. Currently he is professor and researcher at the University College of Teacher Education Vienna.

Peter BAUMGARTNER is a full Professor for Technology Enhanced Learning and Multimedia at Danube University Krems. He graduated in sociology and did his habilitation thesis on "Background Knowledge – Groundwork for a Critique of Computational Reason". His recent research focuses on Higher Education didactics, theories of teaching and learning, e-Education and distance education, e-Learning implementation strategies and the evaluation of learning environments. He has been key speaker at various TEL conferences and has published 8 books and over 120 articles.

Sayfan G. BORGHINI is currently a Lecturer at the Master in Integrated Design, and Responsible for Business and Collaboration Dev. of AIH – Academic Innovation Center – at the Holon Institute of Technology, Israel. Graduated as a doctor in Physics at the University of Rome, she leverages her background to maintain an up to date dialogue among science, technology and design. Her interest focuses on the application of complexity theories at the intersection of social and technological forces, among her projects: stigmergy applied to social environments, mapping of generative systems, biomimicry for social innovation.

Uwe BREITENBÜCHER is a research associate and Ph.D. student at the Institute of Architecture of Application Systems (IAAS) at the University of Stuttgart, Germany. His research vision is to ease the provisioning and management of cloud applications by automating management patterns. Uwe received a diploma in software engineering from the University of Stuttgart.

Michael FALKENTHAL is a research associate and Ph.D. student at the Institute of Architecture of Application Systems (IAAS) at the University of Stuttgart, Germany. He studied business information technology at the Universities of Applied Sciences in Esslingen and Reutlingen focusing on business process management, services computing and enterprise architecture management. Michael gained experience in several IT transformation and migration projects at small- to big-sized companies. His current research interests are fundamentals on pattern language theory as well as cloud computing.

Christoph FEHLING is a research associate and Ph.D. student at the Institute of Architecture of Application Systems (IAAS) at the University of Stuttgart, Germany. His research interests include IT architecture patterns focused especially on cloud computing. Christoph received a Dipl.-Inf. in computer science from the University of Stuttgart. He is a member of the Hillside Group and author of the book „Cloud Computing Patterns" (Springer, 2014).

About the Authors

Helene FINIDORI has a background in business strategy, branding and organizational development. She is a Senior Research Fellow at the Schumacher Institute, a PhD student at the Centre for Systems Studies - Business School, at the University of Hull and until recently she taught Management and Leadership of Change in the International Program of Staffordshire University. She is mainly interested in social change and systemic perspectives. Her focus is on the development of tools and approaches for transformative action, and in particular those connecting dots and building bridges between people, organizations, cultures, disciplines, types of knowledges and languages.

Tina GRUBER-MUECKE is the head of the Educational Technology Research Center at Danube University Krems. Before she was full professor for Organisational Learning at the University of Applied Sciences Upper Austria (School of Informatics, Communication and Media). She finished her PhD in Social and Economic Sciences with a focus on learning during Internationalization processes. Her recent research focuses on Entrepreneurship Education and Work Based learning as well as collaborative team learning processes. She has published articles in leading business management journals, such as the Journal of Business Economics, the International Journal of Emerging Markets and teaches Corporate Learning as well as Innovation and Change Management at several Universities of Applied Sciences.

Aristotelis HADJAKOS is Professor for Music Informatics at the University of Music Detmold, Germany. He is the head of the Center of Music and Film Informatics, a joint institution of the University of Music Detmold and the University of Applied Sciences OWL, Lemgo. He is conducting research on Human-Computer-Interaction in the area of music and media. His research interests include Digital Humanities in music and film, sensor-based music interfaces and interactivity in music scores.

Thomas HENFREY is Senior Researcher at the Schumacher Institute and a Research Fellow on the EU-funded BASE Project (Bottom-up Climate Adaptation) at Lisbon University. A transdisciplinary scholar and active sustainability practitioner, he has degrees in the natural and social sciences and professional training in solar power installation, permaculture design and shamanic healing. He coordinated development of the Pattern Language for Transition Research, a collaboration between researchers from several UK universities and practitioners from the Transition and Permaculture movements.

Jessie HENSHAW began her study of new ways to combine systems principles of physics (laws of control) with architecture (design of services) some 40 years ago, with recognizing both as views of the same world natural systems. Her research on innate patterns found in individual natural whole systems, led to many important findings about their system designs and transformations for fields of science and policy. Her methods also provide much better ways of discussing and accounting for their origins, growth and change as organizational development and adaptive learning.

Frank HENTSCHEL is a full Professor of Musicology at the University of Cologne. He studied musicology, philosophy and German literature in Cologne and London. He received his Ph.D. in musicology in 1999 in Cologne and his habilitation in 2006 in Berlin (Free University). He spent one year at Harvard University Cambridge with a Feodor Lynen fellowship in 2004/2005 and was Professor at the Universities of Jena and Giessen. His recent work focuses on film music and the history of emotions.

Takuya HONDA is a graduate from the Faculty of Policy Management, Keio University, Japan. He researches a methodology for the creation of pattern languages for enhancing organizational creativity. He made some pattern languages on human actions, including collaboration, and education. He is currently working on the practice of creating pattern languages with employees from Japanese companies.

Takashi IBA is an associate professor in the Faculty of Policy Management and the Graduate School of Media and Governance at Keio University. He received a Ph.D. in Media and Governance from Keio University. He is a board member of The Hillside Group, which promotes pattern languages. Collaborating with his students, he authored Learning Patterns (2014), Presentation Patterns (2014), Collaboration Patterns (2014), Words for a Journey (2015), and also many books in Japanese such as the bestselling Introduction to Complex Systems (1998), Social Systems Theory (2011), and Pattern Language (2013).

Taichi ISAKU is a student at Keio University, Japan. His studies are centered around the creative process in people, and uses Patten Languages as a tool to scribe out the practical knowledge involved in people's creative acts. He is especially working on ways to enhance people's creativity through cooking, and is applying the theory of patterns into the new area. His past works with patterns include the Collaboration Patterns (2012), Global Life Patterns (2013), Generative Cooking Patterns (2014), CoCooking Patterns (2014), The Cooking Language(2015), and the Parenting Patterns (2015).

Tomoki KANEKO is an undergraduate student in the Faculty of Environment and Information Studies at Keio University. He is researching a methodology for the creation of pattern language for enhancing creativity. He is a member of the Dementia-Friendly Japan Initiative, a cross-sector network that reassesses issues related to dementia as issues of social design, and is one of co-authors of Words for a Journey (2015).

Arisa KAMADA is a graduate student in the Graduate School of Media and Governance at Keio University and model for a fashion magazine. She graduated from Keio University with a Bachelor of Arts in Policy Management. She created Personal Culture Patterns, a pattern language for supporting youth in creating active, engaged lives, and facilitated many workshops such as the Self-Travel Cafe. Ms. Kamada is one of co-authors of Collaboration Patterns (2014) and Words for a Journey (2015).

Norihiko KIMURA is a student who belongs to the Faculty of Policy Management in Keio University. He is a member of professor Takashi Iba's laboratory. He researches on pattern applications and developed „The 4th Place," a web service using a pattern language. Papers on this system have been published in Asian PLoP 2014 and PLoP 2014. He is currently working on Student Build Campus Project, which is a new campus-planning project of Keio University, making pattern languages for this project.

Emi KUBONAGA is a BA graduate of Keio University who has a strong passion for fashion and technology. She is also an experienced fashion photographer, a start-up CEO, and a radio show anchor. Her academic work includes the Cooking Language (2015) and the Parenting Patterns (2015).

Frank LEYMANN is a full professor of computer science and director of the Institute of Architecture of Application Systems (IAAS) at the University of Stuttgart, Germany. His research interests include service-oriented architectures and associated middleware, workflow- and business process management, cloud computing and associated systems management aspects, and patterns. Frank is co-author of more than 300 peer-reviewed papers, more than 40 patents, and several industry standards. He is on the Palsberg list of Computer Scientists with highest h-index.

Sumire NAKAMURA is a researcher at Keio Research Institute at SFC. She graduated Keio University with a Bachelor of Arts in Policy Management, receiving the SFC Graduation Project Award. As one of the founders of Change Making Project, she has facilitated social entrepreneurship among youth through educational programs in Japan and in the Philippines. Sumire has also been engaged in international development projects in Israel, India, and Cambodia for spreading awareness on social issues in Japan. She is one of co-authors of Change Making Patterns (2015) and Collaboration Patterns (2014).

Hajo NEIS is director of Portland Architecture Programs University of Oregon, and of Research Labs PUARL and CIU. Professor Neis teaches architecture design and urban theory. He previously taught at the University of California, FH Frankfurt, Prince of Wales UDTF, Dresden TU, Duisburg-Essen, and Meiji University Tokyo. His main interest in research and design include the question of quality and value in architecture and urban structure and the question of process and sequence. He works together with Chris Alexander (CES) and also heads his own architecture office (HNA), with projects in the US, Japan, and Germany. Dr. Neis has published in English, German, Japanese, Spanish and Greek Journals, and he is also a co-author of several books.

Makoto OKADA is a senior manager in charge of management of technology (MOT) in the R&D Strategy and Planning Office, Fujitsu Laboratories, Ltd.; a visiting research fellow in the Center for Global Communications, International University of Japan; and a Senior Researchers in Keio Research Institute at SFC. He is also a founder member and the current co-director of the Dementia-Friendly Japan Initiative and an advisory board member for the Dementia Friendship Club. He is a co-editor of Words for a Journey (2015).

Sergio PORTA is full Professor of Urban Design and Director of UDSU (Urban Design Studies Unit) at the Department of Architecture of the University of Strathclyde in Glasgow, UK. His recent research is on various aspects of Sustainable Urban Design, including: spatial networks analysis, urban morphology and evolution, masterplanning for change, community design, construction and therapy. He has published over forty papers on international peer-reviewed journals and sits on the editorial boards of three leading journals in urbanism and science.

Yodan ROFÈ is a senior lecturer of Urban Planning and Design at the Switzerland Institute for Dryland Environmental and Energy Research, and the Department of Geography and Environmental Development, Ben-Gurion University of the Negev. His recent research is on understanding the pattern language of informal settlements of the Negev Bedouin, in order to improve planning for their formalization and development; modeling accessibility and equity in metropolitan areas; and modeling pedestrian movement and safety in urban areas. He published The Boulevard Book with Allan Jacobs and Elizabeth Macdonald.

Ya'ara ROSNER-MANOR is a PHD student at the Albert Katz International School for Desert Studies, Ben-Gurion University of the Negev. Ya'ara is also an architect and an urban planner working as part of a planning staff, who is dealing in the possibility of regulating the Unrecognized Bedouin Villages by the state of Israel. The work presented here is based, partly, on data and analysis that were made in the office of Arch. Ari Cohen, in the framework of checking possibility of regulating the Unrecognized settlements.

About the Authors

Heizo SCHULZE is full Professor for Audiovisual Design at the faculty Media Production at the University of Applied Sciences, Lemgo, Germany. He graduated in Design for Electronic Media. His recent work and research focuses to combine traditional linear media (e.g. film) with the latest interactive and mobile options. He published various essays, papers, linear and nonlinear works, such as films, videos, installations and apps. He is a member of the internal research group Perception Lab and of the Center of Music and Film Informatics, a joint institution with the University of Music Detmold.

Richard SICKINGER is head of the Special Field for Conceptual Architecture at the Department for Building and Environment at Danube University. He graduated in architecture and is currently working on his thesis "The Concept of Coherence in the work of Christopher Alexander". His recent research focuses on sustainable building design and pattern language.

Nao TAMAKI is a student in the Faculty of Policy Management at Keio University in Japan. She is researching a methodology for the creation of pattern language for enhancing creativity. She has created many pattern languages concerning human actions, including Global Life Patterns. She is one of the co-authors of Words for a Journey (2015).

Mariapia VIDOLI is PhD student at the University of Strathclyde of Glasgow. She graduated in Philosofy with a thesis on "The man in Ernest Cassirer. An active metahaphysics". Her research sits in the area of movement and therapy as applied to cases of live-build construction in education and profession. Her work aims at building on Christopher Alexander's legacy in a "Costruction & Therapy" perspective. She is co-author of "Construction and Therapy: an integrated approach to design build", a paper presented at the ACSA Conference in Halifax, NS, Dalhousie University, in October 2014.

Perrin WRIGHT holds a Professional degree in Architecture with a minor in business administration from the University of Oregon. He had the opportunity to diversify his education, gaining a wide range of skills and experience. Some of his alternate focuses included construction techniques & management, regenerative design, and sustainable design. He is currently working as a project assistant for a developer in Portland on a series of multi-unit residential projects. Perrin is interested in systems thinking and discovering ways to initiate changes to complex socio-ecological systems through resiliency and adaptive processes.

From Noam Chomsky and Christopher Alexander to Heinrich Lausberg: Rhetorical Framing for Pattern Analysis

Aspalter, Christian
University College of Teacher Education Vienna, Austria
christian.aspalter@phwien.ac.at

Bauer, Reinhard
University College of Teacher Education Vienna, Austria
reinhard.bauer@phwien.ac.at

Describing living languages from a universalistic point of view is rather challenging. Building a system of pattern is one possible way to work out a consistent theory for diverse disciplines and various fields similar to a universalistic approach for languages. Because of that, this paper looks at the work of Noam Chomsky, Christopher Alexander and Heinrich Lausberg in the context of framing educational patterns. It focuses especially on mutual parallels and dissimilarities of their search for systematization, for universals or generalized postulates, in order to provide a first draft of the model of Rhetorical Pattern Analysis (RPA). Finally, this article works out the difference between traditional pattern analysis and the RPA by giving an example of appliance in the field of education (First Encounter). It can be said that the RPA-model has the advantage of being a smart tool for analysing educational situations and for planning them.

Education; Educational Patterns; Pattern Analysis; Pattern Language; Rhetoric; Theory of Universal Grammar

1. Introduction

Within the educational context, pattern analysis searches for universal patterns that provide solutions for educational problems as well as universal assistance with learning and teaching in general. So this approach can be compared well with the efforts in linguistics that, according to Chomsky, aim at making language accessible by linguistic universals (cf. Bauer, 2013). This universalistic focus on pattern analysis also forms the basis of Christopher Alexander's approach that attempts to derive linguistic universals in architecture from a highly stable basis (one may even be tempted to think of a pattern ontology) of natural phenomena (cf. Alexander, 1984, particularly pp. 14-16). The universalistic approach of pattern analysis against the background of Chomsky and Lausberg is still overstrained with the variability of its application (pragmatics). To solve this theoretical problem we have to focus on the pragmatic aspect of pattern analysis itself. But where can a solid theoretical background for systematisation of pragmatic aspects of language be found? The anticipated answer is within the tradition of rhetoric.

Therefore this article provides an introduction and a brief overview of a possible way to frame educational patterns by relying on rhetorical scholarship. We focus on the following research questions by using rhetoric, the ancient art of argumentation and discourse as an analytic lens:

1. What can be derived from the works of Noam Chomsky, Christopher Alexander, and Heinrich Lausberg for understanding and framing a concept of educational patterns?
2. What are the main issues concerning a model of Rhetorical Pattern Analysis (= RPA) in the field of education?

In what follows we are going to present Chomsky, Alexander and Lausberg's core ideas with regard to (educational) patterns. Based on this, we are going to point out our first steps towards a rhetoric of educational patterns, describe the nature and extent of our RPA model and give an example of appliance.

2. Theoretical Fundamentals

2.1 Noam Chomsky and the Theory of Universal Grammar

"What do natural languages have in common?" - is the first question that arises when we are thinking about linguistic universals. Despite the fact that languages are different from each other - pronunciation, word order, case forms, etc. - they still have much in common.

For instance, almost all languages have sentences that consist of words. Figure 1 illustrates the structure of such a common language starting from the morpheme level. In the present case, our main focus lies on the sentence level, even though the text level is the highest one.

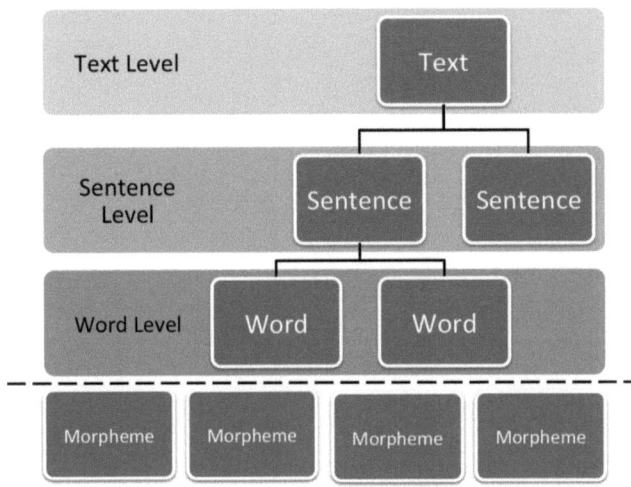

Figure 1. Simple structure of a common language, starting from the morpheme level (cf. Bauer, 2013, p. 131)

"Why do languages have so many things in common?" - is the second question to be addressed. For non-linguists, grammar is merely a set of structural rules that enable people to make a sentence with a couple of words and finally, to generate a coherent text out of different sentences. They assume that people acquire this ability by simply imitating, listening to and repeating others. For linguists like Noam Chomsky, however, grammar is a theory that (ideal) speakers-hearers of a certain language possess implicitly, intuitively, and automatically. Using this theory of an innate "universal grammar", speakers-hearers are able to distinguish between correct and erroneous sentences and they are able to form any number of new and correct sentences from a limited repertoire of linguistic means, i. e. words. With this in mind, it is quite easy to understand the meaning of "generative grammar": It is because of generative grammar that we say "Sincerity may frighten the boy" rather than "Sincerity frighten may boy the" (cf. Chomsky, 1964, p. 76).

As for utterance production, it is important to note that a sentence is much more than the sum of its words. A sentence only gains its meaning according to the relationship between the words forming it. In general, three types of relationships can be distinguished: *syntagmatic* (concerning positioning), *paradigmatic* (concerning substitution), and *semantic* (concerning the meanings of words). The same applies to educational patterns. The pattern language "SEMINARS" (Fricke & Völter, 2000), for instance, might be an appropriate example for it.

"SEMINARS" has the same structure as a common natural language (cf. Figure 2):

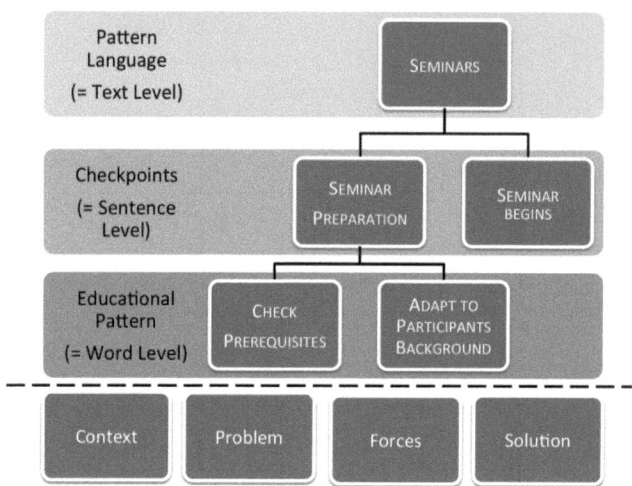

Figure 2. Structure of pattern language SEMINARS (cf. Bauer, 2013, p. 143)

At sentence level, the text level (= "Seminars") splits up into so-called checkpoints such as "Seminar Preparation", "Seminar Begins", and, at the word level, into educational patterns like "Check Prerequisites", "Adapt Participants' Background" which comprise the basic pattern structure "Context", "Problem", "Forces", and "Solution". The individual patterns are syntagmatically, paradigmatically and semantically interrelated.

2.2 Christopher Alexander and the Nature of Order

Seamon (2007) provides a very concise overview of the basic principles of Christopher Alexander's four-volume work "The Nature of Order":

> [It] can be understood as his effort to incorporate life-evoking geometry and step-by-step construction into a process of making that sustains environmental and place well being. To deal with the matter of geometry, he identifies a set of fifteen geometric properties […] that he claims recur in all things, buildings, places, and situations sustaining wholeness and life. To deal with the matter of step-by-step design and construction, he develops a method of making whereby each step in the process becomes a pointer for what is to come next through the recognition, guided in part by the fifteen principles, of creating more and more

centeredness, density, order, and life. His means toward this end is ten structure-enhancing actions that he claims potentially intensify the life and wholeness of the thing made [...]. (Seamon, 2007, [pp. 4 et seq.])

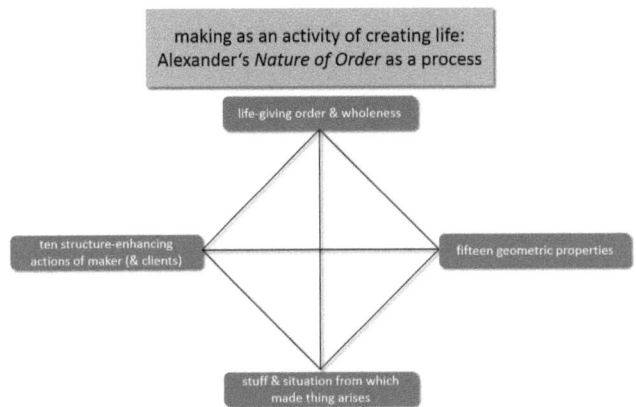

Figure 3. Basic principles of Alexander's "The Nature of Order" (cf. Seamon, 2007, [p. 6])

Against this background, more or less successful attempts have been made to transfer Alexander's pattern approach into pedagogy and education in the past few years (cf. Bauer, 2014, 2013; Bauer & Baumgartner 2012, 2010; Bergin, 2012; Iba, 2014; Kohls & Wedekind, 2011, to name but a few). However, an overall framework and general principles for educational pattern analysis are still missing.

Bauer and Baumgartner (2010), for instance, investigated the potential of Christopher Alexander's fifteen properties of living centers (cf. Alexander, 2004, pp. 143-242) as a foundation and starting point for the analysis and classification of different stocks of educational scenarios, the "phrases" in a system of pedagogical patterns. In their perception, the lack of an agreed educational taxonomy and a common educational language related thereto are based on some misunderstandings: while defining educational scenarios different didactical levels (i.e. micro, meso and macro level) are usually confounded and, with regard to taxonomies, the importance of a holistic approach is usually forgotten. They underline that in the field of education there are very divergent views:

> *This is all the more important when working with (very abstract) didactic models. The more general you get, the less specific (and arbitrary) it becomes [...] The classical abstraction tries to find the "unity in multiplicity", with the result that multiplicity gets lost. Traditional educational models reduce and thus lose the real multiplicity of teaching processes. (Bauer & Baumgartner 2010, pp. 1 et seq.)*

In his doctoral thesis on educational patterns, Bauer (2014) dealt with the same issue. He identified the need for exploring a unified educational model that enables and facilitates the embedding of and the work with educational patterns.

According to these findings and Gesche Joost's (2007) attempt to apply Alexander's pattern approach in combination with rhetorical scholarship for the analysis of film, we assume that it is possible to do the same in the field of education. We argue that our model of Rhetorical Pattern Analysis (= RPA) could be very helpful for both the description of potential educational patterns and the analysis of already existing and defined educational patterns.

2.3 Heinrich Lausberg and his Ars Rhetorica

As we have seen so far both Chomsky and Alexander tried to derive a universal and thereby stable system of language. In the content of educational patterns such stable constructions are always confronted by the act of teaching. Teaching opens a huge variety of concrete possibilities for using (language) universals/patterns. This wide variety is evoked by interaction. Therefore we have to look for an option to systemize this "language in action". As a result, we have to focus first on pragmatic aspects of this teaching language which is always an intentional language because it is effect-oriented.

Linguistic analysis that is primarily oriented on the effect of its application, i.e. the pragmatic aspect of language, can be found in the tradition or rhetoric (cf. Aristoteles, 1995). The starting point of a formative language development and language application is always the concrete objective of a linguistic action. What we have to give up when using this theory is that something in (this) language is invariable or natural.

Rhetoric has been an artificial system from its beginning on. The orator has to construct his speech very carefully for a certain purpose. His speech is always a masterpiece of design. That is why it is part of the ancient "arte":

1. An ordered process that strives for perfection can occur naturally (φύσις [physis] = naturā), thereby corresponding to the natural course of events (e.g. the growth of a tree). If it fails to correspond to the natural course of events it can still occur by chance (τύχη [tyche] = casu) or by means of the deliberate action (τέχνη [téchne] = arte) of a rational creature (human being) […].

3. Therefore, an ars (τέχνη) is a system of instructive rules, gained through experience (εμπειρία) but subsequently thought-through logically, for the correct implementation of a perfection-oriented repeatable action that does not belong to the naturally inevitable course of events and should not be left to chance […].

> 4. Every ars [...] can be taught (doctrina, "instruction") and learned [...] by communication of the rules [...] of ars in question [...]. (Lausberg, 1998, pp. 1 et seq.)

In this context some important references to nature (e.g. the 'ethos' of the speaker) remain within rhetoric, but as a system 'of the deliberate action' this order of language is no longer natural, it is artificial. It is the result of a virtuoso construction work that is designed for a concrete moment in time and space with a concrete intention of a speaker and the presence of a concrete audience.

3. The RPA-Model

In order to design an initial footprint of RPA we first have to look at the shape of the rhetoric system. From a bird's eye view we can see core principles of structuring persuasive language linked to main question each (cf. Göttert, 1994, pp. 15-74):

1. The three "genera orationis" (cf. Lausberg, 1998, pp. 62-111) - What is the pragmatic purpose of the speech in general?
2. The "status orationis" and its four possibilities of questioning (cf. Lausberg, 1998, pp. 42-61) - What is the speaker's general position in relation to the matter of speaking?
3. The "officia oratoris" - the three tasks of the speaker (cf. Lausberg, 1998, pp. 151-155) - What main strategy of speaking helps me to reach the goal of my speech?
4. The five "partes artis" - inventio, dispositio, elocutio, memoria, actio (cf. Lausberg, 1998, pp.112-480) - How does the speaker have to find, construct, narrate and present her/his speech in detail?

The discussion about rhetoric is mainly reduced to only one part of the five "partes artis", to the "elocutio" and its system of analysing and developing the "ornatus". Here we can find all the definitions of rhetoric figures like metaphor, hyperbole, rhetorical question etc. Joost works on this level (2007) in her 'rhetorical pattern analysis of film' as well.

However, for pattern analysis in the field of education the general structure of rhetoric and its main questions are much more interesting. We can easily derive a general didactical model by assigning the three main forces in rhetorical language to the three main operators of an educational/didactical design: ethos to speaker/teacher, logos to subject/content, pathos to audience/learners. In this way we get the basic components of our RPA model (cf. Figure 4).

In Figure 4 the left triangle shows the common structure of pattern analysis as it is derived from the theoretical work of Christopher Alexander. The three basic points of these triangle are the solution, the problem and the pattern user. Within these three main issues we have to think about the content and the forces. When we try to find patterns we start from the point of the solution, then analyse content and forces and finally define the problem of the solution (cf. Bauer & Baumgartner, 2012, pp. 33 et seq.).

The triangle in the middle is the traditional "Didactic Triangle", where we can see the terminological shift form "Solution" to "Content", "Pattern User" to "Teacher" and "Problem" to "Learners".

The right triangle represents the basic structure of our RPA model. The three basic points here are the subject of teaching/content, the audience/learners and the speaker/teacher. Within that we have to think about the context, the forces that can be obstacles as well as chances. When we try to find patterns through our RPA model we also have to start from a problem, which has already been solved, i.e. from a successful situation of teaching. But in the next step, in case of finding educational patterns, we look towards the audience/learners, who, however, cannot easily be defined as a problem. In fact, they are our main object of teaching or to be more precise: Their learning process is the main object of teaching. To optimize this process it is not enough to solve a simple problem. In addition, this means for a teacher to define his professional role – through her/his intention(s), her/his goal(s) of teaching – and design the learning context carefully. And rhetoric gives us a great opportunity to do this successfully.

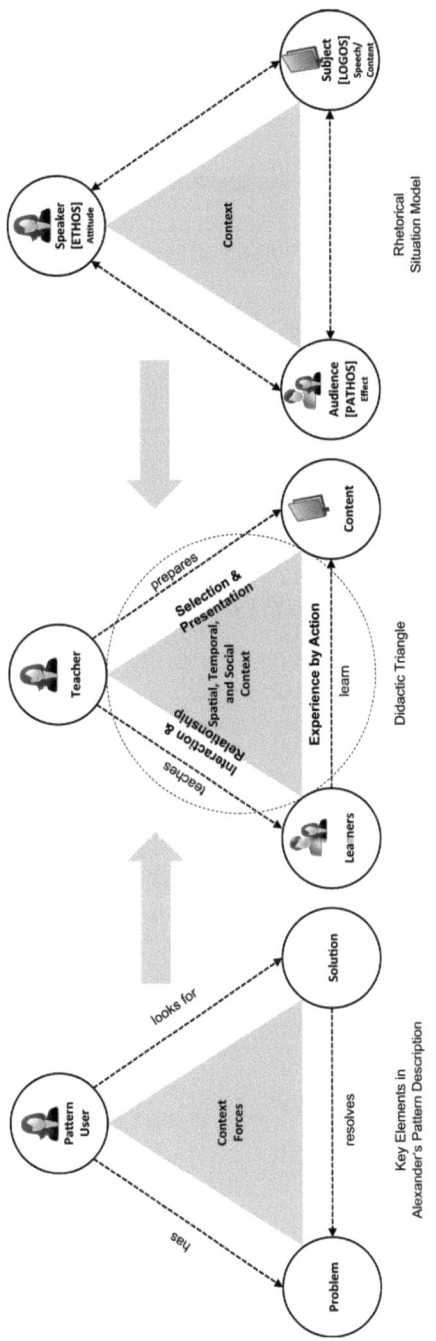

Figure 4. Basic components of RPA model

When we design sequences of teaching we can do that along the five production stages of a rhetorical speech, the "partes artis", supplemented with a pre-consideration (*intellectio*). In this way we get a practical application of our RPA model for planning and analysing teaching sequences (cf. Table 1):

	Production Stages	Rhetorical Process	Problem-Solving Process
Analysis	Intellectio (= knowledge of the cause that motivates the need for the speech)	Intention Analysis	**Current Situation/Context Analysis:** *What are the origins of the problem? Which scenario illustrates the problem? In which situation/ environment is the pattern useful to the user?*
			Goal/Problem Analysis: *What is the core problem that the solution addresses?*
Synthesis	Inventio	Obstacle Analysis	**Identification of Possible Solutions (= Combination of Methods and Actions):** *What are the indications and contraindications for the pattern? What are the goals and constraints, the motivating factors and concerns that the solution is supposed to balance?*
		Choice and Application/Implementation of Methodology Concerning Intention and Obstacles	
	Dispositio		
	Elocutio		**Choice of Solution and its Application/Implementation**: *What is the solution that resolves the conflicting forces? How can the solution be implemented? What needs to be considered for implementation? What are the benefits of the solution? What negative consequences must be accepted?*
	Memoria		
	Actio		
Evaluation			

Table 1. Application of RPA model

4. An Evaluation Example: "First Encounter" in the "Patterns for Supervising Thesis Projects" by Axel Schmolitzky & Till Schümmer

4.1 The traditional pattern approach by Schmolitzky & Schümmer

In order to make the difference between traditional pattern analysis and rhetoric pattern analysis (RPA) explicit, the following example is taken from the field of education: the pattern of first encounter in the "Patterns for Supervising Thesis Projects" by Axel Schmolitzky, Till Schümmer. The pattern begins with the description of the context:

> *Context: A student is looking for a subject for her/his thesis. You fulfill the formal prerequisites for being a supervisor. The student asks you if you would be willing to supervise her/his thesis. (Schmolitzky & Schümmer, 2009, p. 6)*

Afterwards the authors define the "problem" for which this pattern should offer a solution:

> *Problem: You need to find out whether cooperation with the student can work out. If you do not clarify expectations upfront, there is too much room for misunderstandings and conflict. (Schmolitzky & Schümmer, 2009, p. 6)*

Finally we get the solution of the problem:

> *Solution: Meet the student to tell her/him how you handle thesis projects. Give as much information about your way of supervising as possible. (Schmolitzky & Schümmer, 2009, p. 6)*

This pattern is definitely useful because Schmolitzky and Schümmer give a lot of advice to potential supervisors about asking questions concerning the students' resources. But there are also many questions open for the pattern user. Especially questions about the possibilities and intentions of the potential supervisors themselves.

4.2 RPA-approach (1): The step back – clarifying intentions and roles

At this point it is necessary to take a step back and make some further differentiations, be more precise and accurate with the help of rhetoric: At the beginning of every performative speech there is a general aim (intention) which shall be achieved (What is the pragmatic purpose of the speech in general?). This includes a thorough clarification of the position of the speaker her/himself (status orationis) as well as the role which she/he takes during a speech (officia oratoris) to reach the intended goal. This is a substantial difference to traditional pattern analysis and offers an essential precondition in the field of didactics for successful teaching processes - the definition of roles.

According to this, the preliminary questions in the process of RPA are:

1. What is the general aim / the intention of my action?
2. What is my general status / my personal attitude?
3. What is my strategic role to achieve my aim?

The most important point is that the strategic role arises from the aim of the teaching sequence and the status of the teaching person. This role is more (aim-oriented) or less (status-oriented) changeable. The general status is more persistent but not unchangeable. It corresponds to a more or less individual psychological or social construct (a self-concept) within a group.

Concerning the above-mentioned example of "first encounter" this implies the following preconditions:

1. Aim: making a decision whether to supervise
2. Status: supervising tutor who might have high standards, prefer quality before quantity, be benevolent but strict, suffer from excess of work etc.
3. Speaker's role: informing and being informed / selecting convincing offers only

The counterpart to the clarification of the self-concept of the speaker is the knowledge about the audience. Therefore a large part of rhetoric deals with questions like who is the recipient of the speech, what does he/she already know, think to know, assume etc. Equally, rhetoric analyses its role during the action in advance. On this side clarification about status and role is important as well. In our example this means for the students:

1. Aim: finding a supervising tutor
2. Status: Which skills and knowledge does the learner already have? Is the student motivated, ambitious, so far hardly interested but wants graduation etc.?
3. Speaker's role: in this case only noticeable during the conversation

We assume that there is a lot of potential in a thorough and systematic analysis of speaker and recipient like this in regard to generalizing aims, status and role for pattern languages in the area of education.

4.3 RPA- approach (2): From obstacles to potentials

For the remaining context analysis we would like to claim for our model that we also search for obstacles like traditional pattern analysis does but in the educational context it is more important to look for supporting factors, for opportunities. This is another obvious difference of our RPA model. The traditional model of pattern analysis starts by describing (not finding) a solved problem and then focuses on possible obstacles which have to be surmounted. In contrast, the RPA model starts with the definition of a generalizable aim and then focuses on analysing the context, especially on analysing opportunities and supporting factors rather than obstacles. This approach implies changing the paradigm from a negative to a positive perspective, i.e. the potentials of a learner. As a result, the didactic action of RPA is less the solution of a problem but rather a supporting action on the basis of a learner's potential.

4.4 RPA- approach (3): Process designing along the five "partes artis"

The third and last part of RPA is process design, in our case the precise planning of a didactic action. Here, the structure of the five partes artis can be adapted and applied (cf. Table 1):

1. Inventio: core idea of a learning sequence / didactic action
2. Dispositio: draft of a learning sequence / didactic action
3. Elocutio: thorough planning, methods of a learning sequence / didactic action
4. Memoria: preparation before a learning sequence / didactic action
5. Actio: learning sequence / didactic action

Another aspect, which does not belong to the original system of rhetoric but is essential for finishing a pedagogical/didactical process, is evaluation/reflexion, which has to be the starting point of subsequent actions. Hence, the wheel turns full circle at our RPA-model and new patterns can be found, analysed and designed rhetorically as well as applied and evaluated.

5. Conclusion

As we have seen, both Chomsky and Alexander provide a unique system of universalistic generalisation in the field of language respectively architecture. The structure of their systems give researchers the idea of patterns and the possibility to transfer these systems into the field of education. The rhetoric approach offers a very similar possibility to search for systematization but by using the theory of rhetoric we always focus on an artificial system (Lausberg) of linguistic effectiveness, which makes the analytical system much more flexible. In other words: The RPA has the advantage that it starts from changeable practice rather than from a hypothetical construct of stable preconditions. As a first result, we figured out that we can describe the preconditions and the planning-process of an educational action more precisely. The next step has to be the practical appliance and verification of the RPA model in various educational situations.

6. References

Alexander, C. (1984). Eine Pattern Language: Auszüge aus: „Die zeitlose Art zu Bauen" und „Eine Pattern Language". In Arch+: Zeitschrift für Architektur und Städtebau, (73), pp. 14-37.

Alexander, C. (2004). The Phenomenon of Life: An Essay on the Art of Building and the Nature of the Universe: Bk. 1. Berkeley, California: Center for Environmental Structure.

Aristoteles. (1995). Rhetorik. (F. G. Sieveke, Übers.) (5th Ed.). München: UTB Wilhelm Fink.

Bauer, R. (2014). Didaktische Entwurfsmuster: Diskursanalytische Annäherung an den Muster-Ansatz von Christopher Alexander und Implikationen für die Unterrichtsgestaltung. Dissertation. Alpen-Adria-Universität Klagenfurt. Retrieved May 14, 2015 from http://ubdocs.uni-klu.ac.at/open/hssvoll/AC10776663.pdf.

Bauer, R. (2013). Den Unterrichtenden eine Sprache geben: Was didaktische Entwurfsmuster für die Gestaltung von Unterricht leisten können – eine Überlegung. In G. Reinmann, M. Ebner & S. Schön (Eds.), Hochschuldidaktik im Zeichen von Heterogenität und Vielfalt: Doppelfestschrift für Peter Baumgartner und Rolf Schulmeister (pp. 129–149). Norderstedt: Books on Demand.

Bauer, R. & Baumgartner, P. (2012). Schaufenster des Lernens: Eine Sammlung von Mustern zur Arbeit mit E-Portfolios. Münster et al.: Waxmann.

Bauer, R. & Baumgartner, P. (2010). The potential of Christopher Alexander's theory and practice of wholeness: clues for developing an educational taxonomy. In Proceedings of the 15th European Conference on Pattern Languages of Programs (EuroPLoP ,10). ACM, New York, NY, USA, Article 12, 21 pages. DOI=10.1145/2328909.2328924. http://doi.acm.org/10.1145/2328909.2328924.

Bergin, J. et al. (2012). Pedagogical Patterns: Advice for Educators. Joseph Bergin Software Tools.

Burke, K. (1950). A Rhetoric of Motives. New York: Prentice-Hall Inc.

Chomsky, N. (1964). Aspects of the Theory of Syntax. Cambridge, Massachusetts: The M.I.T. Press.

Fricke, A. & Völter, M. (2000). SEMINARS: A Pedagogical Pattern Language about teaching seminars effectively. Retrieved May 14, 2015, from http://www.voelter.de/data/pub/tp.pdf.

Göttert, K.-H. (1994). Einführung in die Rhetorik (2nd Ed.). München: W. Fink Verlag.

Iba, T. (2014). Learning Patterns: A Pattern Language for Creative Learning. Yokohama, Kanagawa, Japan: CreativeShift.

Joost, G. (2007). Die rhetorische Pattern-Language des Films. In G. Joost & A. Scheuermann (Eds.), Design als Rhetorik: Grundlagen, Positionen, Fallstudien (pp. 229-245). Basel, Boston, Berlin: Birkhäuser.

Kohls, C. & Wedekind, J. (2011). Investigations of E-Learning Patterns: Context Factors, Problems, and Solutions. Hershey, Pennsylvania: IGI Global.

Kutschera, F. v. (1993). Sprachphilosophie (2nd Ed.). München: W. Fink Verlag.

Lausberg, H. (1990). Handbuch der literarischen Rhetorik: Eine Grundlegung der Literaturwissenschaft (3rd Ed.). Stuttgart: Franz Steiner Verlag.

Lausberg, H. (1998). Handbook of Literary Rhetoric: A Foundation for Literary Study. Leiden: Brill.

Schmolitzky, A., & Schümmer, T. (2009). Patterns for Supervising Thesis Projects. Retrieved May 05, 2015 from http://ceur-ws.org/Vol-610/paper16.pdf

Seamon, D. (2007). Christopher Alexander and a Phenomenology of Wholeness. Annual Meeting of the Environmental Design Research Association (EDRA), Sacramento, CA, May 2007. Retrieved May 03, 2015, from http://www.arch.ksu.edu/seamon/Alexander%20as%20phenomenology%20of%20wholeness%20dec%2008.pdf.

Leveraging Pattern Applications via Pattern Refinement

Falkenthal, Michael
Barzen, Johanna
Breitenbücher, Uwe
Fehling, Christoph
Leymann, Frank
University of Stuttgart, Germany
{lastname}@iaas.uni-stuttgart.de

Hadjakos, Aristotelis
University of Music Detmold, Germany
hadjakos@hfm-detmold.de

Hentschel, Frank
University of Cologne, Germany
frank.hentschel@uni-koeln.de

Schulze, Heizo
University of Applied Sciences Ostwestfalen-Lippe, Germany
heizo.schulze@hs-owl.de

In many domains, patterns are a well-established concept to capture proven solutions for frequently reoccurring problems. Patterns aim at capturing knowledge gathered from experience at an abstract level so that proven concepts can be applied to a variety of concrete, individual occurrences of the general problem. While this principle makes a pattern very reusable, it opens up a gap between the (i) captured abstract knowledge and the (ii) concrete actions required to solve a problem at hand. This often results in huge efforts that have to be spent when applying a pattern as its abstract solution has to be refined for the actual, concrete use cases each time it is applied. In this work, we present an approach to bridge this gap in order to support, guide, and ease the application of patterns. We introduce a concept that supports capturing and organizing patterns at different levels of abstraction in order to guide their refinement towards concretized solutions. To show the feasibility of the presented approach, we show how patterns detailing knowledge at different levels of abstraction in the domain of information technology are interrelated in order to ease the labor-intensive application of abstract patterns to concrete use cases. Finally, we sketch a vision of a pattern language for films, which is based on the presented concept.

Pattern Refinement; Pattern Application; Cloud Computing Patterns; Costume Patterns

1. Introduction

Christopher Alexander explains the essential characteristic of patterns by the following definition: „*Each pattern describes a problem which occurs over and over again in our environment, and then describes the core of the solution to that problem, in such a way that you can use this solution a million times over, without ever doing it the same way twice*" (Alexander, 1979). Hence, pattern authoring focuses on abstracting the essence of concrete problems and solutions within a specific context to formulate reusable knowledge into documents. Beyond that, pattern authoring is supported by systematic approaches, which define methods to collect problem and solution knowledge in order to organize it into patterns and pattern languages (Fehling et al. 2014; Barzen & Leymann, 2015). Such approaches are additionally supported and eased by pattern repositories, which are IT-based libraries – often realized as wiki systems – to author, store, edit, and search patterns (Fehling et al., 2015; Reiners, 2013; Cunningham & Wehaffy, 2013). Such systems typically enable to interrelate patterns with each other to form *pattern languages* that enable to combine patterns to proper solutions (Alexander, 1977; Fehling et al. 2015). In summary, pattern research mainly focuses on pattern authoring and pattern organization. However, detailed knowledge about concrete solutions is lost during this authoring process as use case-specific details are not captured by patterns (Falkenthal et al., 2014, 2015). While this principle of abstraction makes patterns very reusable, because patterns preserve the so called *gestalt* of the investigated concrete solutions, nevertheless, it opens up a gap between (i) the captured *abstract knowledge* and (ii) the *concrete actions* required to solve a concrete and specific problem at hand – as depicted by the abstraction gap in Figure 1: the abstract solution of a pattern has to be refined towards the respective concrete use case each time the pattern is applied.

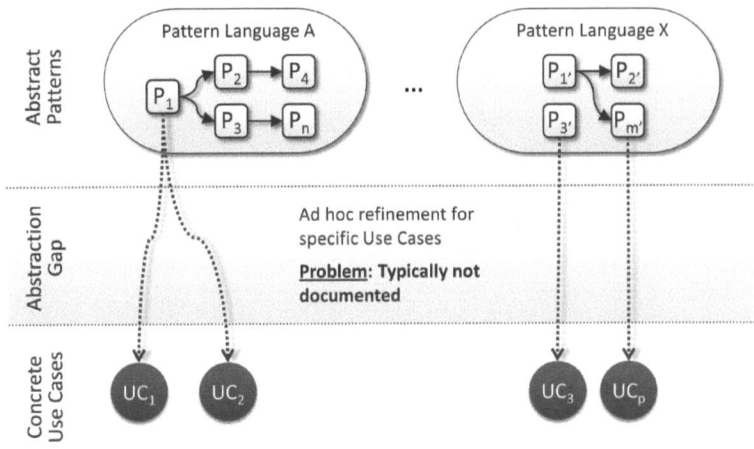

Figure 1: Abstraction Gap

This gap of abstraction seems to be a domain-independent phenomenon due to the above described characteristics of patterns, which leads to abstract descriptions of problems and solutions within a context in any domain. The patterns of Fehling et al. (2014) are examples from the IT-domain of cloud computing, which is a technology that enables to efficiently share computing resources between different applications. They provide patterns, which help to design applications in order to be streamlined for the technological possibilities of cloud computing. In order to keep these patterns reusable in a manifold of use cases, they are formulated in a technology- and vendor-agnostic manner. Thus, specific knowledge on how to implement a pattern utilizing specific technologies is not provided in detail by these patterns. Software architects are, therefore, not supported at designing software architectures taking account of specific technological constraints, which results in a gap of abstraction between the patterns and their concrete realizations. Hence, a software architect has to transfer the documented abstract solutions of the patterns into technology-specific designs ad hoc, i.e., without guidance and support by the patterns. This *ad hoc refinement* requires either much expertise or immense efforts because additional knowledge beyond the applied patterns has to be researched and adopted to the concrete use case at hand.

For another example, we can observe the gap of abstraction in the domain of costumes in films in the pattern language of Schumm et al. (2012). These patterns provide proven solutions in the area of the so-called vestimentary communication. Vestimentary communication describes the communication taking place through clothes, for example, to communicate a specific character trait by, e.g., the material or the color of the worn costume to the audience. The costume patterns provide general patterns as well as genre-specific patterns, resulting in corresponding different costume pattern languages (Barzen and Leymann, 2015). They need to be combined and refined to support a costume designer in detecting appropriate clothes to communicate the intended character. To get from the abstract solution of a costume pattern to a concrete costume, as stated as the abstraction gap, the domain of film points to a second problem: a film is a complex artifact where many various areas come together and influence each other. The setting, the light, the camera perspective, the film music and the makeup, for example, influence the effect of a costume and the other way around. These difficult dependencies lead to immense efforts in the preparation of a film. So, this example shows that isolating pattern languages covering just one aspect of films from the many other influencing elements leads to a lack of documented deep expertise on how to originate the desired effects in films. Therefore, the lack of systematic, easily accessible, and searchable documentation of such dependencies makes film productions very expensive.

Recapitulating, we can state the following shortcomings in current pattern research: while patterns aim to provide abstract and general solution knowledge, it is time consuming to apply them for concrete use cases and the gap of abstraction between patterns and concrete solutions leads to huge efforts because of the required ad hoc refinements. These issues open up the research question „*How to systematically support, guide, and ease applying abstract patterns to concrete use cases?*". To answer this question, we argue that pattern languages have to be augmented by explicit relationships between patterns, which indicate the semantics that one pattern refines another pattern towards concrete solutions.

The remainder of this paper is structured as following: we discuss related work in Section 2 and identify the lack of support for actual pattern applications in state of the art pattern research. In Section 3 we introduce a concept to bridge the gap of abstraction in order to ease the application of patterns for concrete use cases. We show the feasibility of the presented approach in Section 4 in terms of a case study focusing patterns of the domain of cloud computing. We sketch a vision for a pattern language of films, which is based on the presented approach in Section 5. Finally, we conclude this paper in Section 6 and show open topics for future work.

2. Related Work

The presented approach is based on work from decades of pattern research and extends the state of the art in this discipline by the capability to manage pattern languages align with the issue on how to efficiently apply patterns considering specific constrains for concrete use cases at hand. To show how the approach presented in this paper extends the state of the art, fundamental related work is discussed in the following and shortcomings are identified, which show the lack of guidance at pattern application.

In his work on pattern languages Alexander (1977) introduces how patterns can be organized as generative chunks of knowledge that inherently connect reoccurring problems with proven and for many use cases reusable solutions. However, the main organization structure of his pattern language is from large-sized things like cities to more fine-grained things like streets, houses and even parts of houses like rooms and configurations of them. Besides, he discusses relations to other patterns within each pattern and describes how patterns are affected from each other and how they solve overall problems in combination. He shows that patterns are powerful means for solving complex problems once they are applied in combination. While he provides an approach to connect patterns on different levels of scale, he lacks guidance on how the presented patterns and, thus, the abstractly provided solutions can be applied for concrete and specific use cases at hand. Further Alexander (1979) describes the power of a pattern language to unfold a new whole solution by applying patterns from a pattern language step by step. Each pattern adds specific new qualities and properties by adapting the structure of the solution. This follows the principle of piecemeal growth and shows how pattern languages unfold their generativity. Nevertheless, Alexander just focusses on how humans can be supported by patterns at the process of creating things and structures of things but his general pattern approach lacks guidance on how already realized concrete solutions can be reused – which is indeed one of the major challenges in the domain of IT reflected by the simplified question on how to develop code so that it can be reused seamlessly in many different programs.

Zimmer (1994) introduces categories of relationships between patterns of object-oriented software design (Gamma et al., 1994). In this pattern collection he identifies the relation categories „X uses Y in its solution", „X is similar to Y" and „X can be combined with Y" between pairs of patterns. These relationship types are used to organize the pattern collection of Gamma et al. in order to indicate, which patterns are related to each other, which ones solve a similar problem but in different valid ways and, finally, which patterns can be applied together to solve an overall problem in combination. Especially the last relationship type is used to indicate that several patterns in combination can be used as larger building blocks to handle design problems, while pattern combinations can encapsulate combined solutions as more abstract building blocks than just single patterns do. Nevertheless, he doesn't provide a means to reflect refinement paths through a collection of patterns towards concrete use cases and, therefore, towards concrete solutions.

Van Welie and van der Veer (2003) present a methodology to organize patterns into a pattern language by focusing on the decomposition of coarse-grained patterns to more fine- grained ones. The level of granularity is defined by the process of user interface design and therefore the hierarchy levels are only domain-dependent. Decomposition in the sense of the presented approach means that high-level respectively coarse-grained design problems are detailed into smaller design problems. Nevertheless, the decomposition focuses on describing more fine-grained structures, which can be used to build up more coarse-grained ones, i.e., more fine-grained patterns are building blocks from which other patterns can be built. Thus, the presented decomposition does not consider concrete refinements towards pattern implementations for concrete use cases at hand.

Salingaros (2000) describes how patterns are formulated on different levels of granularity align with systems theory. Patterns on more detailed levels act as artifacts, which patterns of more coarse-grained levels are made of. Thus they do not refine solution concepts of coarse- grained patterns towards concrete implementations but show how details of the abstract solution can be described as more fine-grained patterns.

Kubo et al. (2007) introduce a metric to determine the abstraction level of patterns in order to support users to find the most relevant pattern for their problem at hand. Further, besides „Uses" and „Provides Context" they use „Refines" semantics between patterns to distinguish the abstraction levels of different patterns, i.e., these semantics are used to specify the distance between patterns regarding their level of abstraction. Nevertheless, they do not introduce an approach on how to specify refinement by means of semantic links between patterns nor they provide a technical implementation in order to make pattern languages navigable along semantic links to ease the elaboration of concrete realizations of patterns.

Mullet (2002) discusses the organization of patterns within pattern languages by means of different relationship types. Besides the relationship types „Aggregation", which is used to indicate „has-a" relationships between patterns and the general „Association" relationship type, which covers all other non-hierarchical dependencies between patterns, they introduce the type „Derivation". Derivation corresponds to an „is-a" relationship, and, thus, covers semantics of pattern specializations. While specialized patterns inherit functional and non- functional properties described by the more-general pattern and extend them by new properties such specializations do not translate abstract solution principles towards concrete implementations.

Hallstrom and Soundarajan (2009) introduce the concept of design refinement in the IT-domain of object-oriented design and development. They introduce abstraction concepts to formalize patterns and more specialized sub-patterns. The correctness of software designs using patterns and sub-patterns as guidelines is provable because pattern requirements and behavioral guarantees are defined by pattern contracts and subcontracts, respectively. Considering pattern contracts and subcontracts, design refinement leads to pattern hierarchies, which lead from abstract and general patterns to more specialized ones. Nevertheless, specialization in the context of their work leads to variants of solutions in sub- patterns, which are related to general solution concepts in an abstract pattern but the actual refinement towards concrete and specific implementation is not addressed. Further, the approach is tailored to tackle the problem of correctness of design and software and, thus, is not formulated and validated to be feasible for patterns in other domains, i.e., the question is left open if the presented abstraction concepts and contracts are appropriate in general.

Kohls (2011a, 2011b, 2012) provides a detailed discussion on the structure and qualities of patterns and pattern languages. The key elements of patterns – context, forces, problem, solution and consequences – are clearly described and translated into the metaphor of a path. He discusses the qualities of patterns and pattern languages and especially the concepts of wholeness and gestalt utilizing that metaphor. Patterns are described to capture knowledge on a mid-level of abstraction, which means that they are instructive enough to elaborate solutions and, coincidently, are generic enough to be applicable for designing solutions for many different specific use cases. However, the work does not discuss how already existing pattern languages, which are authored on different levels of abstraction can be linked in order to enable navigation from more abstract patterns to concretized ones in order to guide the design of solutions in a more specific context.

Noble et al. (2006) discuss patterns from a semiotics point of view. They introduce that patterns can be grasped as signs and focus on how meaning of patterns and references between patterns are communicated between recipients. Transferred to the domain of IT signs connect the intended effects that a programmer wants to realize and the actual realizations in program code. In their approach they address research problems like how to identify differences in patterns that are very similar, how to organize pattern variants that lead conceptually to a similar solution but each having a very distinct gestalt than the others, how to it can be expressed that one pattern can solve more than one problem depending on the context, or how relationships between patterns can be carried out that a clear semantics is achieved. Their work provides a basis for this paper by discussing how one pattern can have a multitude of concrete implementations. So, Noble et al. provide a communication theory-centric basis applied to the object-oriented design patterns by Gamma et al (1993).

Zimmermann et al. (2009) discuss the modeling on architecture decisions from a problem-driven point of view. They formalize model entities in order to support the decision making process by clear semantics. Design Issues are the leading modeling elements and can be refined from abstract issues to more fine-grained ones. Thus, they discuss the concept of refinement regarding issues in the decision making process for designing application architectures. Issues in their decision models are closely related to problems and forces that are solved and balanced by patterns. The presented approach in this paper extends the concept of refinement of issues to the structure of patterns, which also incorporates the description of a context and a solution.

The meta pattern language by Meszaros and Doble (1996) guides pattern authors at the writing process of patterns and pattern languages. They describe *Pattern Name, Problem,*

Solution, *Context* and *Forces* to be mandatory elements of a pattern so that the main idea carried by a pattern is unambiguously communicated. They further describe optional elements, which can be elaborated if they are helpful to understand the essence of the pattern and to provide guidance for the application of a pattern. The elements *Examples* and *Code Samples* closely related to the concept of concrete solutions as presented in this work. However, they do not discuss a systematic approach on how to support and guide the actual application of a pattern. They also miss a discussion on how to interrelate existing pattern languages, especially, for the case that the pattern languages are authored on different levels of abstraction.

3. A Concept to Close the Abstraction Gap

In this work, we answer the raised research question by generalizing findings from the domain of information technology. In this domain, different pattern languages exist, which capture proven knowledge for different contexts and on different levels of abstraction. For the sake of comprehensibility, we foster the concept of pattern refinement by a definition of the term *refinement* in the next subsection, followed by an explanation on how patterns and refined patterns can be linked. Finally, this enables to select a collection of patterns from different levels of abstraction to ease and guide their realization to concrete solutions.

3.1 A View on Pattern Refinement

The approach presented in this paper is based on refining proven solution knowledge from abstract patterns towards concrete solutions. In our former work (Falkenthal et al., 2014, 2015), we introduced the term *Solution Implementation* to circumstantiate a concrete realization of a solution described in a pattern. For the sake of a better interdisciplinary understandability, we revise the IT-inspired term *implementation* and make a rename in the present work to *Concrete Solutions*. Consequently, we define a concrete solution to be an individual, use case-specific realization of the abstract, generic solution principles described by a pattern.

As described above, the abstraction gap between patterns and concrete solutions often leads to time consuming efforts when patterns have to be applied to concrete use cases at hand. However, in the domain of IT, pattern languages exist, which present proven solutions on different levels of abstraction, i.e., there are pattern languages, which provide technology agnostic solution principles (Fehling et al., 2014) while other pattern languages tackle similar topics but describe the solutions considering specific IT environments and technologies (Amazon Web Services, 2012; Microsoft, 2014). To grasp the terminus *refinement* in this constellation, for this discussion we reduce the structure of patterns to a minimal canonical form consisting of the three parts *problem*, *context* and *solution*. While the problem part provides information about the problem, which is solved by the pattern, the context part describes under which circumstances the pattern is applicable and which forces influence the elaboration of concrete solutions. Finally, the solution part of a pattern describes proven solution principles in an abstract textual and human readable form. Since the solution part of a pattern summarizes the essence of a multitude of concrete solutions, i.e., the solution principles that have proven to be good in practice, this opens a whole solution space of concrete solutions, which can be constructed. This characteristic is pointed out by the phrase "*...you can use this solution a million times over, without ever doing it the same way twice*" by Alexander (1979). Therefore, we can state that the size of the solution space of a pattern is directly related to the level of abstraction of the pattern's solution principles: the more abstract the documented problem, context, and solution, the more use cases can be solved. This is because at higher levels of abstraction the number of constraints, which limit the applicability of a pattern, decreases. Kohls (2012) refers to this as the "*abstraction to emergent qualities*". He points out that more abstract solution descriptions are less instructive but open up more choices at realizing concrete implementations of a pattern. Vice versa, the size of the solution space is significantly smaller if a pattern provides solution principles that are closer to a concrete solution or use case, respectively. This results from *implementation-specific* knowledge and, thus, *implementation-specific constraints* that are part of the more concretized pattern. Nevertheless, this is exactly the kind of knowledge that can be used to close the abstraction gap towards concrete and use case-specific realizations.

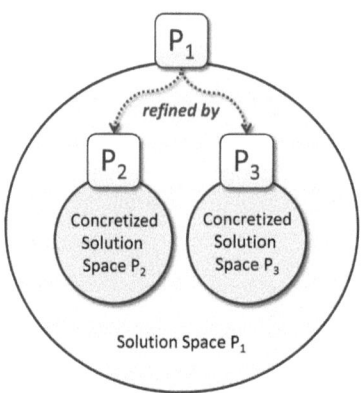

Figure 2: Concretized patterns and solution spaces

In consequence, pattern refinement means that a pattern's problem, context, and solution are getting more specific and precise towards concrete realizations and use cases. Nevertheless, the core of the problem and the provided solutions remain the same. This is conceptually depicted in Figure 2, where abstract pattern P1 opens a solution space and the patterns P2 and P3 refine P1 to more concrete solutions and, thus, open smaller but *concretized solution spaces* within the one of P1. Therefore, P1 can be applied to more use cases than P2 and P3, while they document and provide knowledge about how to realize solutions for certain concrete use cases at hand.

3.2 The Concept of Refinement Links

If one pattern refines another pattern, this refinement can be documented by a semantic link, which determines a navigation path from the abstract solution of the former pattern to the more concretized solution of the latter one. This improves the usability of patterns, which were authored isolated from each other – especially, if they are part of different pattern languages. Thereby, formerly isolated knowledge can be connected via explicit refinement links, which bridge the abstraction gap in order to avoid manual, unguided, and ad hoc refinements.

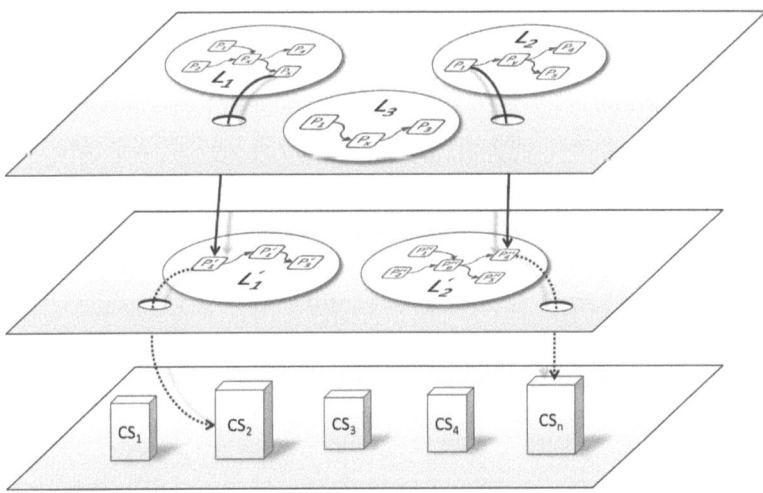

Figure 3: Patterns on different levels of abstraction connected by refinement links

This is conceptually depicted in Figure 3, where patterns (Pi) are organized into pattern languages (Lj). For the sake of simplicity, the depicted layers illustrate that the pattern languages provide solution knowledge on different levels of abstraction - even though pattern languages are not necessarily authored and stuck to just one specific abstraction level.

Refinement links from abstract patterns of the languages L1 and L2 to more concretized patterns of the languages L'1 and L'2 are illustrated by solid arrows, while dotted arrows indicate refinements that have to be done manually.

In this scenario, the pattern languages L'1 and L'2 bridge the abstraction gap by providing concretized solution knowledge to refine the more abstract patterns of L1 and L2 towards concrete solutions (*CS*) for use cases at hand. So, a pattern reader can choose pattern P5 of pattern language L1, which provides a huge solution space and, therefore, only abstract solution principles. Then, he navigates to P'1 in L'1, which provides more concretized solution knowledge to elaborate the concrete solution CS2 that is actually the solution of the specific use case. Nevertheless, it is not obligatory that there is refinement knowledge in the form of more concretized patterns, as depicted by the missing refinement links between other patterns. Especially, there is no refinement guidance for pattern language L3 as there are no concretized patterns that refine the ones in L3.

3.3 Easing Pattern Application by Inter-Pattern Language Solution Graphs

The concept introduced above can be leveraged to ease the application of patterns for concrete use cases. Patterns are often used in combination to elaborate concrete solutions, which is supported by references between patterns in different pattern languages. Thus, a pattern language can be grasped as a graph whose nodes represent patterns and whose edges represent references between the patterns. So, a reader can select a pattern that solves a particular part of the problem at hand and then navigate to related patterns, which provide additional solutions that typically need to be combined to elaborate a proper concrete solution. Navigating and selecting patterns in this fashion results in a subgraph, which we call *Solution Graph*. This concept extends the approach of solution paths by Zdun (2007), because subgraphs are not limited to represent just sequences of patterns, but also branching paths within a pattern language.

The concept of solution graphs is specifically important when we extend the expressiveness of pattern languages by the formerly introduced concept of refinement links in order to enable the navigation towards concretized solutions, too. As depicted in Figure 4, references between patterns enable to navigate within a pattern language of a specific level of abstraction. We call this kind of navigation *horizontal navigation*, since navigation remains on the same level of abstraction. Refinement links also support to navigate towards concretized patterns in other languages, which provide refined solution knowledge. This kind of navigation is called *vertical navigation,* since it targets towards concretized solutions. Therefore, horizontal navigation enables to unfold the power of pattern languages to create a *"new whole out of incoherent pieces"* as Alexander (1964) points out. This means, the abstract patterns allow for designing a new solution conceptually, whereby each pattern adds particular new qualities and, therefore, enables piecemeal growth of the solution. On the other hand, the vertical navigation enables to replace abstract parts of a solution by more concrete ones towards concrete solution artifacts. Thus, the *wholeness* of the abstractly designed solution and its *gestalt* is concretized towards an overall concrete solution, which itself is a new whole.

Given the situation that P5 of pattern language L1, P1 of L3, and P1 of L2 are selected by a reader to solve his problem at hand, he can also navigate to the more concretized patterns P'1 of L'1 and P''4 of L'2 to be guided towards concrete solutions. The selected patterns are part of the solution graph indicated by the surrounding area in Figure 4.

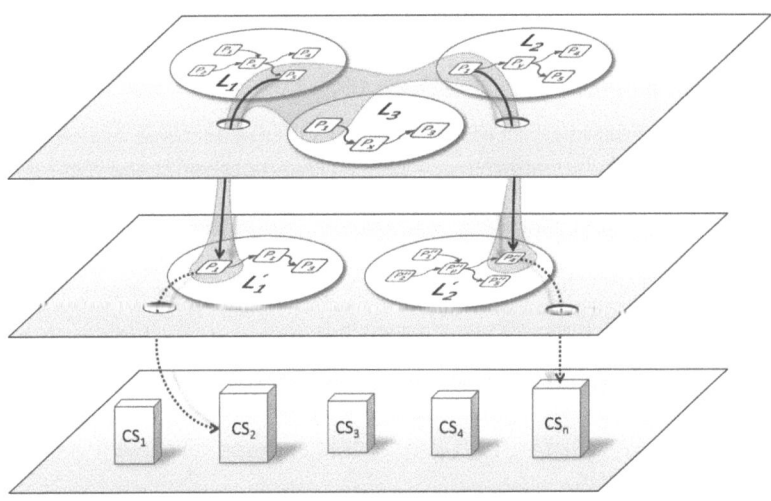

Figure 4: Solution graph spanning multiple pattern languages

Since the refined patterns P'1 of L'1 and P''4 of L'2 are part of the solution graph, this example shows that following refinement links leads to solution graphs that span several pattern languages on different levels of abstraction. Thus, besides the combination of patterns on the same level of abstraction, also refinement of abstract patterns towards concretized ones, and, therefore, more concretized solutions, is represented by the depicted solution graph. Nevertheless, Figure 4 shows that refinement knowledge is not necessarily available for each pattern of a pattern language, which is indicated by the fact that there is no refinement link, e.g., from P1 of L3 to a concretized pattern. This means that the solution principles provided by this pattern have to be manually and ad hoc refined to elaborate a concrete solution. But since refinement links are available to navigation from the other two abstract patterns of the solution graph to concretized solutions, the application of the patterns within the solution graph is at least partly guided and eased.

4. Case Study: Cloud Computing Pattern Refinement

We discovered the above presented concepts of pattern refinement and refinement links by investigating pattern languages in the IT-domain of cloud computing. There, the pattern language of Fehling et al. (2014) describes problems and solutions in an abstract, cloud provider- and technology-independent manner. Besides these patterns, the cloud providers Amazon Web Services (2012) and Microsoft (2014) developed their own pattern languages that focus on realizing applications in their concrete cloud environments. Their languages are, therefore, more concrete in contrast to Fehling's abstract pattern language: indeed, they describe similar problems, contexts, and solutions, but on a significantly more detailed level with respect to their proprietary offerings in order to bind customers. Thereby, the ability to reuse these patterns is decreased in comparison to the patterns of Fehling et al. (2014) because the contexts and solutions of these patterns are concretized to the technical circumstances of the respective cloud environments. This reveals that these provider-specific patterns are not applicable for developing applications for other cloud environments. However, they capture knowledge to realize abstract patterns of Fehling et al. in the environments of Amazon Web Services and Microsoft. Thus, this scenario provides an interesting example of pattern languages on different levels of abstraction, which may be linked to ease applying an abstract pattern by a stepwise refinement via other pattern languages towards concrete solutions.

In total, we discovered 16 patterns in the pattern languages of Amazon Web Services and Microsoft that provide guidance for translating the abstract solution concepts of Fehling et al. (2014) into technological building blocks (and combinations of these) within the respective cloud environment. In Figure 5, we illustrate this exemplarily by the four patterns: *Elastic Load Balancer (ELB)* and *Stateless Component (SC)* from the pattern language of Fehling et al. (2014) as well as *Scale Out Pattern (SO)* and *State Sharing Pattern (SSh)* from the respective pattern language of Amazon Web Services (2012).

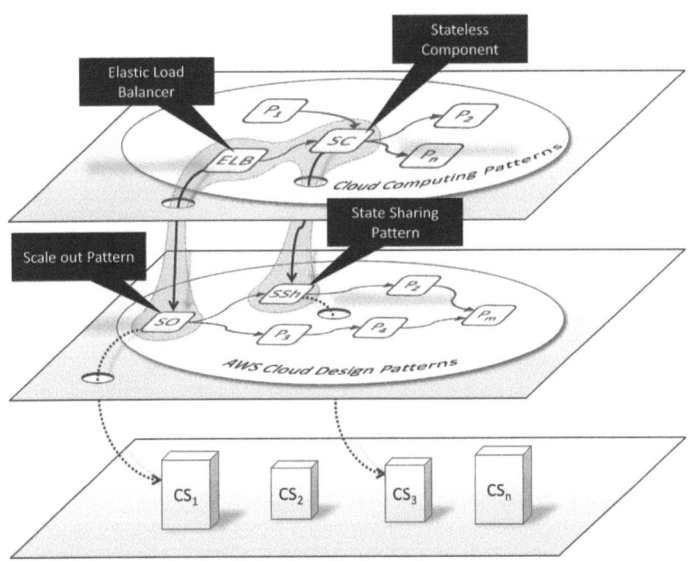

Figure 5: Cloud computing patterns on different levels of abstraction connected by refinement links

The patterns ELB and SO tackle the problem on how the number of application components can be dynamically provisioned and also decommissioned to process changing workloads. This means that, based on measured workloads, new instances of an application component are launched in order to spread and balance high workloads among them. Besides, instances can also be stopped and terminated in situations of low workloads. This behavior is called *elastic scaling* in the terminology of cloud computing. The abstract pattern ELB describes these principles technology-agnostic and does not provide a solution with respect to specific cloud offerings like those of Amazon Web Services or Microsoft. On the other hand, SO refines the general solution concepts of ELB into terms of the Amazon Web Services Cloud Offering.

The SC pattern describes how application components should manage state in a cloud application to ease the above-mentioned scaling functionality and enable failure resiliency. The session state, which is the state of the interaction with the component, should be provided with every request to the component. The application state, which is the data handled by the application, such as a customer database, should be handled outside of the component. Preferably, this application state is handled in provider-supplied storage offerings. This ensures that the application components themselves become stateless, thus, they do not manage an internal state that would have to be synchronized or extracted upon component instance provisioning and decommissioning, respectively. The SSh pattern details this concept of stateless components in scope of Amazon Web Services. Components take the form of virtual servers that rely on key-value stores provided by Amazon for external state management.

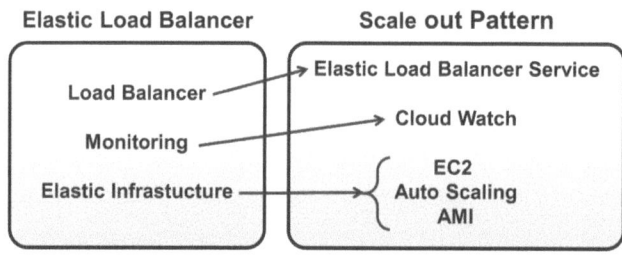

Figure 6: Corresponding concepts in the ELB Pattern and the SO Pattern

In detail, the refinement of the Elastic Load Balancer (ELB) pattern to the Scale out (SO) Pattern was identified by analyzing the textual description of both pattern documents for similarities, which are exemplarily shown in Figure 6. The abstractly described concept of a *Load Balancer* – that is the component, which spreads workload across a number of application instances – in the Elastic Load Balancer pattern on the left, is refined in Scale out Pattern to the concept of *Elastic Load Balancer* Service, which is a service in the ecosystem of Amazon Web Services to spread and balance workload across a number of application instances. So, the Scale out Pattern provides a concretized solution about how to implement load balancing at Amazon Web Services. The same applies to the concept of *Monitoring* actual workloads in the Elastic Load Balancer pattern. It is refined in Scale out Pattern by the technological approach of *Cloud Watch*, which is a service of Amazon Web Services that provides capabilities to monitor actual workloads. Finally, the abstract Elastic Load Balancer pattern describes an *Elastic Infrastructure*, which provides functionality to automatically provision and decommission instances of application components.

In the Scale out Pattern, this concept is refined by the description on how *EC2* (service to provision compute resources within the Amazon cloud), the *Auto Scaling* service (service to configure automatic elastic scaling) and *AMIs* (Amazon Machine Images, that contain the actual application components), have to be combined in order to elicit elastic scaling in the cloud environment of Amazon.

To enable navigation from the abstract pattern Elastic Load Balancer towards the concretized pattern Scale out Pattern, we implemented a refinement link between these patterns in our pattern repository PatternPedia (Fehling et al., 2015). There, we collected the abstract cloud computing patterns of Fehling et al. (2014) and also the more concrete patterns of Amazon Web Services (2012). The result is depicted exemplarily in Figure 7, where Elastic Load Balancer is shown as a wiki page within PatternPedia. On the right, all links to other patterns are listed within the groups "*Related To*", "*Consider Next*", "*In Context Of*" and "*Refined By*". Thus, the refinement link to Scale out Pattern is listed under "*Refined By*", which indicates the specific refinement semantics of the link. Technically, these links are implemented by the Semantic MediaWiki (2015) technology, which provides means to define semantic links in PatternPedia.

Since patterns are stored as *wiki pages*, which are build upon the concept of web pages, refinement links are implemented using the technologies of the semantic web – *RDF-Schema* (W3C, 2014) and *RDF* (W3C, 2014a). Via RDF-Schema, patterns can be defined as typed *pattern resources* and refinement links as properties of the type "*refinedBy*" of these resources. Using RDF, a refinement link between two patterns can be expressed as a RDF triple. The abstract pattern is the *subject* of the RDF triple while the concretized pattern is the *object*. Both are identified by unique URIs that correspond to the URLs of the wiki pages of the respective pattern. Conceptually, the refinement link is the *predicate* of the RDF triple, which indicates the relation between *subject* and *object*. It is represented as a *property* of the type "*refinedBy*", which is part of the subject pattern and contains a reference to the concretized pattern identified by its URI. Since this URI corresponds to the URL of the wiki page of the concretized pattern, the "*refinedBy*" relation can be rendered by Semantic MediaWiki (2015) as a hyperlink, which is indicated in Figure 7. Thus, the creation of semantic links between patterns is fully supported by Semantic MediaWiki (2015), and, therefore, shows exemplarily how the above introduced concept of refinement links is implemented in PatternPedia.

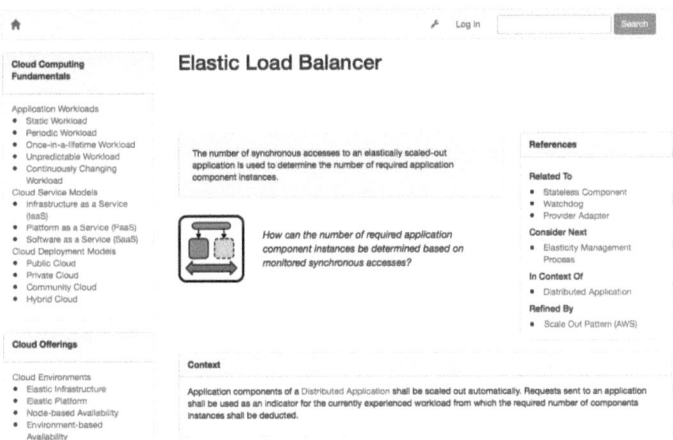

Figure 7: Refinement link from Elastic Load Balancer to Scale out Pattern in PatternPedia

5. Vision: Towards a Pattern Language for Films based on Costumes, Setting, and Music in Films

To prove the generality of our approach and our method, we present how it can be applied to a domain totally different from cloud computing: the domain of films. Because a film is a complex artifact, whose expressional power arise from many diverse areas like the sound and music, the setting, the light, the costumes, the camera perspective and many more, capturing of knowledge about how films reach an effect on a recipient is a difficult task. Because each of these areas focuses on rather diverse subjects, actions and topics, it is challenging to describe their core issues in a uniform manner that allows comparison and combination of this knowledge. Therefore, the concept of patterns gives a powerful means to identify the relevant parameters, to capture this knowledge, and to store it in a reusable way for others working on films.

The costume pattern language of Schumm et al. (2012) gives an example on how patterns can extract and store the knowledge provided by concrete films, especially for the domain of costumes. The costume pattern language aims at capturing the established conventions in terms of an abstract solution about how, for example, stereotype clothes are used to communicate a certain character to the audience.

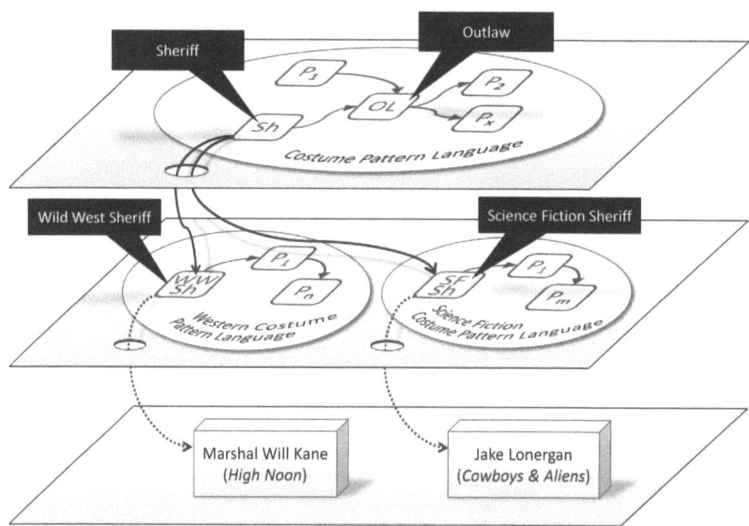

Figure 8: Costume patterns on different levels of abstraction connected by refinement links

When taking a closer look at the Wild West Sheriff Pattern introduced by Schumm et al. (2012), it becomes obvious that the concept of refinement links towards a concrete costume solution is also applicable and valuable in the domain of films. As depicted in Figure 8, there are also different levels of abstraction in the various costume pattern languages in the domain of costume in films. On the highest level the *Costume Pattern Language* is located, containing the highly abstract costume patterns like *Sheriff Pattern* or *Outlaw Pattern*. But, because each film genre has its own Costume Pattern Language (as assumed in Barzen and Leymann (2015)), there are quite different Sheriff Patterns in the genre-specific pattern languages. The genre-specific pattern languages like the *Western Costume Pattern Language* or the *Science Fiction Costume Pattern Language* are less abstract than the Costume Pattern Language and are, therefore, located at the second level. The Sheriff Pattern, thus, can be refined by the *Wild West Sheriff Pattern* from the Western Costume Pattern Language or the *Science Fiction Sheriff Pattern* from the Science Fiction Costume Pattern Language if needed, as indicated by the refinement links in Figure 8. This simplifies the navigation to a suitable concrete solution in terms of a real costume someone wears in a film: The Sheriff Pattern refined by the Wild West Sheriff Pattern can be refined a second time to the concrete solution. This could be, for example, by refining the Wild West Sheriff Pattern to the concrete solution of *Marshal Will Kane* (Gary Cooper) in the Film *High Noon* (1952, Director: Fred Zinnemann) or by refining the Science Fiction Cowboy Pattern to *Jake Lonergan* (Daniel Craig) in the film *Cowboys & Aliens* (2011, Director: Jon Favreau). Using refinement links to navigate through different pattern languages closes the abstraction gap between a very high level and abstract solution to a concrete solution to support, for example, a costume designer to find the right costumes for a certain character.

But, as stated above, a film is a complex artifact, whose expressional power arises through many diverse areas, and the costume area is just one of them. Even more, the expressional power arises through the interaction of these diverse areas, which requires to not only capture the knowledge of a single area, but of many of them as well as their dependencies. For example, a red dress worn in a blue room has a signaling effect, while a character wearing a blue dress in a blue room rather disappears and has a totally different effect than the red dress. The same is true for combining, for example, a forest setting with different music. The effect of the forest can range from seeming a rather safe place to being a very dangerous place according to the music. Therefore, in our vision the diverse pattern languages need to be combined, not only by refinement, but also in dependencies to each other. Therefore, we plan to store all these pattern languages in PatternPedia (Fehling et al., 2014) in order to enable semantic links between patterns from the respective areas. Especially investigating refinements of combinations of these patterns, and representing them in

PatternPedia seems to be a promising means to support and ease pattern application from different areas in the domain of films.

6. Conclusion & Future Work

In the present work we introduced the concept of pattern refinement that eases pattern application. Therefore, we showed how pattern languages on different levels of abstraction can be interrelated by refinement links and, thus, navigation from abstract patterns towards concretized solutions is enabled. We further extended the concept of solution paths within pattern languages to solution graphs, which represent a selection of patterns from different pattern languages, also including refined patterns for solving problems at hand. Based on these concepts, we finally sketched a vision of a pattern language for films, which inherently connects solution knowledge from different disciplines in the domain of films.

To realize our vision, we have to do follow up research on how combination of patterns from different pattern languages can be supported. We also work on a more detailed description of the concept of pattern refinement, especially, in respect to situations where the application of a combination of more specific patterns provide a refinement of an abstract pattern. We are also going to further develop our pattern repository PatternPedia to support the selection of concrete solutions from patterns in an unelaborate way. To approach the vision of a pattern language of films that combines the different art domains and their dependencies, we started to work (in addition to our continuing work on costume patters) on music patterns and are currently developing the basic taxonomies to capture music in its relevant parameters. We also started working on a pattern language for film settings that is based on the tool setscene (HZO Film & Medien, 2014), which already provides numbers of concrete solutions of film settings. We also plan to interweave the pattern languages of different areas of the domain of films and support their application by semantic links within PatternPedia.

7. References

Alexander, C. (1964). Notes on the synthesis of form. Cambridge: Harvard University Press.

Alexander, C., Ishikawa, S., Silverstein, M., Jakobson, M., Fiksdahl-King, I., & Angel,S. (1977). A Pattern Language: Towns, Buildings, Construction. Oxford: Oxford University Press.

Alexander, C. (1979). The Timeless Way of Building. Oxford: Oxford University Press, 1979.

Amazon Web Services (2012). AWS Cloud Design Pattern. http://en.clouddesignpattern.org.

Barzen, J., & Leymann, F. (2015). Costumes Languages as Pattern Languages. Proceedings of PURPLSOC (Pursuit of Pattern Languages for Societal Change). The Workshop 2014. Neopubli.

Cunningham, W., Mehaffy, M. W. (2013). Wiki as Pattern Language. Proceedings of the 20th Conference on Pattern Languages of Programs (PLoP 2013). Articel No. 32. New York: ACM.

Falkenthal, M., Barzen, J., Breitenbücher, U., Fehling, C., & Leymann, F. (2014). From Pattern Languages to Solution Implementations. Proceedings of the Sixth International Conferences on Pervasive Patterns and Applications (PATTERNS 2014). Xpert Publishing Services.

Falkenthal, M., Barzen, J., Breitenbücher, U., Fehling, C., & Leymann, F. (2014). Efficient Pattern Application: Validating the Concept of Solution Implementations in Different Domains. International Journal on Advances in Software (Vol. 7(3&4)).

Fehling, C., Barzen, J., Breitenbücher, U., & Leymann, F. (2014). The Process of Pattern Identification, Extraction, and Application. Proceedings of the 19th European Conference on Pattern Languages of Programs (EuroPLoP 2014). Accepted for publication.

Fehling, C., Barzen, J., Falkenthal, M., & Leymann, F. (2015). PatternPedia - Collaborative Pattern Identification and Authoring. Proceedings of PURPLSOC (Pursuit of Pattern Languages for Societal Change). The Workshop 2014. Neopubli.

Fehling, C., Leymann, F., Retter, R., Schupeck, W., & Arbitter, P. (2014). Cloud Computing Patterns. Wien: Springer.

Gamma, E., Helm, R., Johnson, R., & Vlissides, J. (1993). Design patterns: Abstraction and reuse in object-oriented design. Proceedings of ECOOP'93 (pp. 406-431). Berlin: Springer.

Hallstrom, J. O., & Soundarajan, N. (2009). Reusing Patterns through Design Refinement. In Formal Foundations of Reuse and Domain Engineering (pp. 225-235). Berlin: Springer.

HZO Film & Medien (2014). Setscene - The Compendium of Film Sets. http://www.setscene.org.

Kohls (2011a). The structure of patterns. Proceedings of the 2010 Conference on Pattern Languages of Programming (PLoP 2010). New York: ACM.

Kohls (2011b). The structure of patterns – Part II – Qualities. Proceedings of the 2011 Conference on Pattern Languages of Programming (PLoP 2011). New York: ACM.

Kohls (2012). The path to patterns – introducing the path metaphor. Proceedings of the 17th European Conference on Pattern Languages of Programs (EuroPLoP 2012). Article No. 9. New York: ACM.

Meszaros, G., & Doble, J. (1996). MetaPatterns: A Pattern Language for Pattern Writing. The 3rd Pattern Language of Program congress. Monticello.

Microsoft (2014). Cloud Design Patterns: Prescriptive Architecture Guidance for Cloud Applications. https://msdn.microsoft.com/en-us/library/dn568099.aspx.

Mullet, K. (2002). Structuring pattern languages to facilitate design. CHI2002 Patterns in Practice: A Workshop for UI Designers.

Noble, J., Biddle, R., & Tempero, E. (2006). Patterns as Signs: A Semiotics of Object- Oriented Design Patterns. International Journal on Communication, Information Technology and Work (Vol. 2 (1)).

W3C (2014). RDF 1.1 Concepts and Abstract Syntax. http://www.w3.org/TR/2014/REC-rdf11-concepts-20140225/.

W3C (2014a). RDF Schema 1.1. http://www.w3.org/TR/rdf-schema/.

Reiners, R. (2013). An Evolving Pattern Library for Collaborative Project Documentation. PhD Thesis. Aachen: RWTH Aachen University.

Salingaros, N. (2000). The Structure of Pattern Languages. Architectural Research Quarterly (Vol. 4(02)).

Semantic MediaWiki (2015). Semantic MediaWiki. https://semantic-mediawiki.org.

Schumm, D., Barzen, J., Leymann, F., Ellrich, L. (2012). A Pattern Language for Costumes in Films. Proceedings of the 17th European Conference on Pattern Languages of Programs (EuroPLoP 2012). New York: ACM.

Van Welie, M., van der Veer, G. C. (2003). Pattern Languages in Interaction Design: Structure and Organization. Proceedings of Human-Computer Interaction (INTERACT) ,03: IFIP TC13 International Conference on Human-Computer Interaction. IOS Press.

Zdun, U. (2007). Systematic pattern selection using pattern language grammars and design space analysis. Software: Practice and Experience (Vol. 37(9)).

Zimmer, W. (1994). Relationships between Design Patterns. Pattern Languages of Program Design. Addison-Wesley.

Zimmermann, O., Koehler, J., Leymann, F., Polley, R., & Schuster, N. (2009). Managing Architectural Decision Models with Dependency Relations, Integrity Constraints, and Production Rules. Journal of Systems and Software (Vol. 82(8)). Elsevier.

All links were last accessed on 13.06.2016.

Towards a Fourth Generation Pattern Language: Patterns as Epistemic Threads for Systemic Orientation

Finidori, Helene
University of Hull, United Kingdom
hfinidori@gmail.com

Borghini, Sayfan G.
Vrije University, Belgium
sayfanst@gmail.com

Henfrey, Thomas
The Schumacher Institute, United Kingdom
tom@schumacherinstitute.org.uk

This paper charts the emergence of a fourth generation of pattern languages that continues the generational progression identified by Takashi Iba. In order to characterize Pattern Language 4.0 in the context of societal change, we start by describing some of the complexities of social change processes: the systemic nature of the challenges involved, its pluralistic nature and the consequent need for a semantic approach capable of reconciling multiple perspectives and issue framings. We subsequently describe the systemic potential of pattern languages and outline general features through which fourth generation pattern languages realize this potential and address these complexities. Finally, we describe PLAST (Pattern Languages for Systemic Transformation) as a concrete example of a fourth generation project and in conclusion return to consider prospects for societal transformation and how the use of pattern languages can contribute to this.

Pattern Language; Social Change; Generative Systems; Emergence; Complexity; Wicked Problems

1. Pattern Languages and Societal Change

Pattern Languages originated in architecture, in the work of Christopher Alexander and colleagues at the Centre for Environmental Structure in Berkeley.[1] Alexander's team sought to codify the implicit knowledge underlying vernacular architectures and responsible for them being evocative, in culturally specific ways, of a general feeling of beauty and life enhancement.[2] Alexander's intention was to help reproduce in replicable and scalable ways the morphological and moral coherence that makes such environments nurturing for human beings. He sought to create a process that people could use in a self-directed way, adapted to their time- and place-specific needs, and apply in ways that become self-generating after the fashion of organic processes in living systems.[3]

The barely tangible life-enhancing property sought by Alexander has been defined in various ways. Social activist Tom Atlee refers to it as Goodness,[4] physicist David Bohm as Wholeness,[5] cultural theorist Jean Gebser as Diaphaneity,[6] Gregory Bateson as 'The Pattern that Connects'.[7] Alexander describes it as something desirable, ineffable yet readily perceivable with high levels of intersubjective agreement, calling it the 'quality without a name':[8]

> "There is a central quality which is the root criterion of life and spirit in a man, a town, a building, or a wilderness. This quality is objective and precise, but it cannot be named."

He goes on to elaborate on its context-dependence...

> "[I]t is never twice the same, because it always takes its shape from the particular place in which it occurs."

He later describes the conditions under which it can arise:

> "This quality [...] cannot be made, but only generated, indirectly, by the ordinary actions of the people, just as a flower cannot be made, but only generated from the seed."

Pattern languages as originally formulated, therefore, were vehicles seeking to convey a holistic purpose, to direct designed objects and processes towards a specific quality; hence, instruments for sense-making and purposive design. They aimed to support self-generated societal thriving by articulating fundamental design principles to guide holistic and life-serving applications within a given domain.

---
1 Alexander, C., S. Angel & M. Silverstein, (1977). A Pattern Language. (New York: Oxford University Press).
2 Alexander, C. (1979). The Timeless Way of Building. (New York: Oxford University Press).
3 Alexander, Christopher. 1996. "Patterns in Architecture" presented at OOPSLA '96, October 8, San Jose, California. <bit.ly/1LnXvyP>[Retrieved 15 September 2015]
4 Atlee, T. (2014). The Tao of Democracy. (North Atlantic Books). Pp. 35.
5 Bohm, D. (1980). Wholeness and the Implicate Order. (London: Routledge).
6 Gebser, J. (1984). The Ever-Present Origin. Authorised translation by Noel Barstad. (Ohio University Press). Pp. 6-7.
7 Bateson, G. (1979). Mind and Nature: a Necessary Unity. (New York: Dutton)
8 Alexander, C. (1979). The Timeless Way of Building. (New York: Oxford University Press). Pp. 19 & 26.

Subsequently, setting aside somewhat Alexander's moral preoccupations to concentrate on technical design improvements, pattern languages were quickly and widely adopted as a standard knowledge format in software programming. Their use became standard practice in object-oriented programming, where patterns are a format for exchange and reproduction of building blocks among experts, resolving complex communication issues within this domain.[9] This consecrated their role as lingua franca: formalizing tacit knowledge within specific domains of practice.

They later entered interdisciplinary fields such as design of human-computer interfaces[10] and technology-enhanced learning.[11] In these fields they facilitate communication of expert knowledge across specialized disciplines, partly reflecting Alexander's original intention to undermine architects' control over construction processes by making their specialized technical knowledge accessible to wider groups of stakeholders.

Pattern Languages subsequently expanded into many other domains of activity: pattern theorist Helmut Leitner estimates around 30,000 pattern languages and half a million patterns to exist in domains as varied as movie costume design, organizational design, fire fighting, scrum, and music composition (Leitner 2014).[12] Of particular importance to this paper are their applications in fields of social change and sustainable innovation.[13] These include bio-regional development,[14] community action on climate change,[15] the Transition movement of community-based sustainability initiatives,[16] permaculture's approach to designing sustainable human habitats,[17] as well as other human interaction and action domains such as learning, collaboration, co-creation, innovation, and conflict resolution.[18] Some applications stress their potential as tools to advance democracy, inclusion, and social justice, notably the Public Sphere Project's work on pattern languages for use as emancipatory tools.[19]

---

9   Lea, D. (1994). "Christopher Alexander: An introduction for object-oriented designers." ACM SIGSOFT Software Engineering Notes, 19(1): 39-46. Gamma, E., Helm, R., Johnson, R., & Vlissides, J. (1994). Design patterns: elements of reusable object-oriented software. (Pearson Education).
10 Pauwels, S. L., Hübscher, C., Bargas-Avila, J. A., & Opwis, K. (2010). "Building an interaction design pattern language: A case study." Computers in Human Behavior, 26(3), 452-463.
11 Winters, N. & Y. Mor (2008). "IDR: A participatory methodology for interdisciplinary design in technology enhanced learning." Computers and Education 50: 579-600.
12 Leitner, H (2014). Christopher Alexander – "Introduction and Crash Course" <http://bit.ly/16iRiEw> and <http://bit.ly/1Bw3Is2> [Retrieved 13 December 2014]
13 Schuler, D. (2014). "Pattern Languages — An Approach to Holistic Knowledge Representation" <http://slidesha.re/1IMvMa5> [Retrieved 13 December 2014]
14 Reliable Prosperity website <http://www.reliableprosperity.net/> [Retrieved April 5th 2015)
15 Community Pathways website <http://communitypathways.org.uk/> [Retrieved April 5th 2015)
16 Hopkins, R. (2011). The Transition Companion. (Totnes: Green Books).
17 Jacke, D. & Toensmeier, E. (2006). Edible Forest Gardening. Volume 2: Ecological Design and Practice for Temperate Climate Permaculture. (Vermont: Chelsea Green Publishing). Pp. 63-115. Bane, P. (2012). The Permaculture Handbook. (Gabriola Island: New Society Publishers). Pp. 57-95.
18 Leitner, H. (2015). Pattern Theory. Introduction and Perspectives on the Tracks of Christopher Alexander. (HLS Software).
19 Schuler, D. (2008). Liberating voices: A pattern language for communication revolution. (MIT Press).

2. Three Generations of Pattern Languages

One approach to outlining the development of Pattern Languages comes from the work of Takashi Iba, who identified three distinct phases, or generations, since the end of the 1970s.[20] He distinguishes these in relation to their 'object of design', 'act of design' and 'purpose', and respectively labels them Pattern Language 1.0, 2.0 and 3.0.

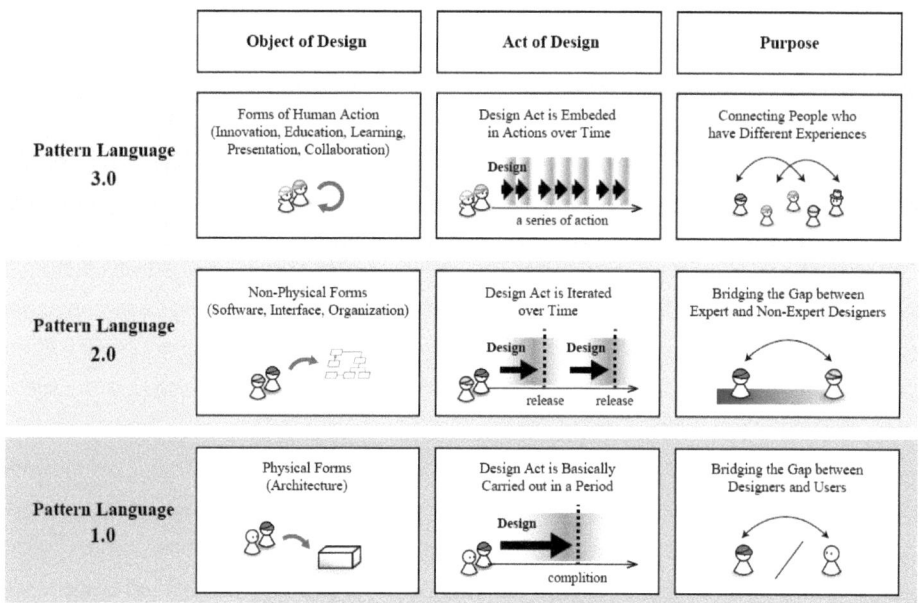

Figure 1: Three generations of pattern languages

2.1 Pattern Language 1.0

The first generation includes Alexander's original pattern languages for settlement and building design and construction.[21] The objects of design are mainly material forms. The act of design consists of a discrete and bounded initiative, such as a specific construction project. The main purpose of patterns is to aid communication (and hence overcome power disparities) between designers and users. As descriptions or hypotheses of sets of invariant properties and systems of forces to resolve given problems,[22] they are sufficiently abstract to be adapted to users' preferences and local conditions, with each principle amenable to

---
20 Iba, T. (2013). "Pattern Languages As Media For The Creative Society." In: Proceedings for Coins13. <http://bit.ly/1Bw0ors> [Retrieved 13 December 2014]
21 Alexander, C., M. Silverstein, S. Angel, S. Ishikawa & D. Abrams (1975). The Oregon Experiment. (New York: Oxford University Press).
22 Alexander, C., S. Angel & M. Silverstein, (1977). A Pattern Language. (New York: Oxford University Press).

diverse forms of manifestation. Pattern languages of the first generation are oriented towards the practice of participatory design with a set purpose.

2.2 Pattern Language 2.0

The objects of second-generation pattern languages are non-material, intangible forms or structures such as organizations, learning programs, software or interfaces. Design acts incorporate multiple successive iterations over time. The purpose of patterns is to bridge gaps of understanding between expert and non-expert designers; they differ from those in first generation pattern languages in the possibility that non-material, intangible forms hold for successive improvement through incremental and iterative redesign. Patterns contribute to revealing, interpreting and communicating domain-specific tacit knowledge, allowing it to be understood, unpacked, and recomposed to address specific challenges and needs by interdisciplinary groups of collaborators lacking any other form of common technical language. They are themselves regularly redesigned to assist and follow adaptations and keep their edge in technical performance. Examples include those cited above in object-oriented programming and related fields where programmers work collaboratively within interdisciplinary teams.

2.3 Pattern Language 3.0

Third generation pattern languages have as their objects of design social processes, being oriented towards process and interaction among actors and the forms they design. Acts of design are again iterative, consisting of self-referential cycles of action learning through which actors learn to identify and express their own tacit knowledge, and collaborate on designing their own interactions. The purpose of patterns is to bridge gaps among people with different backgrounds, experiences, perspectives, and knowledge. They function as a medium for conversation and self-reflection, introducing feedback loops into design processes and allowing structural coupling of design and practice. Such processes foster individual development of consciousness and awareness, new forms of communication within and among groups, and new modes of innovation and action.[23] Examples include Takashi Iba's pattern languages on creative collaboration[24] and learning,[25] and the Groupworks pattern language for group processes.[26]

---

[23] Iba, T. (2010). "An autopoietic systems theory for creativity". Procedia-Social and Behavioral Sciences, 2(4): 6610-6625.
[24] Iba, T. (2014). Collaboration Patterns: A Pattern Language for Creative Collaborations. (Kanagawa: CreativeShift Lab).
[25] Iba, T. (2014). Learning Patterns: A Pattern Language for Creative Learning. (Kanagawa: CreativeShift Lab).
[26] Groupworks deck: Pattern language for group processes <http://groupworksdeck.org/>

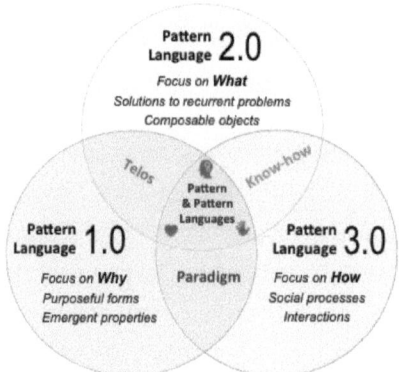

Figure 2: Three generations of pattern languages and the why, what, and how of design

Development from Pattern Languages 1.0 through 2.0 to 3.0 can be viewed as a shift from attention to the intent of design and emergent properties (the ‚why' of design) in the first generation, to the pattern as an element of an agreed solution to a complex problem (the ‚what' of design) in the second generation, to patterns as characterizing social processes (the ‚how' of design), each generation bringing a new dimension to designing for transformation. Pattern Language 4.0, whose emergence we propose to chart in this paper, links the why, how and what and explicitly seeks to employ pattern languages as tools in social change processes that self-evaluate, in ongoing fashion, in relation to a set of common underlying goals. In order to characterize pattern language 4.0, upcoming sections describe some of the complexities of social change processes: the systemic challenges it faces (Section 3), and its pluralistic nature and the consequent need for a semantic approach capable of reconciling multiple perspectives and issue framings (Section 4). We subsequently describe the systemic potential of pattern languages (Section 5) and outline general features through which fourth generation pattern languages realize this potential and address these complexities (Section 6), describing PLAST as a concrete example of a fourth generation project. In the conclusion we return to consider prospects for societal transformation and how the use of pattern languages can contribute to this.

We use the term fourth generation here neither to be prescriptive as to future directions of pattern language research and practice, nor to imply superiority of any generation or generations over any other. The term identifies one emerging trend among possible potentially useful and valid directions in pattern research. Fourth generation builds upon and seeks to integrate insights from the entire history of Pattern Language research.

3. Systemic Challenges and Societal Change

Most present-day societal challenges are systemic in nature. Lacking clear resolution or even problem definition, they exist as 'wicked problems', intractable to causal analysis and impervious to simple and concrete remedies.[27] Wicked problems defy attempts at definitive formulation because they accommodate many different perspectives on an issue and proposed pathways to change.[28] Multiple intervention points exist; some problems can be symptoms of others; solutions are partial and contingent, and may be contradictory and involve trade-offs. Proven experience, practice and expert knowledge do not exist, data are uncertain and often absent, and the information necessary to understand the problem is dispersed across multiple different contexts.

Lock-ins, path dependencies, and unpredictable unintended outcomes are all common features of complex societal problems, emergent upon dynamic processes affected by the behaviors of multiple agents (human and non-human). Consequences of these dynamics often manifest at levels other than those at which they originate. Initially invisible, they may over time gather momentum and become self-reinforcing, and in turn become structural features that shape the choices available to agents in the system. This is the source of phenomena like carbon lock-in:[29] a set of linked technological, institutional and political barriers to decarbonization of industrialized economies that ensure that, regardless of levels of apparent political will and investment, dependencies on fossil fuels and associated infrastructure remain entrenched.[30] This highly undesirable state subsequently propagates as path dependencies built in to new or rapidly changing systems, for example as emerging economies like China and India preferentially invest in market-ready, technologically proven energy conversion technologies with high levels of technical understanding and infrastructural support.[31] Innovation that can escape situations of lock-in is restricted either to the margins of the system, or to localized niches deliberately insulated from wider societal pressures.[32]

Our examination of the relationship between pattern languages and systemic constraints upon change is informed by the concept of stigmergy: indirect coordination of action among different agents based on the changes they make in the landscape.[33] Francis Heylighen describes how agents shape their environment, or medium, as their tracks aggregate and consolidate, up to a point where the medium itself becomes the mediator that directs

---
27 Rittel, H. & Melvin W. (1973). "Dilemmas in a General Theory of Planning". Policy Sciences: 155-169
28 Leach, M., I. Scoones & A. Stirling (2010). Dynamic Sustainabilities. (London: Earthscan).
29 Unruh, G. C. (2000). "Understanding carbon lock-in". Energy Policy 28(12): 817-830.
30 Mitchell, C. (2008). The Political Economy of Sustainable Energy. (Basingstoke: Palgrave MacMillan). Leggett, J. (2014) The Energy of Nations. (London: Earthscan).
31 Unruh, G. C. & Carrillo-Hermosilla, J. (2006). "Globalizing carbon lock-in". Energy Policy, 34(10): 1185-1197.
32 Grin, J., J. Rotmans & J. Schot (2010). Transitions to Sustainable Development. (London: Routledge).
33 Bonabeau, E. (1992). „Editor's introduction: stigmergy." Artificial Life 5(2): 95-96.

the agents.[34] For example, ants leave pheromone traces on the ground to direct others to food sources, creating a positive feedback loop as the pheromone signal strengthens with increased traffic and in turn attracts more ants. Similarly, cross-country trails start as barely distinguishable paths made by the first people to walk them, become more visible as people travel them, and eventually become persistent roads and highways that funnel the majority of traffic. Heylighen notes that the medium effectively manages communication processes, retaining the most useful pathways while the others are abandoned.

Lock-ins and path dependencies arise when the most traveled roads solidify as a dominant infrastructure from which escape is difficult: in more general terms, when norms and structures restrict choice and agency. When a behavior or a strategy is acknowledged as the fittest it becomes a benchmark, standard, or other form of institutionalized model, in such a way that other actors maximize their benefit by seeking to emulate it or directly cooperating. The major criterion for evaluating performance becomes the rate of application of the winning strategy, not its outcomes, and there are no embedded feedback mechanisms that would assess whether it remains fit for purpose over time. Obscured by the strength of this dominant trajectory, alternative routes towards system renewal and regeneration in the system become difficult to identify as such. These mechanisms underlie the establishment of internet monopolies such as Amazon, Facebook and Google, which when achieving critical thresholds of user numbers became able to shape user behavior over the internet more widely. Those same mechanisms are also the source of many of the unwelcome and even perverse outcomes of a global economy based on the scaling up of structures and behaviors optimized for smaller scales and under very different circumstances.[35]

In the techno-social environments in which most present-day humans live, institutionalized models very soon become embedded in cultural codes: sometimes non-materially as accepted customs, norms and habits; sometimes, particularly as computers and computer programs increasingly structure socio-technical realities, physically as algorithms that remain hidden from view in black boxes.

Where humans differ from ants is in the difficulty of changing what has become solidified into structure or coded into algorithm. Once they deplete their food source, ants begin to forage elsewhere and the pheromone track dissipates leaving room for new pathways to emerge. Human tracks are more persistent. As suggested by Heylighen, positive feedback that characterizes goal-oriented stigmergy is a great driver for both action and outcome. This however only applies until continued following of the most traveled tracks and over-

---

34 Heylighen, F. (2008). "Accelerating socio-technological evolution: from ephemeralization and stigmergy to the global brain". In Globalization as evolutionary process: modeling global change: p. 284 (London: Routledge). <http://bit.ly/1yfQyZN > [Retrieved 15 November 2014]
35 Boyle, D. & A. Simms (2009). The New Economics: A Bigger Picture. (London: Earthscan).

shadowing alternative opportunities destroys the functioning of the medium and so endangers the whole system.

Alexander has experienced this in his own work, when established perspectives and practices in the mainstream construction industry directly conflict with the life-enhancing aims of his user-centered projects.[36] The new architectural paradigm implied by Alexander's approach has failed to appear, not for reasons to do with its inherent features, but because the discipline is trapped in the tracks of processes that simply can not accommodate it.[37] More generally, the anti-patterns identified by the Public Sphere Project, describing factors responsible for the creation and persistence of various forms of injustice, inequality and oppression, illustrate how thoroughly pervasive they can be in global society, despite obviously being socially dysfunctional.[38]

The normalization of specific forms creates system dynamics that may be hard to perceive. The underlying structures and practices that continue to generate and reproduce the systems in which we live, whatever their initial purpose, may limit possibilities for engagement and the effects of active agency in projecting and shaping future trajectories. Consequently, actions focused on setting and achieving defined goals without relating to underlying patterns may be ineffective. Alexander opened this discussion by highlighting correlations among built forms and systemic social outcomes, and such discourse has now become evident in multiple areas of social change. Design patterns, especially when located in networks of interrelationships as pattern languages, have the potential to capture and operationalize systemic properties of relevant domains. This is illustrated in the first elements of the pattern language for the productive city, integrating principles regenerative of natural systems, presented by Howard Davis at the Purplsoc 2015 conference.[39] Systemic properties and the dynamics they generate need to be made visible, and over time monitored for truth to purpose and regularly challenged. Weak signals that may announce breakthroughs as well as breakdowns, and indicate possible alternative system trajectories, need to be identified in order to disrupt predetermined dynamics and deliberately design for the Quality Without a Name. Douglas Schuler drew attention to this when including systemic orientation among the key features of pattern languages for social change in his Purplsoc 2014 keynote.

---

36 Alexander, C., HJ. Neis & M. Alexander (2012). *The Battle for the Life and Beauty of the Earth*. (New York: Oxford University Press).
37 Grabow, S. (1983). *Christopher Alexander: the search for a new paradigm in architecture*. (Stocksfield: Oriel Press).
38 Public Sphere Project - Anti-patterns < http://bit.ly/1Nz7I5O>[Retrieved 15 September 2015]
39 Davis, H. (2015). "Pattern Languages and the New Productive City". Keynote presentation at Purplsoc 2015 Conference, Krems.

4. The Multiple Facets of Social Change

While weak signals may be inconspicuous in the face of entrenched dominant societal norms, they are nonetheless present at the margins. Edgar Morin describes this multiplicity of pathways in La Voie (the Way):

> *On each continent and in each nation one can find creative bubbling, a multitude of political initiatives in the direction of economic, social, political, cognitive, educational, ethical or existential regeneration.*
>
> *But everything that must be connected is yet dispersed, compartmented, separated. These initiatives are not aware of each other, no institution enumerates them, and no one is familiar with them. They are nonetheless the livestock for the future. It is now a matter of recognizing, aggregating, enlisting them in order to open up transformational paths.*
>
> *These multiple paths, jointly developing, will intermesh to form a new Path which will decompose into the paths each of us will follow and which will guide us toward the still invisible and inconceivable metamorphosis.*[40]

For systemic change to take place, and to be meaningful and endure in the long term, it needs to occur in a variety of ways and arise from many different locations, interconnected as networks and networks of networks. Isolated silos of thought and action need to become linked in a fabric of interventions that is compatible with the diversity of appropriate forms of action, creating synergies that leverage their variety, their complementarity and the richness of possible pathways they create.

Plurality of interventions is a vital condition for systemic transformation.[41] This needs to be acknowledged, and represented in a way that allows coordination of action across domains without imposing any centralized form of organization, or necessarily demanding coalition among events. Fourth generation pattern languages can accommodate multiple problem framings and describe the consequent emergent complexity in ways that allow change agents to take advantage of and build upon existing links across domains of action, whether or not those domains are aligned in terms of their internal descriptions and defined aims.

Figure 3 illustrates one way to represent and group approaches within this necessarily multidimensional landscape.

---
40 Morin, E. (2011). *La Voie: Pour l'avenir de l'Humanité* (Paris: Fayard). p 34. Citation translated by H. Finidori.
41 Leach, M., I. Scoones & A. Stirling (2010). *Dynamic Sustainabilities*. (London: Earthscan).

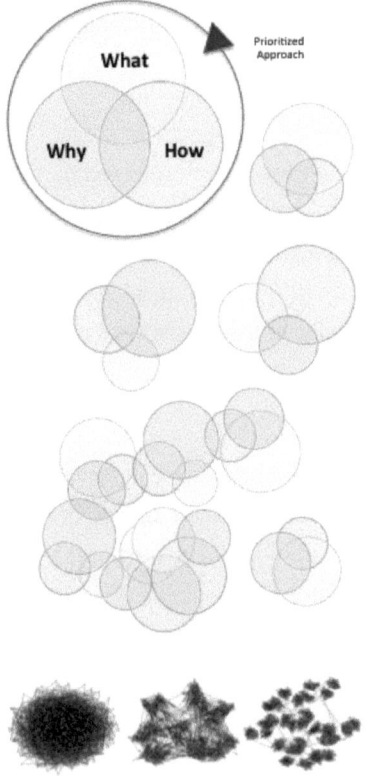

Our values and beliefs influence **why** we do what we do, our intentions, our purposes.

Our mental functions, learning and creative styles influence **how** we function and process information, how we interact with systems and people.

The two drive our logics of engagement and action, and our preferences for **what** we build and care for, and the languages and types of knowledge we develop.

This also determines whether we prioritize the why, the what or the how in our approaches to change and design, and the pathways we chose, creating multiple bubbles of agency.

These bubbles of agency, or islands of language and knowledge are effective in their own cohesive domain of focus.

They function effectively and convergently within their own boundaries, with new ideas that permeate through areas of overlap with other clusters. A network of interventions on whys, hows and whats that can cross pollinate each other.

Networks that are very diffuse (left) make it hard for ideas to catch on, while networks with very strong group boundaries (right) make it almost impossible for ideas to spread. A network that is moderately "grouped," with interconnections between groups, is most conducive to spreading complex ideas." Source: University of Pennsylvania

Figure 3: Interconnecting islands of agency and engagement[42]

Achieving cognitive understanding within cohesive domains of action is easier than achieving cultural understanding across action logics, but not necessarily realized in practice. For example, in addition to any differences of perspective, particular groups of change agents may prioritize intervention on the 'target' itself (the 'what': quality and effectiveness of the object transformed). Others may focus on practices and processes (the 'how': quality of the process and experience), others still on the intentions and motivations of stakeholders (the 'why': quality of the intention and overall direction of the emergent design). Accordingly, the same phenomenon may be a strategic/tactical concern (how) or justification (why) for one group, and at the same time the primary object of attention and care (the what) for another. Equally, development of a tactic (how) or an object of attention (what) may be invoked as a motivating reason (why). All this makes coordination for change rather complicated. What we consequently observe is a multitude of islands of agency and engagement. Each has its own tacit knowledge and language that are effective in the specific domain on which it

---

[42] Centola, D. 2015. "The Social Origins of Networks and Diffusion" in *American Journal of Sociology* Vol. 120, No. 5, pp. 1295-1338

focuses. As Figure 3 shows, different islands either can not or do not need to align on any of the dimensions of how, why and what. However, they may converge in several of their applications.

Pattern languages as they have evolved to date enable change agents, whatever their core areas of interest, to identify their own goals and design their own preferred pathways towards them. Various types of pattern language exist, catering for multiple forms of why, what and how in diverse domains of knowledge and action. Each nurtures opportunities for learning and collaboration, and possibilities for mutually supportive action. By making visible previously covert processes and the tacit knowledge that underlies them, a pattern language provides a common vocabulary for design and so opens up new channels of communication and understanding.

The question we now pose is whether there are valid ways to interconnect pattern languages in order to provide a basis for aggregating diverse separate bodies of actionable knowledge and enabling coordinated action towards common higher purposes that reflect deeper systemic features shared across domains (Figure 4). Douglas Schuler mentions in his Pattern Languages for Public Problem Solving the need to accommodate greater levels of interconnection and sharing through syntactic formalization and creation of shared tag sets to mark up the systemic components of patterns.[43] The next step would involve finding meta-languages for tagging, according to their systemic implications, a multitude of patterns belonging to pattern languages of different types, across domains of know-how and cultures.

Figure 4: Interconnecting pattern languages for synergy and coordinated action

43 Schuler, D. 2014. "Pattern Languages for Public Problem Solving. Seven Seeds for Theory and Practice." Presentation to the Purplsoc Workshop 2014 <http://bit.ly/1GBPQIT> [Retrieved 10 October 2015]

5. The Systemic Orientation of Pattern Languages

Understanding the way pattern theory builds upon systems theory is fundamental to appreciating how elaboration of a fourth generation of pattern languages can support the interlaced meta-network of social action described in the previous section. Across all three prior generations of pattern languages, and in Alexander's core conceptualization, pattern languages provide inter-related units of organization (whether physical, immaterial or relational) that aim to generate systems recognized by their users/designers as creative, healthy, living wholes sustaining multiple types of function.

Alexander wrote in a 1968 article Systems generating Systems:[44]

> *There are two ideas hidden in the word system: the idea of a system as a whole and the idea of a generating system.*

This distinction is crucial to understanding pattern languages. The same article continues:

> *A system as a whole is not an object but a way of looking at an object. It focuses on some holistic property which can only be understood as a product of interaction among parts.*
>
> *A generating system is not a view of a single thing. It is a kit of parts, with rules about the way these parts may be combined.*
>
> *Almost every 'system as a whole' is generated by a 'generative system'. If we wish to make things which function as wholes we shall have to invent generating systems to create them.*

The article predates *A Pattern Language* but it clearly articulates how this systems perspective influenced Alexander's later work[45] and his notion of pattern languages as evocations and instances of generative processes fundamental to the unfolding of natural phenomena, operating in conjunction with intentional behaviors.

Alexander indeed questioned later on in his work whether pattern languages such as derived from *A Pattern Language* (in their context - problem - solution format) didn't actually limit design to assembling fragmented structural ideas or objects (i.e. sequences of good ideas) into static forms rather than helping to create living generative entities and diachronic models (i.e. incorporating a time dimension) able to effectively address contempo-

---

[44] Alexander, C. (2011). "Systems Generating Systems." In Computational Design Thinking, edited by Achim Mengers and Sean Ahlquist, 58–67. Chichester, England: John Wiley & Sons. Reproduced from "Systems Generating Systems", Architectural Design, volume 38 (December), John Wiley & Sons Ltd (London), 1968, pp. 605-610. Originally published in Systemat, a journal of the Inland Steel Products Company.

[45] Alexander, C. (2001-2005). The Nature of Order. (Berkeley: Center for Environmental Structure). Alexander, C. (2003). "New concepts in complexity theory arising from studies in the field of architecture an overview of the four books of The Nature of Order with emphasis on the scientific problems which are raised". <http://bit.ly/1MmRBli>[Retrieved 15 September 2015]

rary societal challenges.[46] The question of the adequacy of the A Pattern Language pattern approach for societal change was at the center of David West's Purplsoc conference talk on Missing Pattern Languages.[47] This talk provided a reminder of lessons from Alexander's earlier book *Notes on the Synthesis of Form*,[48] in particular the idea of patterns as composable diagrams, key to the process of creating form.

The pattern as, "[A]bstract pattern of physical relationships which resolves a small system in interacting and conflicting forces," of the Notes became a problem-solution construct as a means towards descriptive simplicity. More than ever, however, we need patterns to support our understanding of complexity and the richness of our diverse perceptions, interpretations and representations, in order to help us expand opportunities for collective interventions. Recent decades have achieved greater maturity in the understanding of organized complexity, allowing us to begin to reformulate and reintroduce the process of orientation inherent in the idea of patterns and give it an explicit presence.

Most important for the purpose of this paper is the concept of 'generative', which points at emergent structure and behavior. The notion of emergence is invoked when a system's observed global properties cannot be predicted from the known properties of its elements. Emergence therefore refers in particular to the onset of a new level of functional properties in a system. A system presenting such a property is defined as complex and described as having complex behavior.[49] Complexity is a basic organizational feature of all living systems;[50] its emergence is a central feature of biological and social evolution.[51] Many complex behaviors are generated by local and relatively simple rules of interaction, as observed for example when colonies of social insects build and maintain extremely sophisticated nests[52] or in the 'nearest neighbor' rules of flocking birds.[53] The specific behavior of elements is unpredictable, but the global outcome can be modelled by specifying the rules of interaction among elements - as happens, for example, in computer simulations of swarms.

---

46 Alexander, Christopher. 1996. "Patterns in Architecture" presented at OOPSLA '96, October 8, San Jose, California. <http://bit.ly/1LnXvyP> [Retrieved 15 October 2015]
47 West, D. 2015. "Missing Pattern Languages". Talk at the Purplsoc 2015 conference <http://bit.ly/1OIC3bG> [Retrieved 15 September 2015]
48 Alexander, C. 1964 Notes on the Synthesis of Form (Harvard University Press)
49 Prigonine, I. & I. Stengers, (1984). Order out of Chaos. (New York: Bantam Books).
50 Jacob, F. (1989). The Logic of Life. (London: Penguin).
51 Kauffman, S.A. (1993). The Origins of Order. (Oxford: Oxford University Press).
52 Theraulaz G., Gautrais J, Camazine S, Deneubourg JL, (2003), "The formation of spatial patterns in social insects: from simple behaviours to complex structures". Phil. Trans. R. Soc. Lond. A 361, 1263–1282.
53 Reynolds, C. W. (1987) "Flocks, Herds, and Schools: A Distributed Behavioral Model, in Computer Graphics", 21(4) (SIGGRAPH ,87 Conference Proceedings) pages 25–34.

There is a correlation between **structural aspects** of a system, the emergent **behavior** of it, and the ways in which it **evolves** successful form-function solutions over time, that pattern languages can encode and decode, allowing to maneuver and orient intentional behavior in conjunction with systemic phenomena.

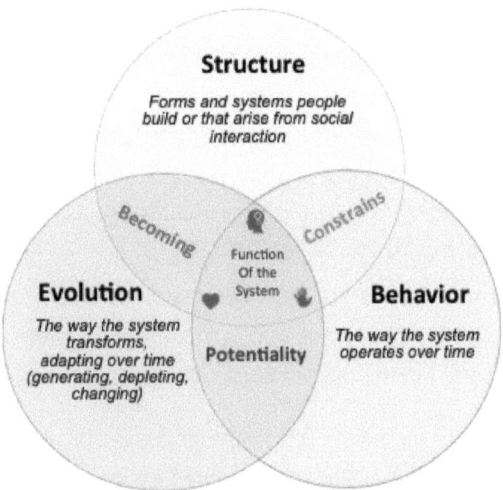

Figure 5: Adaptive development of systems

Using the notion of emergence, "Generative patterns can be understood to work indirectly; they work on the underlying structure of a problem (which may not be manifest in the problem) rather than attacking the problem directly."[54] The pattern approach to systems, while maintaining awareness of inherent uncertainty, allows identification of relevant points of contact and interaction of elements (articulated by the patterns) at levels other than the problem or phenomenon as a whole. It thus orients intentional behavior in relation to systemic phenomena. Generative patterns address the physical connections, designed forms, organizing protocols and processes[55] that give rise to emergence, synergies and other complex properties responsible for the wicked nature of societal challenges.

Understanding how complexity acts together with intentional design in social systems also requires examination of the telos - purpose or directionality - of complex systems and how this can be influenced through design. Considering biological systems, O'Grady and Brooks distinguished three types of complex behavior: teleological (outcome is defined by human or other external agent); teleonomic (outcome is ‚programmatic', setting defined limits within which possibilities can unfold in many different ways, such as those of the genetic

---
54 Coplien, J. O. (1996). Software Patterns. SIGS Books. From Ing, David "Systems generating systems - the architecture of Christopher Alexander (1968) < http://bit.ly/1Eq8N3A> [Retrieved 15 September 2015]
55 Jones, P.H. "Systemic Design Principles for Complex Social Systems" Chapter 4 in: Social Systems and Design, Gary Metcalf (editor) Volume 1 of the Translational Systems Science Series, Springer Verlag

code) and teleomatic (outcome is contingent, the consequence of concomitant forces, like in ecosystems).[56] Similarly from a social design standpoint, systems thinker and design thinker Peter Jones distinguished purposive systems - well structured or institutionalized social systems that embed deterministic mechanisms dedicated to prescribed outcomes - from those that are purposeful or purpose-seeking. Purposeful systems target pre-determined outcomes and fulfill specified purposes through diverse means. A purpose-seeking system seeks to converge towards an ideal future state, and upon attainment of any of its intermediate goals then seeks another goal that more closely approximates its ideal.[57] Living, non-human, systems exhibit behavior that is teleonomic/purposeful and/or teleomatic/purpose-seeking rather than teleological/purposive. Human techno-social, socio-economic and socio-environmental systems are hybrid complex systems whose directionality derives from a variety of underlying processes and forms of telos, generating different combinations of deterministic and intentional behaviors and allowing variable degrees of agency.

In relation to the foregoing formulation, pattern languages provide the basis for the type of design for emergence that Jenny Quillien proposes for addressing organized complexity.[58] They attempt to replace purposive processes, prescriptive as far as interventions are concerned (such as prior specification by an architect of all details of how a building will be built and used), with generative processes whose nature is either purposeful (for example, when designers, builders and users co-design a building within specific parameters to produce certain types of behavior through inclusive and organic processes) or purpose-seeking (if no end is specified at the onset, but rather a 'quality' or property as an ideal that is then pursued through intermediate stages).

Present-day understanding of ecological systems has moved beyond static equilibrium models based on homeostasis and the teleological notion of progress towards climax formations to more dynamic notions incorporating phases of rapid change whose outcomes are contingent on interactions between the system's internal dynamics and factors in its external environment.[59] Similarly, in social processes, particularly in a context of rapid societal change, emergent behaviours are inherently unpredictable. Moreover, the development over time of hidden informal structures can change intended or stated goals. This mean we find ourselves in the area of purpose-seeking, needing to orient and adapt processes through a number of intermediate stages.

---

[56] Mayr, E. (2006). "Teleological and Teleonomic: A New(er) Analysis" <http://bit.ly/1GilErG> [Retrieved 15 September]; O'Grady, R. T., & D. R. Brooks, (1988). "Teleology and biology". Pp. 285-316 in B.H. Weber, D. J. Depew, and J. D. Smith (eds.) Entropy, information, and evolution: New Perspectives on Physical and Biological Evolution. (Cambridge, MA: The MIT Press). Unseen, cited in Abel, T. (1998). "Complex adaptive systems, evolutionism, and ecology within anthropology: interdisciplinary research for understanding cultural and ecological dynamics". Journal of Ecological Anthropology, 2(1), 6-29.

[57] Jones, P.H. Ibid

[58] Quillien, J. 2015 "Parsing systemic change: And the Three begot the ten thousand things" in: Spanda Journal VI,1/2015. Systemic Change, Finidori, H. (Ed) (The Hague: Spanda Foundation)

[59] Gunderson, L. & C.S. Holling (eds.) 2002. Panarchy. (Washington DC: Island Press).

While searching for generative mechanisms, we can neither map causal processes to structures in any simple fashion, nor can we assume that the relation of processes to structure will remain unchanged over time. The option we do have is continuously to explore and monitor the landscape of possible solutions as it evolves. This is where the system may continue to develop new functionality, which we can evaluate in relation to desired properties. In nature, we observe a massive parallel exploration of strategies that constantly optimizes structures in relation to the fitness landscape.[60] Artificial systems perform similar processes (if parameters can be accurately formulated) through simulations by recursive algorithms that explore multiple options in parallel towards successful generative relations. In relation to social phenomena, studying a sufficiently wide selection of case studies or data, when they are available, will provide a similar type of output.

The evolution of pattern languages can also be understood from this perspective. Alexander's meticulous study of recurrent structural patterns in vernacular architecture while constructing the first ever pattern language provided a wide set of case studies, with demonstrated capacity to maintain fitness, from which to formalize knowledge in the relevant domain. The second generation built upon the format thus developed, in order to allow successful transfer and production of adaptive knowledge across different domains. This allowed exploration and optimization of solutions over an extremely wide and diverse range of users and problems. The third generation introduces self-referential processes that reconnect the structures being designed to the systems they produce, in real time and easy to observe at human scale. It thus creates an iterative loop that is both generated by the structure (relational) and generative of it, and so brings reflexivity about social processes to center stage.

This understanding is fundamental for work in domains changing so rapidly that past change in similar systems cannot alone provide the information necessary to inform effective strategies. Even if we are able to define the 'quality without a name' as an end, we have to reintroduce processes of orientation and attention to telos, evident in Alexander's original thinking, in order to create frameworks for guiding unpredictable dynamic processes.

Once the dimension of orientation is acknowledged and actively iterated, the broad plurality of active agency and the multiplicity of approaches discussed earlier allow a wide-ranging exploration of the landscape of possibilities that can orient the search for workable and effective generative interventions. The next step is to reveal the potential for active and adaptive knowledge development and transfer across wide and heterogeneous networks, and monitoring and orientation of the development of the systems thus generated.

---

60 Kauffman, S., 2007. "Beyond reductionism: Reinventing the sacred". Zygon, Journal of Religion and Science 42: 903–914.

6. Fourth Generation Pattern Languages

Fourth generation pattern languages respond specifically to these needs for interconnection and diachronic orientation. Different pattern languages can be semantically interconnected to provide an epistemological thread and a collective coordination medium connecting capacity for action across separate domains of application. As Figure 6 shows, in this way they help set the conditions for effective societal change by leveraging collective intelligence and catalyzing agency at aggregated levels.

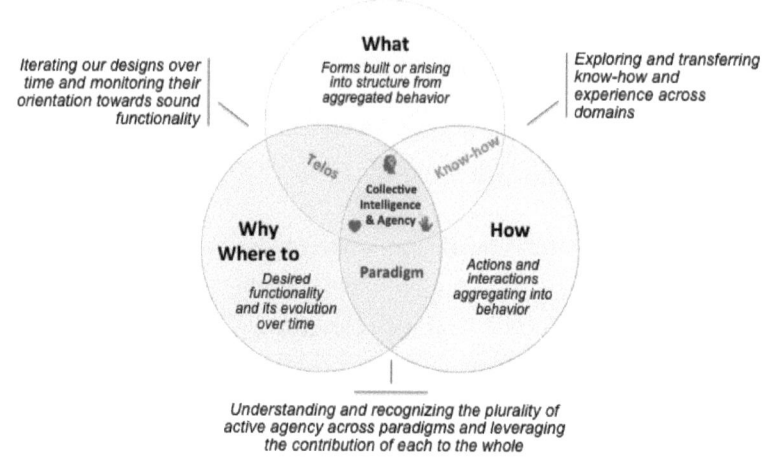

Figure 6: Leveraging collective intelligence and catalyzing agency at aggregated levels

Extending Iba's framework, the objects of design of fourth generation pattern languages are dynamic systemic forms (structures, systemic behaviors, relationships and effects). The act of design is generative: emergent, stigmergetic and self-organizing over time. The purpose of design is to connect different types of agencies and intentions across domains of practice in order that the search for functionally sound generative patterns converges on optimal solutions.

We see Pattern Language 4.0 as a system of knowledge to:

1. Help decode and encode systems' directionality (potential emergent behavior and evolution of design objects)

while

2. Mediating among multiple knowledges and cultural contexts, perceptions, interpretations and representations by semantically connecting existing pattern languages.

We here relate to pattern languages primarily as operating generative structures in recursive interaction with the systems they are intended to produce, and thus having strong systemic connotations. Summarizing the above arguments, we describe them as empirical and phenomenological tools with the capacity to:

» Investigate and capture interacting components of situations and systems, and formalize tacit practices that have generative properties;

» Create suitable media for the collective processing of knowledge about constructive responses to complex challenges;

» Render visible and accessible for iteration the feedback loops that support inquiry into the desired functionality of context-related systems;

» Thus allow collective orientation of emerging systems, at the same time facilitating the formalization, monitoring and iteration of the desired functions adaptively provided by a system.

To accommodate the last aspect we added a fourth attribute to Iba's comparison matrix: orientation. It refers to the ability to actively monitor and orient our interventions within the systems being produced. This supports a process of successive approximation to desired and iteratively formulated qualities that are understood as emergent. It can also be understood as the capacity for collective interpretation of the evolving directionality of the resulting system (which is different from the purpose of the design). This is a fundamental aspect of working with increasingly complex systems and wicked problems - as is the case in societal change - where direct interventions are part of knowledge building in the field and demand continuous processes of observation, interpretation, orientation, design, action, monitoring and adaptation. Processes of this kind are involved in frameworks such as Charles Pierce's cycle of pragmatism[61] (observation, induction, abduction, deduction, testing, action), John Boyd's OODA loop for situational awareness[62] (observe, orient, decide, act) and more recently, Dave Snowden's Cynefin approach to complex adaptive systems[63] (probe, sense, respond).

---

61 Peirce, C. S. (1903). "Pragmatism as a Principle and Method of Right Thinking", The 1903 Lectures on Pragmatism, ed. by P. A. Turrisi, SUNY Press, Albany, 1997. Also in [18], pp. 131-241.
62 Boyd, J. (1996). "The Essence of Winning and Loosing". Slideshow <http://bit.ly/1MomGyU>[Retrieved 10 October 2015]
63 Kurtz, C. F. & Snowden, D. J. (2003). "The new dynamics of strategy: Sense-making in a complex and complicated world" in IBM Systems Journal, Vol 42, NO 3 pp 462-483

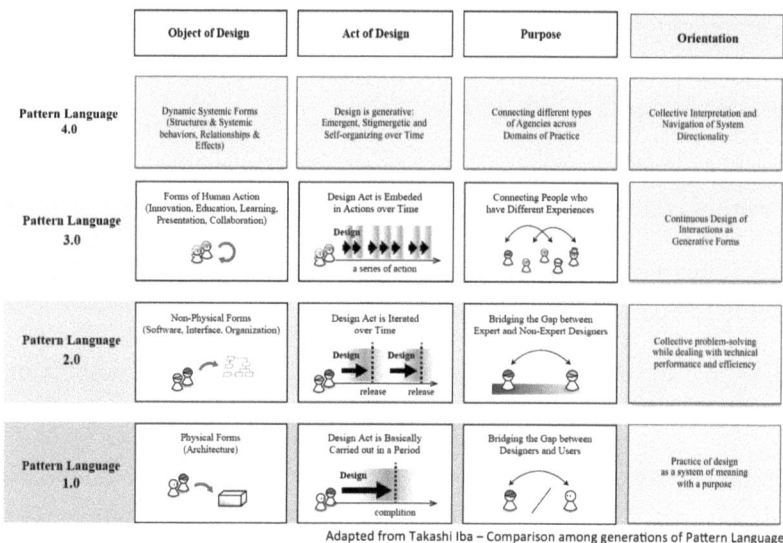

Figure 7: The four generations of pattern languages

In the newly proposed matrix of comparison we see that while Pattern Language 1.0 is about orientation of the practice of design as a system of meaning with a purpose, Pattern Language 2.0 is about orientation of collective problem-solving while dealing with technical performance and efficiency of the objects transformed, and Pattern Language 3.0 is about orientation of the continuous design of interactions as a form of engendering creativity (like in collaborative discovery and sense-making), Pattern Language 4.0 is about orientation of the collective interpretation and navigation of system directionality as an enactment of agency.

PLAST: a concrete example of a fourth generation project

The PLAST project aims to develop a pattern language of the fourth generation.

PLAST is a collaboration of individuals and communities of practice (pattern language practitioners, permaculturists, change agents, facilitators, educators and designers) and scholars in various disciplines (pattern languages, complexity theory, network theory, systems thinking, mathematics, algorithmic design, economics, linguistics, graphic design…) gathered in an open source network to create tools and methodologies for collective interpretation of systems' behavior and directionality, and to share experiences, while understanding each other across domains of knowledge and culture, in order to have more impact in bringing about societal transformation.

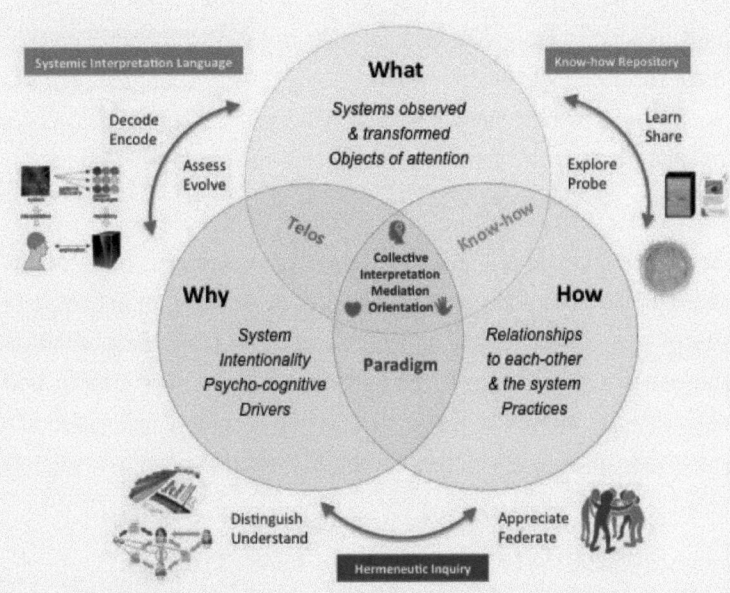

Figure 8: PLAST - A collective interpretation and systemic orientation system

The sets of tools and methodologies PLAST aims to develop comprise: a visual language (vocabulary, grammar, syntax) composed of systemic interpretation elements;[64] systemic patterns and various semantic connectors to encode and decode systemic orientations, structure and interactions, emergent dynamics and behaviors; and associated heuristics in order to assess and advance system design.

PLAST will be operationalized offline through design and facilitation methodologies that support both the design of the PLAST language and tools and a process for hermeneutic inquiry based on action research, shared discovery and mutual recognition across communities of practice and experience. It will thus enhance systemic awareness and systemic literacy. The approach is part of a peer-to-peer learning process that will help communities distinguish and understand different perspectives and engagement logics in order to appreciate their differences and complementarities and federate a diversity of actions.

A first set of components sourced both from theory and pilot practice has been tested in workshops, including during the Purplsoc conference, which helped generate systemic stories that enabled comparisons and rich discussions about various systemic conditions and situations. PLAST will grow organically by expanding through community encounters during conferences, workshops, and hackathons.

---

64 Finidori, H. (2014). "A Pattern LAnguage for Systemic Transformation (PLAST) - (re) Generative of Commons", in Baumgartner, P & Sickinger, R (Eds) PURPLSOC: The Workshop 2014 (Krems: Conference Edition) <http://bit.ly/11xD2oF> [Retrieved 13 December 2014]

The language itself - and in particular the systemic interpretation elements - will be used for indexing and connecting various elements, and for mapping the web of pattern languages and domains of social change. Envisioned technological applications include standards for indexing solutions and pattern databases, qualification or tagging of projects and models, and indexing algorithms as a systemic interoperability standard, in addition to indexing pattern languages.

PLAST will be operationalized online mainly as a digital platform comprising a repository of various layers of patterns and pattern languages by domains of application or function (such as PatternPedia[65]), with a social network component to evaluate and discuss problematiques and patterns, along with design tools that support synchronous and asynchronous co-design (graphic as well as text/code), forking and merging, migration, combining, sequencing, such as currently enabled by Github[66] or Ward Cunningham's Smallest Federated Wiki.[67]

PLAST will strive to enable the following experiences and capabilities:

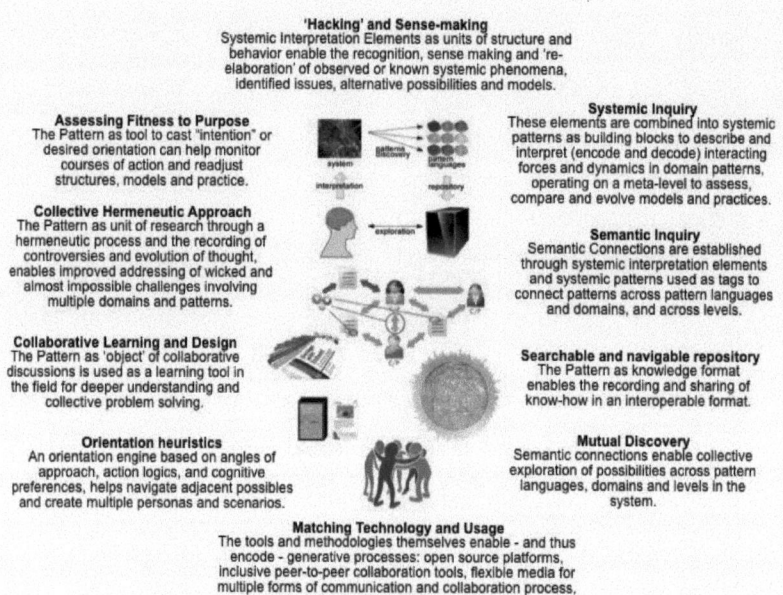

Figure 9: Main elements of PLAST (experiences and capabilities)

---

65 Fehling, C., Barzen, J., Falkenthal, M., & Leymann, F. (2014). "PatternPedia. Collaborative Pattern Identification and Authoring". In: Proceedings of Pursuit of Pattern Languages for Societal Change - Preparatory Workshop 2014.
66 Github features: <https://github.com/features>
67 Smallest Federate Wiki Welcome Visitors page <http://bit.ly/1kri2tI> [Retrieved 15 September 2015]

7. Conclusion: a code for systemic transformation

Fourth generation pattern languages such as PLAST can become emancipatory tools, as they can bring to light knowledge and understanding about the workings of interconnected techno-social, socio-economic and socio-environmental systems that are normally hidden from view and that, when consciously articulated, allow people to propose and act upon ways to transform the directionality of these systems and, hence, their own situation. The approach of decoding and encoding is a way of 'hacking the system', to understand its components and interactions in order to build anew or transform.

Alexander saw pattern languages as tools for supporting what he referred to as System-A, a life-centered, human scale alternative to the globally dominant social, political, economic and cultural configuration he called System-B.[68] Discussions on the feasibility of systemic transformation, on structure versus agency, have been going on for a long time in many disciplines.[69] French philosopher and sociologist Jean Baudrillard defined an ungraspable order in the System, a simulacrum made of indefinite chainings of simulations he called 'the code'.[70] This code, in its unbounded (de-finalized in Baudrillard's own terms) space-time, dissolves and absorbs any final cause for change such as political economy or revolution. In this logic, trying to 'fight' The System from within is vain, because any attempt will be neutralized by dilution in the code: the medium taking control of the agent as described earlier in the paper.[71]

For Baudrillard, dissent could only succeed by transcending 'the code': when applied at a higher logical order than that it wishes to overcome. It is difficult to imagine in this logic, with an open-ended medium that is not 'circumscribable' and that we can't step out of to ‚transcend' or ‚overcome', that this could happen through anything else than a totalitarian enterprise. Hence the deadlock he evoked. We suggest that dissent could materialize through the insertion of new pieces of code at multiple levels and scales via distributed praxis, in an approach akin to hacking, in order to ‚dilute' the existing dominant code in an emergent process.

This is probably what Alexander had in mind when he noted,[72] in his talk at the Object Oriented Programming, Systems, Languages and Applications conference in San José in 1996, the increasing influence of computer programs in shaping almost all aspects of the

---
[68] Alexander, C., HJ. Neis & M. Alexander, (2012). *The Battle for the Life and Beauty of the Earth*. (New York: Oxford University Press).
[69] Bateson, G. (1979). *Mind and Nature: a necessary unity*. (New York: Dutton). Giddens, A. (1984). *The constitution of society: Outline of the theory of structuration*. (Cambridge: Polity Press). Sewell Jr, W. H. (1992). "A theory of structure: Duality, agency, and transformation". *American Journal of Sociology*, 1-29.
[70] Poster, M. 1988. *Jean Baudrillard Selected Writings*. 1st edition Stanford University Press p 110 to 148
[71] Poster, M. Ibid
[72] Alexander, Christopher. 1996. "Patterns in Architecture" presented at OOPSLA '96, October 8, San Jose, California. <http://bit.ly/1LnXvyP> [Retrieved 15 September 2015]

world in which we now live in (for example in manufacturing, transportation, construction management, diagnosis, printing or publishing…even before the advent of social networks and their increasing power to orient choices and shape behavior), and deplored the lack of discussion about how programs and therefore code could help change the world. Software programmers, he argued, have a responsibility to generate living structures in the world and could write code as sets of instructions for generative processes and procedures.

As a set of 'meta' languages, used to encode and decode systemic directionality, emergent behavior and evolution of design objects, pattern languages of the fourth generation could well pave the way towards achieving this purpose. They would help make visible the various hidden 'codes' of the system and enable a hermeneutical inquiry of systemic, semantic and paradigmatic nature that would help the emergence of new more generative encodings. Unlike conventional code, which usually operates in black boxes, this 'code' would operate in plain view.

Guiding Patterns of Naturally Occurring Design: Elements

Henshaw, Jessie Lydia
HDS natural systems design science, USA
sy@synapse9.com

Pattern language can be used to describe transformative ways of resolving disparate forces in complex contexts, making explicit the ancient practices of holistic architectural design, creating new forms with living quality. Discussed here are ways to use pattern language for learning from recurrent design patterns of nature. Common patterns of naturally occurring organization and transformation are used to search in great repositories of natural design patterns, and find diverse living examples to learn from. For example, the familiar way designers work from early concepts to finished products is can be described as a recurrence of the natural process of complex designs developing from small beginnings to emerge in new forms. The technique of "pattern search" uses a "dual paradigm view" to separate the subjects of conceptual models and of observed natural forms, allowing attention to turn back and forth from one to the other as one studies their connections.

Pattern language; natural design; pattern repositories; living quality; dual paradigm; object oriented science

1. Introduction

The organization of this report, the choice of topics and their order, came from needing to introduce a broad field of research. Many years of natural systems science research on the complex patterns of naturally occurring design proceeded this, and needed to be translated into a pattern language vernacular for communicating with a wider audience. It originated with the author's years of original work on the complex natural patterns of eventful energy use in natural systems (1979, 1995-9). The paper is arranged somewhat as a series of vignettes, introducing numerous related topics, alternating general discussion with deep dives into advanced topics.

That is a somewhat pedagogical choice too, of presenting core subjects as a way to introduce a broad complex subject. The alternative would be to condense a general survey of the field, sure to be incomplete and likely to be less informative given the space and time available. The approach is both hoped to follow a logical sequence and to cover subjects both sufficiently developed to present and of general interest. The main interest is to provide a good sampling of the field giving readers places to start their own thinking on it. So each topic presents various parts of interesting problems and some of the kinds of solutions explored, thought of as a good way to give both advanced and beginning readers interesting and useful points of entry.

1.1 Origins

Christopher Alexander's motivation for developing pattern language seems to first appear in "A city is not a tree" (1965), written when teaching architectural theory at Berkley. He recognizes a missing richness in the patterns of modern design, "some essential ingredient missing from artificial cites", compared with treasured traditional cities if the past. He linked it with a loss of rich interconnections, that made modern urban design relatively dull and lifeless both aesthetically and unwelcoming as places to live. What was missing seemed to him to be a pattern of overlapping complexly in natural opportunities for connection, what he called "a semi-lattice" form of relationships, that would offer a richness of unplanned possibilities.

My own interest in the general subject came from struggling with many of the same concerns with a lifelessness in modern design, but in the early 70's a few years later. It was while studying architectural and environmental design in Philadelphia[1]. His starting point was seeing inconsistencies between natural patterns of design and mathematical hierarchies, as

---
1   GSFA MFA in Archt.& Environmental Design, 1974

"trees". Mine was recognizing a difference between what I'd studied in physics[2], a world of fixed rules, and the eventful nature of designs that would develop as individual unified wholes. Architecture is all about working with individual circumstances and perfecting uniquely individual designs for them. That's a subject that physics treats only as "undefined". My questions weren't focused at first, but led to finding that "individuality" and "the liveliness of events", are among the things most defined in nature, but the sciences generally leave unstudied, looking for universal laws.

What I eventually found was that the great success of physics as a language for nature was also very selective. By focusing only on natural relationships that can be defined mathematically, one inadvertently excludes all questions about things that work and behave individually, noticing ways that selectivity was a costly kind of trade-off. In the field of design, then, one studies the wonderful things that are possible, more or less in-between the laws for what things are necessary, requiring an interest in both. That not only includes learning to create individually whole systems of design, but also create designs to provide fully satisfying services. One controls many things, but the usual intent is to create a good home for some set of services and to understand the cultures providing and receiving them. It's a comprehensive task, for serving independent interests, not an issue of imposing laws of control.

That confronted me with much the same basic dilemma Alexander faced, a feeling that what seemed increasingly dominating my world seemed so "lifeless". I eventually understood that what physics actually defines are not "determinant causes", really, but "knowable limits". It's between those limits where the liveliness emerges, in the complexity of the uncertainties, the part of our information that traditional science discards. That's the space that design and natural systems work within. That kind of insight really only came as a result of my graduate studies, doing studies of the how energy naturally moved in passive buildings, where I found a very lively pattern of emerging design in how organization develops around energy use, a sort of pattern language quite different from Alexander's (Henshaw 1979, 1995).

My first real hints of how organization develops around energy use were during school, observing the work in the design studio. With every design we'd begin with relaxed exploratory efforts that lead successively to more and more intense investments of energy that then tapered off again with the last finishing touches. Great crescendos of effort typically were needed to bring any design to conclusion, building as if following a natural course of expanding on some simple concept. In studio one occasionally pauses and sits up to notice

---
2   St. Lawrence Univ., Physics, 1968. See also JLH CV (2015)

what's happening around you. Observing the textures of sound in the room changing in nervous energy with the intensity of work going on is one of many things reflecting the big wave shape of the energy being expended as the designs develop. Studio projects always develop from scratch, with everyone working on the same problem, looking for how to start, then adding to the complexity and effort while staying focused on making it whole in the end, or it fails. Most often the projects in the studio all go off in different directions, with each individual's effort leading to something distinctly individual.

I also recall being inspired by hearing of Alexander's ideas back then too, well before his first general description of a pattern language (1977). I recall just from discussing in school, hearing about how he had studied the evolution of urban designs and changing shapes of public spaces. In the evolving shape of the Piazza San Marco he had found evidence of the environment having served as a pattern repository (Henshaw 2015b). The notable feature was how new patterns of design sometimes revived discarded features from the past, displaying a kind of environmental pattern memory for the future. It made me think about how that happened all the time during the work on any design project too. Having an accumulating pile of old versions and experiments as a design progressed allowed you to go back and find a version of something that had been discarded and later turned out to be really needed. Today there may no longer be piles of drawings to go back through physically, page after page, and review the whole evolution of a project and see how you got where you did, and what was lost. One hopes that still goes on somehow, and that the evolution of designs as accumulations of alternatives and experiments is still studied.

I also did a thesis length paper on micro-climates and how they characterized local places, and for my thesis then focused on a design for sustainable town planning. Where that thinking really became a study in new science was in the studies I began a couple years later, with the field research on how solar energy moves in homes. I purchased portable instruments for recording building climates over 24 hour periods. After setting it up I would spend the whole day and night taking notes and tracing the development of both individual air currents and their evolving pathways, by which most natural energy movement travels. It always takes a tricky bit of organization, since for air to move anywhere other air needs to get out of the way. So the energy is effectively "trapped" by that, until the organization to make a pathway develops. So that very quickly became a study of the individuality of those designs, and how they evolved over the day as the sunlight changed direction. The flow patterns would kick up in the morning, reorganize and move several times in a day, and then fade away at night as the energy dissipated (Henshaw 1979a).

After a few months that led to recognizing a fundamental pattern, that all the emerging systems of organization evolved much the same general way, they developed and subsided by *progressive* patterns of accumulative development, step-wise design that multiplied and transformed. My first attempt to describe it as a natural pattern was in "An Unhidden Pattern of Events" (Henshaw 1979b). It seemed to imply a very clear opportunity studying how individual systems developed as wholes, particularly given that the emergence of new organization seemed associated with emerging energy use too. That also made it seem particularly surprising that it also appeared not to have been studied before. I think what happened was that I found a fairly practical to approach to studying whole organizational patterns, but the sciences that relied on equations lacked a way to study individually emerging systems. Having no mathematical way to represent them would make their organization "undefined" and so left unstudied.

What eventually drew me to Alexander's pattern language was how it developed to offer me this way to translate my earlier work. In later years it began to be adopted by other fields, and becoming a kind of universal language of design that any profession or field could use. I was mostly unaware of how it was emerging as it was making its important contribution of "object oriented design" for software development. My own introduction was in just the last couple years, as pattern language started being part of the systems thinking used in the commons movement (Finidori 2014, 2015)(Bollier, Helfrich Eds. 2014)(Roy & Trudel 2011) (Nahrada 2013), and led to my work with UN organizations finding ways to make a commons approach work, and learning to make explicit the patterns of relationships required for a commons approach to work (Henshaw 2013, 2014).

What was most useful was how the general model for pattern language had evolved fairly simple basic structure, a basic plan for identifying all the competing "forces" in a given context and a lasting way of resolving them all together. It would usually aim to be with some "recurrent principle" of elegant design. It's not always possible but it sometimes wonderfully is. One then adds other details for describing the context and means of fitting the pattern to it. Altogether it captures the heart of the ancient principles of holistic design, an organization for unifying the forces, that incidentally produces wonderful emergent qualities.

It's not quite how Alexander presented it, but way of describing the common elements of Alexander's approach in the form that seems to be spreading to multiple professions and communities. Like everyone else, I constantly have to work on defining these "gems of good design", how to describe and applying them, define terms and standards, etc. To develop into a common language what remains essential is retaining the simple organizing principles common to all approaches, so they can be translated back and forth as they are added to. So this paper for PURPLSOC, and a companion paper for the October meeting of PLoP (Henshaw 2015c), are my initial attempts to apply a pattern language approach to recording a number of very interesting naturally occurring patterns of design. A few other mentions of those who inspired my work are listed in Acknowledgements.

1.2 Natural design patterns

The "object orientation" of pattern language rests on the whole pattern and the whole design of the things being discussed, not as theoretical objects, but actual designs. They are designs for unifying responses to some set of "forces" in some "context" creating a "center" of organization in the context that can act as a whole. This is a very common set of characteristics in natural environments, where you see tremendous varieties of distinctly individual systems, as organisms, cultures, or their working parts, as well as environmental and weather systems, and economic and communication systems. They all generally have both their own individuality of design and of roles in related contexts. It's both the ability to see the separations of these individual organizations as wholes, as objects that work independently, and also how they can combine to work together as "wholes of parts". It makes you think of diagrams, but the only adequate 'diagram' would be the actual thing, the service, place, community process or event and the relationships that unify it. So pattern language is more a language of generalities, than of abstractions, though it might certainly sound abstract sometimes.

The focus is also on versatile "recurrent patterns", that are more or less universal design concepts. For example a "door" is a "closure for an opening", a really wonderful solution to the need for both privacy and openness. It's something that can be used to bring satisfying resolutions of complex differences in numerous situations. Another example would be "seating things comfortably" as a way to mutually adjust the needs of many things at once, getting them to really fit. So those elemental patterns become both "design elements" and "end purposes" as well as suggestive models to learn from. More More complex design patterns, maybe called "house" or "government", become discussed as guides to what complex design for unifying the forces of common situations. You might perceive a frequent kind of discord to understand, and perhaps call it "friction" or "misfit parts" and try to identify the pattern of forces that is out of balance, perhaps. Sometimes you'll need to formalize the description, and get input from others, and do random trials. Sometimes patterns are just discussed as observations and passed around informally.

So, design patterns are not actually '*solutions*' as much as they are '*guides*'. You use them to help you learn, either about 1) any particular context where they might be applied or 2) to find how to study working examples and their contexts. Here we are more focused on the second, becoming familiar with the world of natural design patterns we have to learn from, and using them as keys to unlock some of the secrets of natural circumstances where they are found to work.

For example for intentional design, for a product or service perhaps, designers may finish their own plans and direct any sort of work for implementing them, but it's always nature that really finishes the design. That applies equally to software or to buildings that designers produce, or public policies or laws passed. How the nature of the living systems to which the designs are applies respond is what actually finishes the design of how they'll work. What will matter is how well such designs happen to really work for both the communities that are serving the design and those being served by it. Purposeful designs are generally means of delivering services from one community to another. How those and associated communities "heal in" around the new service, is nature's living response.

As with a new product, new restaurant, new law or idea, it's the environmental response that determines if and how it thrives. Lifeless places are ones the living environment doesn't respond to, and doesn't take into its living designs. So in functional terms what design patterns may describe as "solutions" are not the really solutions. The real solutions are the matching of the living relationships being served. Some designs make that easier some harder. So what design patterns do is describe promising frameworks for getting things to work, to allow some part of nature to grow into and welcome or not.

From the software community, Jan Borcher (2001) nicely states "a pattern is a proven solution to a recurring design problem", one that "pays special attention to the context in which it is applicable, to the competing forces it needs to balance and to the positive and negative consequences of its application". Jennifer Tidwell (1999) touches on the heart of why framing them as simplifying ideals of design makes that possible: "They are not abstract principles that require you to rediscover how to apply them successfully, nor are they overly specific to one particular situation or culture. Instead, they are somewhere in-between: a pattern describes possible good solutions to a common design problem within a certain context, by *describing the invariant qualities of all those solutions.*" [italics added]

That design patterns define "whole working units" on which to base "object oriented design", appears to have played an important role in reshaping the thought processes used in programming. It offered a way to define and give names to versatile modules of complete software design serving holistic purposes, independent of the software itself. Whether sufficient, it certainly seems essential for allowing software development to become "engineering", and certainly greatly increases the ability of software developers to communicate.

So while pattern language is still being uses as an art, it also seems possible to spread to diverse other fields, like education, community building, firefighting or even medicine perhaps, all finding a better way to understand the needs of their work. The possibility that it might create "object oriented science" is briefly discussed at the end. The focus here is not on applications, though, but applying pattern language concepts to learning from naturally occurring patterns of design.

The companion paper (Henshaw 2015c) is on a particular application, a design pattern for guiding software engineers in bringing "living quality" to their software designs. The simple idea is to use the intentional parts of the design to lead you to finding better ways to serve both the system resources being used and the users of the service it provides. , It's like an extension of "getting to know your providers and customers", usually very productive thing to do. Knowing who your users are helps you know what they need, understand what attracted them, might disturb them, discover other unmet needs.

The method here generally starts with using one pattern to look around for others, displaying new variations to broaden the understanding, learning to look for how it might apply elsewhere. Using one pattern to look for relates ones involves generalizing a subject pattern to be "search template" and doing a "pattern search", to find instances of it in other places in the same environment or in other kinds of environments. For a general example, you might generalize a pattern called "home" to search for the diversity of examples to learn from. Starting with its simple design as both "enclosure" and "connector", you'd find it's a generally a location where some culture develops its own individual way of living, withy very complex meanings.

You find out all sorts of things that way, like how the enclosures that living cultures make for themselves to live in are generally made as they grow, and then become what they use to transmit and exercise their cultures. The shell of a home both secures a culture's domain like a kind of exoskeleton or "external body", but may be outfitted with diverse services for what takes place inside. It's the diversity of living examples you find that lets you discover the many ways the design pattern can work, suggesting good questions and examples of solutions to consider, not possible to know about any other way.

This approach also helps one get "unstuck" in one's own thinking or that of others you work with too, just being exposed to unexpected natural ways for things to work. A pattern language approach helps you recognize them as unusual combinations of forces being brought into play in novel unifying ways. What you find is that *"a door without a latch"* seems perfectly normal until you've see a door with a latch. Then you can't think of a door as complete without one. Various combinations of things tend to be found to play critical roles like that, each transforming the meaning of the whole, as essential "simplifying ideals" needed to make it. Once the design is made "whole", though, it can be hard to tell what the essential parts are, only seeing the whole. So the study of natural designs can take time, involve seemingly crazy thought experiments, waiting impatiently for something to jar your thinking, to help you stop seeing only the of smoothly working complexly of the parts. You look at the how connecting parts have opposite roles to work together and try to imagine what else could work if some random thing were removed.

As you learn from natural designs looking for their variations and opposites, to see every quality and feature in perspective, the useful alternatives become recognizable. As you do the essential features come clear, easy to recognize, letting you see the variation in how designs are adapted to different contexts. Almost anything we design is a variation on some natural model. Say the model pattern is called "vehicle", and you are working on a design that needs one... Nature displays all sorts of different kinds you might think about, that can suggest unexpected options for your situation. 'Vehicle' might be "a conveyance" as for moving on something, or it might be a "channel" for moving along something, or it might be a "medium", for moving in something, or moving a reaction like a "catalyst" that just alters the local chemistry of the situation. That the corresponding metaphors brought up by variations on a common pattern of meaning often directly correspond to variations of common patterns of organization is not really coincidental. It seems to come from what the meanings of language developed for, importantly for conveying how things work. So exploring the terms associated with patterns of design this way is just using the natural associations of natural language, exploring language as a repository and guide to patterns of design, something discussed more in Section 3.5.

1.3 The dual paradigm

One difference between "design patterns" and "natural patterns" is the presence or absence of "the designer". Natural science describes nature as following the conceptual designs of the equations we find for making predictions, using mathematical rules as a metaphor for the designs of nature. Where we observe nature producing highly complex and often self-contained forms of design, what you can initially discuss are only the observable patterns of organization or traces of how they developed.

It doesn't really describe them functionally to just have words for them, of course. The meaning of the words one uses for what is observed then mostly just identify parts one might go back to study later. As one attempts to sketch out the "anatomy" of natural systems step by step that way, trying to understand things like the subcultures of a business, upstart social movements, how an ecology works, or an industry or professional community, one quickly notice they're beyond description. We see they behave cohesively somehow as if well defined by nature and so important for us to respond to, but they are also so complex and composed of individuals of undefined number and relationships, we need a new model for understanding them.

To further focus the problem, it's common to find such natural systems traceable to their origins, new cultural display or new product, as a relatively insignificant point of beginning. It leaves us close to nothing to point to for explaining the enormous consequences. With a business case at least you can often see a very purposeful "start-up" event, as burst of activity using external resources, then the business plan using profits to multiply its systems with records kept you can follow over time to get a clear picture of how the small upstart becomes a giant. It turns out that general pattern is rather universal, and offers a way to organize one's observation of the patterns of operation within a system as they develop.

These lively systems that define themselves as they grow also display a common tendency to retain the patterns they began with from their origins. Partly it's just that as how they grow they are adding onto their original patterns. The irony is that at the origin there's often no evidence of any pattern as if the systems develops from nothing, and so denying us literally every possible avenue of explanation. Efforts to explain them with "cause and effect" only seem to imply "lawless laws", producing great complexity without any "requisite variety" for explanation in an information theory sense (Ashby 1956).

Still, in the case of an organism or a business, an industry or culture, or other kinds of naturally occurring organization, we can plainly see the complexity emerging as the system develops. It appears to start simply and then develop enormous variety in the design as it develops in a way that is never predictable. We can recognize the continuity in the design from its earliest origins, and various systematic behaviors, but we're left in the dark as what is really happening. The net result is that we get a much better match between subject and explanation just focusing on the general patterns observed, than on any explanatory theory. The visible patterns don't tell you everything, but they tell you something, often quite solid things you could build on.

So we apparently need at least two kinds of language for relating what we can predict, our rules for deterministic parts and the various clear patterns of design for organized wholes. Each addresses things the other omits, what I'll call a "dual paradigm" view, of a world needing both forms of explanation. What's common to studying either, a) natural patterns of design or b) deterministic theories with equations, is the same basic relation to nature (Figure 1). Any science is based on a practice of turning one's attention back and forth, between the subject in nature and the method of description. One does it for studying natural design patterns and also for studying deterministic equations. The two are parallel conversations with nature that we need to have work together.

In the study of natural patterns the observer is exploring the limits of the patterns they find in a way intended to be well enough documented to return to them for further study and confirmation by others. If the observer has few preconceptions like an artist or a child they will make more objective observations.

• Rosen Model Relating Theory & Things •

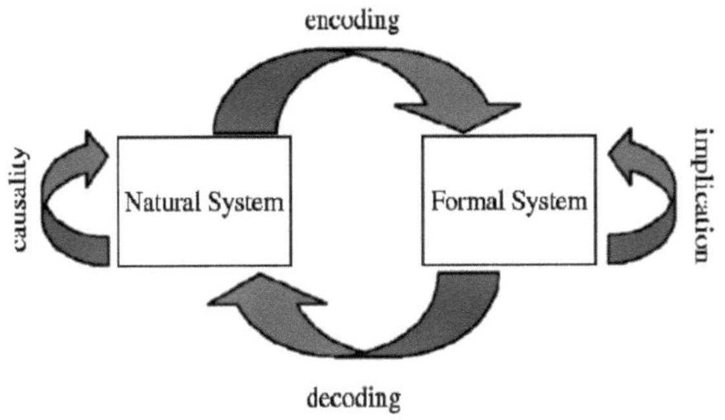

Figure 1: Going back & forth between nature and theory

Figure 1 is Robert Rosen's model for the relationship between science and nature, a diagram of how its done (1991). It shows science engaging in process of learning from nature, turning its attention back and forth between "Natural Systems" and "Formal Systems", learning then testing and applying (encoding then decoding). Information is collected from natural subjects and used to develop formal theory, and then the theory is used to raise more questions about how the theory applies. The same operates for pattern language. The formal language of design develops by an accumulative process of finding the hart of what brings about complete resolutions. Pattern language differs from deterministic science in using natural language for its natural meanings, as that permits discussing holistic design patterns of common things. Traditional science uses mathematics to describe deterministic rules common things.

Both approaches rely on the human ability to maintain undivided attention on subjects of interest, being inquisitive in collecting objective impressions, as if directly "imprinting" one's mind with the forms of the subjects studied. They both lead us to ask questions for expanding our understanding. For pattern language the subjects are both more complex and the descriptions often a bit simpler, generally defined by appreciating what is observed rather than by analysis. So it's a matter of collecting observations forming good questions then testing and applying in a way like fitting a glove of description on the hand of nature. They differ in that pattern language descriptions are more for fitting nature in a way that is comfortable and responsive to its self-organizing parts, rather than as for deterministic science fitting tightly the forms of nature that described rigidly.

One need not make a whole research project of it. It starts with a natural way of learning, as partly just a better way to pay attention to the relationships we rely on, the 'natural objects' of our lives. Then you learn to switch paradigms and talk about them conceptually, noticing when you switch from one view to the other.

To solidify your thinking as you learn about the subject you can take any paragraph that introduces a new idea and think of yourself as being in a study group, and think it through from different points of view as a group would. You might even invent different characters, being a stickler for details, the 'big picture' person, just looking for whacky views. It shakes up your assumptions and helps raise other perspectives to broaden you understanding as the experience becomes more memorable.

The test of doing it right seems to be whether if every time you recheck the patterns you learn something new. It's a simple way to validate what you're learning. That test also seems be how one most directly validates the design patterns you write, by seeing if using them teaches you more about the subject.

2. Two Primary Patterns

2.1 The Natural Process of Design

Perhaps the most universal pattern of natural design is one I first noticed it in design studio projects, that design always takes time and follows a pattern of increasing then declining effort and energy. It varies a lot in how, but every project at home, in business, or any process of emerging change in nature as well, starts with small initial steps that lead to others getting progressively bigger, and then reverse and get smaller. So over all its a pattern of escalating and then reducing intensity at the end, a "storm" of efforts that grows and subsides.

It's easy to examine closely in how design projects proceed. You first start with no idea how to start… and look for small hints and collect resources to use, and at the very end find a similar pattern of looking for finishing touches as the work approaches completion. That happens whether you "run out of time" or not, just altering the hurry of the process, either for getting started of finishing. If you think through any other kind of project the same applies. The phases of getting things started and finishing them up are critically important, as when "launching a product" or even when "making dinner". If you "get off on the right foot" everything can go much more smoothly, and the same with "bringing things to resolution" as an end. As a phrase, we just say "*designs develop*" or "have a cycle". They might develop either by well-practiced or wholly unfamiliar stages of rethinking, with each stage building upon the one before, so every step changes and is important to the whole as well. In the process the whole design tends to change form again and again, a combination of projecting patterns and trial and error in guiding them.

For intentional design, as for designing buildings, the formal design and its construction are separated, with the formal design and its energy expenditure done before being turned over to others to expend their energy in executing (Figure 2, 3). The designer will often still be involved in watching the work take place, providing some finishing touches and clarifications during construction, but their work quickly tapers off till the final "check list" of defects is prepared, at the very end when the "key is turned over to the client", and the "house becomes a home".

In nature, of course, the design of complex organizations has no separate designer doing their work ahead of the development of the design, but the two occur at the same time, not following a predetermined course but following an evolving course of growth as the product is created (Figure 4). To really use this pattern you just need to recognize that studying how these steps of "searching for the next step" work as you do a design, make dinner or complete any other project, is at the same time a study of the kinds of steps nature has to go through too, not following a "design" but something more like a "search".

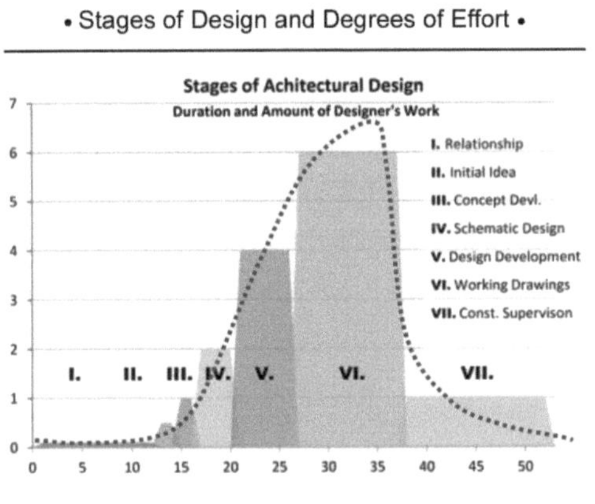

Figure 2: The general development pattern of design

In nature the same pattern of rising then falling scales of developing change and energy use are found in what we call "natural growth", usually leading to either a stable level of perfection or to a peak when something goes wrong. Just as for intentional design, natural growth generally originates from some initial pattern to build on, sometimes a visible start-up system or "seed" that "germinates" to get a larger system going. That "start-up" is usually followed by many stages of accumulative reorganization as development proceeds, you can call "graduations", to liken them to how our own educations proceed as we advance. In natural design, with the design of the system at the same time as the building of the system, the energy sources for the design and the building may be the same, or may be somewhat separate. The energy used for adding new parts and for finding new parts to add can be alternating too. When a formal design precedes the development, as for intentional designs, those energy uses are clearly separate.

In economies the energy for simply operating and maintaining businesses comes directly from earnings for the sale of its products or services, with the profits put aside and accounted for separately. The energy for starting new businesses and expanding existing ones generally comes from one or another source of accumulated profits, used as a resource for starting new things. The spending of profits as investment in making things is for a limited time, stopping when they become self-sustaining (Figure 4). So the development and life of a system start together, but end very differently. The reason to notice these details is to learn to see the patterns of intentional design (Figure 3) as a "recurrence" and "special case" of the general patterns of natural design, just coordinated a bit differently for the advantages people get from it.

In architectural studio practice, distinct stages of design follow a fairly standard pattern, shown here as: *I.-The Client Relationship, II.-Conceptual Design, III.-Schematic design, IV.-Design Development, V.-Contract Documents,* and *VII.-Construction Observation*. They correspond to distinct changes in the types of "search for what to add" taking place, reflected in the a) complexity and funding of the work, b) the organization and size of the team, c) the deliverables, d) hazards, e) length of meetings, f) kinds of legal work, etc,. Each generally progresses from tentative and immature stages toward delivering robust and refined products. Looked at from beginning to end like that, the same general pattern of stages is found in all kinds of organizational processes, as changes in the character and content of emerging and going to completion.

As any design progresses the added tasks branch out again and again. That tends to creating an explosion of details needing to be completed, increasing the intensity and complications of the design effort. Just to "get it out the door" as if in a panic, pressed to deliver on time becoming a separate driving motivation concentrating everyone's attention. It's not a matter of poor planning, but completely natural, that as a design progresses it creates multiplying demands for finishing things, caused by each added part having become a place to add more. It originates from the "elemental pattern" at the beginning, that to initiate growth has to have a built-in pattern for adding parts that need more parts to be added, for later stages are built upon. So something else has to occur to reverse that progression before it exhausts the energy available to resolve the design as a whole, or things fall apart.

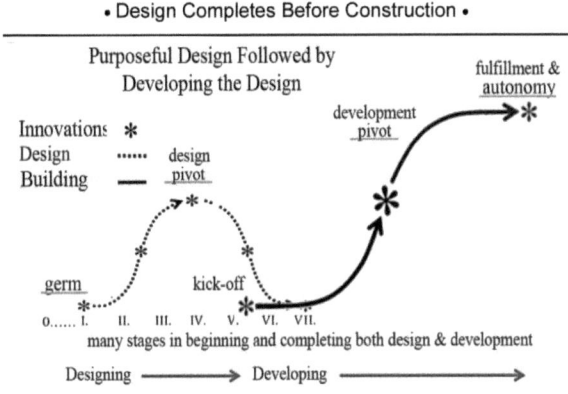

Figure 3: Intentional design preceeds the process of development

One can see in biological growth where that middle stage of most rapid increasing complexity occurs. It's called "differentiation", the time when the "basic frameworks" of different kinds of cells, different organs, the skeleton and other major systems all emerge. That framework basically "sets the plan" and creating a real explosion of places to add more parts. That's similar to the stage in architectural design called *design development* (IV.) when the specific form of building frame and infill systems are all decided, and there's suddenly loads more work for figuring out the details and connections.

You see these same generic stages in the work needed to produce a Thanksgiving dinner. You see a smaller scale version the lunch next day. You always have the three major milestones, the *start-up* or "germ", the turning point or '*pivot*', and the *completion* point or "*fulfillment*". Watching those thresholds being crossed also gives you more of a better idea of how the natural processes that exhibit them work too. Variations on those stages are there in the project to send a man to the moon. They are there in the stages of establishing anyone's career. Every step takes a bit of inspired invention, starting with small tentative steps, to follow a pattern to take it a long way, on which the series of larger and then smaller steps toward fulfillment rely.

If you look at the common pattern of getting an education it all starts with early childhood, and one's absorption of language and culture at home. Then there's the long ladder of ascending levels, each usually seeming like an impossible challenge as you begin them. They are usually completed with a sense of mastery and joy, though, reflecting the real creative success story each represents, again and again. These stages of growth in learning correspond to stages of organizational complexity of our knowledge too, and generally correspond to growing scales of energy use as well. It's maintaining that combined view of the progression of design and of energy use together that is the main way the design science and physical science become connected, as a link between the two different sets of "laws". A swelling and subsiding use of energy doesn't tell you what design process is taking place, but it does tell you where… and that helps a lot if you have some general idea of what to look for.

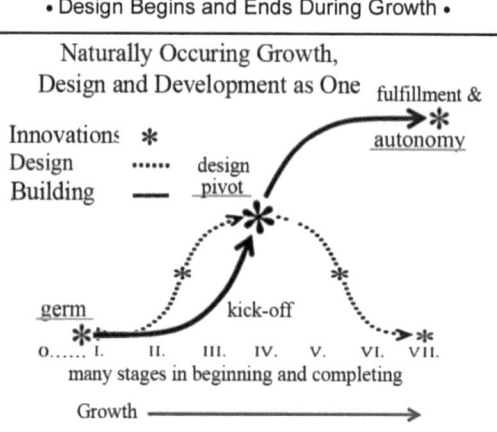

Figure 4: Organic design occurrs during development

Thinking of design as swelling and then subsiding energy use also gives it a series of mathematical markers to add to the three most directly visible, for use in tracing its course. The mathematical markers include the peaks and saddles and points where the curvature of the curve reverses. They also include changes in the character of the noise in the data, and mathematical evidence of strong continuity (flow) in the progression. If there is continuity there are also the implied accelerations and shifts in accelerations to signal to an observer what may be happening. Those are all quite informative for characterizing the identified whole system, what and how its' doing.

The most important, though, do seem to be those three "existential" points. Those are the points marking the "germ", "pivot" and "fulfillment" as the end point of growth when the new form tales its role in its new environment. With a little experience these signals of systemic change can be fairly easily recognized, something solid as a pattern for beginning to learn how developing systems navigate their natural transformations.

2.2 Elemental forms of "Homes"

Homes are enclosures that allow good access to the resources of the world around them and within which cultures can create their own ways of living relatively free of outside interference. That "simplifying ideal" resolution of the forces is found extremely widely used. Homes create private worlds, for very individualized working relationships, with regulated relationships with the outside. Three simple types are depicted in figure 5, a '*hut*', a "*family home*", and a "*town hall*" to represent a community home.

A biological cell is also a home, for the living chemistry within its enclosure, the enclosure giving that interior design selective access to the outside. It would be hard to count the great differences between the way of living within a cell and that within a family home, or that within a meeting hall for a community. What you can see quite clearly is the commonality of the pattern of home. You can also describe many of the essentials for any home that each kind has. You can also notice frequent design elements with special functions, like how the internal life of family homes and biological cells both generally have a kind of "nucleus" around which the life of the cell is organized. In the family home or community center it's the place for intimate communication, where the culture of the home is shared. In the cell it's the place where the culture of the cell as the genetic code of the body is shared. The center of a family home may vary, but is usually a main room where people gather, often in a circle, and surrounded by symbols of its culture. In my family home it was around the kitchen table and dining room table as centers of conversation that alternated in location.

Whatever way a family centers its conversations is rather important in forming its individual way of living, to talk about family matters and share their common culture. With people so versatile it might be lots of things, but it has to work. Meeting in a circle as around a table, each person has the attention of all the others and is a witness to all the communication between the others, as a shared experience. It's private as when sitting around a campfire at night, in a circle of well-lit faces. That design is a simplifying ideal for equitable communication, meeting around an open space that equally separates and connects all the individuals. It has been central to the life of homes in most human cultures for a very long time.

The Western design tradition of homes actually descended from the enduring Bronze Age Aegean culture centered on its design for "hearth homes", as a way to bring the campfire relationship indoors! That distinctive architectural design also became a model for public architecture in the various advanced Aegean cultures that followed, later becoming the model for early Greek democracy's public halls and the starting point for Greek formal architecture too (Dinsmoor 1902). The historic design is roughly sketched in the figure. It's been so central to the early culture for so long, though there's no recorded history it seems the attachment to a pattern for ideal human communication was, sitting around the large circular hearth in a wide room, tending small fires, was likely the reason for the endurance of the tradition and its presence in our world too. Like the campfire it brings people together as it holds them apart too, giving each person an equal audience with every other, sharing cultural roots far older than formal designs.

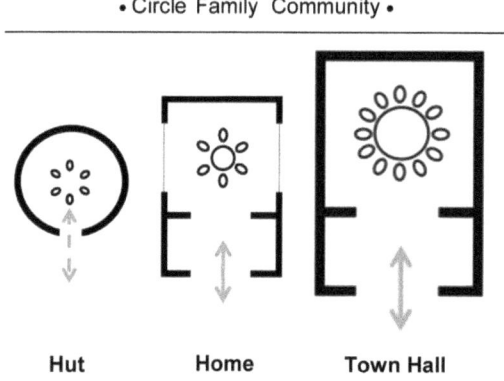

Figure 5: Homes shelter cultures of equitable living

It's where we regularly got together to eat and talk about family matters, as a common culture. Around a table each person has the attention of all the others, and is a witness all the communication between the others, as a shared experience. The simplifying design for equitable communication shown in Figure 5, meeting around an open space that equally separates and connects all the individuals, has been central to the homes of our cultures for a very long time.

The Western tradition at least, descended from the early Bronze Age design of Aegean "hearth homes", becoming a model for public architecture by many early Aegean cultures and later becoming the model for early Greek society public halls and formal architecture too (Dinsmoor 1902). The historic design was much like these figures, so central to the early culture for so long it seems it must have been for people sitting around the large circular hearth in a wide room, tending small fires in a vented "great room", defining the way of life and the home. Much the same relationship exists when sitting around a camp fire too, though, with the fire bringing people together as it holds them apart too, giving each person an equal audience with every other, having cultural roots far older than formal designs.

How strong and unique a family bond that special design serves is not appreciated until you experience "inclusion in the circle" or exclusion from it, and recognize how complete a kind of privacy is created by it. From the outside family cultures are literally invisible to others who don't participate in them, and from the inside they are common universe with ancient roots, that invisibly passes on its ancient inherited ways of living. Because they are indeed invisible from the outside, even if we can see through the windows, we still cannot see the relationships that hold the culture of the home together. So we tend not to think about these inner worlds we know both so much and so little about, until crossing the boundaries of their personal space and feel uncomfortable, embarrassed by not knowing how to act. The greatest separations can be between "homes" with invisible boundaries, like the walls of open cultures that serve as great homes for their societies having little to do with others. For the invisible domains of neighborhood gangs or other groups averse to strangers, crossing the hidden lines can get one in trouble.

As children we first find other people's homes deeply mysterious, the homes of neighbors and relatives, full of special things that surprise us and show us how differently they live. As adults we are still frequently surprised if we go to someone else's home, and find they have their unexpected ways of living. We learn so little about how others live privately it also can take quite a long time to correct our initial misimpressions, being unable to understand who they are until we have had a long close association. So every culture is a "cult" in that way, an "alien" culture and way of life with its own deeply rooted manners and practices. To an insider small cues carry large meanings, which to any outside observer can go quite unrecognized.

As a result many of us, if not most, find ourselves living somewhat "invisible lives", as what makes private lives so private in many ways is rather universal. It's that they are designed from the inside. We may also have grown up in one of the many old inherited family cultures that are not the subject of the news or stories so much, perhaps filling the work places but not the media, mostly unrecognized and undiscussed publically. It's just in the nature of homes for the culture to not to be understood except by participants, a tradeoff for also being places where cultures most deepen and thrive. They tend to be private physically, organizationally and also in heritage. It keeps outsiders from understanding anything at all, up until something breaks their preconceptions, they develop empathy for the hidden ways of life they have long seen around but been unaware of.

3. A Starter Kit for natural patterns of design

The idea of offering a "starter kit" of techniques is to offer a collection of things to explore a bit and perhaps master later. They're intended to have some easy uses, with room to grow, offered as a way to introduce a complicated subject. It takes the "core" approach, offering general discussion along with advanced technique, rather than attempting a general survey. It's for giving people ideas of what to experiment with on their own. So to start one might first get a sense of your own place on what I show as the ladder of learning for the subject, depicted roughly in Figure 6. We all start with a great wealth of inherited cultural knowledge, our very broad foundation in knowledge of life's patterns, so we're not on the bottom rung.

We may not have ever thought of it that way, of course, but more than likely we already have a variety of concentrated interests we've build up several layers of learning about. So this approach might be used to help extend and broaden those as well as begin interests in new ones. Some references that have been helpful to my working with pattern language include the collections of the Pattern Language Association (2015) and the Hillside Group (2015) and the meetings the latter sponsor. It's useful to search for discussions of Christopher Alexander and his formative and more popular writings (1965, 1977, 1979, 1987, 2001-6). There are the books by the urban design critic Jane Jacobs, on the natural patterns of economies and cities and their sources of creativity (1961, 1970). Sophisticated patterns identified by of Doug Schuler (2008) and Sebastian Denf (2012), as well as software pattern design essays by Jan Bochers (2001) and Jennifer Tidwell (1999) were all very helpful to me too.

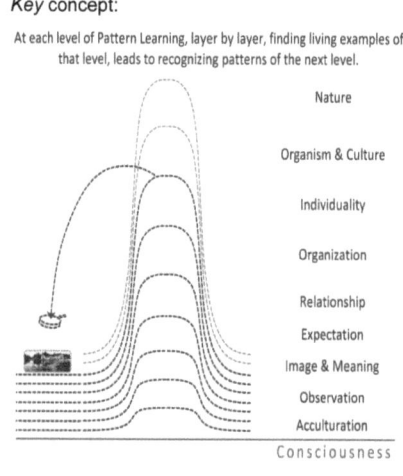

Key concept:
At each level of Pattern Learning, layer by layer, finding living examples of that level, leads to recognizing patterns of the next level.

Levels of Natural Pattern Learning[3] we look at levels of accumulating learning, added layer by layer, here starting from a base of biological consciousness, plus cultural absorption, then observation, information and experience. It's then using the model patterns at one level of abstraction, to explore their natural instances, that leads to recognition of the patterns at the next level.

Figure 5: Homes shelter cultures of equitable living

General introductions and Slide sets by Takashi Iba (2013) and Helmut Leitner (2014) are current and very helpful. Good books on ecology and living systems from a naturalist or "deep ecology" approach are a big help, such as books by or referencing D'arcy Thompson (1961) and Brian Goodwin (1994). Books that tell the stories of history, such as on the history of civilization, language, science, society and technology are all helpful, as are books on comparative anthropology and subjects like competitive strategy. Books on myths and children's tales often addressing the same issues of "how things work" from a cultural view are all helpful, as well as the Bible and other ancient texts if read as documenting our earliest ways of thinking. Of course finding great teachers sometimes just carefully listening to things you hadn't before, are invaluable as well.

3.1 Steps of Natural Pattern Study

The patterns of naturally occurring design one finds become 'guides' when somewhat generalized, to use as "model patterns" for searching the environment for working examples. Examples found that way are usually varied and rely on features and connecting relationships you wouldn't expect. Those are what you learn from, adding to your own mental library of "ways things can work". So the simple image in the mind connects you with the rich related patterns of natural cases. What you find lets you see how the real subjects work. Maybe more importantly it lets you see the kinds of designs that serve both their internal and external worlds of relationships at the same time.

3.1.1 Perception

If your pattern idea is 'tree', you can reduce in your mind to the universal pattern of systems nested in their environments (Figure 7),. You then use that general design pattern in your mind to look for and learn from partidular examples. When you find them you'll both increase your understanding of the natural subject and its variations of design, as well as your own natural limits for understanding them, noting what seems to get lost in translation perhaps. It helps you collect images of variations needed to get things to fit well, to experiment with when developing a pattern description or employing them in your own work. It also helps eliminate the ironic habit of many people, of interpreting nature as conforming to their own image (rather than the reverse), and so converting the mental images they construct as mental rules and beliefs about the things the images roughly imitate. What is a lot more useful is a way of seeing that is not misleading like that, and exposes the differences between what we observe and how we think it works, like retaining one's raw impressions for continuity to compare with one's theory. What helps with that is a habit of using simplified patterns we recognize in nature to find new working examples, needing to be understood from how they do and don't differ from what we've seen before.

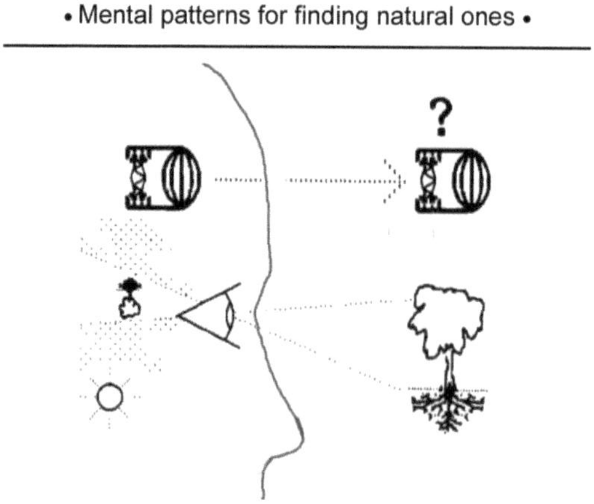

Figure 7: Creating a pattern to search for its recurrances

For example, a community might have the idea of 'growth' as a pattern of increasing wealth for relieving strains, and want to know will sustain that, relying on patterns of working design for it found naturally occurring. That would let them see more clearly the variations on the pattern that naturally develop, and the diverse results and varied consequences that result. That growth is a process of building something, usually to become a home for some culture would come from seeing the varied examples.

The basic designs for it change over time, 1) a 'germ' of design to get a chain reaction of change going to build on itself and 2) a 'pivot' to turn the process toward resolution in a fulfilling end as better goal than unbounded replication (Figures 2,3,4). There are obviously lots of secrets to be found or invented, as any stage of growth does seem to rely on original innovation at every step. What one also discovers is that growth is about conquering your own world, not numbers, and the period of it relieving strains is temporary, and something to come to terms with too. The natural way the 'forces' being faced change with growth is into relationships with new partners to preserve, in a world to join instead of conquer.

3.1.2 Architecture

Alexander's pattern language approaches these issues of natural design as a way of making the traditional methods of holistic design explicit. That's to identify all the forces of a particular circumstance to be resolved, doing so with a unifying design for satisfying services, contributing what he called 'living quality' to their surroundings. The practice of holistic design developing from his work applies well beyond architecture though, creating an art and science of holistic design potentially applicable to any field. What seems to pull it all together is this new way of defining the usually unstated "motive to serve". 'Patterns' carry an implied intent to be responsive to the needs of varied individuals, their living cultures and environments. Out of that need to serve, a tension between responding to forces and the ideals of doing it holistically arises, that is answered only completing them with a new form of design.

• The General Pattern •

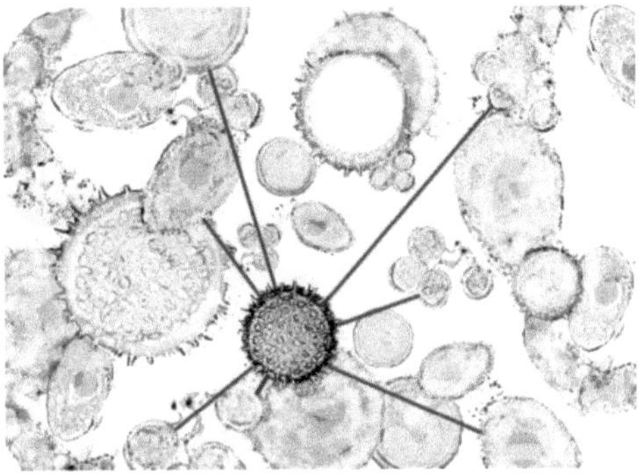

Figure 8: Cultures finding their roles in a complex worlds

That ideal of making things that serve helps one understand Lou Kahn's curious ways of expressing it, urging designers to ask "what does it wants to be", and to always begin every design by "reading book zero", the book of all things without preconception (Henshaw 2015b, Youd 2014). Such designs begun that way, in any circumstance, ideally find a point where everything else falls into place as if by itself, the way a crystal crystalizes, but in the living relationships being touched. If you don't find that the opposite tends to occur, however many 'Band Aids' applied, opposing unresolved forces tend to lead to endless struggle.

The greatest difficulty of ideal design is really its central purpose, looking for holistic bit counter-intuitive ways of combining things to be resolved together, hoping to discover "emergent properties" in satisfying new forms of design as the reward. One's knowledge is naturally limited by how many kinds of natural holistic design are quite hidden from outside view; leaving observers blind to how other they work (Figure 8). For that reason one is in constant need of breaking away from one's own perspectives, to allow small hints to be suggestive and begin to see things from fresh points of view. It calls for having various productive means of widening one's search, in a very neutral way. That lets your mind move easily between viewpoints without carrying assumptions with you to gain real perspective. Ideal design is also not always ideal too. One part may really need to be sacrificed to serve another perhaps, or it just may not be what you are asked to do. Still, asking what really needs to be served seems to be what allows anything to be controlled to have the purpose it can.

3.1.3 Practice

The good subjects to study this way could be anything of interest, but much better if something you know quite well, having some complexity and changes you are already familiar with to study. Your home town or city could be good to study fir hints of a variety of different local cultures and the niches they create for themselves. You can often find signs of multiple local cultures on virtually any street corner, and aware of the boundaries between subcultures in familiar neighborhoods. You don't see it much, but those differing culture groups share common histories, connections and demographics, for each profession, age group and social group. So you just practice following your curiosity about them, reproaching them enough to start expanding your understanding of them. I tend to find that a combination of broad impressions and close detail produces the best follow-up questions for the next time, to build on what I learned before. Study of your own or another business community you have some connection with might be approached the same way, or your own or connected social network or professional culture too.

As you study their varied patterns of living relationships that get things done you get better at recognizing their variations. As a casual way of just paying attention to how things work it adds to the general ability to follow how anything works, as well as associations with the patterns you find. For finding applicable patterns to apply for balancing the forces in some other context you may or may not apply what your general practice of paying attention has shown you, but you will apply the comfortable way of exploring the context you're in. Designers don't design the living things that later inhabit their designs, but only the frameworks of services to make available to the expected users. That's what the real design is, a "facility". It's those common services that the coding, the pleasing of the client and the beauty of thing as well, all need to work together to harmonize in the end. A building or a program gets used by a great many people of many kinds, so most any design is a design for serving a whole community. So you might think of design as a kind of ecological service or caretaking, things for which there are patterns to study, but no specifications.

What anchors the process is still the work of accumulating reliable observations of how things work, noticing all the variations in how things are organized to work as a way of developing perspective, alert to the:

1. The ways of resolving forces by creating new forms of design
2. The inside and outside relationships,
3. The tradeoff's, special connections and conditions
4. The Stages of change, and how innovations discover new roles

That awareness of nature as full of creative design that works better if you see it is the solid foothold one develops. It's what lets you return again and again to validate what you found and find out more. It then lets you share what you've found with others and give them ways they can check and for themselves and add to what you shared with them too. Surprisingly often the most valuable part of this kind of scientific observation is the gaps in the patterns you find, recognized as something missing and kept as place holders for things yet to be found.

In looking for where to apply this method in your own work you might consider just looking around for places where "something's missing" as a good place to start, perhaps considering how to approach situations like the following.

1. A community adapting to climate change,
2. A business that changed culture unexpectedly and no longer feels itself
3. A disorganized start-up that wants to become well organized
4. Software platforms that become monopolies and are stagnating
5. Communities that need to resolve cultural conflicts,
6. News organizations trying to get our world stories straight
7. Town meetings on disruptive social, crime or drug use cultures.

These are all also "healing problems" of one or another kind. You need as long a view of what is being healed as possible, of the established relationships and what they are struggling with, going back and forth between completely fresh thinking and studying the familiar. Generally you'd be looking around in hopes of finding what it is that will let the existing sets of relationships, and the new ones, all pull together to generate a fresh living quality for the place and to share with others.

3.1.4 Exploration

In searching for a true purpose for a design you might clear your thinking and explore the context with "fresh eyes" as if opening up pages of "book zero" but you need something to be looking for. For just learning from your environment having some neutral guiding pattern helps you look for the varied circumstances where it occurs. Using Alexander's 15 common patterns found in designs expressing wholeness (Table 4) is one collection that can be used to search with, for "pattern search". These spatial design patterns depict very recurrent shapes and natural forms, you can use to trace natural occurring designs and patterns of organization. The varied circumstances and ways they connect can tell you a lot. My most useful group of elemental patterns to trace for finding how things work are the natural process patterns, of growth and development as natural progressions of design (Figures 3 and 4), an of communication between whole systems through "mediums of exchange" (Figure 9).

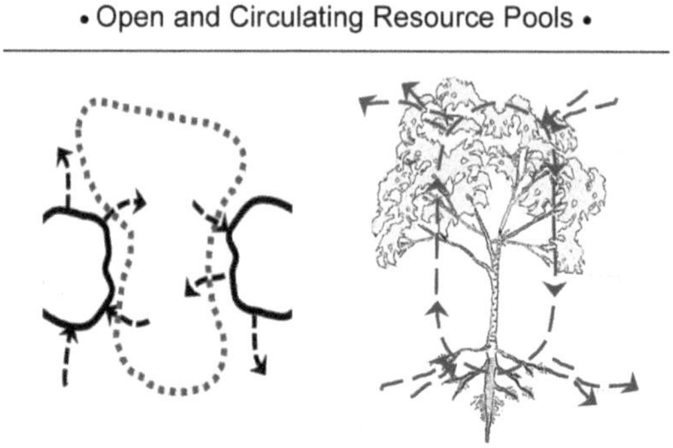

Figure 9: Mediums of exchange link diverse varieties

Nature makes very extensive use of "mediums of exchange", allow separated things to communicate. They teach us lots of things, like that communication really only occurs between separated things, a counter force to nature organizing so many to work by themselves. Mediums of exchange serve as continually replenished reservoirs of resources, information and patterns of design, often easily located by being what human and natural ecologies gather around. So mediums of exchange are natural centers of rich living quality and variety, allowing individuals to both complete and have freedom to work their own way at the same time, another simplifying ideal design like the design of 'homes', that allows things to thrive.

To look for natural mediums of exchange sometimes they're recognized as what diverse cultures swarm around, another kind of "center" for living things. Looked at closely they're most notable for their loose organization rather than their dense organization, the actual role they play is not as "centers" but as "in-betweens", as collections of great varieties of things that are quite unattached and free to take. So they're not "systems" in that sense, if also playing very important roles within and for working systems to operate.

The common specialized mediums of exchange we see that living systems use to communicate are things like economic "markets" or "ecologies", a fresh water pond for one example and the blood stream for circulating one, but also "compost piles" and the social spaces where people like to congregate. Each of these varied spaces of free resources are great designs for communication of different kinds. You can use their easily recognizable patterns for "pattern search" like the others mentioned above, to find diverse working examples. That might be useful if you are designing a community center and want to know what connecting patterns create the diversity of resources that makes a community center thrive.

The natural patterns of "centers" that will be easiest to find and learn from, are then the ones you can recognize as serving common "cultures". They generally have recognizable external boundaries and show evidence of highly creative internal designs. Those are most often the active parts of the environment too, leaving trails of artifacts we can often trace. It's not only spatial designs and patterns we can trace, but also patterns of temporal change we can trace too. Natural designs leave trails of evidence that may expose their perhaps quite eventful histories and processes of development, leading you to how they originated from some common origin.

As you begin to explore these working relationships there may come times when you want to speed it up some, and quickly survey the field for issues related to a particular question. When exploring an environment searching for one natural design pattern you can't do that. A nice adaptable way came out of my work at the UN as a versatile workshop design, called the 3Step process for working with nature (Henshaw 2013). It's a design that frees up the thinking of the whole group to contribute observations of what matters in an environment for their concerns.

The trick to the design is that's done by focusing not on a "problem" (presuming some theory) but on a group "ideal" (as an absolute). Then the group can freely explore for all the forces in the environment that would affect their ideal. It nicely puts off the thinking about how and what to do till later, and just collects a large and diverse collection of mostly unbiased fresh observations, which the group quickly organizes a bit at the end.

3.2 Mining Patterns Of Transformations

Learning to read records of change to recognize what in the environment is changing form, is probably easier done with storytelling than empirically at first, and even that takes a little experience. In a world in which ancient cultures and environments seem to be changing ever faster, it's of course then also very important. That's one of the side effects of "growth". It naturally produces a design panic of a sort, a moment of "being a bit too pregnant" with juggling changes, like the panic in design projects as the tasks multiply as you're trying to deliver the finished product. I don't know a better way to introduce it than to just help people become fascinated by these amazing changes that go on all around us.

3.2.1 The Emerging Phrase "Pattern Language"

The frequency of the term "pattern language" in the books Google scanned[3] provides a great example of a found "proxy" for cultural transformation. It's the shape of the curves that are so telling (Figure 10). Both the curve for books in English and German show "progressive proportional change", at least from ~1985, very suggestive of spontaneous growth for an emerging new form of culture. The data source has definite limitations as scientific evidence. Here we are fairly certain what the term is referring to, as there was no prior use and it does name an emerging discussion. We may not be able to update the curve, for example, due language moving away from books to online sources changing what the measure means, as a common problem for historical data. There are also the irregular changes.

So instead of relying only on clearly defined and sourced information, the study of natural patterns assumes information is partial and not exactly defined. It makes the job of interpretation one of putting together a testable pattern on which to base good new questions about the subject, as a forensic research process. Some secondary sources might be found, for example, like media and journals. Still, the apparent explosion of the term's use show here still looks like strong evidence of an emerging culture. It is cultures that grow like that you'd look to for signs of the compound growth of the system producing it. It's a fairly universal sign of something new defining its own individuality as it expands its presence and makes its home. It's a kind of evidence that gives you a lot of pattern language kinds of questions to talk about.

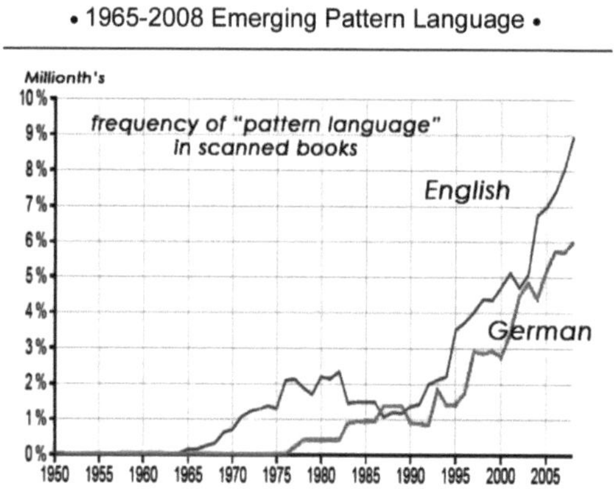

Figure 10: Growth shows the pattern of organic emergence5

Here it lets us see differences in how the discussion of pattern language developed in English and German language communities. The two curves end up following about the same explosive growth trend from 1990 on, with the curve for English showing rise and fall in

---
3 Google Ngram for "pattern language" in books in English or German https://books.google.com/ngrams/graph?content=pattern+language&year_start=1960&year_end=2008

the frequency, a wave that peaked in ~1980. The German trend shows hints of a smaller related bump that peaked a little later, ~1987. The overall appearance is that the early wave of use might have reflected the original discussion about urban design and building architecture. That might be easy to check. That did not lead to widespread adoption, and so the later rapid growth then seems certain to mainly reflect the much wider spread of pattern language principally for computer software development. It might include some spread to other professions, but that seems more recent.

If you accept that interpretation of the pattern the curve does seem to be a remarkable record of a transformational change, and shows us a variety of things we would not have known about otherwise. Seeing the two records of change as responses of two different communities, with slightly differing shapes, side by side, seems clearly to be two responses to the same transformative design method and conversation, a historic event in itself. It gives us "found data" that tells a story that could be followed further. The data was actually found by picking out shapes of this kind form the flood of new data sources now available, and so demonstrates a new use of "big data" too.

Found data is one of the more common sources for discovering unexpected change taking place, as things that were happening hidden from view, and questions were not being asked about. Exposing dynamic continuities of natural developments like this helps locate the centers of organizational transformation producing the data. The shapes of the curves are also fairly good evidence of some culture behaving as a whole. The two curves seem to have close to the same doubling rate, ~7.5 years, indicating their coupling, with the curve for English having a little head start. If we had other knowledge of what was happening we might find other ways to look at what is going on internally, and externally. Growth curves are generally also proxies for the growing scale of energy use and money invested, so there are a lot of things a systemic change of this kind would affect that might be looked at. Of course, from a pattern language view you'd want to know if the services to its communities and its environment that are making it thrive.

Rates of word use can be tricky to interpret, of course. An increase in word use fall off even if the associated change continued, but just wasn't news any more perhaps. Of course a minor spelling change, or a switch to using an acronym in favor of a phrase would also confuse the data. So as elsewhere, what you're really looking form is not 'data' but information that teaches you something that can be confirmed. The general impression is that these curves seem to fit what I generally know of the timing and relative sizes of interest in pattern language in American architecture, followed by the worldwide interest in it for software development. So, curve interpretation like this is built piece by piece like that, as forensic inquiry is generally done.

3.2.2 Big Data

Finding good proxies for what is happening in your own environment might possibly be automated, mining the data of all sorts now available. The "big data" now available are generally not being looked at this way though. It would certainly associate data with real events to use it to locate the great waves of organizational change we all feel, but people have nothing to point to talk about yet. It would also let you collect diverse cultural responses and their informative perspectives to draw general attention to newly emerging phenomena, speeding the work of understand the patterns of organization that are growing. That could be greatly aided by having computers scanning the flood of statistics available for this and other patterns of whole systems of things working together in various ways, to prompt community and professional interest.

The shapes in the data don't say what is there, but just tell you *where* to look. Someday the various big data projects might publish online resources on how the world is changing in generally searchable formats, displaying emerging centers of ecological, cultural and economic change for people to study and find and work with. Some of the work on these pattern recognition methods has been done (Henshaw 1995-9, 1999) to offer a starting point. Ways of teaching pattern recognition of this kind, and using workshop methods for accessing the insights of people involved with it have also been proposed (Henshaw 2013 2014).

In addition to the wealth of economic data from national accounts, there's a flood of data in the form of "community indicators" and "comprehensive sustainability reports" for city and business sustainability reports becoming available. Combined with commercial data sources, the potential resource is enormous. Of course libraries, research centers and governments are all actively developing new ways to use the flood of data already. The UN has a major worldwide data collection and coordination effort for the Post 2015 sustainable development plan. That includes a focus on collecting a broad spectrum of information on what is generally called "ESG factors", for monitoring interrelated environmental, social and governance conditions worldwide. The interpretation of data still largely relies on isolated statistical correlations between numerical "goals" and "targets", treating societies as working by numerical pushes and pulls between categories we define for them. The UN's statistical programs and innovative Data Revolution council[4] as well as CIVICUS civil society organizations[5] and others are certainly trying to invent marvelous ways to use all this data.

It's not clear that's happening, though, as the paradigm shift to using data to find how whole systems of change are developing seems not to be happening. The main use of data still

---
4   UN Data Revolution panel: http://www.undatarevolution.org/
5   CIVICUS 'DataShift' project http://civicus.org/thedatashift/

seems very strongly fixed on setting numeric targets. That treats complex cultural changes as working by statistics rather than as networked living systems. So work would need to be done to reorient the search toward finding patterns in the data revealing the forms of natural systems we need to work with. For cultures to respond you actually need to find how to feed their own internal motivations to make them the leaders of their own changes and learning. You'd rather not rely on the plans of business interests maximizing their profits given credits to meet certain statistical targets. As well-meaning as it may be that's just neocolonialism. The study of our changing economies, ecologies and cultures is not taking place as a study of how their parts work as whole systems though. That makes the business model for responding to public demands the likely fallback strategy, even though that's not what the UN or anyone else really wants.

3.2.3 Locating Centers by Their Boundaries

We all become expert in recognizing boundaries, like between the sidewalk and street, or entering some private group's conversation or some unfamiliar culture's neighborhood. We quickly notice if we're approaching or crossing them, often tipped off by a gut feeling of either caution or anticipation that tells us to think of acting differently. Then we realize we should think of changing behavior as we approach. It's a well-tuned environmental alertness we all have, that prompts us to sharpen our senses and look closely for signs of what to do next. It may be to open up and become engaging, or to expect threats and be more cautious. What those signals are about is our entering or leaving someone else's home territory, its 'niche', "private space", "near environment" or "back yard", their peripheral space that mediates the separate worlds within and without.

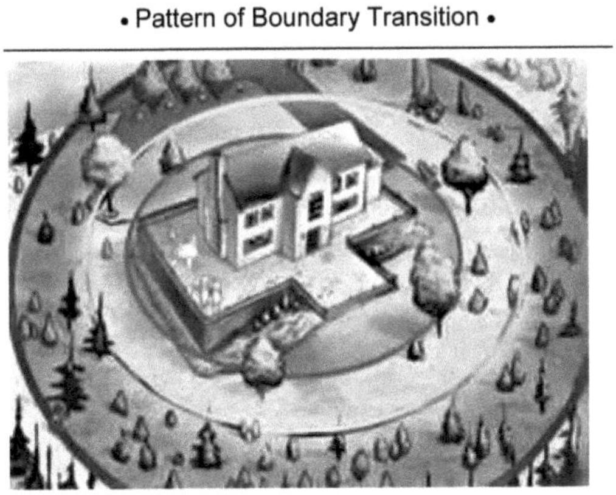

• Pattern of Boundary Transition •

Figure 11: Centers surrounded with niche boundary zones

You can think of the general pattern in terms of walking through the woods and coming across someone's home (Figure 11), unaware of people or animals but seeing it as a well maintained place. You probably wouldn't approach to say hello unless you needed to. But coming across a boundary and being curious you'd look for where it goes, and for signs of how the relationships differ inside and out. If you had a question perhaps you'd judge whether you'd be comfortable walking up to the door, or had better keep to the fringes of the yard.

If it seemed OK and you did need some help, you'd look at details of the entrance for hints on how approach the door and get an idea of what response to expect. We might stop before knocking if we noticed signs that the resident isn't really home. We might see the shades drawn, the patio unswept and the plants on it untended, realizing it must have been a hired service that recently mowed the lawn. Much the same sort of encounter may be experienced approaching a strange vendor's stall at a green market or crafts fair. We read the signs the same way, noticing details of the stalls that are more or less well-kept and arranged with joy, reading all the odors and visual signs.

As you approach you are encouraged to come close, but then you still need to size up how to interact with the vendor. Crossing into someone's personal space is a matter of presence, little ceremony, like a handshake. When you make contact with others you ideally want the timing to be right, and for both parties to engage in the greeting together, like using a mutual homing device to synchronize the contact motions. Those same fine details of negotiating boundaries might be found literally anywhere messages need to be passed from one domain to another.

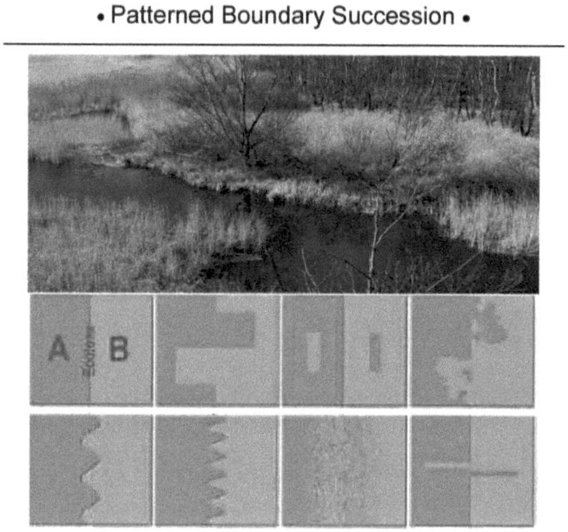

• Patterned Boundary Succession •

Figure 12: Centers found with diverse boundary shapes

The natural shapes of boundaries are fascinating, hard to define but once noticed often then easy to pick out. We learn to be expert in reading them too, anywhere there's a "territory", it's likely to be filled with boundaries that define separations between one home culture and another. You find them between industries and business cultures. The variety of shapes one finds in all kinds of natural spatial boundaries are generally similar in character. Figure 12 shows one collection of geometries characterizing natural boundaries, these drawn for plant ecological zone transitions. They're complex and overlapping yet as distinctive as the signatures of people, both rather hard to explain but distinctive.

3.2.4 Following the energy

Locating centers of design is often a matter of locating centers of energy use, and found by following the traffic to and from them. The "desire lines" of trails across a snowy campus show where the foot traffic goes, and "where the energy" is. They're much like the pheromone trails that insects follow to a new food source. That's what the idea of "stigmergy" is based on too, as a programmable model for how behaviors develop following signs left by others returning from some place of interest. Energy uses leave traces behind of many kinds, as artifacts of what the energy was used for, leaving trails of interesting patterns of design that can be traced to their pattern uses, as well as their sources. In the case of economic energy uses, the trails of energy use eventually lead back to the homes of families and communities where the knowledge of how to use and get energy is concentrated, for example.

Patterns of melting snow on the roofs of houses shows interesting signs of energy use, but doesn't show much about the knowledge culture inside those houses, that is their real source of energy. The evidence of energy use just shows where such knowledge cultures are located. It's generally the hidden internal life of homes that is both drawing in the flows of energy they need and giving their occupants the insight and means of going out to get more. You'd learn a little more looking at all the other signs of the culture a group of similar homes arrange around themselves, the kinds of shops, public and private space, travel and other artifacts of how a community lives.

The money people bring home is a direct proxy for energy resources too, as are the products of energy use brought home with it. So money use can lets you trace where society puts its energies of all sorts, in a far more truthful and inclusive way than the stories we tell. The homes of its families are arguably society's largest infrastructure and capital investment, where people both bring and enjoy the end products of using energy and exercise their own culture for how to enjoy products of their own energies. There's a reason for that.

If you didn't "follow the energy" to understand what is being done with it, you wouldn't come to realize that the energy used in homes is being invested in enabling its occupants' work in the world. The energy invested where we center our lives yields direct "returns on investment", enabling the occupants to go out and bring back money and goods to sustain their home cultures. Though rarely mentioned what it reveals is that, homes of all kinds are the real energy centers of a society, where the internal "flame of hearth and home" burns as a culture, teacher, motivator and source of healing, to enable our roles in the world. A healthy home then contributes its energy to enlivening surrounding centers of the community and culture too, in both direct and metaphorical senses. Being so private and hidden from outside view, our homes remain largely protected from any invasions of privacy, or judgment, as they empower the world.

A software program object it can be read somewhat the same way. Like a private home with its own internal culture within a larger network of software objects, any one has both a named pattern description and stated role in the system, as well as an actual electrical current use. The current use need not reflect the importance of its information process, but it tells you more about its users, and indicator of how it's service is being used in the network. It's adds a new perspective on what the design object does by learning about what it serves. If using a lot of energy it is probably deserving of attention.

Perhaps the most profound if confusing aspect of a natural world organized around serving cells of hidden internal design is that in the development of ecologies that hidden information is not needed. If an internal culture has a motive to relate to its external world in a way that avoids needless conflict, it seems only a very vague sense of how that culture works is needed by any other. The ecologies where species become so close knit and interdependent, responding only to external patterns, are dramatic examples. That's at least the implication, of tight interdependence between species that live so differently having nothing but external contact with each other. Nothing would seem to work but each taking care of itself, allowing others to build solid relationships without information on how or why. It helps you understand a bit of what you are looking at when you see boundaries indicating where something has made its home, as a kind of separation that connects.

3.3 Pattern Writing Templates

The usual way of design patterns are described is as a concise overview of its place in a complex world and how it is made. One collects diverse observations on the conditions and issues to be resolved, the simplifying ideal for resolving them and means of doing it, giving it a suggestive name and visual image. The focus is often some gem of expert knowledge, or way to achieve some natural change of state. Leitner (2014) and Schuler (2008) describe styles of pattern description using stacks of cards for group discussion. Table 1 shows a somewhat standard template for technical pattern writing, attempting to show the common elements of pattern writing for software design, social relationships, and other fields, based on the model of Iba (2014), including:

1. A suggestive name, and characterizing image
2. The circumstances where the design would apply,
3. The unresolved 'forces' to be balanced and resolved
4. A problem, or untapped opportunity presented
5. The unifying response that satisfies the whole,
6. The actions to take and outcomes expected

The intent is not to provide instructions, but to clearly record a holistic objective, that will be of particular help when trying to implement a design that manner. So it's both a recording device and a guide to what needs to be achieved in local circumstances. It's a way to start a very organized "conversation with nature" in that sense, as someone uses it to become an expert themselves in responding the actual complex relationships with which they work. So its greatest value is for describing truly fulfilling purposes. The "object" is both the intent to resolve the forces in a fully unifying way, as well as a unit of design, for producing versatile working parts to work in larger systems. The written pattern is to make those relationships and intentions explicit, as an achievable ideal (Table 1, 2).

Every situation will require a unique response, of course. The ideal designs are often "counter-intuitive" and context dependent, and the realization not exactly duplicated in most cases, but to be discovered as fulfilling the ideal. If it is reasonably well validated and doesn't produce the expected change in form and emergent properties, there should be some clear reason. For implementing a design the design pattern is really just a place to start you learning about the actual circumstance addressed, having identified an apparent pattern match with its needs. Learning how to satisfy the needs of the real situation may then be either simple or complex, take minutes or years, depending on what kind of organizational transformation is involved. It's a process of learning from the real context and its actual forces to find what they will actually respond to, that produces the final fulfillment of the pattern design.

Name	Context	Forces
Image	Problem	
	Solution	
Subject	Actions	Results

Table 1: A Template for Design Pattern Writing

Table 2 shows some of how you might expand the template for describing naturally occurring design patterns. The main difference is needing to describe the emerging development process that occurs as the intended organization develops. For naturally occurring designs development is a natural process of self-organization, what conceptually takes the place of the "designer". Describing it would include identifying characteristics of its own stages of developmental transformation, its "Origins, Growth & Integration", depicted as a succession of stages that have already occurred to need to be arrange for or anticipated occurring later.

You'd try to relate the stages of development to the changes in the systems of organization at each stage. The stages of transformation themselves generally follow a pattern, generally progressing from "naïve" to "immature" to "adolescent" and then "mature" at the pace of the systems development. That would be a good general naming for a series of stages if no other is available. Each stage would also be thought of as a "cycle" of step-wise change, of pattern accumulation. It's a series of smaller steps that that gets somewhere as the growth progresses, going from level to level.

For a design teams applying a pattern there are numerous models for "action learning", the most ancient being the design studio method of every individual pinning up their work and engaging in a group discussion with stakeholders, each working independently on their ideas for how to advance the group objective. A modern method for "agile design" of software products that has been widely adopted and varied is called SCRUM. Its organizing principle is somewhat like that of the studio model, but around delivering a testable product for every scheduled design review. From my own work, a learning cycle that could be used to augment any action learning process was developed to including a holistic sweep of the knowledge base for the problem to follow the design review, that I've discussed as a 4D principle of design. At each cycle you'd review the Internal and External relationships of the design, its Distant, connections, risks and purposes, and find a way to add up its Total

Balance of tradeoffs[6]. That accounting for tradeoffs would include accounts of resource dependencies and energy costs. The whole cycle of self-examination starts rather simply and develops holistically with the rest of the design.

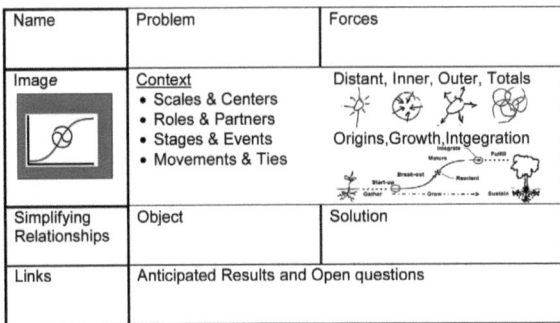

Table 2: A Template for Natural Pattern Writing

3.4 Great Repositories for Natural Patterns

One of the more surprising discoveries when applying Alexander's idea of design patterns to patterns of naturally occurring design is how many rich repositories of natural design patterns there are. It's more or less inherent in nature to accumulate traces of everything, both simple and complex. Some remnants are like echoes of the past others more like a compost pile or junk yard of designs, recording the accumulating variations on how old designs are being used too. Then there working patterns of the systems of nature themselves, what amounts to their genetic code of working patterns, the habits and practices of that organize our own lives that follow rituals with patterned design, the "night out" or the "day at the beach" or "school", etc. They're all resources, to build on, stores of reminders of things that worked before, often refined again and again.

Human cultures themselves are the living storehouses of all the learning we inherit and build on, containing all our accumulated ways of knowing and living, offering endless reminders of the tricks we might not come upon during our whole lives if not reminded by bits of ancient wisdom and practice. One could even define a new meaning for 'culture' that way, as our evolving connection with our specie's shared experience of life. Cultures are a living memory and way of reproducing a community's total experience. Today we still learn from traces of lives lived a million years ago, and we clearly still have much to learn from our current way of living to record in our culture for those who follow.

Nearly every person knows a great deal about their own culture. That makes their acculturation a great resource of recorded natural patterns of response to common circumstances

6   Henshaw- 4D Sustainability http://synapse9.com/connection/

and familiar meanings for them. Of course, maybe more than anything else we all tend to take our own culturally inherited knowledge for granted, as we perhaps should. It really is our foundation on which all our understanding is built upon.

The natural patterns we know of from our own cultural inheritance would be hard to stand apart from to critique or compare, they are so deeply rooted in our feelings. They're often "too close" to recognize in that sense. It's a source of miscommunication that much of our tacit knowledge and ways tend to be hidden from us, so left out of our thinking about how we might affect others. So using your culture to discover natural designs can both awaken and refresh long held assumptions for current circumstances, rediscovering the real genius of their original sources perhaps. In other cases bring out hidden patterns offers security in finding things more solid, to help in living down some discovered mistake.

3.4.1 Cultures as Stores of Natural Patterns

It is curious how unaware people are regarding their own cultures, their natural designs built up silently over the centuries. Our cultures really do contain all our ways of living and knowing about life though. Somehow there seems to be a highly evolved complexity wrapped up in our every gesture and thought, meaningful only in its environment, and its environment reverberating with it. Individual expressions of people in one culture seem both as individually unique as if from different species as well as to display the recognizable patterns of every expression of others in the culture. Open connections between cultures appear unexpectedly often enough, with moments of empathy during shared experiences, but changing cultures seems as rare as grafting a plant onto new roots.

Bridges to connect differing cultures can be found by more practical means too. One is by comparing independent observations on the same naturally occurring patterns of design. It can add to the richness of the meanings of the pattern to combine differing perspectives of the same thing that way. If different views add useful perspective it can be of critical necessity for getting things to work too. I mention it here not because of having some neat way to make that easy, as we're often not so culturally open.

Just being attached to certain styles of expression can keep us from listening to unexpected views, and people invent styles of expression to use as codes for their cultures in great variety. If they code for different common emotions it's easier to translate than for differing abstract theories. Theories following differing defined principles are not possible to connect, and we may be unaware entirely of why. That's the pattern that seems to be present to keep the fabled "six blind men" from being unable to describe "the elephant". They are kept from communicating with each other by each one abstracting the elephant as being the part they are touching. It seems to be a very common cause for intellectual confusion.

How so much of this cultural foundation of how we know and live is deeply hidden from our own view is expressed in Figure 13, showing a range of visible and hidden aspects of human cultures. It adds to the richness of the heritage to expose it, and study its roots. The majority of consists of tacit understandings that are quite unconscious, very vital and active but unspoken and hidden, with only surface features exposed like the tops of icebergs. Though people speak a lot and use words for all kinds of communication, the real foundations of our knowledge and ways of living seem largely in non-verbal experience, and well worth exploring.

So this list of the visible and hidden natural layers of culture is hardly complete, very sketchy really. We just don't have any explicit record or statement of what a culture is, except that it's the root of everything we know and every way we live. Cultures are really remarkable living "artifacts" of lives lived and shared over time, easily more complex than our genetic codes, retaining patterns of relationships, lived by others, kept alive for the ages and always open for accumulating new variations too

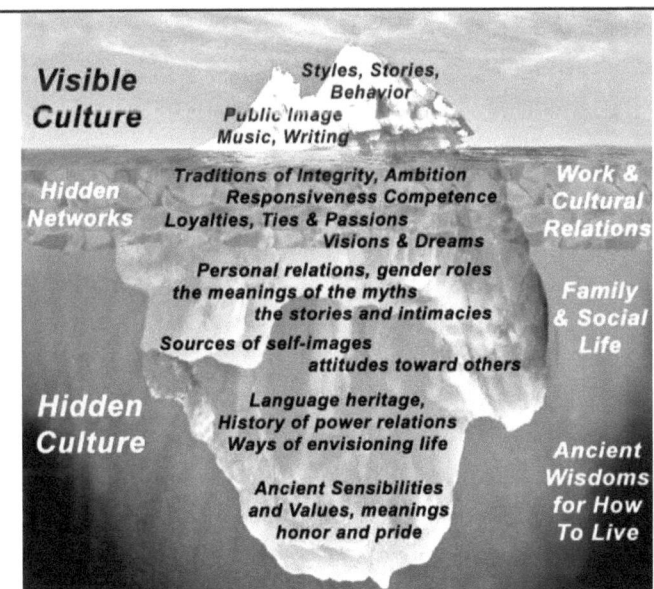

Figure 13: Cultures hold all our accumulated ways of knowing & living

3.4.2 Natural Language as a Pattern Repository

If you think about where natural language came from, it appears the role of words in our lives is for connecting our cultural meanings with the natural design patterns we found meaningful, and needed the words for referring to. Nouns, verbs and adjectives may have many related semantic meanings, but would mean little if they had nothing to refer to. Take the word "noun" for example. Without words that name things, the word 'noun' would not have much meaning.

Before exploring a few details, I should mention the ways this rich resource of natural patterns can be used. Any time you see a word in a sentence you can use this approach to search for the naturally occurring pattern of experience the word originated from. It might be a word noticed for having some pivotal meaning to an author or to the story or circumstance you want to better understand. Another pattern writer, Takashi Iba, uses a similar technique. He draws on what he calls "center words" that he finds in pattern descriptions to start his search for images to illustrate design patterns (Iba 2015). A good dictionary is of course also a good resource for learning more about what experience of nature a word refers to, but here we're also focusing on using words to study the germ of design in nature being responded to.

If you trace words to their subjects like that, what we generally find is that words are used for common traits that apply to numerous and richly varied examples, like "apple" referring to all the kinds of apples and our cultural uses and associations with the word. Looking for the natural design patterns being referred to uses natural language as a repository of references to natural designs we find meaningful. It can be either done simply or with more effort, but we essentially only need to explore the "contexts" the word refers to identify the "forces" that are brought into balance in our experience, to give them the meaning we find in their nature.

An easy example might be the word "frigid", which quickly brings to mind a number of situations where you'd use that. You just think over the natural patterns of relationships it brings up to see the combination we are responding to. It's a feeling of being somewhat exposed and almost attacked by the cold, not just about a temperature. So the way we use words to express qualities, most anywhere that word seems to apply it is likely the circumstance leaves someone both somewhat exposed and attacked, as the pattern. I find it works very often and produces surprising insight, just from the use of words that seem intuitively right for the circumstance.

That way of looking at words as a reference to a natural pattern also makes the word a name for design pattern referred to, as well as for the collection of semantic and cultural meanings associated with it, a gigantic reservoir of associations really. I understand this probably seems unfamiliar at first, and may take searching around for how to become comfortable with at first. We start from thinking of words only in relation to the meanings that come immediately to us, with no thought of them referring to anything else, such as natural relationships and experiences.

For mining natural design patterns from words it can help to study families of words with related meanings. When taken out of normal context and looked at as a group, the meanings for a group of words can then stand out better, and be seen in relation to the original subjects they refer to. In English it can be done by looking at how words are built combining meaningful parts, a 'root' word with its modifiers, as 'prefixes' and 'suffixes'. What we find is that a modifier sometimes adds associated natural meaning to all the root words it modifies, sort of like a seed does the same job for every plant.

Take simple words ending with "-or", for example. That suffix adds the natural design meaning "doer" to each one, as in the words "tractor", "actor", "projector" or "progenitor". The root words mean something by themselves, but together with their action mean a lot more. The combination gives the new word strong "emergent properties", and most compound words seem to be built with combined meanings work like that.

The patterns of meaning added are clearer when looking at lists of words with the same modifiers. As you look at a number of them you recognize the common action being referred to, and see the richness the modifier adds, that highlights the pattern of the natural design referred to. You might think of these powerful combinations of simple meanings as "events", imagined as the "ah ha moments" at some moment in time when the two parts were put together to create the burst of new meanings. There are large collections of these kinds of words.

Figure 14 shows how the parts of the word "community" are assembled, combining "comm-"meaning '*together*', and "unity" meaning '*one*', so referring to things brought together as one, another word structure with curious transformative properties, referring to an important natural design. One would then need to study a number of root words transformed this way to become really clear as what forces are balanced and how that unifies the connection of two thoughts. From there the next step would be to study the overall pattern of natural relationships as a nameable design, and identify the implied "forces" and the "unifying organization" that presents them as a nameable ideal.

> • Pattern words that identify natural 'centers' •
>
> Community: *[comm·unity]*
> ***Bringing "together" a "unity"***
>
> The word structure turns our attention:
> - to the common natural occurrences,
> - to it having natural properties and design
> - to a great variety of examples we each know of,
> - and the diverse and layered associations we are all familiar with.

Figure 14: Words built from names for natural designs

To better understand how modifiers amplify root meanings with their roles in nature, it helps to look at whole lists of similarly modified root word meanings. Below, for example, are a very few of the over 2,000 common words in English that have the "*-tion*" suffix. It helps to study some of the whole list to appreciate the kind of action the suffix fairly consistently associates with the root[7]. That then helps you turn your attention back and forth between the meaning of the word root[8] and how the modifier[9], transforms its meaning, in this case to create names of common transformative processes and the ends states that result.

What these richly meaningful terms of English have in common is this simple way of being elevated in meaning. It's a linguistic invention that came to English from the Latin of early Rome[10]. The added meaning the device produces has one more twist. What seems very curious and important is that these "-tion" words are used to both name how a transformation takes place and the end state it results in, a double meaning of both temporal and spatial designs. I was shocked when I first found that. The third part of the meaning is the association of those natural designs with all our accumulated cultural experiences of them. It is like a whole textbook of complexly related meanings in every word! (Figure 15).

So as for each word in Table 3, the compound word refers to both the end state and how it came about. "*Abbreviation*" refers to both the shortened form as well as the way it was shortened, along with all our cultural associations with both. To understand any state of being you'd surely want to know all three, but who would have guessed that combining 1)

---
7 OneLook dictionary search for words ending in "tion": http://www.onelook.com/?w=*tion&scwo=1&sswo=1
8 'root' http://www.thefreedictionary.com/root "The element that carries the main component of meaning in a word and provides the basis from which a word is derived by adding affixes or inflectional endings or by phonetic change."
9 'modifier' http://www.orbilat.com/General_References/Linguistic_Terms.html "a word or phrase that makes specific the meaning of another word or phrase."
10 - tion: suffix of Latin origin, to form abstract nouns from verbs or stems, to express actions, states or associated meanings - http://dictionary.reference.com/browse/tion

our recognition of important natural patterns, 2) our understanding of how they developed and 3) our cultural experience of them, would be all combined in the meaning of our words for them?

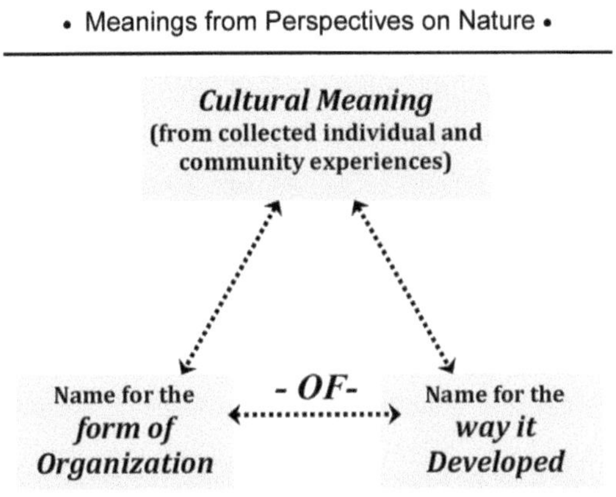

Figure 15: Words with 3 Dimensions of grounded meaning

Examples root words expanded in meaning with "*-tion*"

Root + Suffix	The Action	The Result
comm ∘ uni ∘ cation:	The process	What was made one
co ∘ oper ∘ ation:	The practice	What was achieved
vocal ∘ iz ∘ ation:	The expressing	What was expressed
abbrev ∘ iation:	The shortening	The short form
dele ∘ tion:	The removing	What was removed

Table 3: Words modified to name transformations and their end states

So as for each word in Table 3, the compound word refers to both the end state and how it came about. *"Abbreviation"* refers to both the shortened form as well as the way it was shortened, along with all our cultural associations with both. To understand any state of being you'd surely want to know all three, but who would have guessed that combining 1) our recognition of important natural patterns, 2) our understanding of how they developed and 3) our cultural experience of them, would be all combined in the meaning of our words for them?

This approach is easily done for very casually like this, or as a research. In either case it is likely to deepen your appreciation of the many living qualities that common language gives us access to, and to give you more ready access to them where it matters.

3.4.3 Individuality as a Repository of Unique Designs

Individuality is somewhat puzzling, seeming to refer to the uniquely special inventions of nature, which have no equals, grand examples of what the sciences call "emergence". What we see in individually seems to be unique designs that can't be imitated, and are never to be seen again. It can be complex designs like species or cultures, or singular achievements. It can be singularly simple new forms of design with extraordinary influence, as if adding a new dimension to life.

Truly individual things seem to come about unexpectedly, and not to be exemplars or ideals of some category, but "true originals" with a form and category all their own. So individuality seems not to be a repeatable or recurring design. It makes "individuality" another mysterious property like "wholeness", but for identifying things of extraordinary unrepeatable kind, good and bad. Of course, a problem with categorizing individuality that way is that, technically, nothing in nature is repeatable particularly for complex designs, as they all do seem to develop in individually unique ways. As they say, you can never step into the same river twice.

Still individuality is a very commonly used word, and easily spoken of as having varying degrees. So it evidently refers to something valuable for us to recognize and consider from many points of view. But it's not clear we can really study the individuality of things. What our minds are better suited for is studying the common patterns of things that we can put in a category. So it appears individuality may be something special, expressing the limits of our perception as as the aspect of designs that we admire but find beyond our understanding. So it may refer to the quality of natural designs that are so very original we find it hard to see them as having patterns, a matter of perception.

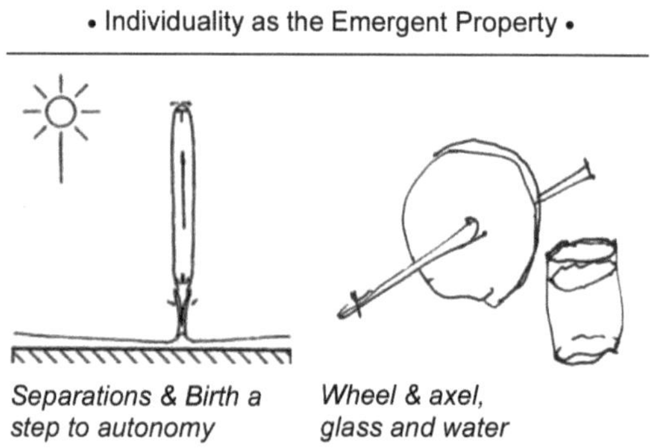

Figure 16: Emergent individuality with abrupt change of state

As we get to understand naturally occurring designs we do often notice their uniqueness seems to undefinably pervade every part, like the body of work by a great artist, or a great culture, that has readily identifiable ineffable traits we could never define. In that way we sometimes recognize it as containing something like having its own "science" or "language". Every person is like that too, both having familiar traits as well as being truly unique individuals too, a duality of being both comprehensible and incomprehensible at the same time, having a lot of meaning for us.

Not knowing quite how to categorize individuality, I've just chosen some examples of "rapid" and "slow" emerging individuality. Figure 16 shows three images of rapidly emerging individuality. The individual air currents shown as having a rapidly rising column of hot air at its center is also in the process of abruptly separating from its hot air source, to become detached and independent. The combining of a wheel with an axel and water with a glass depict profoundly transformative simple dualities. They depict uniquely individual and influential innovations that take place abruptly and change the whole meaning of their parts. The funny thing is that these simple combinations that perform something quite new are not at all rare. Almost anything people use is used for joining complementary parts to benefit from their emergent properties when combined., as "what we 'do' ". These three are just classic examples.

• Eventful forms of Relationships •

Relationships   Monuments of Art & Design

Figure 17: Emergent individuality with long development

Individuality is also seen in the variety of new forms with emergent properties that take extended periods of time and go through many stages of development. That's the deeper story I notice behind the story of any really happy couple, for example, as well as for the great moments in time, such as the advent of Greek architecture as monument in the history design (Figure 17). These are just special examples how great designs commonly involve long series of development, for both intentional and naturally occurring designs (Section

2.1). So perhaps "individuality" also about how such long gestation periods, perhaps allowing very little of the design or how it developed to be noticed, sometimes result is such dramatic moments when they mature.

Part the reason individuality appears to occur suddenly, even when it has taken a long time to develop, is that in early stages it may not be recognizable. The developing form may be too immature, or its roles not yet discovered. So to turn into the completed pattern that our minds are able to register, just needs to wait, to when recognition may occur suddenly. For example, though nothing changes when we graduate from school or achieve professional recognition, the meaning of all that went before can become suddenly apparent.

We also see individuality that very much puzzles us in mankind's way living on earth, following the very long gestation of modern society, maturing with inventing ever more radical ways or reorganizing ourselves and monopolizing the earth that appear to lack real meaning. Like any growth process in nature, it leads to creating a new kind of species. In this case it's as an experiment partly of our design and it seems we need to now look for a purpose. That would be a learning process, of engaging our conceptual thinking with nature's systemic world (Figure 18), shown here as a variation on the Robert Rosen's model of science as a cycle of encoding and decoding nature (Figure 1). It seems the challenge is to find meaning in our new way of living on earth, organized largely by the pursuit of wealth, as it seems to lose meaning.

The real point is about how hard it naturally is to recognize individuality when it is still immature. We might indeed not recognize who we really are until after we find out where we're going with our creativity. The picture only shows a general diagram of the process. It does not show whether the "chicken and egg" cycle on its way to becoming a really fulfilling object oriented design or not. For all appearances we are in a difficult struggle to find how to make the earth our good home, but not yet really thinking about how homes work or even what homes are for. We will find whatever we find, by turning our attention going back and forth the usual way, between interpreting and acting on our world, hopefully learning to appreciate both what is found and lost in translation.

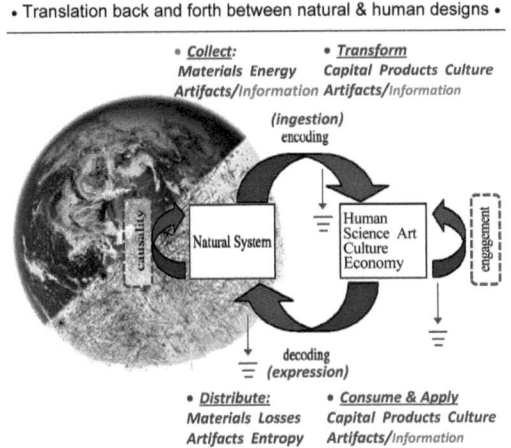

Figure 18: Relationships between cultures as systemic learning

3.4.4 Alexander's 15 Principles

Table 4 shows various illustrations of Alexander's 15 recurrent features of wholeness (2002). The intent is to suggest using varied illustrations, examples for varied perspectives in the description of design patterns, as expressing richness "worth a thousand words". They help suggest where these or other rudimentary features are found and what they do. I've shown some of my illustrations and with those of two others, along with a few questions and suggestions.

Appreciating any complex subject takes looking at it from multiple viewpoints. So just as the fabled "six blind men" describing an elephant are handicapped by not looking for commonalities that would let them communicate, they are also handicapped by failing to "look around" for what else might be connected to their initial impressions. Looking at different views of the same thing 1) helps expose unexpected connections, and 2) helps keep one's own thinking fresh and avoid becoming stuck on any one view.

Alexander initially developed his 15 principles from an unusual pattern repository, a study of the timeless beauty of ancient Turkish carpets (1995). An interesting view of it from a carpet trader's view is found in Detlev Fischer's sort online article (2010). I see Alexander's 15 features of wholeness as a very useful collection of shape patterns found in natural whole systems, though not inclusive. They're all 'spatial' patterns, and a similarly diverse collection of 'temporal' patterns, like the "phases of growth", or ecological processes of allowed by "mediums of exchange" might be collected along with other design and pattern primitives too.

I see primitive pattern like these as most useful when used for "pattern search", used to trace the working parts of natural designs such as the communities that intentional designs are served by or serve. You could think of them somewhat abstractly as for pattern 'stigmergy', a way to use patterns to trace the origins and roles of things that an observer can follow as trails. So one can use the 15 principles and their variations for either helping to explain things where you find these patterns, or just to help explore what's living. For example Pattern 01 here, "Strong Center", is shown with three images of 'centers', a point, a cathedral plan, and a discussion circle under a tree. Those are totally different kinds of "strong centers" that never the less have a lot in common. Many others could be added. But you need to think of the variety to begin to understand both the common principles involved, and to become free with discovering and using their varying use in other circumstances.

Table 4: Images of Alexander's 15 characters of wholeness

Illustrated by Leitner (2013), Reckard (2011) with related images and suggested occurrences in naturally occurring design by the author (Henshaw 2015b)

[01] Strong Center

[02] Level of Scales

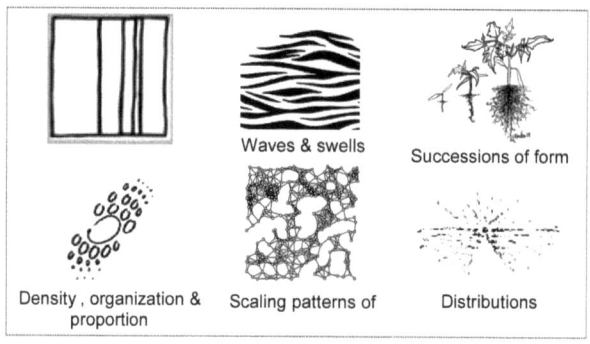

Guiding Patterns of Naturally Occurring Design: Elements

[03] Boundaries, Geometry, Walls, Transitions, Limits

- paths of growt as natural bounds
- ranges of behavior as natural bounds
- Margins of ecologies -, trophic scales, neighborhoodscircles of relations
- Limits of Visibility, - of Reach, of Scale, of Change, of Versatility

[04] Alternating, Repetition, Recurrence

- Vitality, Resilience, Responsiveness
- Cycles and waves of change
- Practice & training, perfecting
- Looking back and forth, inside and out, foreward and back, poking around
- Successive addition or subtraction, of layers of design, or branching from designs
- Hysterisis, Action learning, Exploration
- Semi-lattice (as added complexity with added variety of opportunity)
- Stigmergy (trail reinforcement)

[05] Positive Space, complementarity

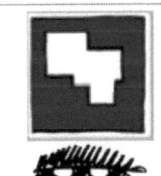
- Open environments
- Spaces of free association and adaptation
- Proximity with separation
- "In-betweens" and freedoms of movement.

Openings Permeability

[06] Good Shape & form

- Simplicity of design
- Comfortable and Complementary fit
- Serves intersecting needs
- Serves exclusive needs

137

[07] Local Symmetries

- Polarities: roots and branches
- Approaches and arrivals
- Interiors and exteriors

[08] Deep Interlock and Ambiguity

- The impossibly complex overlap of so many things working independently
- How nature can only organize separate things and our reason can only organize mutually defining things, looking for one world in a life of so very many worlds

[09] Contrast, difference

- A bridge between information and matter
- Revealing things hidden from view
- The potentials for complementary fit
- Signs of transition

[10] Gradients

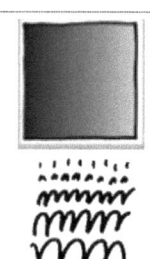

- Energy gradients to power orgaization
- Proximities, potentials, distance, values
- Margins, ranges, cushions, resilience, flexibility, continuity, versatility

Guiding Patterns of Naturally Occurring Design: Elements

[11] Roughness, diversity

- Inconsistency, consistencey, texture,
- Intermittance, irregularity, courseness
- Surface, ground, skin,
- Fabric, aggregation, collection, granularity

[12] Echoes

- Spreading and lingering reflections; elastic vibrations; memories of lost places, events; artifacts of periods of change
- Environments as repositories of fragments and footprints, a compost of discards,
- Traces of history as memory of all past learning and change, ornamenting things new

[13] The Void

- A lack of form, absence,
- 'Book zero', the potential of formlessness,
- The uncertain silence, the moments of stillness, pauses, suspense, immobility

[14] Simplicity

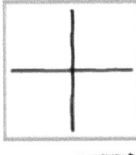
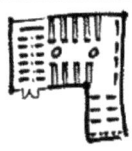

- Inner Calm
- Freedom of direction
- Balance
- Observing, listening, receptiveness
- Emergent couplings, organization
- Individuality

[15] not-separateness, "QWAN"

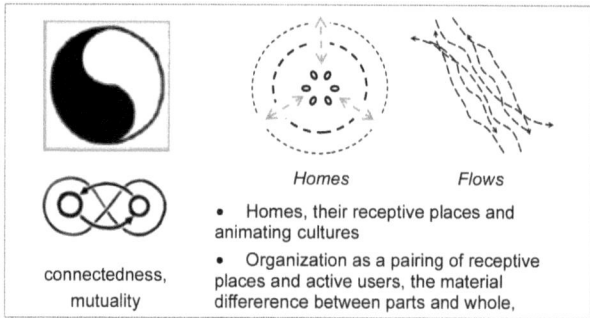

4. Discussion

I hope to have presented an interesting introduction that readers can use to explore natural patterns of design and expand the value of pattern language methods. The qualities and real meanings of both purposeful and naturally occurring designs seem to rest on having organization with emergent properties of the whole. I'm certainly very grateful for having found how Alexander's pattern language has evolved. As a general method for communicating sound principles of holistic design, it seems to give me a way to translate years of prior work to make it communicable. It lets me separate the discussion of purposeful designs and naturally occurring designs. It lets me serve them both equally and by being separated then better show how they can be understood as usefully connected. It adds "new forces" to my world, that allow the cooperation of previously disparate ones.

That serendipity gave me a freedom to discuss the details of two of my favorite natural patterns, the Two Primary Patterns discussed in Section 2, 'homes' as the strong centers of whole natural world, and stages of growth as its process of self-organization and means of energy use, characterizing both purposeful and naturally occurring design. I hope that brief look at these two key patterns was adequate, for then offering the "Starter Kit" for the method offered in Section 3. That "kit" composed of a few dozen variously simple and advanced ways for readers to branch out with their own thinking, presents a collection of naturally occurring designs to explore that have fascinated me tremendously. I'd like for others to find as well their own recognitions of the bridges between our purposeful designs and naturally occurring ones such as the one I presented that opened the door to everything else I found.

I've mostly referred to natural patterns of design as something we might study, but without discussing much of how they appear to work by themselves. I've also been critical of mainstream science, for representing nature with equations that omit many of nature's more prominent features. So below I offer remarks on those two subjects, first on how apparently autonomous natural design processes really "do it", and then pointing to where I think science may be heading in the near future.

4.1 Natural Patterns of Learning

If you consider how new art forms develop, say "impressionism" as a style of fine art painting, or "Hip Hop" as a popular culture and style of rap music, it's clear they originated with a burst of innovation, but not clear quite what it came from. You do notice that the patterns of design they began with they also continued with, though, elaborating on it over time but remaining faithful to it as well.

That seems to be a common pattern in anything that develops by growth, forming complex systems that work as wholes. Natural designs of that kind seem to remain "true to their roots" that way, as if only able to extend the pattern they began with. It seems to be virtually universal, for any new design to develop by itself to need to have an original design for adding new parts that extends the same pattern for adding more parts. It needs to be have a "pattern of replication", making copies, as an essential function for designs that will "emerge", adding layers in a way that makes new places for more layers. Beyond that is seems the variety of natural patterns that replicate is exceedingly varied, perhaps as numerous as snowflakes, but also as uniquely individual.

It appears to mean that the small beginnings of things set a pattern that only attaches that extend the pattern, as if in the manner of a snowflake starting a pattern of crystallization that catalyzes more of the same pattern of crystallization. In a general way that also appears to be the natural form of adaptive replication, as the general pattern of what we notice replicating. It's also a fairly apt depiction of what people spend their days doing too, looking around for the next thing to extend their pattern.

It might set a somewhat new, but as a pattern for extending a pattern it can't be so different to break the replication. So for the evolutions of designs by growth, that we observe as accumulating creatively rather than deterministically such as what we see is resulting from growth, the original pattern needs to be replicated in an exceptionally faithful way, just to continue to do so for a great many replications..

So that process of extended replication also seems to be necessity for something small to get big, and so to seem universal. What a replication of parts also allows is a multiplication of faithfully replicated parts, another feature of the general pattern for how small things get big that seems universal. If faithful replication were to be linear in how it progressed, a single fertilized cell in the womb adding another cell every week, it would take 19 billion years to reach birth weight with about a trillion cells! With every cell made doubling every week it only takes nine months. So it seems real complexity would not be remotely possible without it.

Figure 19: Snowflake design developing from the center

You can see these patterns of growth directly in the shape of a snowflake (Figure 19). The new layers don't exactly replicate the first ones, but add onto them while providing new locations that get added to, and so elaborate on, or branch from, the original. How the whole becomes so distinctive is by some crystal edges being more receptive than others for new crystal formation as "hot zones" for catalyzing new crystal formation. The form of the whole is then being determined by whatever parts replicate their crystal pattern the fastest.

The interior parts of the snowflake are highly symmetrical and repetitive, but outer branches actually become fairly irregular, so it seems the replication pattern deteriorates somehow. So, it appears the evolution of complexly organized designs is a matter of finding a very successful design for continually having an answer to the question "What's next?" but more of an open question than one answered by laws.

Much that same general kind of growth pattern can be seen in the course of the world economy (Figure 20). The way it builds on itself is by using the profits of businesses to add to the scale and kinds of businesses that make profits, the chain pattern of reliable replication that readily multiplies. That's expands the system by making more options for expanding the system. The big difference, of course, is that it is a highly complex cultural/*technological system*, guided by decisions based on information about monetary profits. That's a big difference, but other than the very different design for replication they start with, the two are similar in having to be faithful to their start and having no design for ceasing their replication.

The snow flake keeps attracting more layers of crystalizing water vapor as it falls, until the water vapor runs out or it meets warmer temperature at lower elevations. What would make the replication the world economy's parts stop before exhausting its resources or making economic environment unprofitable?   You'd think the latter cause, general decline in profits as we are actually starting to see now, would only stop growth if profits declined toward zero, and investors withdrew their assets from risk. It's the logical end point of a growth system with not goal but growth, a "pattern problem", and "imbalance of forces".

• Design starting from an origin pattern •

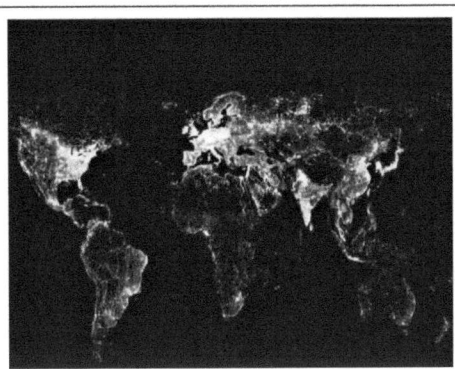

Figure 20: World economy growing from all cells at once

It's one that would ideally call for some "unifying design" to resolve it holistically, rather than simply letting it run its course. To attempt that you'd first spend a lot of time looking for patterns that embody the same circumstance, to find working examples other transformations that are possible, and their "simplifying ideals" for resolving the forces. Nature does indeed seem to display all kinds of creative ways of furiously replicating patterns that then smoothly resolve the imbalances that come naturally from it.

Whether it's a snowflake or a world economy, pattern language now seems to offer a way to identify and find ways of studying complex designs of many kinds, in terms of their recognizable recurrent design patterns. It could result in better understanding of both of our real subjects and our deep common roots of human understanding. Most importantly it allows individual forms of both intentional and natural design to be recognized as objects of organization based on natural design principle, each individual with its own separate origin and development by replication.   We can identify and verify many of their stages of development, to be considered from many perspectives, based on what many can observe in common. It changes our perception of all these emergent forms, making them much better understood and relevant as tangible realities to work with. We might still find them mysterious, certainly, while we still become more and more able to confirm them as individually occurring and possible to study, mutually observed, and opening a new kind of discussion well-grounded in nature.

4.2 An "Object Oriented Science"

In the introduction and elsewhere I've long been fairly critical of mainstream science, for limiting its study of natural design to the invented equations we based on the categories of data we collected. That approach completely overlooks the dense centers of organization exhibited by individual energy using systems. Those include all the kinds of living organisms as well as living cultures, as well as any number of other kinds of complex energy using systems that develop their own organization by growth, giving them organizational independence while leaving how they work hidden from view.

It's those classes of "objects" that I see the sciences needing to find how to study. So here I'd like to briefly describe what I see as a way for mainstream science to recognize and start to explore this new territory, without abandoning the mathematical tools it uses. The sciences have mostly restricted themselves to looking at the rich multi-dimensional designs of nature through a lens of one dimensional measures, "data". Now science can potentially begin to also refer to the whole objects of nature, in their own forms, just by recognizing where they are by their locations. One can then study their uses of energy, for one thing, studied using the same "black box" methods as for machines. It won't reveal everything inside the box of course, but at least you'd have a "natural box", as the location of what is being studied, and to associate with what is learned about its inside. It's really just an incremental change in methods of boundary definition, that recognizing the boundaries of "whole systems" (Henshaw 2011)

With learning to recognize boundaries of independent organizations the potential is then clearly there to greatly expand the subjects that the sciences can define and study, that were never studied before. The individual systems then possible to study are found throughout nature on every scale, and if recognized as having boundaries could be named and studied as individually organized wholes. These objects of nature that do appear to work as wholes would then be recognizable as the units of design that life works with, expands the potential view of science further.

The expansion of subjects could also come directly from current conventional research methods in the mainstream sciences. It might be from scientists seeing a need for a better way of "taking notes", in following the hotly pursued search in complexity science for way to understand the emergence of new properties and forms. Feynman had a wonderful notation system that helped speed the advance of physics, for example (Moody 2009). It might be a notation, just to help with keeping track of shifts in organization observed while studying the uncontrolled behaviors of complex AI systems that spread to other uses, perhaps. It might also come from some taxonomy method used in forensic science, maybe later borrowing concepts from Alexander's pattern language, or not. All the methods that worked would get their validity from being means of learning from the same natural forms, and so be interconnected and interrelated by that.

Given the demonstrated potential power of a pattern language view, the emerging new views of nature in the complexity sciences and those of pattern language will eventually approach each other and meet in the middle. Each is likely to retain its individuality, and while using differing technique also learn from each other's perspective, producing a greater view than either when combined.

One can also imagine barriers to doing that arising, like institutional investment in old ways and resistance to change. Perhaps each science would insist on sticking only with its own somewhat proprietary way of describing a different world. That would have each continuing to wandering off in its own direction more or less continuing the historic pattern, of studying very bodies of information as if different "realities", that as for the "six blind men" and the elephant, seeing realities that don't connect. To upset an entrenched habit you might need some unexpected event. It might possibly be like the BIG NEWS that a very useful way of making the ancient principles of holistic design explicit had been found. Upon hearing that, perhaps some new generation might look up from its boredom and "blink", to then take off on the task of connecting the new with the old and expand our whole way scientific thinking.

There are various names for it one mighty consider. Often new forms are named by happenstance and that's OK. As a "working name" I think the simple "object oriented science" is perhaps best. It's neutral, directly descriptive and already used as an expression that way. One can probably trust that interest in the qualities of "aliveness", "living quality", "individuality" and "wholeness" found in both the most appreciated kinds of intentional and natural forms of design, will carry over. Helmut Leitner and Franz Nahrada propose the more direct "liveliness science" as "lebendigkeit science" (2014), a nice way of saying it. I called my own research archive on the subject "the physics of happening" so I have affection for that. The first question I had that became productive for my studies was: "What makes life lively?" We could call the science "liveliness" then, or perhaps just "individuality" or "nature". With one of those terms non-scientists might more quickly get the whole idea... that the name actually refers to the real subject of study.

If we want it to spread, though, it needs to stay faithful to its roots while continuing to be clarified and made more relevant to users. It also needs to become more adaptable to new domains, shareable across disciplines, maintained as a broad common language, and to expand to new areas and disciplines, like this effort to introduce a direct way to learn from naturally occurring design.

5. Acknowledgements

I have quite a number of people and fortunate circumstances to acknowledge. It was the clear way that Christopher Alexander's pattern language was discussed in the software community that first made it clear to me I could use it too, which I greatly appreciate. It allowed me to translate my prior natural science work on these subjects into this more communicable way of discussing them. I had a fine education in physics too, at a small college with a wonderful physics department, professors Peckham and Rohmer at St. Lawrence Univ. They encouraged my odd studies of how lab experiments always misbehaved. I found inspiration at the Univ. of Pennsylvania school of design too, both from visionary faculty and the pervading presence of Lou Kahn's deep ways of thinking about the nature form. Of course I am also indebted to being taught how to observe natural patterns from a very early age by my father Clement L. Henshaw, a professor of physics at Colgate. His idea of teaching was to show students where to find explanatory principles for themselves. I also owe thanks to a friend from high school, John A. Blackmore, who became a social scientist and I must credit with many of my key insights, as well as being a constant intellectual partner with a wonderful appetite for any subject we could think of talking about, through all the years.

6. References

Alexander, C. (2001-6). The Nature of Order, Books 1-4. Center for Environmental Structure, Berkeley, California, USA. Book, 1. Center for Environmental Structure

Alexander, C. (2002). The nature of order: the process of creating life. Taylor & Francis.

Alexander (1995). A foreshadowing of 21st century art. Center for Environmental Structure, Vol 7 SBN-10: 0195208668

Alexander, C., Neis, H., Anninou, A., King, I., (1987) A New Theory of Urban Design. Oxford Univ. Press.

Alexander, C., (1979). The Timeless Way of Building. New York: Oxford University Press.

Alexander, C., Ishikawa, S., Silverstein, M., Jacobson, M., Fiksdahl-King, I., Angel, S. (1977). A Pattern Language. New York: Oxford University Press.

Alexander, C. (1965) A city is not a Tree. Architectural Forum, Vol 122, No 1, April 1965, pp 58-62 (Part I),Vol 122, No 2, May 1965, pp 58-62 (Part II): online in the Pattern Language archive online - http://www.patternlanguage.com/archives/alexander1.htm

Argyris, C. (1982). Reasoning, learning, and action: Individual and organizational (pp. 85-101). San Francisco, CA: Jossey-Bass.

Ashby, W. R. (1956). An Introduction to Cybernetics. Chapman & Hall, London, UK. Online - www.pespmc1.vub.ac.be/ASHBBOOK.html

Bollier, D., & Helfrich, S. (Eds.). (2014). The wealth of the commons: A world beyond market and state. Levellers Press.

Borchers, J. O. (2001). A Pattern Approach to Interaction Design. AI & Soc 15:359-376 Springer-Verlag London

Dinsmoor, W. B. (1975). The Architecture of Ancient Greece. W W Norton & Co. Reprint of 1950 3rd ed,, first published 1902. ISBN 0-393-00781-2

Denef, S. (2012). A Pattern Language of Firefighting Frontline Practice to Inform the Design of Ubiquitous Computing. in Constructing Ambient Intelligence, AmI 2011 Workshops, Amsterdam, The Netherlands, November 16-18, 2011. Revised Selected Papers, Wichert, R., Van Laerhoven, K., Gelissen, J. (Eds.)2012, pp 308-312 DOI: 10.1007/978-3-642-31479-7; Excerpt of pattern abstracts for quick introduction, as author recommended: http://synapse9.com/ref/Denef-FireFightingDesignPatterns.pdf

Finidori, H. (2015). Towards a Fourth Generation Pattern Language:Patterns as Epistemic Threads for Systemic Orientation. PURPLSOC 2015 Proceedings, Krems Austria.

Finidori, Helene (2014) An Open Source Pattern Language. DebateGraph wiki, H. Finidori Ed. online - http://debategraph.org/Details.aspx?nid=329727

Fischer, D. (2010). Alexander's theory: The color and geometry of very early Turkish carpets'. review of: Alexander, C. (1995). A foreshadowing of 21st century art. Online www.oturn.net/rugs/tor/alexander.html

Goodwin, B. (1994). How the Leopard Changed It's Spots. Princeton Univ Press edition, 2001

Henshaw, J., (2015c) Guiding Patterns of Natural Design, Mining Living Quality, A Pattern Language Approach. PLoP conf. Oct 2015. Online - draft http://synapse9.com/drafts/2015_PLoP-draft.pdf

Henshaw, J., (2015b) Illustrations from author's collection.

Henshaw, J., (2015a) Current Jessie Henshaw CV. online - http://synapse9.com/jlhCV

Henshaw J., (2014) Reports to UN bodies on whole system designs for sustainable development. in J. Henshaw Publication List. online - http://synapse9.com/jlhpub.htm#UN

Henshaw J. (2013) 3Step process for Working With Nature, an brainstorming environmental design method, proposed for use in developing sustainable development goals, during the UN post 2015 development goals process. online - http://synapse9.com/signals/2013/07/03/3steps-process-for-working-with-nature/

Henshaw, P., King, C., Zarnikau, J. (2011) System Energy Assessment (SEA), Defining a Standard Measure of EROI for Energy Businesses as Whole Systems. Sustainability 2011, 3(10), 1908-1943; doi:10.3390/su3101908

Henshaw, P. (1999). Features of derivative continuity in shape, International Journal of Pattern Recognition and Artificial Intelligence (IJPRAI link to article), for a special issue on invariants in pattern recognition, V13 No 8 1999 1181-1199. Online - http://www.synapse9.com/fdcs-ph99-1.pdf

Henshaw, P. (1995-9) The Physics of Happening. An archive of studies and natural system pattern recognition methods. online - http://www.synapse9.com/drwork.htm & drstats.htm

Henshaw, P. (1979b). An unhidden Pattern of Events. republished 2014 in An Open Source Pattern Language, "Patterns of Complex Natural Systems" by H. Finidori. Originally in book of same name, self-published edition, Denver 1979. online -http://debategraph.org/Details.aspx?nid=360233

Henshaw, P. (1979a). Sneaky Invisible Things, Air Currents of Classic Passive Solar Homes, Rain Magazine, Tom Bender Ed. V5 No6 Apr 1979 Portland, OR. online -scan http://www.synapse9.com/pub/1979RainSneakyInvisThings.pdf, text http://www.synapse9.com/airnets.htm

Hillside Group (1993-2015) Sponsoring PLoP Conferences and Pattern Language use. online - http://www.hillside.net

Iba, T., (2014) A Journey on the Way to Pattern Writing: Designing the Pattern Writing Sheet. PLoP 2014 proceedings.

Iba, T., (2013) Evolution of Pattern Languages. Keio Univ

Jacobs, J., (1970) The Economy of Cities. Vintage Books, New York

Jacobs, J., (1961) The Death and Life of Great American Cities. Vintage Books, New York

Leitner, H., Nahrada, F. (2014). The concept of ‚liveliness' and the program of „aliveness Science". Lebendigkeitswissenschaft, Theoriekultur-Wiki. – online http://www.theoriekultur.at/wiki?Lebendigkeitswissenschaft: Google English trans

Leitner , H. (2014). Pattern Language and Christopher Alexander, intro & crash course. Guest lecture at Danube University Krems, Jul 31, 2014. online video https://www.youtube.com/watch?v=Q4R7dDtLYgU

Leitner , H. (2013). Illustrations for Alexander's fifteen properties of living structures from the The Nature of Order Book 1. online - http://peter.baumgartner.name/wp-content/uploads/2013/05/15-properties-leitner.png

Maslow, A.H. (1943). A theory of human motivation. Psychological Review 50 (4) 370–96. Found online - http://psychclassics.yorku.ca/Maslow/motivation.htm

Nahrada, F. (2013). The commoning of patterns and the patterns of commoning", in The Wealth of the Commons, David Boiler & Silke Helfrich ed., the Commons strategy group. online - http://wealthofthecommons.org/essay/commoning-patterns-and-patterns-commoning-short-sketch

Pattern Language Association (2015) PatternLanguage.com. a program of the Center for Environmental Structure (CES). Online- http://www.patternlanguage.com/index.html

Reckard, W. (2011) Sketches of Christopher Alexander's Fifteen Fundamental Properties of Wholeness, TKWA Architects, Cedarburg, WI. online - http://www.tkwa.com/blog/edra-42-reflecting-on-alexander-and-the-use-of-patterns-as-a-design-tool/

Rising, L. (1998) The Pattens Handbok. – Techniques, Strategies and Applications. Cambridge Univ. Press.

Rosen, R. (1991). Essays on Life Itself. Columbia Univ Press. ISBN 0-231-07565-0

Roy B., Trudel, J., (2011) The Conception-Aware, Object-Oriented Organization. Integral Leadership Review, Integral Publishers, Creative Commons ISSN 1554-0790. Online http://integralleadershipreview.com/3199-leading-the-21st-century-the-conception-aware-object-oriented-organization/

Schuler, D., (2008) Liberating Voices: A Pattern Language for Communication Revolution. Cambridge, MA: MIT Press.

Tidwell, J. (1999). A Pattern Language for Human-Computer Interface Design. (c) 1999 Jenifer Tidwell. online http://www.mit.edu/~jtidwell/common_ground.html, resources http://designinginterfaces.com

Youd, B. (2014). Louis I. Kahn: The Prophetic Creative Genius. University of Nottingham Department of Architecture and Built Environment. Online - http://benjaminyoud.co.uk/wordpress/wp-content/uploads/2014/11/Youd_Benjamin_4078785.pdf

Words for a Journey: A Pattern Language for Living Well with Dementia

Iba, Takashi
Keio University, Japan
iba@sfc.keio.ac.jp

Kaneko, Tomoki
Keio University, Japan
t14236tk@sfc.keio.ac.jp

Kamada, Arisa
Keio University, Japan
arskmd@sfc.keio.ac.jp

Tamaki, Nao
Keio University, Japan
s12552nt@sfc.keio.ac.jp

Okada, Makoto
Fujitsu Laboratories, Japan
okadamkt@jp.fujitsu.com

This paper presents Words for a Journey, a pattern language for living well with dementia. This pattern language consists of 40 patterns, which are categorized into three different groups: words for those living with dementia, words for caring families, and words for everyone. These patterns can be used in three ways: (1) reading them and putting those into practice, (2) using them as a part of their vocabulary to speak with other people about matters related to the patterns in daily life, and (3) talking with others about experiences based on the patterns. This paper demonstrates some cases of workshops utilizing Words for a Journey for sharing experiences, expressing positive feelings in a day care center, enriching nursing education, and inventing new products and services to help people in the situations described by the patterns. Finally, we discuss ideas for the pattern language's use by various stakeholders.

Pattern Language; Pattern Language 3.0; Dementia; Dialog; Idea Generation; Design, Quality of Life

1. Introduction

In Japan, the number of elderly people over 65 years old with dementia, including mild cognitive impairment, is estimated to be 8.46 million (the Ministry of Health, Labour and Welfare, 2012). This represents one in four people over the age of 65 or one in 15 people overall in Japan. Dementia is a syndrome of deterioration of the memory, thinking, behavior, and the ability to perform daily life activities. Dementia has physical, psychological, social, and economic impacts on affected people and their families and society. Worldwide, 47.5 million people have dementia (WHO, 2015), and it is an emerging global social issue.

While medical and welfare support for those with dementia is growing, support for daily activities with the condition is still inadequate. In Japan, the Ministry of Health, Labour and Welfare announced "A New Orange Plan: A Comprehensive Strategy for the Promotion of Dementia Measures," and while it promotes early diagnosis, it asserted that support after diagnosis is not yet sufficient. Furthermore, the stigma surrounding dementia is present not only in society but is also deep-rooted in persons with dementia and their families. Consequently, promoting "early diagnosis" leads to "early despair."

On the other hand, some people live well with dementia. They do not give up everything in their lives just because they have dementia. In 2014, the Japan Dementia Working Group was established and met for the first time in Japan, working toward the elimination of the "early diagnosis = early despair" notion. Masahiko Sato, a joint representative, expressed the following view: "Even though I have dementia, the many things I can no longer do are also accompanied by many things I can do. I have introduced ways to be creative in my lifestyle without giving in to despair and continue living with hope" (Sato, 2014). There are many like him who live well with dementia.

Social movements that convey the voices of such people have already emerged; however, they need more powerful tools to reframe the concept of dementia and to change behaviors to make a social impact. To that end, in this paper, we present a pattern language for living well with dementia, which we call *Words for a Journey*. Pattern Language is a method of sharing practical knowledge in a target domain. We mined the knowledge from deep interviews, revealing the principles behind cases, and describing them in a certain format. In the following sections, we will overview the pattern language *Words for a Journey*, present the patterns, show cases of workshops using them, and discuss the advantages of using the pattern languages.

2. Overview of Words for a Journey

The pattern language for living with dementia, Words for a Journey, contains positive, practical wisdom about daily life, which was extracted from interviews about their experiences with people who are living well with dementia.

The method of pattern language was invented by Christopher Alexander for architectural design (Alexander et al., 1977; Alexander, 1979) and then applied to software design (Beck & Cunningham, 1987; Gamma, et al., 1995). Recently, this method has been applied to various domains related to creative human actions (Iba, 2015), which we call "Pattern Language 3.0," including education (Pedagogical Patterns Editorial Board, 2012), innovation (Manns & Rising, 2005; Manns & Rising, 2015), learning (Hoover & Oshineye, 2009, Iba & Iba Lab, 2014a), collaboration (Iba & Iba Lab, 2014b), presentation (Iba & Iba Lab, 2014c), change making (Shimomukai, et al., 2015), disaster prevention (Furukawazono, et al. 2015), beauty in everyday life (Arao, et al., 2012), and cooking (Isaku & Iba, 2015). *Words for a Journey* is the first pattern language in the social welfare domain.

The core of *Words for a Journey* is the pattern "A New Journey" which offers a new perspective on living with dementia. Although it is not easy to accept the fact that you, a family member, or someone close to you has dementia, if you think of it as the start of a new journey, you can live more positively. For example, if you have dementia, you will be spending more time with your family, which will be a good opportunity to get to know them better. You will be going together to places where you used to go alone, and you will get a chance to reflect on each other's lives and notice things about them that you did not know before.

The rest of the patterns in this pattern language provide practical and comparatively more concrete knowledge to live well with dementia. These patterns are categorized into three different groups: words for those living with dementia, words for caregiving families, and words for everyone (Figure 1). From the perspective of the pattern language method, this structure is unusual and quite new. Although existing pattern languages are designed for only one type of people for solving problems, *Words for a Journey* helps several types of people solve problems collaboratively with other types of people.

This means that it is not enough for only people with dementia to do their best; it is not enough for only caring families to do their best; and it is not enough for only others, for example, neighbors and care staff, to do their best. A dementia-friendly society will emerge only with their mutual cooperation. *Words for a Journey* enables spontaneous collaboration among them without requiring them to consciously think about collaboration (Figure 2).

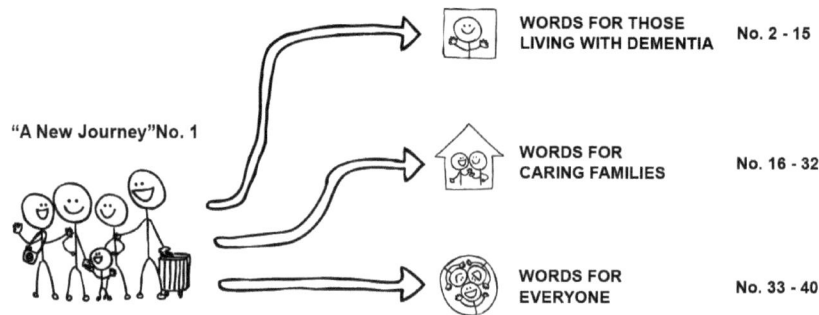

Figure 1: The three groups in Words for a Journey

Figure 2: Interrelations between patterns among the groups

Each pattern is written in the same pattern format: Pattern Name, Introduction, Pattern Illustration, Context, Problem, Solution, and Consequence. The Pattern Name defines the pattern with a short memorable word for easy reference, and the Introduction helps readers understand a living image of the pattern. Pattern Illustration shows the pattern's essence, including characters expressing human movements and feelings. The Context describes the situations in which the pattern should be used. Followed by the words "In this context," a Problem that is likely to occur in the context is presented. Then, followed by the word

"Therefore," a solution to the problem is presented. Finally, after the word "Consequently," the Consequence describes how things can change when this pattern is put into practice.

Note that the Pattern Name is not just a headline or summary for the pattern but a new word that can be used in conversations. Furthermore, Pattern Illustration is not just a complementary figure illustrating the pattern but an important element symbolically representing the essence of the pattern (Harasawa, et al., 2014; Miyazaki, et al., 2015; Iba & Iba Lab, 2015). Therefore, we elaborated on the name and illustration. Figure 3 shows an example of the pattern "Daily Chore" from the "Words for Those Living with Dementia" group.

Pattern Number	No.7
Pattern Name	**Daily Chore**
Introduction	Even the smallest things matter if you do them every day.
Pattern Illustration	
Context	You increasingly need the help of other people to do things for you.
	▼ In this context
Problem	**If you start to think you shouldn't do something on your own and should have everything done by others, you will start to become unable to do even the tasks that you can do now.** You might be worried about whether you can still do a task in the same way that you used to. On top of that, your family may offer to do everything for you out of concern. However, if you accept having everything done for you, your brain will receive less stimulation, and your symptoms may progress more rapidly.
	▼ Therefore
Solution	**Talk with your family and create a chore that you can do by yourself every day.** It can be simple tasks such as watering a plant and giving the pet dog his/her food. Tasks such as folding the laundry and making coffee for the family… anything similar to this is important. Reference your "Can-Do List" to look for chores that you can do.
	▼ Consequently
Consequence	You can actively engage in the actions around your life. The chores will create a steady rhythm in your day, making it easier for you to maintain control over your life. The chores would also become a good starting point to have conversations with your family.
Related Patterns	▷ 6. Can-Do List ▷ 21. Chance to Shine ▷ 38. Inventing Jobs

Figure 3: Format and Contents of the "Daily Chore" Pattern

Words for a Journey is available as a book and a card set. The book contains the full contents of the patterns (Figure 4). Each pattern is printed in a double page spread; the left page contains the Pattern Number, Pattern Name, Introduction, Pattern Illustration, and Context; and the right page contains the Problem, Solution, Consequence, and Related Patterns. We took care to keep the size of letters of the text large enough for elderly people to read easily. In addition, we left wide margins and plenty of blank space to comfortably emphasize the sentences for the pattern. On the cover, we intentionally used positive, gentle colors and faces with positive—but not too strong—expressions.

The card set is designed with the same design standards of simplicity, gentleness, and comfort. The card set consists of the same patterns but contains only a summary of each pattern (Figure 5). It is intended for workshops in which people talk about their experiences using the patterns. Each pattern is printed on one side: Pattern Name, Introduction, Pattern Illustration, Context, a key sentence of the Problem, a key sentence of the Solution, and Pattern Number. The omission of the details is quite important because it makes people initiate conversations rather than reading in the workshop.

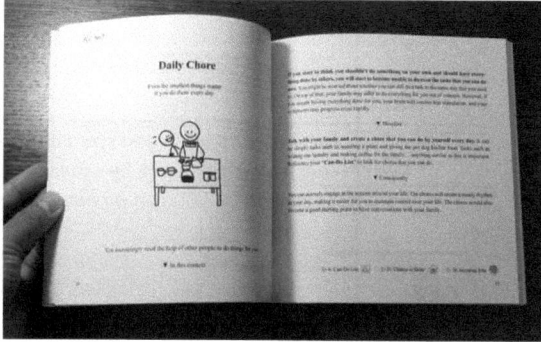

Figure 4: Words for a Journey Book

Figure 5: Words for a Journey Cards

3. Patterns in Words for a Journey

As we mentioned earlier, the core pattern is "A New Journey." Table 1 shows a summary of the pattern: Pattern Number; Pattern Name; Pattern Illustration; Context; and key sentences of Problem and Solution. The rest of the patterns in *Words for a Journey* are categorized into three different groups: words for those living with dementia, words for caring families, and words for everyone.

The first group of patterns, for those living with dementia, contains 14 patterns: The First Step, Departure Announcement, Travel Plan, Fellow Traveler, Can-Do List, Daily Chores, Self-Reflecting Room, Favorite Place, Voice of Experience, Turning the Tide, Live in the Moment, Self-Intro Album, Own Way of Expressing, and Gift of Words (Table 2). These are patterns to help people with dementia live well with dementia.

The second group of patterns, for caring families, contains 17 patterns: Going Together, Team Leader, Family Expert, The Three Consultants, Disclosing Chat, Chance to Shine, Preparation for the Dream, Make It Funny, Usual Talk, The Seen World, Personal Time, Emotion Switch, Casual Counseling, Special Day, Generational Mix, The Amusement Committee, and Hint of Feelings (Table 3). These are patterns to help caring families help those with dementia to live well and also take care of themselves.

The third group of patterns, for everyone, contains eight patterns: Job-Specific Contributions, On-the-Spot Helper, Encouraging Supporter, Personal Connections, Mix-Up Event, Inventing Jobs, Delivering the Voice, and Warm Design (Table 4). These are the patterns for anyone to use to support people with dementia and their families.

CORE			
No.	Pattern Name	Pattern Illustration	Context, Problem, and Solution
1	A New Journey		You, a family member, or someone close to you has been diagnosed with dementia. In this context, you may at first have trouble accepting the fact, from the fear that you may not be able to pursue the life plans that you previously had. Therefore, you must accept the fact that you will have to make some changes in your life, and learn to think of it as the start of a new journey.

Table 1: A Pattern in the CORE category

| \multicolumn{5}{l}{**WORDS FOR THOSE LIVING WITH DEMENTIA**} |

No.	Pattern Name	Pattern Illustration	Context, Problem, and Solution
2	The First Step		You recently became aware of the possibility that you may have dementia. You may have noticed that you have become more forgetful, or people around you may have noticed symptoms. In this context, if you are reluctant to visit a doctor and do not receive proper care, it will hinder early detection and treatment and may cause your symptoms to worsen. Therefore, think of your first visit for an examination as the start of a journey: a journey to live well, with others, as a strong individual.
3	Departure Announcement		You are at the beginning of 'A New Journey.' In this context, your family won't know how much they should get involved with your disease, especially if the symptoms are still mild. Therefore, take the opportunity to tell your family about your disease.
4	Travel Plan		You have taken 'The First Step' of your journey, and made your 'Departure Announcement' to your family. In this context, the life plans that you had before this New Journey may not work out exactly the way you planned. Therefore, get help from family, friends and even specialists to arrange a new life plan so that you can still live up to your full potential, even with dementia.
5	Fellow Travellers		You have come to the beginning of 'A New Journey,' made your 'Departure Announcement,' and have made your 'Travel Plan'. In this context, although you are carrying out your 'Travel Plans', sometimes you may lose confidence in yourself and have a hard time cheering yourself up. Therefore, find people that you can mutually empathize with and have fun with those people.
6	Can-Do List		You are trying to live positively with dementia, but there will still be times when you feel down. In this context, you may feel trapped by sad feelings caused by fright and worries about your future. Therefore, make a list of the things that you can still do now.
7	Daily Chore		You increasingly need the help of other people to do things for you. In this context, if you start to think you shouldn't do something on your own and should have everything done by others, you will start to become unable to do even the tasks that you can do now. Therefore, talk with your family and create a chore that you can do by yourself every day.

8	Self-Reflecting Room		You sometimes become afraid of gradually losing your memories. In this context, it is sad if, in the near future, you do not remember what things once composed your identity. Therefore, make your room reflect yourself by filling it with the things you think are beautiful, the things that you treasure, and the things that tell stories about moments from your life.
9	Favorite Place		You have begun spending less time outside and more time inside your home. In this context, staying inside your home all the time is not fun and may be tiring. Therefore, find a place where you can go by yourself without any trouble, and make sure your family knows about the place too.
10	Voice of Experience		You have read and heard advice on living with dementia and are thinking of putting it into practice. In this context, in your head, you understand what you should do, but actually putting it into practice is hard. Therefore, find a person who has been living with dementia and seek first-hand advice from them.
11	Turning the Tide		You are starting to get used to your journey of living well with dementia. In this context, you feel inconvenience in the environment around you and wish for that to change, but keeping this discontent to yourself or within your family will not solve anything. Therefore, you can start by sharing your experience and discontent to make people become aware of the problems.
12	Live in the Moment		A fun event such as a party or vacation is coming up. In this context, the event seems like fun, but somewhere in your mind you are hesitating to go. Therefore, jump into the event and enjoy the moment.
13	Self-Intro Album		You recently have many opportunities to meet new people. In this context, you sometimes have trouble introducing yourself with words. Therefore, keep a small item with you, such as an album, which you can use to show who you are.

No.	Pattern Name	Pattern Illustration	Context, Problem, and Solution
14	Own Way of Expressing		You feel you are having trouble expressing your thoughts and emotions with words. In this context, having trouble expressing yourself and not being understood is stressful and takes away from your confidence. Therefore, find a way that you could enjoy expressing yourself that doesn't use words.
15	Gift of Words		You are gaining support from many people around you. In this context, you are feeling thankfulness towards these people, but they will not understand if it is just in your mind. Therefore, express your thankfulness in words.

Table 2: Patterns in the WORDS FOR THOSE LIVING WITH DEMENTIA category

WORDS FOR CARING FAMILIES			
No.	Pattern Name	Pattern Illustration	Context, Problem, and Solution
16	Going Together		You recently became aware, due to forgetfulness or other behavior that a family member may have dementia. In this context, if you do not take them to the doctor to receive proper care, it will hinder early detection and treatment and may cause symptoms to worsen. Therefore, think of the first visit for examination as the start of a new journey to live well with others as a strong individual with dementia and help them by taking the 'First Step' with them.
17	Team Leader		You are going to be the closest person to support the family member with dementia. In this context, trying to do everything by yourself is very stressful and tiring. Therefore, name yourself as the 'leader' of the support team and determine who will be on the team and how the team will be organized.
18	Family Expert		You have been collecting information about dementia care from books and the Internet. In this context, there is no guarantee that all of the information will work perfectly for your situation. Therefore, become an expert in the house at searching for and collecting information that would be specifically helpful at your home.

Words for a Journey: A Pattern Language for Living Well with Dementia

19	The Three Consultants		You have started providing care for your family member with dementia and are facing numerous problems. In this context, the problems are spread across a broad range of areas from daily life to expert knowledge, and it is difficult to find the right person to ask for help. Therefore, select three different types of consultants according to their expertise: medical help, caregiving help, and family help.
20	Disclosing Chat		You have not got the opportunity to tell the people around you that a family member of yours has been diagnosed with dementia. In this context, if people around you do not know about the situation, you will not be able to ask for help, nor would they be able to help you. Therefore, do not set a special occasion to disclose the disease, but mention it casually during brief conversations with the person.
21	Chance to Shine		You are putting effort into caregiving. In this context, if you do everything for the person with dementia, including the tasks that they can do on their own, eventually they would become unable to do anything. Therefore, provide small opportunities for the person with dementia to contribute to the family.
22	Preparation for the Dream		You have found out that the person you are caring for has a dream or goal that they wish to achieve. In this context, you want to help achieve their goals, but you think you should wait until they recover a little before they start. Therefore, even if the goal seems hard to achieve, start now and move little by little towards its actualization.
23	Make it Funny		You are giving care to your loved family member. In this context, when caregiving continues for a long period, topics of conversations tend to be centered around the disease itself and its care. Therefore, pick up signs of enjoyment in their words, and reply to amplify their fun feelings.
24	Usual Talk		You talk to your loved family member, but sometimes they 'space out' and you do not get an answer. In this context, if you decide they would not understand this topic and end the conversation, eventually you will have less and less to talk about with them. Therefore, continue the conversation even if they do not understand you and you do not receive an answer.

25	The Seen World	Your loved one with dementia sometimes says things that differ from the facts and reality. In this context, just plain neglect of what they are seeing will hurt the person's feelings. Therefore, do not affirm or deny what they are saying or feeling.
26	Personal Time	You are spending much of your time giving care for your diagnosed family member. In this context, if you become too devoted to caregiving, you will eventually become emotionally tired and lose yourself in being so busy. Therefore, gain cooperation from the people around you and take time off for yourself.
27	Emotion Switch	Even if you have the deepest love towards them, there will come times when you feel frustration or anger when giving care for someone with dementia. In this context, if these negative emotions pile up, one day they may explode. Therefore, have a way to switch your emotions to something more positive and move on.
28	Casual Counseling	You are bearing most of the caregiving responsibility in the house. In this context, you are experiencing problems and worries that you try to handle by yourself and have not had the opportunity to talk about it to the rest of the family. Therefore, find a casual opportunity to lightly disclose your feelings to family members.
29	Special Day	The days are passing by and each day seems similar to the one before. In this context, when the days are monotonous, maintaining a positive feeling both for the person with dementia and caring families is hard. Therefore, put aside time for a 'Special Day' once in a while, where the person being cared for can experience something different from the usual.
30	Generational Mix	The ones giving care are always the same few people. In this context, when the same people are always around, the person with dementia will be confined to a very small world. Therefore, set up opportunities for the person with dementia to meet and talk to children and adults of various generations.

No.	Pattern Name	Pattern Illustration	Context, Problem, and Solution
31	The Amusement Committee		Some family members are taking central roles in caregiving. In this context, family and relatives who live far away rarely get a chance to spend time with the person with dementia. Therefore, set up a fun event and get different people from family and relatives involved in planning it.
32	Hint of Feelings		You are starting to get used to giving care to your loved family member diagnosed with dementia. In this context, when you are busy giving care for the person, you may be unknowingly making them do things against their will. Therefore, look into the actions and words of the person you are caring for and search for hints of what they truly want.

Table 3: Patterns in the WORDS FOR CAREGIVING FAMILIES category

WORDS FOR EVERYONE

No.	Pattern Name	Pattern Illustration	Context, Problem, and Solution
33	Job-Specific Contributions		In Japan alone, approximately 8 million people are believed to have dementia today, including those at risk; in addition, one in four elderly have either dementia or show early symptoms of the disease. In this context, though the people with dementia need help in a wide variety of areas in their daily life, little effort is made to provide assistance outside the medical and welfare fields. Therefore, set an opportunity to think about how you can help with the issue of dementia hindering your work, and put the ideas into practice.
34	On-the-Spot Helper		You are walking in town and see someone showing unusual behavior. They may be walking in an uncoordinated manner or having trouble controlling a machine. In this context, that person may have dementia and may need help. Therefore, become an 'On-the-Spot Helper' and offer to help for a short amount of time.
35	Encouraging Supporter		You have a friend who is giving care to a family member with dementia. In this context, you feel rude to step into family problems, so you do not touch on the topic. Therefore, have them talk about their situation and what kinds of efforts they are putting in.

PURPLSOC: Designing Lively Scenarios in Various Fields

36	Personal Connections		You are seeking ways to learn more about dementia and get involved. In this context, starting by reading books or taking classes on dementia and caregiving can be overwhelming and hard to continue. Therefore, create a connection with an actual person with dementia, and learn necessary information by spending time with them.
37	Mix-Up Event		You are planning an event for people with dementia and their family members. In this context, it is hard for participants to truly have fun at an event designed specifically for the people with dementia. Therefore, organize the event so that people can enjoy it regardless of if they have dementia or not.
38	Inventing Jobs		A person with dementia wishes to contribute to society. In this context, though the person may have the will to work, it is often difficult to find a job that they are capable of doing. Therefore, create a new opportunity for them to contribute to their society with the help of local companies and government.
39	Delivering the Voice		You regularly spend time among people with dementia, and often work with them. In this context, there are still many people in the world who are unconcerned or uninformed about dementia. Therefore, help deliver the voice of the people with dementia and their families to as many people as possible.
40	Warm Design		As part of your normal job (i.e. 'Job-Specific Contributions') you have thought of a new product or service targeted at people with dementia and the people around them. In this context, if you put all of your effort into its function, but its design is unattractive, your target audience will not want to use it. Therefore, make it so that the user feels the design fits them perfectly and gives them a sense of kindness.

Table 4: Patterns in the WORDS FOR EVERYONE category

4. Using the Patterns Words for a Journey

The primary goal of this pattern language, *Words for a Journey*, is for people with dementia and their families to gain insights into living well with dementia. It enables people to absorb the patterns from *Words for a Journey* into their daily lives and engage with others to expand their understanding of the disorder.

Basically, there are three ways for people with dementia and their families to use these patterns in daily lives. First, they read through the collection of patterns and put those that they find interesting or useful into practice. This should become an opportunity for them to initiate a new action for positive change that they otherwise would not have taken (Figure 6). By reading through the patterns, it becomes easy to incorporate positive thinking into daily life through concrete images. Here, the fact that the abstract patterns are already written is quite important because it is extremely difficult for people to extract wisdom from others' experiences and then apply it to their own situations. The patterns provide a shortcut, so users can simply apply the patterns to their situations.

Figure 6: Reading the book and learning wisdom

The second way to use the patterns is to use them as a part of their vocabulary when speaking with others about matters related to these patterns in daily life (Figure 7). For example, a person with dementia and his/her family can, for example, have the following conversation: "I should put this picture on the wall in my Self-Reflecting Room so we can remember this family trip." By including these words in their vocabulary, they come to be thought of as something to be considered. The current problem suggested by the pattern can be worked on and solved, and the potential risk of future problems can be reduced.

Figure 7: Using words as common vocabulary in daily life

The third way to use this pattern language is to talk about experiences with others using the patterns (Figure 8). This dialog sometimes takes place in a "dementia cafés" or workshop setting. The facilitator picks two, three, or more patterns from among the 40 and invites people to share their experiences with them. For example, a facilitator can introduce the pattern "Daily Chore" and ask attendees if they have such an activity and what it is; their Daily Chore may be growing vegetables in the garden or walking their dog. When listening to their peers' stories, other participants may be able to envision their own daily chore or be motivated to start doing something on their own. Thus, they can learn not only from the patterns but also from the experience of others in light of the patterns.

Figure 8: Sharing experiences using the words

5. Workshops using Words for a Journey

Recently, pattern languages have been used as a media for narrative and dialog in various domains (Iba, 2014a, 2014b, 2015). *Words for a Journey* also can be used in workshops to provide participants with an opportunity to reflect on their experiences, talk about them with others, and make a plan for future actions using the patterns from *Words for a Journey*. In what follows, we describe some cases of workshops using *Words for a Journey*.

5.1 A dialog workshop for sharing experiences

The first case was a dialogue workshop for sharing experiences on supporting people with dementia and their families using the *Words for a Journey* cards (Figure 9). We held this kind of workshop for various groups of people, including care staffs, people from industries, nonprofit organizations (NPOs), government agencies, educators, and students.

This workshop is usually held in the following process: First, participants were divided into medium-sized groups, with each group sitting in a circle. The 34 pattern cards were shuffled, and 3–5 cards were dealt to each person. Each person took turns revealing a pattern card in their hand with which they have had past experience and then shared a story about it with the group.

Next, each person chose and placed on the table a card from their hand that they wanted to hear stories about. If any person in the group had a story about one of these patterns, that person would share it. A person could also choose a pattern that they had already experienced but about which they wanted to hear additional stories. When no cards remained in a person's hand, additional cards could be drawn from the deck.

Every time we held the workshop, participants enjoyed sharing their experiences and looked positive and excited.

Figure 8: Sharing experiences using the words

5.2 Reading time for expressing positive feelings

The second case was that of a day care center, where *Words for a Journey* was used by elderly people to express positive feelings about their lives. Hideki Inada of Care Salon Sakura held such reading periods at the end of their "orange café" (dementia café) because, he said, the patterns in *Words for a Journey* were written with such gentleness and positivity that the elders were able to express positive feelings. In this setting, they sat in a circle, and he chose a pattern from *Words for a Journey* to read together (Figure 10).

Figure 10: Reading time with Words for a Journey for expressing positive feelings in the "Orange Café" (dementia café)

5.3 Workshop for enriching nursing education

The third case was nursing education. Prof. Kikuko Ota from the Faculty of Nursing and Medical Care at Keio University used *Words for a Journey* in her class "Developmental Issues in Geriatric Nursing" to provide an opportunity for students to understand people with dementia (Figure 11).

The goal of this class was for students to understand the features of dementia and consider concrete measures for supporting people with dementia. They divided into groups of six and discussed from a nursing perspective their feelings about the problems of elderly people with dementia and their solutions using seven pattern cards from *Words for a Journey*.

Prof. Ota said that a result of the workshop was that students were able to deepen their understanding even if they had little experience working with the elderly, because they could learn from the experiences of other students. In the practical training after the class, some students were able to make use of their new understanding in actual communication.

Figure 11: Workshop for Nursing Education using Words for a Journey

5.4 Idea generation workshop for inventing new products and services

The fourth case was a workshop to generate ideas for new products and services for people with dementia and their families. In the workshop, the patterns were used in the two following ways as seeds for designing products and services to help people in the situations described by the patterns: one was designing products and services to support actions leading to solutions and the other was designing products and services to correct conditions so that problems do not occur in the first place.

We held an idea generation workshop with *Words for a Journey* for students in the Faculty of Policy Management and Faculty of Environment and Information Studies at Keio University (Figure 12). Few had previous knowledge about dementia, but they were able to learn enough from the pattern language to conceptualize new tools for positive support.

Figure 12: Idea Generation Workshop using Words for a Journey

6. Ideas for use of Words for a Journey by various stakeholders

The use of *Words for a Journey* is intended not only for people with dementia and their families but also for wider audiences. This includes members of family associations, NPOs, volunteers, care providers at medical and other facilities, people working for municipalities and other governmental agencies, educators, companies creating new products and services to make the world a better place, and even people who do not yet have firsthand experience with dementia.

6.1 For people involved with family associations, NPOs, and volunteers in the field

People involved with family associations and NPOs and volunteers in the field can hold discussions for participants to discuss their experiences with dementia. Participants pick two, three, or more patterns from the 40 patterns and invite people to share their experiences with these patterns. For example, one could introduce the pattern "Favorite Place" to a family association and ask participants if they have such a place and how they are using it. Their "Favorite Place" may be a local coffee shop or the library. Then, one could ask them why they consider this their favorite and how their lives would be different if they did not have this place. When listening to their peers' stories, the other participants will be able to envision their own "Favorite Places," which will motivate them to find a place of their own if they do not already have one. *Words for a Journey* will become a conversation starter to facilitate comfortable conversations even among people who do not know each other well yet.

6.2 For people in caregiving and other medical fields

People in caregiving and other medical fields can create opportunities for people with dementia, their families, and others who use their facilities. In addition, their staff can engage in constructive conversations with these people so they can learn from each other and thus add value to the quality of the services provided. *Words for a Journey* is also useful when people with dementia and their family members are experiencing difficulties. The patterns will help them view dementia in a more positive light. These pointers, coming from a non-professional perspective, would be useful in a different way from the usual professional advice.

6.3 For people working with municipalities and other government agencies

People working with municipalities and other government agencies can use *Words for a Journey* to help them talk to people with dementia and their families about how government support can be improved. This will help them share and communicate contexts and problems and enable a constructive discussion.

6.4 For educators

Even if educators do not have personal experience with anyone with dementia, *Words for a Journey* will offer a good peek at what it would be to have the condition or be close to someone who does. For students at any level, from elementary school to college, knowing the people of their community better will be a good experience and make them think more about their futures, develop awareness of the issue, and cultivate a caring attitude toward others.

6.5 For industry leaders

The problems and concerns faced by people with dementia can be used to help industry leaders think about new products and services and reach beyond patterns such as "warm design." However, many patterns can be a good starting point for ideas. If every company were to take a role in resolving issues related to dementia, we would have a great foundation for a society that lives well with dementia.

7. Conclusions

In this paper, we presented a pattern language for living well with dementia and ways to use the pattern language. In order to involve many people, it is necessary to consider how to use the pattern language in various contexts, and these opportunities and efforts to develop the ways can become a trigger for encouraging behavioral changes. Also, we are still searching for new words for living well with dementia, so we will build social networks to enrich the collection of words. We think of this process itself as an activity for building a society that enables living well with dementia. I hope that our study is a trigger for turning the tide toward a dementia-friendly society.

8. Acknowledgements

We would like to acknowledge other members of our project: Aya Matsumoto, Tasuku Matsumura, Takehito Tokuda, Masahiko Shoji, Katsuaki Tanaka, Yasufumi Okui, Tsutomu Ikezawa, Mayu Nagumo, Minami Suwa. Also, we thank Taichi Isaku for translating the patterns into English. Finally, we would like to say thank you to the participants for the help they provided creating this book, including interviews and feedback.

9. References

Alexander, C., Ishikawa, S., Silverstein, M., Jacobson, M., Fiksdahl-King, I. and Angel, S. (1977) A Pattern Language: Towns, Buildings, Construction, Oxford University Press.

Alexander, C. (1979) The Timeless Way of Building, Oxford University Press.

Arao, R., Tamefusa, A., Kadotani, M., Harasawa, K., Sakai, S., Saruwatari, K., and Iba, T. (2012) "Generative Beauty Patterns: A Pattern Language for Living Lively and Beautiful," in the19th Conference on Pattern Languages of Programs (PLoP2012).

Beck, K. and Cunningham, W. (1987) 'Using Pattern Languages for Object-oriented Programs', OOPSLA-87 Workshop on the Specification and Design for Object-Oriented Programming.

Furukawazono, T., Iba, T., with Survival Language Project (2015) Survival Language: A Pattern Language for Surviving Earthquakes, CreativeShift Lab.

Gamma, E., Helm, R., Johnson, R. and Vlissides, J. (1994) Design Patterns: Elements of Reusable Object-Oriented Software, Addison-Wesley.

Harasawa, K., Miyazaki, N., Sakuraba, R., and Iba, T. (2014) "The Nature of Pattern Illustrating: The Theory and the Process of Pattern Illustrating," in the 21th Conference on Pattern Languages of Programs (PLoP2014).

Hoover, D. and Oshineye, A. (2009) Apprenticeship Patterns: Guidance for the Aspiring Software Craftsman, O'Reilly Media.

Iba, T. (2014a) "Using Pattern Languages as Media for Mining, Analysing, and Visualising experiences," International Journal of Organisational Design and Engineering (IJODE), Vol. 3, No.3/4.

Iba, T. (2014b) "Pattern Languages as Media for Creative Dialogue: Functional Analysis of Dialogue Workshops," in the Workshop on Pursuit of Pattern Languages for Societal Change (PURPLSOC2014).

Iba, T. (2015), "Pattern Language 3.0 and Fundamental Behavioral Properties," in the World Conference on Pursuit of Pattern Languages for Societal Change (PURPLSOC2015).

Iba Lab & DFJI (Dementia Friendly Japan Initiative) (2014) Words for a Journey: The Art of Being with Dementia, Taking Action on Dementia: G7 Global Dementia Legacy Event Private Sector Side Meeting

Iba, T. and Iba Laboratory (2014a) Learning Patterns: A Pattern Language for Creative Learning, CreativeShift Lab.

Iba, T. and Iba Laboratory (2014b) Collaboration Patterns: A Pattern Language for Creative Collaborations, CreativeShift Lab.

Iba, T. and Iba Laboratory (2014c) Presentation Patterns: A Pattern Language for Creative Presentations, CreativeShift Lab.

Iba, T. and Iba Laboratory (2015), Pattern Illustrating Patterns: A Pattern Language for Pattern Illustrating, CreativeShift Lab.

Iba, T. and Okada, M. (Eds), Iba Laboratory and DFJI (Dementia Friendly Japan Initiative) (2015), Words for a Journey: The Art of Being with Dementia, CreativeShift Lab.

Isaku, T. and Iba, T. (2015) "Creative CoCooking Patterns: A Pattern Language for Creative Collaborative Cooking," in the 20th European Conference on Pattern Languages of Programs (EuroPLoP2015).

Manns, M.L. and Rising, L. (2005), Fearless Change: Patterns for Introducing New Ideas, Addison-Wesley.

Manns, M.L. and Rising, L. (2015) More Fearless Change: Strategies for Making Your Ideas Happen, Addison-Wesley Professional.

Ministry of Health, Labour, and Welfare. (2015) "A New Orange Plan: A Comprehensive Strategy for the Promotion of Dementia Measures: Towards a Community Friendly to the Elderly with Dementia" (in Japanese)

Miyazaki, N., Sakuraba, R., Harasawa, K., and Iba, T. (2015), "Pattern Illustrating Patterns: A Pattern Language for Pattern Illustrating," in the 22nd Conference on Pattern Languages of Programs (PLoP2015).

Pedagogical Patterns Editorial Board (2012) Pedagogical Patterns: Advice for Educators, Createspace.

Sato, M. (2014), Ninchisho ninatta Watashi ga Tsutaetai Koto [What I want to share as a person with dementia], in Japanese, Otsuki Shoten.

Shimomukai, E. and Iba, T. (2012) "Social Entrepreneurship Patterns: A Pattern Language for Change-Making on Social Issues," in the 17th European Conference on Pattern Languages of Programs (EuroPLoP2012).

World Health Organization (WHO). „Dementia fact sheet N. 362 March 2015." [2015-08-21]. http://www.who.int/mediacentre/factsheets/fs362/en

The Fundamental Behavioral Properties

Iba, Takashi
Keio University, Japan
iba@sfc.keio.ac.jp

Kimura, Norihiko
Keio University, Japan
s13300nk@sfc.keio.ac.jp

Akado, Yuma
Keio University, Japan
s13015ya@sfc.keio.ac.jp

Honda, Takuya
Keio University, Japan
hontakku@gmail.com

In this paper, we present 24 behavioral properties that capture "wholeness" in a lively human activity. In dynamic order like human activity, there is a wholeness, which cannot be understood by separating as parts. Based on Christopher Alexander's theory of wholeness and center, we explore how centers create the wholeness of human activity. The properties are: 1. BOOTSTRAP, 2. SOURCE, 3. SPREADING, 4. ATTRACTION, 5. INVOLVING, 6. TOGETHERNESS, 7. BUILDING UP, 8. ORGANIC GROWTH, 9. REFLECTING, 10. ACCOMPANY, 11. ENHANCEMENT, 12. EMPATHY, 13. SELECTION, 14. SIMPLIFICATION, 15. CONSISTENCY, 16. LOOSENESS, 17. FLEXIBILITY, 18. ABUNDANCE, 19. ENDEAVOR, 20. CONNECTING, 21. POSITIONING, 22. DIFFERENTIATING, 23. OVERLAPPING, and 24. CONTINUOUS RELATION. These properties were found through the investigation of pattern languages of human action, and can be put to use to create new pattern languages or designing human activities.

Behavioral properties; wholeness and center; Christopher Alexander; The Nature of Order; pattern language

1. Introduction

Wholeness is present in an activity where people or organizations work in a lively way. It is difficult to understand wholeness if it is separated into parts. This is because partial activities interact with each other in dynamic order like human activity.

For example, German composer Ludwig van Beethoven was most creative while taking a walk; he brought blank scores and a pen to his walk, and wrote his ideas whenever he needed to. Beethoven is said to have settled on the melodic subject for the second movement, known as the "scene by the brook," of his Pastoral Symphony while walking along the Shriver River. It is impossible to capture his creative activity as a whole when we consider his act of *composing* and *walking* as individual actions. That is because the liveliness of his creative activity comes from the interaction of his *composing* and *walking*.

It is impossible to understand the wholeness of lively human activity by dividing the whole into parts. This means that wholeness is not a sum of separable parts. So in what way can we capture and understand wholeness?

2. Wholeness and Center

Christopher Alexander explains his theory of creating wholeness in his book, *The Nature of Order* (Alexander, 2002a). He defines a basic unit, called a "center," as an element of a lively wholeness. Wholeness is a conception in which parts and wholes work in a holistic way. In order to explain his theory consistently, he called all single elements of the whole "centers." In other words, wholeness, which is not decomposable, is a "system of larger and smaller centers, in their connection, and overlap" (Alexander, 2002a, p. 90). A lively wholeness has a structure where centers reinforce each other.

Since there is also wholeness in lively human activities, we must consider the whole, and the centers that intensify the whole to capture its wholeness. What this means is that there are centers that create wholeness and intensify wholeness by strengthening each other in a human activity, making the activity lively.

For example, a boy might become interested in space and astrophysics by coincidently finding a book on the origin of our galaxy in a library. His curiosity then might grow as he learns more and more. The excitement of his deepening knowledge could push him to know more, and he may finally become a specialist on galaxy. In this example, the interest in the galaxy is a center. The whole activity becomes lively as the center becomes intensified by other centers, such as reading books, meeting people, and hearing their stories.

As above, wholeness in lively human activity is created by the interaction between the centers. In what follows, we will propose properties by which the centers intensify each other.

3. Human Activity and Behavioral Properties

In this section, we will overview of behavioral properties that create wholeness in lively human activities. Through analyzing pattern languages of lively human activity, we found 24 properties of how centers strengthen each other to create the wholeness (Figure 1, Table 1).

The 24 properties we found are as follows: 1. BOOTSTRAP, 2. SOURCE, 3. SPREADING, 4. ATTRACTION, 5. INVOLVING, 6. TOGETHERNESS, 7. BUILDING UP, 8. ORGANIC GROWTH, 9. REFLECTING, 10. ACCOMPANY, 11. ENHANCEMENT, 12. EMPATHY, 13. SELECTION, 14. SIMPLIFICATION, 15. CONSISTENCY, 16. LOOSENESS, 17. FLEXIBILITY, 18. ABUNDANCE, 19. ENDEAVOR, 20. CONNECTING, 21.POSITIONING, 22.DIFFERENTIATING, 23.OVERLAPPING, and 24.CONTINUOUS RELATION.

The way in which these properties were found, the detailed explanation of each property, and its usage are written in sections 4, 5, and 6.

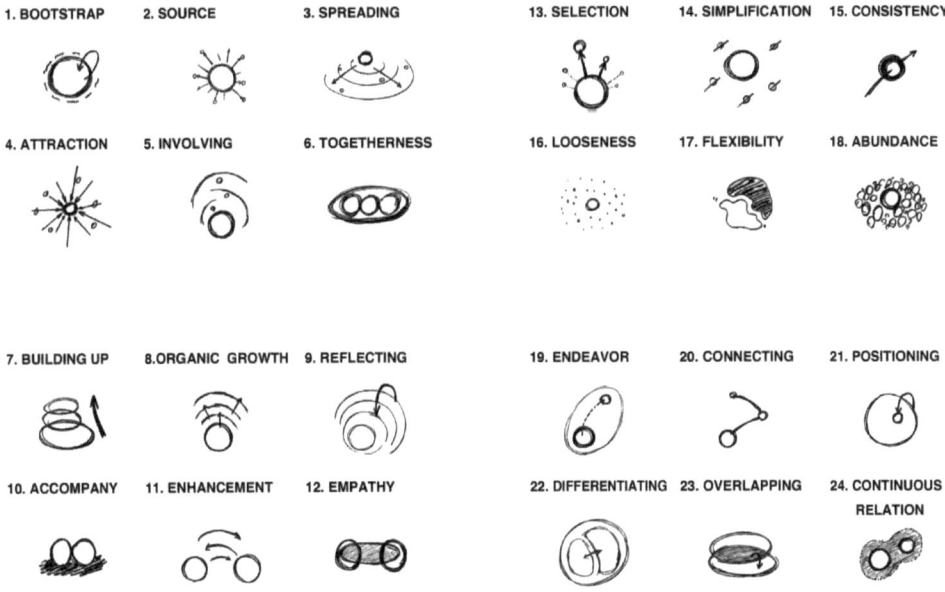

Figure 1: The Overall Picture of 24 Behavioral Properties

No.	Name	Summary
1	BOOTSTRAP	Centers that radiate their own energy recursively strengthen themselves through their own energy, rather than using other centers to strengthen.
2	SOURCE	An overwhelmingly strong center becomes a spring of energy and strengthens the surrounding centers, making the whole lively.
3	SPREADING	Power extends as a center strengthens the surrounding centers, and as those surrounding centers also strengthen their surrounding centers, creating a larger center.
4	ATTRACTION	A center with attractive power extracts the power of surrounding centers, ending up strengthening the attractive center itself.
5	INVOLVING	A center, which functions as a core, makes the whole lively by involving centers that are necessary for strengthening itself.
6	TOGETHERNESS	When small centers strengthen each other, they create a larger center that enfolds them, and as they reinforce each other, it makes the whole lively.
7	BUILDING UP	A whole becomes livelier as centers build up with consistency, repeatedly creating larger centers containing them.
8	ORGANIC GROWTH	By gradually growing while keeping its structure, a center can grow without losing its power, making the whole livelier.
9	REFLECTING	As a center reflects on the trajectory of its change, each trajectory becomes a new center and strengthens other centers, making the whole lively.
10	ACCOMPANY	The center by itself may be powerless, but it becomes affected by the power of the second center, being strengthened as a result.
11	ENHANCEMENT	The chain reaction of mutual enhancement between centers will result in an intensification of the liveliness of the whole.
12	EMPATHY	A center sometimes becomes strengthened when another center shows empathy towards it, and when the center shows empathy back, resonance is created.
13	SELECTION	Selecting centers to strengthen makes a center able to concentrate on specific centers, creating a relationship of strengthening between them.
14	SIMPLIFICATION	The center can effectively strengthen the surrounding centers by cutting off the relationship with incongruent centers.
15	CONSISTENCY	The whole becomes lively when centers with same direction align, creating an inclusive center.
16	LOOSENESS	The whole can be livelier when the relationship of centers is loose.
17	FLEXIBILITY	A center with flexibility adapts to the differences between centers in a relationship, creating numbers of relationships, making the whole lively.
18	ABUNDANCE	The core center of a whole can get strengthened when there are an abundance of centers, strengthening abundance of centers back.

19	ENDEAVOR	Working diligently towards a shining center can strengthen a center, and as the shining center becomes synergistically strengthened, these centers create a larger center and become lively as a whole.
20	CONNECTING	A new connection between centers strengthens each other, creating a larger center with greater power than the individual centers.
21	POSITIONING	Clearly positioned in a whole, centers can release their energy at its best to the surrounding centers, making the whole lively.
22	DIFFERENTIATING	When a center is differentiated into several centers, each center's individual power gets strengthened as those centers strengthen each other, creating a living whole.
23	OVERLAPPING	The whole becomes lively as the overlapped part of overlapping centers becomes a new center and forms a strengthening relationship with the original centers.
24	CONTINUOUS RELATION	Centers having a continuous relationship get strengthened as the relationship becomes extended, and their strength becomes greater as a whole.

Table 1: Thumbnails of 24 Behavioral Properties

4. How Behavioral Properties were found

In order to determine the properties, we analyzed patterns of human action that we had previously created (Figure 2). In *The Nature of Order*, Book 2, Alexander says that a pattern language is an essential way of defining generic centers (Alexander, 2002b, p. 344). This means that it is possible to capture centers by investigating pattern languages. Based on this, we could capture the centers in human activities from the patterns and find the properties with their commonalities.

The basic strategies are as given: investigate pattern languages of human action in order to find out the mechanism that is creating the liveliness behind each pattern; verify the universality necessary for the properties of the mechanism by checking if they can describe other patterns' liveliness; express how the discovered properties generate the mechanism for liveliness by illustration and description while thinking about the relationship between the properties.

4.1 Finding the Mechanism Behind the Patterns

We examined human action pattern languages previously described, which helped us find these behavioral properties. We analyzed three human action pattern languages: *Learning Patterns* (Iba & Iba Lab, 2014a), *Collaboration Patterns* (Iba & Iba Lab, 2014b), and *Presentation Patterns* (Iba & Iba Lab, 2014c), which were created by Iba laboratory. Iba laboratory has been creating pattern languages in order to seek liveliness in human activity. We hypothesized that through an investigation of these human action pattern languages, we could find the core properties shared within lively human activity. Similarly, Alexander investigated buildings and carpets with "life" to find and note the geometrical properties of "liveliness."

We began by reading patterns in order to understand liveliness within the patterns and the kinds of mechanism that create that liveliness. The action of centers behind the patterns is what we call the behavioral properties. For example, a pattern talks about the importance of an environment that creates togetherness when working in a group. In this case, the members of the group can be regarded as interacting centers, and togetherness can be regarded as a larger center. We can then understand that when interacting centers create a larger center encompassing them, togetherness, which is a form of lively human activity, is created. We then grouped the patterns that share similar action in their centers, which led us to find a basis for behavioral properties.

4.2 Refining and Revising Properties

In order to validate our findings, we then used the properties we found to examine the liveliness of other human action pattern languages. By doing so, we were able to verify their universality, also finding some missing properties. Additionally, through this refining process, some properties that had been considered core properties were removed.

We continued to apply this process to other pattern languages in order to check whether the analysis of liveliness of human activity is possible and whether it is useful to use these behavioral properties. Some of the patterns we used for this process are "Generative Beauty Patterns" (Arao et al., 2013), "Creative CoCooking Patterns" (Isaku & Iba, 2015), and *Words for a Journey: The Art of Being with Dementia* (Iba et al., 2015), which were also created by Iba Laboratory. The other pattern languages for human actions such as *Fearless Change* patterns (Manns and Rising, 2005, 2015), Pedagogical Patterns (Pedagogical Patterns Editorial Board, 2012), and Creative Thinking patterns (Kohls, 2012, 2015) were not used as sources when mining the properties. We will examine the properties with these pattern languages in near future.

4.3 Describing Behavioral Properties

Finally, while considering the relationship between these behavioral properties, we added illustrations and descriptions in order to make them shareable (Figure 1, Table 1). Thinking about the relationships of properties helped to validate and clarify them. With the addition of illustrations and words, the behavioral properties appeared to be more useful, particularly in dialogs and for mining more and better patterns for human activity.

Figure 1: The Overall Picture of 24 Behavioral Properties

5. Twenty-four Fundamental Behavioral Properties

In this section, we will explain each behavioral property in detail. The 24 properties are divided into four groups, based on how centers strengthen each other in that property. Note that detailed examples and the description with patterns are shown in Iba et al. (2015), Harashima et al. (2015), and Akado et al. (2016).

First of all, 1. BOOTSTRAP, 2. SOURCE, 3. SPREADING, 4. ATTRACTION, 5. INVOLVING, and 6. TOGETHERNESS are in a group in which centers intensify themselves with their energy.

1. BOOTSTRAP: In a living whole, there are centers that radiate their own energy (Figure 3). Rather than using other centers to strengthen them, these centers are recursively strengthened by themselves. During this process, power spreads out to its surroundings, which eventually actualizes a living whole. These centers are a core element upon which the lively process is built.

Figure 3: BOOTSTRAP

2. SOURCE: The existence of one overwhelmingly strong center in a whole makes it lively (Figure 4). The overwhelmingly strong center becomes a spring of energy and strengthens the surrounding centers. As surrounding centers get strengthened, the strong center gets even stronger.

Figure 4: SOURCE

3. SPREADING: The power extends as a center strengthens the surrounding centers, and those surrounding centers also strengthen their surrounding centers (Figure 5). As power extends, it creates a larger center, which also strengthens the centers within it.

Figure 5: SPREADING

4. ATTRACTION: There is a center that has an attractive power in a living whole (Figure 6). It attracts other centers and pulls out the power of those centers, which end up strengthening the strong center itself. The whole becomes livelier as the attractive power gets stronger.

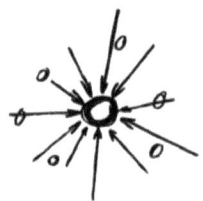

Figure 6: ATTRACTION

5. INVOLVING: A center that works as a core makes the whole lively by involving other necessary centers (Figure 7). The involved centers strengthen each other and, at the same time, they strengthen the core center as well. Thus, the more the centers get involved, the stronger the whole can be.

Figure 7: INVOLVING

6. TOGETHERNESS: At times when small centers strengthen each other, they create a larger center that enfolds them (Figure 8). The large center strengthens the small centers within itself, and small centers strengthen the enfolding center. Thus small centers and the larger center reinforce each other, making the whole lively.

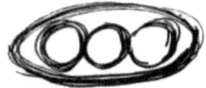

Figure 8: TOGETHERNESS

Next, 7. BUILDING UP, 8. ORGANIC GROWTH, 9. REFLECTING, 10. ACCOMPANY, 11. ENHANCEMENT and 12. EMPATHY are grouped together, as these centers grow by the influence of other centers.

7. BUILDING UP: The whole can become livelier when centers continuously build up with consistency (Figure 9). As centers build up continuously, built-up centers strengthen each other, and create larger centers. As centers are built up into larger centers repeatedly, the whole become livelier.

Figure 9: BUILDING UP

8. ORGANIC GROWTH: The whole may become more lively when a center grows gradually (Figure 10). A center can grow without losing its power if it keeps its own structure. As the center gradually grows, the whole becomes livelier.

Figure 10: ORGANIC GROWTH

9. REFLECTING: As a center reflects on the trajectory of its change, the whole can become livelier (Figure 11). By reflecting on the change in the center, each trajectory becomes a new center and they strengthen each other, creating a living whole.

Figure 11: REFLECTING

10. ACCOMPANY: A center is sometimes intensified when it is accompanied by another center placed right beside it (Figure 12). The center by itself may be powerless, but it may be made more powerful by the second center. As a result, the whole will be livelier.

Figure 12: ACCOMPANY

11. ENHANCEMENT: When a center exists, a nearby center may be influenced by it, and intensified (Figure 13). This second center may then influence the first center to strengthen it. This chain reaction of mutual enhancement will result in the intensification of the whole, to make it livelier.

Figure 13: ENHANCEMENT

12. EMPATHY: A center sometimes becomes strengthened as another center shows empathy towards it (Figure 14). The center that received empathy returns empathy and creates a resonance between the centers. Resonance strengthens the centers even more, making the whole lively.

Figure 14: EMPATHY

Then, 13. SELECTION, 14. SIMPLIFICATION, 15. CONSISTENCY, 16. LOOSENESS, 17. FLEXIBILITY, and 18. ABUNDANCE are in the same group, as the properties become strengthened when centers are in a complex situation.

13. SELECTION: Centers can be strengthened by selecting centers that they want to be in a relationship with (Figure 15). The selection of centers makes it possible to concentrate on specific centers to strengthen. The selected centers can be more intensified by being intensively strengthened. The intensified center can then re-strengthen the original center, creating a strengthening relationship.

Figure 15: SELECTION

14. SIMPLIFICATION: A center can be strengthened as it simplifies relationships with other centers (Figure 16). Cutting off its relationship with incongruent centers prevents the dispersal of its power. In this way, the center can strengthen the surrounding centers effectively, and actualize a living whole.

Figure 16: SIMPLIFICATION

15. CONSISTENCY: The whole becomes lively when centers with the same direction align (Figure 17). As these centers align, the centers strengthen each other to create an inclusive center. The inclusive center then strengthens inner centers recursively, making the whole more living.

Figure 17: CONSISTENCY

16. LOOSENESS: The whole can be livelier when the relationship between centers is loose (Figure 18). The centers can be in a strengthening relationship with various centers by making relationships free rather than fixed. The loose coupling between centers makes the whole lively.

Figure 18: LOOSENESS

17. FLEXIBILITY: There are centers with flexibility in a living whole (Figure 19). Those centers meet other centers, they easily become adapted to a new environment, and they can be in a stronger relationship. The existence of such centers makes it possible to create new relationships, making the whole lively.

Figure 19: FLEXIBILITY

18. ABUNDANCE: The core center of a whole can become strengthened when there is an abundance of centers (Figure 20). The existence of an abundance of centers strengthens the center of the core and the strengthened core center strengthens those centers back.

Figure 20: ABUNDANCE

Finally, 19.ENDEAVOR, 20.CONNECTING, 21.POSITIONING, 22.DIFFERENTIATING, 23.OVERLAP, and 24.CONTINUOUS RELATION are in the same group, where centers intensify with the differences or commonality that centers have.

19. ENDEAVOR: A center can get strengthened when it is working diligently towards a shining center (Figure 21). The shining center is also strengthened by the fact that it is endeavored by another center, and the endeavoring center is strengthened by the act of endeavoring. The relationship between these centers creates a larger center including them and become lively as a whole.

Figure 21: ENDEAVOR

20. CONNECTING: Centers can be strengthened when they are connected with other centers (Figure 22). When a new connection is born, connected centers create a larger center that enfolds them. The larger center can exert a power that could not be created by the included individual centers.

Figure 22: CONNECTING

21. POSITIONING: A center can be strengthened by positioning itself in the whole (Figure 23). As it is clearly positioned in a whole, the center can release its energy to the surrounding centers. As the surrounding centers are strengthened, the whole will become livelier.

Figure 23: POSITIONING

22. DIFFERENTIATING: The whole sometimes become more lively when centers are differentiated from each other (Figure 24). When a center is differentiated into several centers, each center will have a unique power that other centers do not have. This power becomes strengthened as each center strengthens the others, creating a living whole.

Figure 24: DIFFERENTIATING

23. OVERLAPPING: There are overlapping centers in a living whole (Figure 25). When centers overlap, the overlapped part becomes a new center. The overlapped centers strengthen the new center as the new center strengthens them. The strengthening relationship makes the whole livelier.

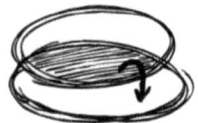

Figure 25: OVERLAPPING

24. CONTINUOUS RELATION: A whole with centers having a continuous relationship has liveliness (Figure 26). As the relationship endures, each center is strengthened, and their strength as a whole becomes greater. As the relationship between centers continues, the whole may become livelier.

Figure 26: CONTINUOUS RELATION

6. Usage of Behavioral Properties

In this section, we will describe how the 24 behavioral properties can be used. This will mainly be for three purposes: pattern mining, pattern writing, and designing.

6.1 Pattern Mining with Properties

Properties can be used to indicate patterns from experience or episodes shared at pattern-mining interviews or workshops. As behavioral properties describe the properties of lively human activities, understanding them makes it possible to estimate how actions from the experiences or episodes make each activity full of life.

For example, a participant in a workshop may share a story about the importance of increasing the number of members in order to accomplish a goal. In this context, the interviewer can conject that INVOLVING causes liveliness in this story, and he may ask a confirmation question such as "Do you talk passionately about your vision or the benefit people will receive in order to get people involved?" Knowing the properties enables the creation of direct questions to approach the core of patterns. If empathy is created within the group or related episodes from other members are pulled out from the question, this shows that these stories, and experiences may become a pattern of lively human behavior.

As above, it becomes possible to grasp the essence of tips, and hints at interviews or workshops with the use of properties.

6.2 Pattern Writing with Properties

Properties are also useful for the accurate verbalization of how patterns contribute to make an activity lively. Behavioral properties are properties of how centers intensify each other to create liveliness in human activities. Therefore, it will assist the writer to capture the centers in the description of a pattern and understand how those centers intensify each other to create the liveliness of that activity. By capturing this, the writer will then be able to improve the description. Thus, properties work as a trigger for inspecting liveliness in specific human activities.

There are patterns that include several properties to make an activity lively. It is necessary to determine whether properties enhance each other or whether they only appear in one series of action. If they appear in one series of action only, there is a need to write them out as individual patterns to verbalize how each property affects an activity.

6.3 Design with Properties

Besides for patterns, properties can also be used for designing. Even though patterns on lively human behavior are small in number, there are various lively human behaviors that have not yet been converted into patterns. It is possible to recognize wholeness by identifying centers of its behavior and how those centers intensify each other.

Behavioral properties were used as inspirations of ideas at some workshops (Iba & Akado, 2015; Yoder & Iba, 2015; Iba, Yoder, & Wirfs-Brock, 2015). Using the properties as a common language assisted the participants to think about how this conference can be "strengthened" from the properties' point of view. Rather than urging the participants to come up with specific ideas, sharing ideas based on the properties also created wholeness in the conference.

7. Behavioral Properties and Geometrical Properties

Alexander discovered how centers intensify each other, proposing 15 geometrical properties (Alexander, 2002a). In this section, we describe the relationship between our 24 behavioral properties, and Alexander's 15 geometrical properties.

The relationship between behavioral and geometrical properties can be compared from the viewpoint of a time series. Alexander's 15 geometrical properties capture the liveliness of the structure at one point in the time series. On the other hand, 24 behavioral properties capture the liveliness of movement through the flow of time.

For example, an organization is in a good state when the goal of the team or individual members matches the trend, when each member has their own role, and when they help each other out. This phenomenon can be captured by the geometrical properties, ECHOES, and POSITIVE SPACE. ECHOES is a property where centers generate a larger center by similarity of orientation, and the property POSITIVE SPACE is where adjacent centers are partially strengthened in order to strengthen a specific center.

From a different point of view, the team is activated by having and heading towards a challenging attractive goal, and involving cases, information, or people related to the project. This phenomenon can be captured by the behavioral properties, ENDEAVOR and INVOLVING. ENDEAVOR occurs where centers working diligently towards a shining center, and INVOLVING is where a core center involves new centers that are necessary for strengthening itself, also strengthening the whole.

This example shows that there are different sets of properties visible from two different viewpoints, namely: geometrical properties that capture liveliness at a certain time, and behavioral properties, which express the liveliness of the process of the change in the flow of time. Geometrical properties are properties on a plane, showing the structure, and the being of things at one point in the series of time. Behavioral properties are properties of movement expressed by time axis, describing movement or how things become another in the transition of time.

Geometrical properties and behavioral properties are not only properties that appear in architecture, nature, or in human activity, but also viewpoints for capturing lively phenomena. Therefore, it is important to capture and generate wholeness from both the point of view of structure and motion.

8. Conclusion

In this paper, we proposed fundamental behavioral properties for capturing the wholeness of lively human behaviors, explaining its usage and its relationship with Alexander's geometrical properties. In addition to the behavioral properties of human activity, we presumed that the investigation of the existence of emotional properties could be done as a future study.

The 15 properties are commonly discussed, as they are basic theory when talking about the wholeness of buildings throughout *The Nature of Order*, but Alexander also reveals the existence of color properties in Book 4 of *The Nature of Order* (Alexander, 2004). He states that colors are also an essential part of wholeness and that there are properties of how they intensify life. Thus, he calls the ways that centers of color create, and intensify life in one another color properties.

Similarly, we consider that not only behaviors but also emotions are important in order to create a lively wholeness in human activity. That is because in order to capture the deep wholeness of human activity, it is necessary to understand the emotions behind the behaviors and actions. For example, "Passion for Exploration," from the *Learning Patterns*, advises you to choose a topic that you can be passionate about while choosing a subject to explore. Additionally, "Mission for the Future" from the *Collaboration Patterns* talks about the importance of having an image of how the future must be and starting work with a sense of a mission, which you must be the one to make this future a reality. These two patterns make the activity lively with passionate emotion from the sense of vocation. As the patterns show, additional properties with emotion may be required to capture the wholeness of human activity.

We hope that additional research will be done on the comprehensive theory of wholeness by systematizing geometrical, color, behavioral, and emotional properties, which have not been discovered yet (Figure 27), and searching for more properties.

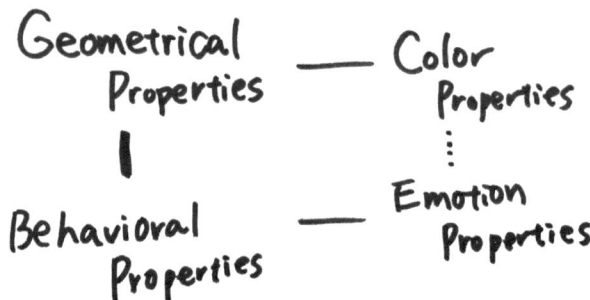

Figure 27: A Vision for the Theoretical Overview of Fundamental Properties

9. Acknowledgement

We acknowledge other members of our project: Arisa Kamada, Yuji Harashima, Tomoki Kaneko, Alice Sasabe, Sakurako Kogure, Tetsuro Kubota, Natsumi Miyazaki, Kosuke Suzuki, Nao Tamaki, Masafumi Nagai, and Tsuyoshi Ishida for the effort of inquiry towards the behavioral properties. We also thank Taichi Isaku, Haruka Mori, and Lena Kurata for their support towards the project. Lastly, we would like to thank Keishi Saruwatari for his great idea on behavioral properties, and the discussion that he initiated within our laboratory.

10. References

Akado, Y., KIMURA, N., ISHIDA, T., and IBA, T., "Fundamental Behavioral Properties, Part 3: Extending the Theory of Centers for Pattern Language 3.0," in the 23rd Conference on Pattern Languages of Programs (PLoP2016).

Alexander, C. (2002a), The Nature of Order: An Essay of the Art of Building and the Nature of the Universe, Book 1: The Phenomenon of Life, Center for Environmental Structure.

Alexander, C. (2002b), The Nature of Order: An Essay of the Art of Building and the Nature of the Universe, Book 2: The Process of Creating Life, Center for Environmental Structure.

Alexander, C. (2004), The Nature of Order: An Essay of the Art of Building and the Nature of the Universe, Book 4: The Luminous Ground, Center for Environmental Structure.

Arao, R., Tamefusa, A., Kadotani, M., Harasawa, K., Sakai, S., Saruwatari, K., and Iba, T. (2012) "Generative Beauty Patterns: A Pattern Language for Living Lively and Beautiful," in the 19th Conference on Pattern Languages of Programs (PLoP2012).

Harashima, Y., Kaneko, T., Isaku, T., and Iba, T. (2015) "Fundamental Behavioral Properties, Part 2: Extending the Theory of Centers for Pattern Language 3.0" in the 22nd Conference on Pattern Languages of Programs (PLoP2015).

Iba, T. and Iba Laboratory (2014a) Learning Patterns: A Pattern Language for Creative Learning, CreativeShift Lab.

Iba, T. and Iba Laboratory (2014b) Collaboration Patterns: A Pattern Language for Creative Collaborations, CreativeShift Lab.

Iba, T. and Iba Laboratory (2014c) Presentation Patterns: A Pattern Language for Creative Presentations, CreativeShift Lab.

Iba, T., Kamada, A., Akado, Y., Honda, T., Sasabe, A., and Kogure, S. (2015) "Fundamental Behavioral Properties, Part 1: Extending the Theory of Centers for Pattern Language 3.0," in the 20th European Conference on Pattern Languages of Programs (EuroPLoP2015).

Iba, T. and Akado, Y. (2015) "Workshop: Thinking Patterns for Human Actions with the Fundamental Behavioral Properties," in the 20th European Conference on Pattern Languages of Programs (EuroPLoP2015).

Iba, T., Yoder, J., Wirfs-Brock, R. (2015) "Workshop: Generative Processes of Community with the Fundamental Properties," in the 22nd Conference on Pattern Languages of Programs (PLoP2015).

Iba, T. and Okada, M. (Eds), Iba Laboratory and DFJI (Dementia Friendly Japan Initiative) (2015), Words for a Journey: The Art of Being with Dementia, CreativeShift Lab.

Isaku, T. and Iba, T. (2015) "Creative CoCooking Patterns: A Pattern Language for Creative Collaborative Cooking," in the 20th European Conference on Pattern Languages of Programs (EuroPLoP2015).

Kohls, C. (2012) "Patterns for Creative Thinking," in PLoP ,12 Proceedings of the 19th Conference on Pattern Languages of Programs.

Kohls, C. (2015) "Patterns for creative thinking: idea generation," in EuroPLoP ,15 Proceedings of the 20th European Conference on Pattern Languages of Programs.

Manns, M.L. and Rising, L. (2005), Fearless Change: Patterns for Introducing New Ideas, Addison-Wesley.

Manns, M.L. and Rising, L. (2015) More Fearless Change: Strategies for Making Your Ideas Happen, Addison-Wesley Professional.

Pedagogical Patterns Editorial Board (2012) Pedagogical Patterns: Advice for Educators, Createspace.

Yoder, J. and Iba, T. (2015) "Workshop: Generative Processes for Assisting with Quality Collaborative Groups" in the 5th International Conference on Collaborative Innovation Networks (COINs15).

Pattern Language 3.0 and Fundamental Behavioral Properties

Iba, Takashi
Keio University, Japan
iba@sfc.keio.ac.jp

In this paper, I present frontiers of pattern languages based on my studies over the past 10 years. First, an overview of the history of pattern languages and the perspectives of categorizing existing pattern languages is presented. In this categorization, pattern language for human actions are in their third generation—thus the name "Pattern Language 3.0." This paper introduces Learning Patterns, Collaboration Patterns, Presentation Patterns, Change Making Patterns, Survival Language, and Words for a Journey as examples of Pattern Language 3.0. The paper also illustrates methodologies of pattern mining, pattern writing, and pattern illustrating. Then, workshops using pattern languages and tools for accessing pattern languages are described. Finally, I propose Fundamental Behavioral Properties as an extension of the theory presented in Christopher Alexander's book, The Nature of Order. I hope that this articulation of the results of my studies will stimulate others to develop future innovations for a creative society.

Pattern language 3.0; human action, dialog; workshop; behavioral properties

1. Introduction

Over the past 10 years, working with my students, I have created more than 20 pattern languages on various topics to describe human actions, consisting of more than 600 patterns in total. By creating these new pattern languages, we have studied and developed methodology to create pattern languages and to use them. Furthermore, we have made theoretical advances related to pattern languages. This paper presents results from such studies and practices: a conception of generations of pattern languages; examples of pattern languages for human actions; and methodologies of pattern mining, pattern writing, and pattern illustrating. There are also descriptions for how workshops contribute to the successful use of pattern languages, tools for utilizing pattern languages, and fundamental behavioral properties of pattern languages for human actions.

2. Generations of Pattern Languages

Pattern languages can uncover design knowledge that exists in particular areas of a profession. Design knowledge refers to both the intelligence to notice problems and the clue to solve them. In other words, pattern languages describe expertise in problem solving under certain conditions and in particular contexts.

The originator of pattern language was the architect, Christopher Alexander who proposed it to develop design knowledge of building and town (Alexander, 1979). His intention was to have people who lived in a community get involved in the process of designing their own towns and houses. In the late 1970s, he wrote a book with his colleagues that contained 253 patterns on practical architectural design (Alexander et al., 1977). Ten years after the book was published, Alexander's idea of pattern language was adopted in the field of software design (Beck & Cunningham, 1987; Gamma, et al., 1995). Since the 1990s, an increasing number of fields have adopted the methods of pattern language (Coplien & Harrison, 2004; Manns & Rising, 2005; Manns & Rising, 2015; Hoover & Oshineye, 2009; Pedagogical Patterns Editorial Board, 2012).

On the basis of this background, I have been creating pattern languages in a new area of knowledge concerning human actions such as learning, presentation, collaboration, education, business, social innovation, policy-making, and even beauty in daily life.

Through these experiences, I have thought a fundamental question "What are pattern languages?" In considering this question, I have organized and refined my views on pattern languages. Human actions appear to differ vastly from architecture and software; nevertheless, they need to be designed with tacit design knowledge, which still consists in a context, a problem, and a solution. In that sense, without losing the essence of design knowledge, pattern languages are continuing to evolve, which has brought us to the Pattern Language 3.0 stage, distinguishing it from previous stages: Pattern Language 1.0 and Pattern Language 2.0 (Iba, 2011; Iba, 2012b). Figure 1 and Figure 2 illustrate the evolution and difference of these generations as they relate to the object of design, the act of design, and the design purpose.

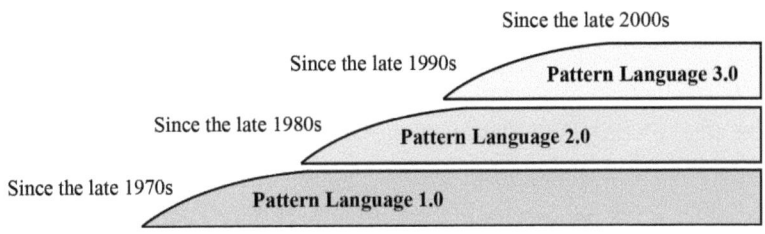

Figure 1: Three Generations of Pattern Languages

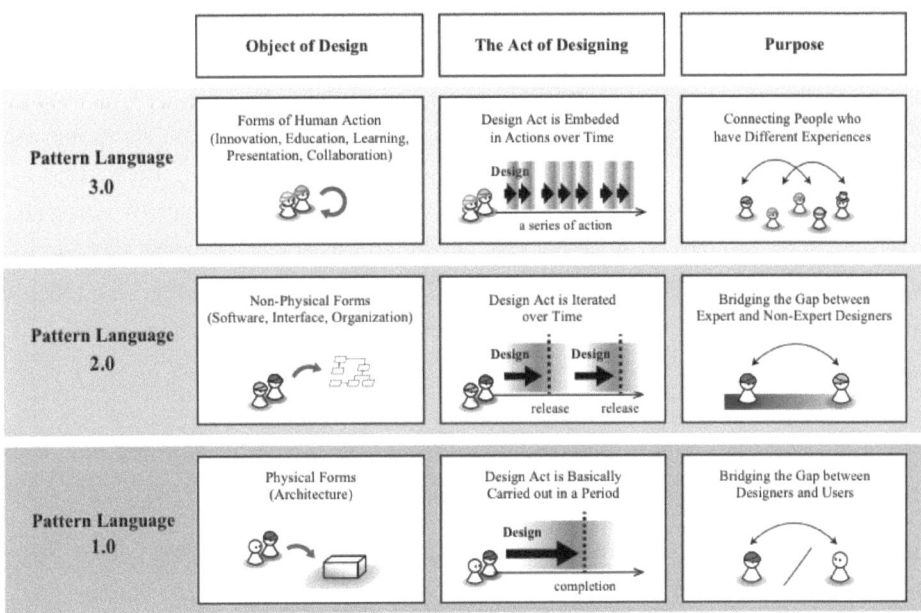

Figure 2: Comparison of Pattern Language Generations

2.1 Object of Design

A pattern language is a collection of inter-related facets that describe aspects of the expertise that is the foundation of design knowledge. The areas of expertise for which pattern languages have been used have changed over time. Initially, the primary object of using pattern language was to describe the design of architecture. Next, it was applied to non-material objects, software programs. Today, in Pattern Language 3.0, the evolution continues as it addresses human actions. An entirely new and unique feature of using 3.0 to create pattern languages is that users develop a type of meta-cognition as they are constantly reflecting on themselves whilst developing their designs.

Examples of the Pattern Language 3.0 areas of human actions being addressed today include: education (Pedagogical Patterns Editorial Board, 2012; Iba et al, 2011; Shibuya et al., 2013), innovation (Manns & Rising, 2005; Manns & Rising, 2015), learning (Hoover & Oshineye, 2009, Iba & Iba Lab, 2014a; Harashima, et al., 2014), collaboration (Iba & Iba Lab, 2014b), presentation (Iba & Iba Lab, 2014c), change making (Shimomukai, et al., 2015), disaster prevention (Furukawazono, et al. 2015), beauty in everyday life (Arao, et al., 2012), living well with dementia (Iba & Okada, 2015), living with continuous self-fulfillments (Nakada, et al., 2013; Kamada, et al., 2014), living in the age of a global society (Matsuzuka, et al., 2013), cultural design (Kadotani, et al., 2013, 2014), academic research (Kobayashi, et al., 2008), project promotion (Naruse, et al., 2008), cooking (Isaku & Iba, 2014; Isaku & Iba, 2015), and policy design (Iba & Takenaka, 2013).

In addition, Pattern Language 3.0 actually includes patterns for creating new pattern languages. These specialized patterns are referred to as "meta-patterns," because they present the fundamental skills to develop new pattern languages. Meta-patterns include: pattern mining (Iba & Isaku, 2012; Iba & Yoder, 2014; Akado, et al., 2015), pattern writing (Meszaros & Doble, 1997; Harrison, 2006), pattern illustrating (Harasawa, et al., 2015), shepherding (Harrison, 2006), writers' workshops (Coplien, 1999), and designing workshops to use patterns (Iba, 2012a).

2.2 The Act of Designing

As pattern languages have evolved, not only has the object of design changed, but the meaning of the design has changed as well.

In Pattern Language 1.0, architectural designing was basically a once-off activity in the process of creating a town or a house. After it had been built, it could rarely be undone. Pattern Language 2.0 updated the design system to accommodate software code to make it easier to identify problems, understand how to fix the problem and rewrite the corrected code to be re-released as a better version of the product. For this reason, Pattern Languages 2.0 are useful for repetitive design.

In 3.0, a new aspect has evolved based on the fact that, in practice, human actions undergo continuous change, as people find better ways to do things. Unlike architecture, with its concrete start and end, or software that requires iterative design to turn out new versions of the software, 3.0 pattern languages for human actions must address nonstop change and it is difficult to recognize a clear beginning or end of a certain phase of an activity. This new level of complexity can be explained by the observation that the difference between designing and practicing a human action is hardly distinguishable. We practice to design and design to practice, creating an endless design process.

2.3 Purpose

In Pattern Language 1.0, Alexander developed pattern languages to serve as a lingua franca to bridge the gap between professional designers and community members. With the shift to the information age, Pattern Language 2.0 was primarily developed to fill technical gaps between experts and less experienced professionals. Software designers who wished to improve their skills read the patterns to acquire design knowledge from more experienced programmers. In this case, both sides became designers and the patterns existed merely to reduce the distance between them. The 3.0 evolution of pattern languages now makes it possible to connect all kinds of people (actor) with all kinds of different experiences. 3.0 patterns help illuminate the less noticeable parts of a person's experience, so the person can reconsider the experience to talk about and share these with others. Stated simply, Pattern Language 3.0 becomes a medium for narrative and conversations between people regardless of the amount of experience or skill a person has. In addition, a person need not understand the concept of pattern languages or background knowledge about the design knowledge written in it to use the pattern to its fullest advantage.

3. Examples of Pattern Languages for Human Actions

This section focuses on some major examples of 3.0 pattern languages for human actions we created: Learning Patterns, Collaboration Patterns, Presentation Patterns, Change Making Patterns, Survival Language, and Words for a Journey (Figure 3).

3.1 Learning Patterns

Learning Patterns consists of 40 patterns (Iba et al., 2009; Iba & Miyake, 2010; Iba & Sakamoto, 2011; Iba & Iba Lab, 2014a) to enhance creative learning by providing an opportunity for learners to reflect on their learning styles, to discover or rediscover good habits, and to obtain new insights into how they can become a better learner.

3.2 Collaboration Patterns

Collaboration Patterns are 34 patterns that describe practical knowledge for performing collaborative interactions (Iba and Isaku, 2013; Iba & Iba Lab, 2014b), whereby teamwork creates new values that could change the world by producing an emergent robustness that cannot be attributed to any one member of the team, but comes with the process of enhancing one another.

3.3 Presentation Patterns

Presentation Patterns are 34 patterns that describe practical knowledge for designing presentations (Iba et al. 2012; Iba & Iba Lab, 2014c; Iba & Isaku, 2014) A Creative Presentation is an imagination provoking presentation inviting the audience to discover new findings. Although we use the word "presentation," this set can be applied to all kinds of presenting such as general public speaking, performance of music, drama, or dance.

3.4 Change Making Patterns

Change Making Patterns describe the secrets for facilitating social change (Shimomukai & Iba, 2012; Shimomukai et al., 2012, 2015; Nakamura & Iba, 2015a, 2015b). The 31 distinctive patterns show how social entrepreneurs identify social issues and create or implement solutions to overcome these issues. This set of tacit knowledge is disclosed for you to not only learn how social entrepreneurship is executed in difficult situations but also start your own change making project.

3.5 Survival Language

Survival Language is a pattern language to support survival when a catastrophic earthquake occurs (Furukawazono, et al., 2013a, 2013b, 2015). There are 20 patterns to teach people to develop practices, including: *Designing for Preparation [for an earthquake], Designing for Emergency Action [in the event of an earthquake],* and *Designing for Life After an Earthquake*. These patterns were formulated based on the lessons Japan has learned from its experience of numerous earthquakes.

3.6 Words for a Journey

Words for a Journey are 40 patterns to assist people living with dementia (Iba & Okada, 2015; Iba, et al., 2015a, 2015c) and those who care for them to improve quality of life for all involved, and to reduce the negative impressions people may have of the disease. This pattern language was developed from a collection of wisdom and stories from people living in this situation and extracts its essence to be shared widely.

Learning Patterns	Core	Opportunity	Creation	Openness	
	Creative Learning	Jump In	Thinking in Action	Community of Learning	
	Opportunity for Learning	Copycat Learner	Prototyping	Serendipitous Encounters	
	Learning by Creating	Effective Asking	Field Diving	Good Rivals	
	Open Learning	Output-Driven Learning	A Bug's-Eye & Bird's-Eye View	Talking Thinker	
		Daily Use of Foreign Language	Hidden Connections	Learning by Teaching	
		Playful Learning	Triangular Dig	Firm Determinations	
		Tornado of Learning	Passion for Exploration	Questioning Mind	
		Chain of Excitement	Brain Switch	The Right Way	
		Quantity brings Quality	Fruit Farming	Brave Changes	
		Skill Embodiment	Attractive Expressions	Frontier Finder	
		Language Shower	The First-Draft-Halfway-Point	Self-Producer	
		Tangible Growth	Acceleration to the Next	Be Extreme!	
Collaboration Patterns	Core	Good Team	Creation Process	Going Beyond	
	Creative Collaboration	Growth Spiral	Emergence Vigor	Power to Change the World	
	Mission for the Future	Sympathetic Union	Loaf of Time	Quality Line	
	Innovative Ways	Response Rally	Collaborative Field	Creative Clashes	
	Create a Legend	Feeling of Togetherness	Activity Footprints	Generative Destruction	
		Part to Contribute	Chaotic Path to Breakthrough	Beyond Expectations	
		Return of Growth	Ideas Taking Shape	Project Followers	
		Spontaneous Commitments	Inside Innovator	Strategic Developments	
		Loose Connections	Roadmap to the Goal	Context of the World	
		Vulnerability Disclosure	Improvised Roles	Endurance to Continue Creating	
		Words of Thanks	Spadework for Creativity	Polishing Senses	
Presentation Patterns	Core	Sharing	Inspiring	Performing	Ultimate
	Creative Presentation	Storytelling	Mind Bridge	Stage Building	Unique Presenter
	Main Message	Exploration of Words	Reality Sharing	Reminders of Success	Aesthetics of Presenting
	Touching Gift	Visual Power	Participation Driver	Construction of Confidence	Be Authentic!
	Image of Success	Dramatic Modulation	Quality in Details	Presentership	
		Unexpected Evolution	Expression Coordinator	Best Effort	
		Doors of Mystery	Discomfort Removing	Personally for You	
		Beautiful Clarity	Significant Void	Invitation to the World	
		Perfect Portion	Activation Switch	Improvised Presentation	
		Cherry on Top	Take-Home Gift	Reflecting Forwards	
Change Making Patterns	Mindset	Mission Defining	Preparation	Implementation	Scale Out
	Know Yourself	Frontiership	Field Diving	Success Prototyping	Inspire Evangelists
	Yes, and	Detective Eyes	Quick Actions	Invite Aliens	Passion Teller
	Energy Checkup	Market Research	Training for Innovation	Excitement Delivery	Outcome Measurer
	Microvision	3W1H		Trustream	Medium Communication
	Trust Your Instinc	Leverage Point	Change Construction	Stage Setting	Idea Catcher
	Idol Imitation		Sustainable System	Pile of Efforts	Professionalism
	Juice Work and Life		Root Rediscovery	Obsession with Everything	
			Roadmap to the North Star		
Survival Language	The Core Pattern	Designing Preparation	Designing Emergency Action	Designing Life After Quake	
	Survival Action Gift	Safe Sleep Zone	Life over Furniture	Kick Signal	
		Storage Area	Evacuation Before Fire-Fighting	Evacuation Initiator	
		Door Space		Repetition of Better Decision	
		Reverse L-Shape Lock	Armadillo Pose	Vinyl Lavatory	
		Biting Lock	Cover and Lock	Breaker Off	
		Roots of TV		Contact by Any Means	
		Extrastock			
		Daily Use of Reserves			
		Crowbar			
Words for a Journey	Core	Words for Those Living with Dementia	Words for Caring Families	Words for Everyone	
	A New Journey	The First Step	Going Together	Job-Specific Contributions	
		Departure Announcement	Team Leader	On-the-Spot Helper	
		Travel Plan	Family Expert	Encouraging Supporter	
		Fellow Travelers	The Three Consultants	Personal Connections	
		Can-Do List	Disclosing Chat	Mix-Up Event	
		Daily Chore	Chance to Shine	Inventing Jobs	
		Self-Reflecting Room	Preparation for the Dream	Delivering the Voice	
		Favorite Place	Make it Funny	Warm Design	
		Voice of Experience	Usual Talk		
		Turning the Tide	The Seen Scenery		
		Live in the Moment	Personal Time		
		Self-Intro Album	Emotion Switch		
		Own Way of Expressing	Casual Counseling		
		Gift of Words	Special Day		
			Generational Mix		
			The Amusement Committee		
			Hint of Feelings		

Figure 3: Pattern Names of Learning Patterns, Collaboration Patterns, Presentation Patterns, Change Making Patterns, Survival Language, and Words for a Journey

4. Methodology of Pattern Mining

Despite the method of pattern language has been applied to various domains, little has been discussed about how to create pattern languages and its methodology is yet to be developed. To start the process of developing a new pattern language, it is important to "mine the seeds" of the patterns from examples of best experiences or practices. Pattern mining is shorthand for discovering thought patterns embodied in our minds or in the activities associated with the target. The term pattern mining is taken from a metaphor of geological *mining* (Gabriel, 1996; DeLano, 1998).

In the pattern mining, first, miners explore their experiences, observations, episodes, or documented past work related to the subject at hand. Through this exploration, they look for and identify hidden knowledge used for the target. This knowledge may include associated rules, methods, tips, or customs. Next, the miner finds critical connections among these related items so that prospective pattern begins to form a meaningful whole. In what follows, I will show three types of pattern mining methods based on our experiences in creating pattern languages: Collaborative Introspection, Mining Interview, and Mining Workshop.

4.1 Collaborative Introspection

Collaborative introspection is usually done by two or more people so that multiple points of view are engaged to avoid patterns becoming skewed, to reflect only the values of a single person. In the process, group members first go through an element mining session together (Figure 4). They write rules, methods, tips, or customs they consider important about the subject onto a sticky note, talk about it briefly to the group, and then place the note on a large sheet of craft paper. The members simultaneously write their notes and each take turns talking about them until no one has any more ideas to share. After collecting their ideas, they organize these by compiling similar ideas and dividing them into groups, and finally the groups are potential seeds of patterns.

Figure 4: Collaborative Introspection (Left: Presentation Patterns; Right: Collaboration Patterns)

Using this method, we created the following pattern languages: the Learning Patterns (Iba & Iba Lab, 2014a), the Collaboration Patterns (Iba & Iba Lab, 2014b), Presentation Patterns (Iba & Iba Lab, 2014c), the Generative Beauty Patterns (Arao, et al., 2012), the Creative Co-Cooking Patterns (Isaku & Iba, 2015), and several meta-patterns. Iba & Isaku (2012) presents the patterns for collaborative introspection and clustering ideas into the seeds of patterns in holistic way. And, Iba, et al. (2010) shows the process of creating the Learning Patterns; Sakamoto & Iba (2011) shows the case of the Presentation Patterns.

4.2 Mining Interviews

If you are motivated to create a pattern language for an area in which you have little or no experience, it is necessary to conduct interviews with experienced people to collect key information needed to write the patterns (Figure 5). During an interview, it is important to ask key questions that relate to the *Solution, Problem,* and *Context*. According to the *Keys Worth Sharing* (Iba & Yoder, 2014), a good way to begin an interview is to first ask what the interviewees really want to share with colleagues and newcomers. This question usually elicits responses that include core ideas about possible solutions; most people enjoy sharing this information. Then, ask what will happen if you don't practice the important points in order to conduct *Problem Digging*. For example, you can ask what drove you to choose this solution? This will help to obtain information about the problem that the pattern solves. Thereafter, ask when or where the problem occurs, in order to conduct *Context Catching*.

The interviewer should take notes during the interview process by either writing them down in their sticky notes, notebook or on a whiteboard. After collecting the ideas by such an interviews, they go on to organizing them by compiling similar ideas and dividing them into groups.

Figure 5: Mining Interview (Left: Words for a Journey; Right: Pedagogical Patterns for Creative Learning)

With using this method, we created the following pattern languages: Words for a Journey (Iba & Okada, 2015), the Change Making Patterns (Shimomukai et al., 2015), Survival Language (Furukawazono et al., 2015), Personal Culture Patterns (Nakada et al., 2013), Global Life Patterns (Matsuzuka et al., 2013), Policy Language (Iba & Takenaka, 2013), and Pedagogical Patterns for Creative Learning (Iba, et al., 2011; Shibuya, et al, 2013). See also Oi et al. (2015) for the method of presenting patterns related to their original interview transcriptions.

4.3 Mining Workshop

Another approach is to conduct pattern mining workshops where the seeds of patterns are collected from dialog among the participants. Interestingly, different goals for participants and organizers can be set for such a workshop (Akado, et al., 2015). Mining pattern seeds would not be a motivation for people from outside the pattern language community. Therefore, it is a good idea to design the workshop as an opportunity to get some practical tips and solutions directly from the workshop, even though one goal of the organizers could be collecting information about problems and solutions for making pattern seeds (Figure 6).

In a pattern mining workshop, ideas about both solutions and problems are mined. It does not matter with which one starts, just so long as both are clarified during the workshop. If someone starts with a solution, ask the person what the problem is. The special type of facilitator, which we call `generator,' tries to discover what that person sees as a suitable solution or asks other participants for suggestions. To easily maintain separation between the sticky notes for comments on Problems and comments for Solutions, it is highly recommended to use two different colors of sticky notes.

Figure 6: Mining Workshop (Generative Beauty Workshop)

We used this method to collect additional pattern seeds for the Generative Beauty Patterns. Based on this experience, Akado et al. (2015) presents five patterns for designing pattern mining workshops. Hong et al. (2015) used this type of mining workshop to understand cultural similarities and differences on beauty in daily life in Japan, Korea, and the United States.

5. Methodology of Pattern Writing

After any of the mining methods pattern seeds are obtained. Next what we need to do is to write them down into a pattern format. Although there are various pattern formats, I usually follow this format: Pattern Name, Introduction, Pattern Illustration, Context, Problem, Forces, Solution, Actions, and Consequence.

The Pattern Name gives the pattern a short memorable name for easy reference that accurately describes the pattern. The introduction provides an entry gate to the patterns, and Illustrations make it easy to imagine a living image of the pattern. These three elements actually provide a summary of the pattern.

The rest of the elements provide more details about the patterns. For example, Context informs when the pattern should be used. Problem is the undesired consequence that is likely to occur in the context under discussion. Forces are unavoidable laws about the aspects of human nature that make the Problem difficult to overcome. A Solution is one way to resolve the problem, and Actions provide some concrete activities. Finally, Consequences describe how things can change when this pattern is applied to the situation.

Even with a simple format of a pattern, we take a different, more complicated order to write the contents of the pattern. This process tends to confuse many beginners in pattern writing. I have emphasized the order of pattern writing in university classes and workshops for pattern writing because I realized that, for some people, it is necessary to have a tool for showing basic order to follow in pattern writing.

On the backdrop, I designed the Pattern Writing Sheet (Iba, 2014a). It provides not only the space to write the contents of a pattern but also instructions on how to proceed thinking about them (Figure 7). This sheet is available online under the Creative Commons license, and I have used it for several workshops (Figure 8).

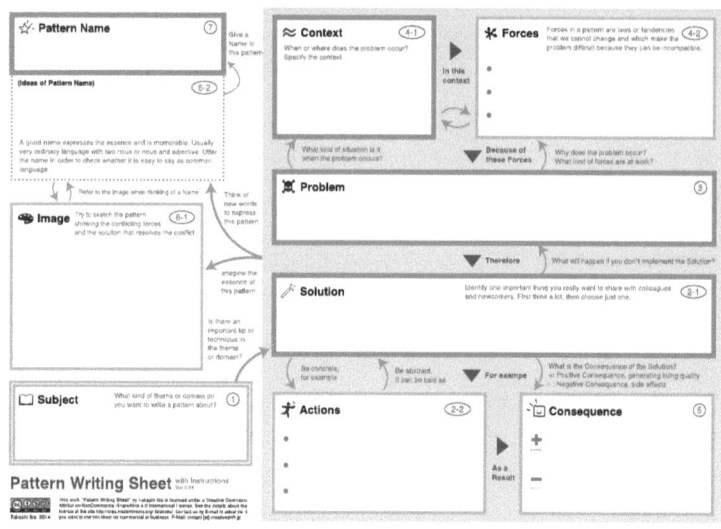

Figure 7: Pattern Writing Sheet

Figure 8: Workshop: Business people write pattern related to their work using Pattern Writing Sheet

6. Methodology of Pattern Illustrating

The most eye-catching part of our patterns is pattern illustration. In my mind, pattern illustrations are not just interesting side drawings, but essential expressions of a pattern, especially in Pattern Language 3.0 for human actions. Pattern Illustrations should meet the following three requirements:

1. It should express the essence of the pattern.
2. It should include character(s) that express human movements and feelings through body language and facial expressions.

3. It should be an iconic representation of the pattern that does not connect multiple scenes with arrows.

Pattern illustrations are carefully designed. We start by understanding the essence of the pattern, draw rough sketches, and revised them several times, much like revising a sentence to get it just right. For example, to get the 34 pattern illustrations for the Presentation Patterns, we drew more than 500 illustrations.

The preference is for simple characters rather than realistic, detailed characters (Figure 9). Manabu-kun is the character for the Learning Patterns (Iba & Iba Lab, 2014a), the Collaboration Patterns (Iba & Iba Lab, 2014b), the Presentation Patterns (Iba & Iba Lab, 2014c), the Survival Language (Furukawazono, et al., 2015), and the Pedagogical Patterns for Creative Learning (Iba, et al., 2011). "Manabu" means "learn" in Japanese, which is why we used it to name the drawing pattern illustrations for Learning Patterns, which was our first pattern language with pattern illustrations. However, there are other characters in other pattern languages that we have created; some examples are shown in Figure 9.

Many writers in our pattern community are interested in pattern illustrating, but they say that it is difficult and want to know where to start and how to proceed through the design process. We have studied pattern illustrating (Harasawa, et al. 2012, 2014), and published two guides about it; one is a picture book (Figure 10) showing the process of pattern illustrating very simplistically (Harasawa, et al., 2015), and the other is comprised of the 28 actual patterns in Pattern Illustrating Patterns (Iba & Iba Lab, 2015; Miyazaki, et al., 2015).

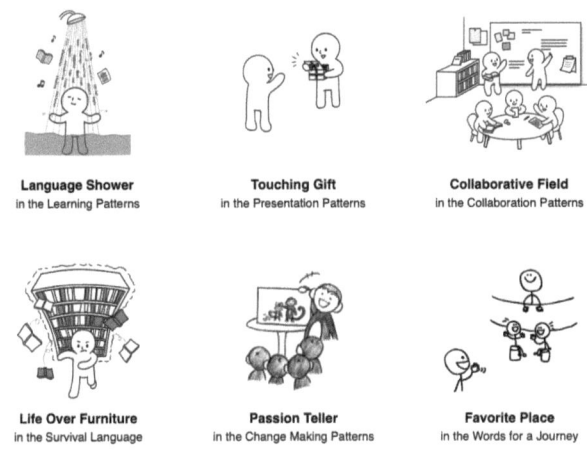

Figure 9: Examples of Pattern Illustration

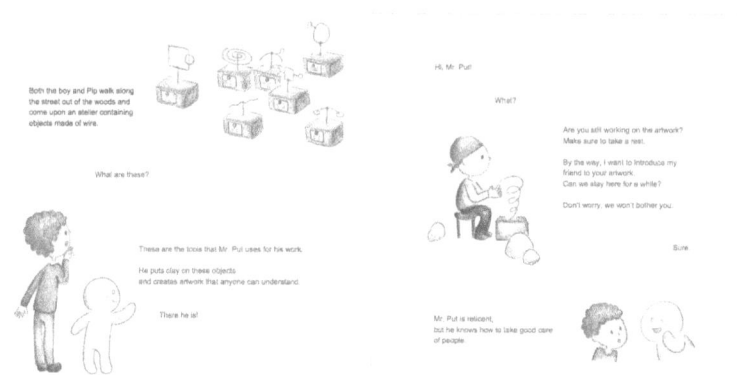

Figure 10: Picture book: A Tale of Pattern Illustrating (Harasawa et al., 2015)

7. Workshops using Patterns Languages

Third generation pattern languages for human actions are used not only for self-study by reading patterns, but also as media for narrative and dialog. For different purposes, I invented some specific types of workshops: the creative dialog workshop, a collaborative improvement workshop, and an idea generation workshop.

7.1 Creative dialog workshop

An implementation of pattern languages as media for creative dialog is an organized workshop (Iba, 2012b, 2014c) that provides participants an opportunity to reflect on their experiences, talk about them with others, and make a plan for future actions using the pattern language (Figure 11).

In this workshop, first, participants are asked to recall their experiences in terms of the provided pattern language. They are asked to choose five patterns they wish to master in the near future. Then, participants are free to mingle and to find and talk with other participants. When they find someone who has experienced a pattern they want to master, they listen to the other participant's story.

Dialog workshops using the Learning Patterns (Iba & Iba Lab, 2014a) have been held at the Faculty of Policy Management and Faculty of Environment and Information Studies, Keio University, since 2011. All freshmen at the two faculties, approximately 900 students, have participated in these workshops and talked about their experiences of learning in light of the patterns. About 4,500 students have participated in the workshops over the past five years. Iba (2014c) presents feedback from workshop participants of the dialog workshop using the Learning Patterns. Based on the results, we realized the following merits of dialog workshops using a pattern language.

First, participants can talk to people to whom they have never talked before. By setting a rule that participants must talk only to people they do not know, the workshop becomes an extraordinary and interesting event and is still feasible even if participants are shy and do not like talking to new people. This is because the atmosphere and rules of the workshop make it more comfortable for people to talk. Moreover, the workshop is fun and interesting and the participants even make new friends, although the theme is learning.

Second, to actualize the patterns they want to implement, the participants gain ideas about specific actions they can take and also learn that the same pattern can have various applications. In this workshop, participants are often motivated by other people's attitudes and experiences, of learning in the case of Learning Patterns, and by seeing the diversity of the experiences of others. Through the workshop, the participants gain a broader viewpoint of the world and themselves to help them share and solve problems they are facing.

Third, the workshops not only allow participants to know something unique about others, but also to discover new aspects in themselves by using the pattern language to talk about themselves. In the dialogs, they also sometimes discover they have experience with a pattern that they did not realize they had experienced. Some participants are already using the pattern names as part of their vocabulary and making emphatic comments about what the dialog workshop actualizes in them.

Thus, dialog workshops facilitate not just simple conversation and trading information, but become places for creative dialog. Iba (2012a) presents a pattern language for designing thus type of workshop and Iba (2014a) introduced the method of pattern language as media for mining, analyzing, and visualizing experiences.

Figure 11: Dialog workshop using a pattern language (Up: Learning Patterns at Keio University; Down: Learning Patterns at the University of North Carolina at Asheville)

7.2 Collaborative improvement workshop

A pattern language can be used to improve design based on a diagnosis of current status. Christopher Alexander calls this function "a process of diagnosis and local repair"(Alexander et al., 1975). Likewise, we can use pattern languages for human actions by diagnosing the current status and finding ways to repair it.

I sometimes hold workshops where participants improve their presentation skills using the Presentation Patterns. First, they give their own short presentation, maybe three minutes, very short. Then, they discuss how they could improve the presentations by giving constructive comments using the Presentation Pattern Cards, which will be discussed later in this paper.

Interestingly, in previous workshops, I have witnessed that younger less-experienced participants can still impart useful advice to comparatively experienced participants, possibly because the participants do not need to think of the advice from scratch based on their experience, but rather can choose patterns and apply them to the presentation during discussion. We have held the workshop for collaborative improvement using the Presentation Patterns (Iba & Iba Lab, 2014c) for graduate students (Figure 12) and my collaborator has had success with a similar workshop at an elementary school.

Figure 12: Creative Improvement Workshop (Presentation Patterns)

7.3 Idea generation workshop

Patterns are usually used to support direct design for the target. In 3.0, this means designing human actions. Recently, however, we utilized patterns as seeds for designing products and services to help people in the situations described by the patterns (Figure 13).

There are two kinds of pattern language use: designing products and services to support conducting actions to solve a problem and designing products and services to change conditions so that the problem does not occur in the first place. The idea generation workshop can be conducted as solution-driven, problem-driven, or a mix of both.

During idea generation using a pattern language, patterns take on several roles: seeds for abductive reasoning, constraints on the scope of ideas, and needs for the emerging ideas. Since patterns provide ideal direction of solutions, people can think out new ideas based using the patterns as clues. These patterns are also constraints on divergent thinking, but the level of abstraction of patterns provides a good level of ambiguity. Moreover, ideas based on solutions of the patterns always have reasons why the idea is important, because every pattern is written as a pair: problem and solution.

We held idea generation workshops using "*Words for a Journey*" patterns for college students (Figure 14). In the workshop, participants invented new ideas for products and services for people with dementia and their families, using Words for a Journey Cards, which are shown in the next section. Few had previous knowledge about dementia, but they were able to learn enough from the pattern language to conceptualize new tools for positive support.

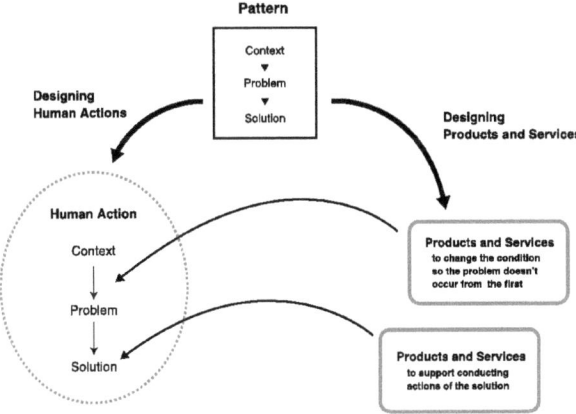

Figure 13: Designing products and services to indirectly support actions with a pattern

Figure 14: Idea Generation workshop (Words for a Journey)

8. Tools for utilizing Pattern Languages

Since Alexander invented the method of pattern language, patterns are now shared in books, papers, and on web pages. These are good for studying the practical knowledge from domain experts. However, these sources are not suitable when pattern languages are used as media for dialog between more than two people.

Accordingly, we created several new tools for using pattern languages, such as pattern cards, pattern stickers, and a web system for sharing quality.

8.1 Pattern cards

The crucial problem of providing pattern languages as books, papers, and web pages is that these are less flexible. It is simply impossible to manipulate patterns in books, papers, or web pages to stimulate thinking or communication. So, I created several pattern cards, which are small-size thick paper cards with a summary of the patterns printed on them. These pattern cards are easy for people to manipulate as they think and communicate about an issue. Figure 15 shows the layout of one of the Presentation Pattern Cards and Figure 16 shows one of the Words for A Journey Cards.

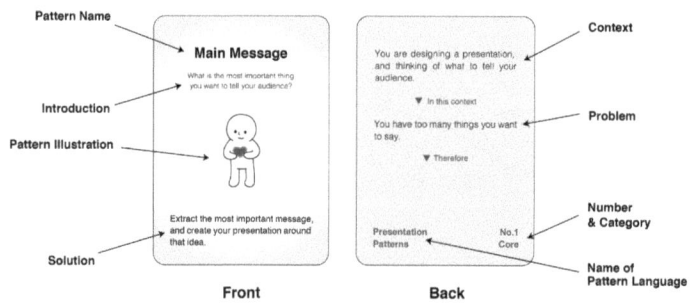

Figure 15: Front and Back of a Pattern Card (Presentation Pattern Cards)

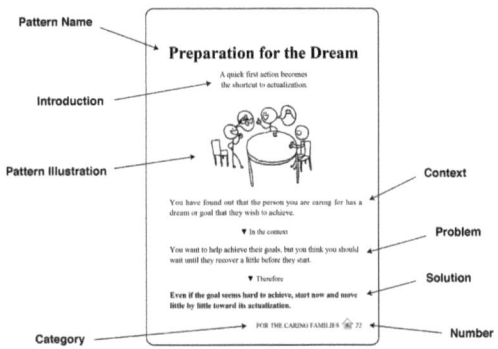

Figure 16: Pattern Card (Words for a Journey Cards)

Although pattern cards can be used in various ways, I recommend the following ways:

1. Diagnosing Yourself: Diagnose yourself by grouping the cards according to whether you have prior experience with each pattern.
2. Drawing Future Visions: Use the Pattern Cards to develop your plan of activity.
3. Improving Your Learning: Use the Pattern Cards to improve your actions.
4. Reflecting on Your Activity: After an activity is finished, the Pattern Cards can be used for reflection on your experience.
5. Case Studies: Use the Pattern Cards as tools for case studies of activities.
6. Dialogs: Use the Pattern Cards to share past experiences of activities.
7. Interviews: With the Pattern Cards, you can interview others to hear stories about the patterns that you want to use in the future.

The upper pictures in Figure 17 illustrate using the Presentation Pattern Cards for (5) case studies in a high school. After becoming familiar with patterns through (6) Dialogs, participants watched a TED talk (www.ted.com) and analyzed the presentation using the Presentation Patterns. They examined all 34 patterns and categorized them into three groups: Practicing, Partially Practicing, and Not Practicing. These categories indicated whether the presenter was practicing any of the patterns or not. Then, they discussed why the presentation was attractive based on the patterns grouped in the Practicing or Partially Practicing groups. Lower pictures of Figure 17 show the same workshop, but for training of high-school teachers.

I have created the following pattern cards so far: Learning Pattern Cards, Collaboration Pattern Cards, Presentation Pattern Cards, Survival Language Cards, and Words for a Journey Cards. These cards can be used for thinking alone or for workshops. Additionally, we have a prototype of a card game of patterns (Okazaki et al., 2011).

Figure 17: Workshop with Pattern Cards (Presentation Pattern Cards)

8.2 Pattern stickers

Although workshops using pattern languages are great and pattern cards are good tools for workshops and daily use, it is difficult to always use them in daily life. How can we make pattern languages something that comes to mind easily in daily life?

One way is to create stickers with the pattern name and pattern illustration and put them on any flat surface, such as the cover of laptop computer, tablet PC, schedule book, cosmetic case, or wall. The stickers can remind you of the patterns whenever you look at them during the day. The sticker not only sticks itself to the flat plane but also can stick the corresponding pattern about life in the mind of the individual.

I have designed pattern stickers for the Learning Patterns, the Collaboration Patterns, and the Presentation Patterns (Figure 18). These stickers were given to participants at the PLoP2013 (20th Conference on Pattern Languages of Programs) conference and at ORF2013 (Open Research Forum 2013). Figure 19 shows some of use cases of the participants who received stickers.

Pattern Language 3.0 and Fundamental Behavioral Properties

Figure 18: Pattern Stickers

Figure 19: Making use of Pattern Stickers

In the near future, I want to create 3D objects that present patterns in the real world using digital fabrication machines such as 3D printers and laser cutters. The research and practice of creating new pattern objects that fit naturally into surroundings while being reminders of patterns are one of several new frontiers.

8.3 Web system for sharing quality

In pattern language workshops, participants exchange their vivid experiences related to the patterns that are being examined. Through the dialog, participants can feel the aliveness of experiences related to the patterns. However, there are few opportunities for workshops, and it is not possible for a reader of a pattern paper or book to communicate with others as they read.

We realized that a new system for sharing personal experiences and feelings of aliveness is the key to dissemination and real application of pattern languages. Therefore, we designed a system that supports people in grasping and sharing the aliveness of personal experiences through a pattern language, and named it the "Feeling of Life System" (FoL) (Iba et al, 2014).

This system lets people express themselves using photos and stories, sharing the aliveness of personal experiences as they relate to each pattern. The system can store the aliveness and continue to share it. Photos show the scenes or objects that invoke the aliveness, or the feelings or objects that express personal feelings. These types of stories tell about real life. The system attempts to personalize a pattern language that is initially universal by using the system users' own photos and stories. As Alexander said, "A language gives you back your confidence in what seemed once like trivial things" (Alexander 1979, p. 545), and to "express life" with different patterns repeatedly helps people realize their aliveness.

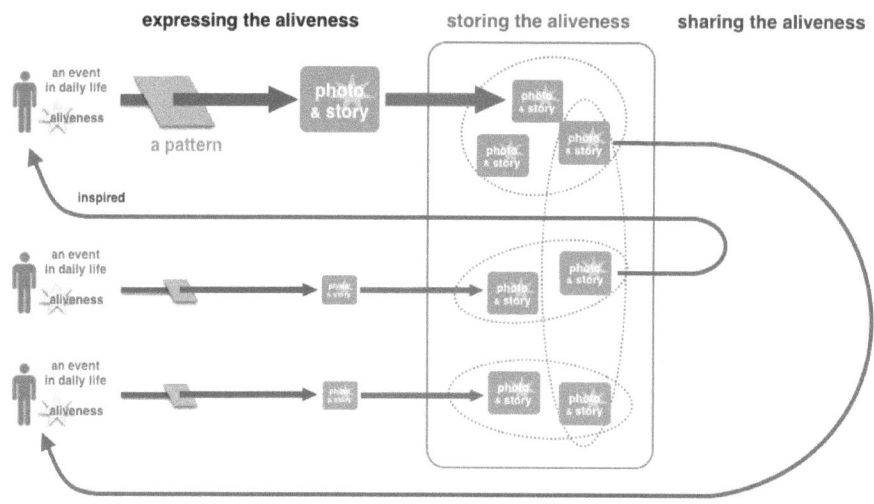

Figure 20: An Overview of the Feeling of Life System (FoL)

The FoL system has three functions: expressing, storing, and sharing. While these three functions are basically different, they impact and give power to each other, so the system can be called cyclic. System users will get *piecemeal growth* by expressing and storing, or being inspired by others and, then expressing new feelings or actions (Figure 20). We also demonstrated the system, "The 4th Place," as an example of the FoL system, which uses the Generative Beauty Patterns, a pattern language for one to live lively and beautifully each day (Figure 21).

Note that a more functional system to keep using a pattern language, the Pattern Diagnostic System was developed by Isaku et al. (2013).

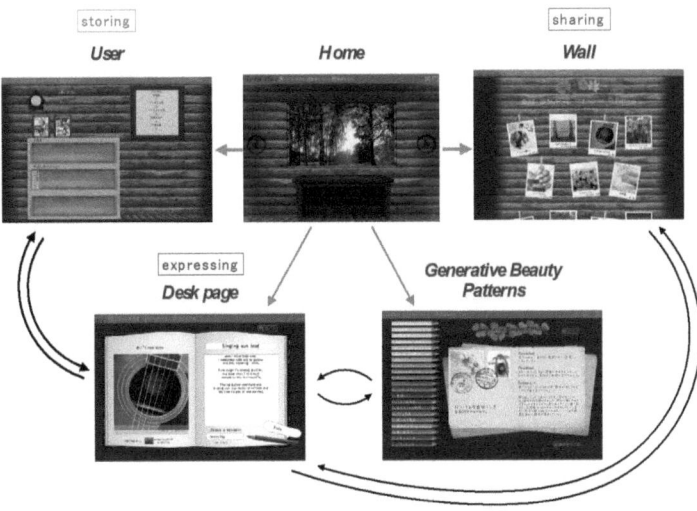

Figure 21: "The 4th Place" system for the Generative Beauty Patterns as the first prototype of the FoL system

9. Fundamental behavioral properties

Christopher Alexander outlined the core properties of the hidden qualities of buildings in his book, *The Nature of Order*. He pointed out that a living whole consists of "centers," which are parts that make up the whole, and that the whole becomes lively when the centers synergistically intensify each other (Alexander, 2002a). He organized how centers intensify each other into 15 geometrical properties, known simply as the „fifteen properties" in *The Nature of Order*: 1. LEVELS OF SCALE, 2. STRONG CENTERS, 3. BOUNDARIES, 4. ALTERNATING REPETITION, 5. POSITIVE SPACE, 6. GOOD SHAPE, 7. LOCAL SYMMETRIES, 8. DEEP INTERLOCK AND AMBIGUITY, 9. CONTRAST, 10. GRADIENTS, 11. ROUGHNESS, 12. ECHOES, 13. THE VOID, 14. SIMPLICITY AND INNER CALM, and 15. NOT-SEPARATENESS (See Figure 22, an illustration of the geometrical properties, which I presented in Iba & Sakai (2014)).

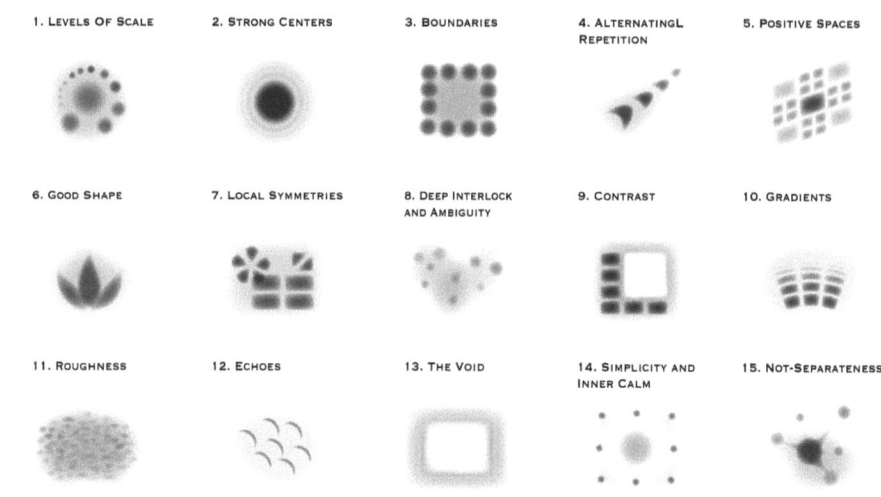

Figure 22: Fifteen Fundamental Geometrical Properties

Recently, there has been a movement challenging the application of these geometrical properties as things other than architectural, e.g. workshop on the Pursuit of Pattern Languages for Societal Change (PURPLSOC) and even within the software community. However, Alexander's properties focused primarily on geometrical, physical objects, such as buildings and items found in nature. Thus, it is still unknown whether they can be applied to things that are hard to perceive, such as human actions or society.

Based on the background, we have identified and defined fundamental behavioral properties within the wholeness of lively human activities; similar to the way in which Alexander defined the 15 properties based on his theory of wholeness and centers (Iba et al., 2015b, 2015d; Harashima, et al, 2015). In order to find these properties, we analyzed human action patterns that we had created in the past. In *The Nature of Order*, Book 2, Alexander says that a pattern language is an essential way to define generic centers (Alexander, 2002b). The implication is that it is possible to capture centers by investigating pattern languages. Based on his idea, we could capture the centers in human activities from the patterns and discover the properties based on their commonalities.

Thus, the basic strategies would be to investigate pattern languages of human action in order to find out the mechanisms that create the liveliness behind each pattern; verify the universality necessary for the properties of the mechanism by checking if they can describe liveliness in other patterns; and finally, express how the discovered properties generate the

Pattern Language 3.0 and Fundamental Behavioral Properties

mechanism for liveliness by illustration and description while thinking about the relationship between the properties.

Through the investigation process, we discovered these 24 fundamental behavioral properties: 1. BOOTSTRAP, 2. SOURCE, 3. SPREADING, 4. ATTRACTION, 5. INVOLVING, 6. TOGETHERNESS, 7. BUILDING UP, 8. ORGANIC GROWTH, 9. REFLECTING, 10. ACCOMPANY, 11. ENHANCEMENT, 12. EMPATHY, 13. SELECTION, 14. SIMPLIFICATION, 15. CONSISTENCY, 16. LOOSENESS, 17. FLEXIBILITY, 18. ABUNDANCE, 19. ENDEAVOR, 20. CONNECTING, 21. POSITIONING, 22. DIFFERENTIATING, 23. OVERLAPPING, and 24. CONTINUOUS RELATION (See Figure 23, an illustration of the behavioral properties (Iba et al., 2015d)).

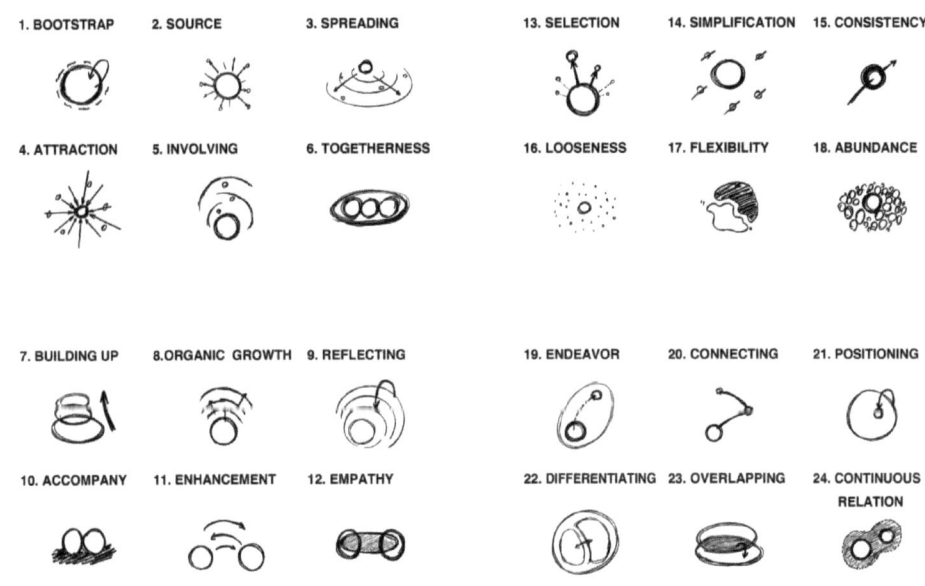

Figure 23: The 24 Fundamental Behavioral Properties

The 24 behavioral properties can be used mainly for three purposes: pattern mining, pattern writing, and designing. First, these properties can be used to indicate patterns from experiences or episodes shared at pattern mining interviews or workshops. As behavioral properties describe the properties of lively human activities, understanding them makes it possible to estimate how actions from the experiences or episodes imbue each activity with life.

Second, properties are also useful for accurate verbalization of how the pattern contributes to make the activity lively. Behavioral properties are the properties of how centers inten-

225

sify each other to create the liveliness of human activities. Therefore, it helps the writer to capture the centers in the description of a pattern and to understand how those centers intensify each other to create the liveliness of that activity so that the writer can improve the description.

Third, other than for patterns, properties can also be used for designing. Even if there are only a small number of patterns already written in a certain domain, there should be plenty of lively human behaviors that have not yet been converted into patterns. It is possible to recognize the wholeness by identifying the centers of behavior and how those centers intensify each other.

Geometrical properties and behavioral properties are not just properties that appear in architecture, nature, or in human activity but two viewpoints may can be used for capturing lively phenomena in general. We anticipate that these properties can support people to experience aliveness and wholeness of phenomena.

10. Conclusion

Thirty years ago, Christopher Alexander said, "The house is no longer an 'object' which is manufactured, but a thing of love, which is nurtured, made, grown, and personal" (Alexander, 1985) and therefore "families would design their own houses" (Alexander, 1985). Similarly, our life is "a thing of love, which is nurtured, made, grown, and personal" and, therefore we would design our own lives. It is my hope that the studies presented in this paper will stimulate people to work for future innovation in pattern language methodologies.

11. Acknowledgements

I would like to thank to Richard Gabriel, Joseph Yoder, Rebecca Wirfs-Brock, Linda Rising, Mary Lynn Manns, Jenny Quillien, Hajo Neis, Howard Davis, Ralph Johnson, Lise Hvatum, Bob Hanmer, Christian Kohls, and Christian Köppe for encouraging our quest to create a new type of pattern language. I want to thank Reinhard Bauer, Peter Baumgartner, and Helmut Leitner for inviting me to be the keynote speaker at a PURPLSOC conference. Finally, my greatest honor goes to all members of Iba Lab at Keio University and collaborators for their wonderful collaboration.

12. REFERENCES

Alexander, C. (1979) The Timeless Way of Building, Oxford University Press.

Alexander, C., Davis, H., Martinez, J. and Corner, D. (1985) The Production of Houses, Oxford University Press.

Alexander, C., Ishikawa, S., Silverstein, M., Jacobson, M., Fiksdahl-King, I. and Angel, S. (1977) A Pattern Language: Towns, Buildings, Construction, Oxford University Press.

Alexander, C., Silverstein, M., Angel, S., Ishikawa, S., and Abrams, D. (1975) The Oregon Experiment, Oxford University Press.

Alexander, C. (2002a), The Nature of Order: An Essay of the Art of Building and the Nature of the Universe, Book 1: The Phenomenon of Life, Center for Environmental Structure.

Alexander, C. (2002b), The Nature of Order: An Essay of the Art of Building and the Nature of the Universe, Book 2: The Process of Creating Life, Center for Environmental Structure.

Akado, Y., Kogure, S., Sasabe, A., Hong, J.-H., Saruwatari, K., and Iba, T. (2015) "Five Patterns for Designing Pattern Mining Workshops," in the 20th European Conference on Pattern Languages of Programs (EuroPLoP2015).

Arao, R., Tamefusa, A., Kadotani, M., Harasawa, K., Sakai, S., Saruwatari, K., and Iba, T. (2012) "Generative Beauty Patterns: A Pattern Language for Living Lively and Beautiful," in the 19th Conference on Pattern Languages of Programs (PLoP2012).

Beck, K. and Cunningham, W. (1987) 'Using Pattern Languages for Object-oriented Programs', OOPSLA-87 Workshop on the Specification and Design for Object-Oriented Programming.

Coplien, J. (1999) "A Pattern Language for Writers' Workshops," in Harrison, N., Foote, B., Rohnert, H. (eds), Pattern Languages of Program Design 4, Addison-Welsey Professional.

Coplien, J.O., Harrison, N.B. (2004) Organizational Patterns of Agile Software Development, Prentice Hall.

DeLano, D.E. (1998) 'Patterns mining,' in Rising, L. (Ed.): The Patterns Handbook: Techniques, Strategies, and Applications, Cambridge University Press.

Furukawazono, T., Seshimo, S., Muramatsu, D., and Iba, T. (2013) "Designing a Pattern Language for Surviving Earthquakes," in the 4th International Conference on Collaborative Innovation Networks (COINs2013).

Furukawazono, T., Seshimo, S., Muramatsu, D. and Iba, T. (2013b) 'Survival Language: A Pattern Language for Surviving Earthquakes', in the 20th International Conference on Pattern Language of Programs (PLoP2013).

Furukawazono, T., Iba, T., with Survival Language Project (2015) Survival Language: A Pattern Language for Surviving Earthquakes, CreativeShift Lab.

Gabriel, R.P. (1996) Patterns of Software: Tales from the Software Community, Oxford University Press.

Gamma, E., Helm, R., Johnson, R. and Vlissides, J. (1994) Design Patterns: Elements of Reusable Object-Oriented Software, Addison-Wesley.

Harasawa, K., Arao, R. and Iba, T. (2012) "A Pattern Language for Pattern Illustrating," in the 19th Conference on Pattern Languages of Programs (PLoP2012).

Harasawa, K., Miyazaki, N., Sakuraba, R., and Iba, T. (2014) "The Nature of Pattern Illustrating: The Theory and the Process of Pattern Illustrating," in the 21th Conference on Pattern Languages of Programs (PLoP2014).

Harasawa, K., Miyazaki, N., Sakuraba, R., and Iba, T. (2015) A Tale of Pattern Illustrating, CreativeShift Lab.

Harashima, Y., Kubota, T., Matsumura, T., Tsukahara, K., and Iba, T. (2014) "Learning Patterns for Self-Directed Learning with Notebooks," in the 21st Conference on Pattern Languages of Programs (PLoP2014).

Harashima, Y., Kaneko, T., Isaku, T., and Iba, T. (2015) "Fundamental Behavioral Properties, Part 2: Extending the Theory of Centers for Pattern Language 3.0" in the 22nd Conference on Pattern Languages of Programs (PLoP2015).

Harrison, N.B. (2006) "Advanced Pattern Writing: Patterns for Experienced Pattern Authors" in Manolescu, D., Voelter, M., Noble, J. (eds), Pattern Languages of Program Design 5, Addison-Wesley Professional, pp. 433-452

Harrison, N.B. (2006) "The Language of Shepherding: A Pattern Language for Shepherds and Sheep," in Manolescu, D., Voelter, M., Noble, J. (eds), Pattern Languages of Program Design 5, Addison-Wesley Professional, pp. 507-529

Hong, J-H, Akado, Y., Kogure, S., Sasabe, A., Saruwatari, K. and Iba, T. (2015), "Understanding Cultural Similarities and Differences by Mining Patterns of Thinking and Doing in Daily Lives," in the 5th International Conference on Collaborative Innovation Networks (COINs2015).

Hoover, D. and Oshineye, A. (2009) Apprenticeship Patterns: Guidance for the Aspiring Software Craftsman, O'Reilly Media.

Iba, T., Miyake, T., Naruse, M. and Yotsumoto, N. (2009) "Learning Patterns: A Pattern Language for Active Learners," in the 16th Conference on Pattern Languages of Programs (PLoP2009).

Iba, T. and Miyake, T. (2010) "Learning Patterns: A Pattern Language for Creative Learners II," in the 1st Asian Conference of Pattern Language of Programs (AsianPLoP2010).

Iba, T., Sakamoto, M., and Miyake, T. (2010) "How to Write Tacit Knowledge as a Pattern Language: Media Design for Spontaneous and Collaborative Communities," in the 2nd Conference on Collaborative Innovation Networks (COINs2010).

Iba, T. (2011) 'Pattern Language 3.0: Methodological Advances in Sharing Design Knowledge,' in the 4th International Conference on Collaborative Innovation Networks 2011 (COINs2011).

Iba, T. and Sakamoto, M. (2011) "Learning Patterns III: A Pattern Language for Creative Learning," in the 18th Conference on Pattern Languages of Programs (PLoP2011).

Iba, T., Ichikawa, C., Sakamoto, M. and Yamazaki, T. (2011) "Pedagogical patterns for creative learning," in the 18th International Conference on Pattern Languages of Programs (PLoP2011).

Iba, T. (2012a) "A Pattern Language for Designing Workshop to Introduce a Pattern Language," in the 17th European Conference on Pattern Languages of Programs (EuroPLoP2012).

Iba, T. (2012b) 'Pattern Language 3.0: Writing Pattern Languages for Human Actions,' Invited Talk, in the 19th Conference on Pattern Languages of Programs (PLoP2012).

Iba, T., Matsumoto, A. and Harasawa, K. (2012) "Presentation Patterns: A Pattern Language for Creative Presentations', in the 17th European Conference on Pattern Languages of Programs (EuroPLoP2012).

Iba, T. and Isaku, T. (2012), "Holistic Pattern-Mining Patterns: A Pattern Language for Pattern Mining on a Holistic Approach," in the 19th Conference on Pattern Languages of Programs (PLoP2012).

Iba, T. and Isaku, T. (2013) "Collaboration Patterns: A Pattern Language for Creative Collaborations," in the 18th Conference on Pattern Languages of Programs (EuroPLoP 2013).

Iba, T., and Takenaka, H. (2013) "Policy Language: Creating a Pattern Language for Policy Design," Pattern Languages: Media for the Creative Society, Keio University Press (in Japanese)

Iba, T. (2014a), 'Using pattern languages as media for mining, analysing, and visualising experiences,' International Journal of Organisational Design and Engineering, Vol. 3, No.3/4, pp.278-301.

Iba, T. (2014b) "A Journey on the Way to Pattern Writing: Designing the Pattern Writing Sheet," in the 21st Conference on Pattern Languages of Programs (PLoP2014).

Iba, T. (2014c) "Pattern Languages as Media for Creative Dialogue: Functional Analysis of Dialogue Workshops," in the Workshop on Pursuit of Pattern Languages for Societal Change (PURPLSOC2014).

Iba, T., Kimura, N., and Sakai, S. (2014) "Feeling of Life" System with a Pattern Language," in the 21st Conference on Pattern Languages of Programs (PLoP2014).

Iba, T. and Iba Laboratory (2014a) Learning Patterns: A Pattern Language for Creative Learning, CreativeShift Lab.

Iba, T. and Iba Laboratory (2014b) Collaboration Patterns: A Pattern Language for Creative Collaborations, CreativeShift Lab.

Iba, T. and Iba Laboratory (2014c) Presentation Patterns: A Pattern Language for Creative Presentations, CreativeShift Lab.

Iba, T., and Isaku, T. (2014) "Presentation Patterns: A Pattern Language for Creative Presentations, Part I," in the 10th Latin American Conference on Pattern Languages of Programs (SugarLoafPLoP2014).

Iba, T. and Sakai, S. (2014) "Understanding Christopher Alexander's Fifteen Properties via Visualization and Analysis," in the Workshop on Pursuit of Pattern Languages for Societal Change (PURPLSOC2014).

Iba, T. and Yoder, J. (2014), "Mining Interview Patterns: Patterns for Effectively Obtaining Seeds of Patterns," in the 10th Latin American Conference on Pattern Languages of Programs (SugarLoafPLoP2014).

Iba, T. and Iba Laboratory (2015), Pattern Illustrating Patterns: A Pattern Language for Pattern Illustrating, CreativeShift Lab.

Iba, T., Matsumoto, A., Kamada, A., Tamaki, N., Matsumura, T., Kaneko, T., and Okada, M.

(2015a) "A Pattern Language for Living Well with Dementia: Words for a Journey," in the 5th International Conference on Collaborative Innovation Networks (COINs2015).

Iba, T., Kamada, A., Akado, Y., Honda, T., Sasabe, A., and Kogure, S. (2015b) "Fundamental Behavioral Properties, Part I: Extending the Theory of Centers for Pattern Language 3.0," in the 20th European Conference on Pattern Languages of Programs (EuroPLoP2015).

Iba, T., Kaneko, T., Kamada, A., Tamaki, N. and Okada, M. (2015c) "Words for a Journey: A Pattern Language for Living well with Dementia," in the World Conference on Pursuit of Pattern Languages for Societal Change (PURPLSOC2015).

Iba, T., Kimura, N., Akado, Y., and Honda, T. (2015d) "The Fundamental Behavioral Properties," in the World Conference on Pursuit of Pattern Languages for Societal Change (PURPLSOC2015).

Iba, T. and Okada, M. (Eds), Iba Laboratory and DFJI (Dementia Friendly Japan Initiative) (2015), Words for a Journey: The Art of Being with Dementia, CreativeShift Lab.

Isaku, T., Yamazaki, K. and Iba, T. (2013) "Pattern Diagnostic System: A Diagnostic Approach to Pattern Applications', in the 20th Conference on Pattern Languages of Programs (PLoP2013).

Isaku, T. and Iba, T. (2014) "Towards a Pattern Language for Cooking: A Generative Approach to Cooking," in the 19th European Conference on Pattern Languages of Programs (EuroPLoP2014).

Isaku, T. and Iba, T. (2015) "Creative CoCooking Patterns: A Pattern Language for Creative Collaborative Cooking," in the 20th European Conference on Pattern Languages of Programs (EuroPLoP2015).

Kadotani, M., Matsumoto, A. Shibuya, T., Lee, Y., Watanabe, S., and Iba, T. (2013) "Creative Language for good old future from Japanese Culture," in the 4th International Conference on Collaborative Innovation Networks (COINs2013).

Kadotani, M., Ishibashi, S, Lim, K., Matsumoto, A., and Iba, T. (2014) "Pattern Language for good old future from Japanese culture," in the 21st Conference on Pattern Languages of Programs (PLoP2014).

Kamada, A., Nakamura, S., Nagai, M., Sakuraba, R., Iba, T. (2014) "Personal Picture Method for Self Design," in the 10th Latin American Conference on Pattern Languages of Programs (SugarLoafPLoP2014).

Kobayashi, Y., Yoshida, M., Sasaki, A., and Iba, T. (2008) "Research Patterns: A Pattern Language for Academic Research," in the 15th Conference on Pattern Languages of Programs (PLoP08).

Matsuzuka, K., Isaku, T., Nishina, S., and Iba, T. (2013) "Global Life Patterns: A Methodology for Designing a Personal Global Life," in the 4th International Conference on Collaborative Innovation Networks (COINs2013).

Manns, M.L. and Rising, L. (2005), Fearless Change: Patterns for Introducing New Ideas, Addison-Wesley.

Manns, M.L. and Rising, L. (2015) More Fearless Change: Strategies for Making Your Ideas Happen, Addison-Wesley Professional.

Meszaros. G., and Doble, J. (1997), "A Pattern Language for Pattern Writing," in Martin, R.C., Riehle, D., and Buschmann, F. (eds), Pattern Languages of Program Design 3, Addison-Wesley Professional, pp. 529-574

Miyazaki, N., Sakuraba, R., Harasawa, K., and Iba, T. (2015), "Pattern Illustrating Patterns: A Pattern Language for Pattern Illustrating," in the 22nd Conference on Pattern Languages of Programs (PLoP2015).

Nakada, M., Kamada, A. and Iba, T. (2013) "Personal Culture Patterns: A Pattern Language for Living with Continuous Self-fulfillments," in the 18th European Conference on Pattern Languages of Programs (EuroPLoP2013).

Nakamura, S. and Iba, T. (2015a) "Collaborative Social Change with Change Making Patterns Workbook," in the 5th International Conference on Collaborative Innovation Networks (COINs2015).

Nakamura, S. and Iba, T. (2015b) "Fostering Changemakers with Change Making Patterns: A Conceptual Framework for Social Change and Its Educational Applications," in the World Conference on Pursuit of Pattern Languages for Societal Change (PURPLSOC2015).

Naruse, M, Takada, Y., Yumura, Y. Wakamatsu, K., and Iba, T. (2008) "Project Patterns: A Pattern Language for Promoting Project," in the 15th Conference on Pattern Languages of Programs (PLoP08).

Oi, S., Kubota, T., Kimura, N., and Iba, T. (2015) "Touching Patterns to Interview Transcriptions," in the 20th European Conference on Pattern Languages of Programs (EuroPLoP2015).

Okazaki, Y., Takaoka, A., Okabe, Y., Sakamoto, M. and Iba, T. (2011) "Learning Patterns Card Game," Artifacts, in the 3rd International Conference on Collaborative Innovation Networks 2011 (COINs2011).

Pedagogical Patterns Editorial Board (2012) Pedagogical Patterns: Advice for Educators, Createspace.

Sakamoto, M. and Iba, T. (2011) "Collaborative Mining and Writing of Design Knowledge," in the 3rd International Conference on Collaborative Innovation Networks 2011 (COINs2011).

Shibuya, T., Seshimo, S., Harashima, Y., Kubota, T. and Iba, T. (2013) "Educational patterns for generative participant: designing for creative learning," in the 20th International Conference on Pattern Language of Programs (PLoP2013).

Shimomukai, E. and Iba, T. (2012) "Social Entrepreneurship Patterns: A Pattern Language for Change-Making on Social Issues," in the 17th European Conference on Pattern Languages of Programs (EuroPLoP2012).

Shimomukai, E., Nakamura, S. and Iba, T. (2012) "Change Making Patterns: A Pattern Language for fostering social entrepreneurship," in the 19th Conference on Pattern Languages of Programs (PLoP2012).

Shimomukai, E., Nakamura, S. and Iba, T. (2015), Change Making Patterns: A Pattern Language for Fostering Social Entrepreneurship, CreativeShift Lab.

The Cooking Language: Applying the Theory of Patterns into Cooking

Isaku, Taichi
Keio University, Japan
tisaku@sfc.keio.ac.jp

Kubonaga, Emi
Keio University, Japan
gyorome@gmail.com

Iba, Takashi
Keio University, Japan
iba@sfc.keio.ac.jp

This paper will introduce a new concept that we call the Cooking Language. This is a new method to understand cooking, derived from the idea of patterns, which provides its users with a new approach to cooking. The Cooking Language is a collection of sublanguages that each focuses on a certain food item, which contains cooking words that describes the food item's functions in a pattern-like manner. Users can use the cooking words as sources for ideas, guidelines for making decisions while cooking, and as a tool to understand recipes and dishes made by other people. As our first set of a Cooking Language we will present the Egg Language with 19 egg words. In the course of creating the language, we have made further discoveries which include the possibility for Cooking Properties and using the cooking words as a tool for scribing out and understanding culture.

Pattern language, cooking, creativity, recipe, culture

1. Introduction

TIn this paper we will introduce a new concept that we call the *Cooking Language*. This is a new method to understand cooking derived from the idea of pattern languages. Cooking, though a widespread conception as a profession exists, is the simplest form of creation that we can experience in our daily lives. If more people become able to cook, it should raise the creative level of the whole society.

When we cook, in many cases we start with a recipe. However, cooking often requires an aesthetic sense, and this kind of knowledge is rarely written in recipes. The *Cooking Language* is a more flexible method to capture this knowledge for a creative and dynamic cooking process. As our first set of a *Cooking Language* we will present the Egg Language that shares the knowledge of cooking with eggs.

2. Background

Cooking has always been a part of the human culture as we flourished on this planet. With both the aspect of survival and pleasure, food and cooking has always been something that us humans were attracted to. Through cooking was how we learned how to use tools, and some even argue that it is our ability to cook that separated us from the rest of the animals [1]. A few thousand years later today, we have a much different view on food and cooking. Though it still continues to be an essential part of our daily lives, thanks to industrialization, much less people cook today than we used to. In our highly organized and sophisticated culture, many food preparations are done inside factories where most of us do not know what happens. Here, every ingredient is perfectly controlled and measured, bringing us the same taste that we love every time. Cheap and tasty (but not necessarily healthy) food has become an essential part of the human culture, excluding more and more people out from the kitchen.

Otherwise, many people consider cooking in the kitchen as a household chore, a profession, or a hobby. It is an activity for someone who is highly concerned about their health, someone who is in need of a sustainable way of feeding themselves and their family, or someone who can purely enjoy the joy of cooking. Nonetheless, many of us still understand the importance of cooking for ourselves from nutritional and economical reasons, but are faced with the challenge of skill in the kitchen. In these situations, the most useful and convenient aid that they can find will be the recipe. But recipes themselves face many difficulties in increasing the literacy for cooking.

2.1 Previous Work

This is part three of our series of papers that explore for a new methodology for cooking. In a previous paper [2] we have applied the method of pattern language into cooking to accomplish a similar challenge of supporting people's creative processes in the kitchen. To explain briefly, the paper introduced a method using patterns called the Generative Cooking Approach, which writes patterns that capture the condition of the dish using one or more of the five senses, and then provides the cook with actions that she can take to take the dish to a different condition. The chain action of the patterns will guide the dish through a process of piecemeal growth, ultimately resulting in a tasteful dish.

Though this method is useful to some extent, we found out that the approach alone was not sufficient to gain the skills of cooking. The patterns in this collection were focused too much around the actual actions that are being taken while cooking (for example, "stir the ingredients so they don't stick to the pan"). These patterns were useful in knowing when to do what while cooking on a technical aspect, but it would not give ideas to its users on what to cook based on the ingredients available, nor how to make the dish tastier from its current condition. Therefore, it was helpful for its users to better understand a certain recipe on why a certain step should be done, but the patterns itself were not sufficient for people to put down the recipe book. And besides, most of these techniques that were captured with these patterns already had their own names that many recipes used as common language. These findings were important for us to take the next step in our inquiry for cooking patterns.

In a different paper [3] we introduced a pattern language for a collaborative cooking session. These patterns focused more on the social aspects of cooking, and contained patterns that would enhance communication and ideas in the kitchen. This was due to our decision that the Generative Cooking patterns focused too much on the mere ingredients, and we needed a system of supporting the human side of cooking. We feel these patterns were successful in creating a social environment that would help people cook more easily and more often. However, the fundamental problems we faced in the first paper were not resolved in the sense that we left teaching cooking skills to the beginning cooks in the hands of skilled cooks, and did not give a systematic methodology of doing so. Hence, we are back to technical side of cooking again in this paper.

With the combination with these past works, we believe the *Cooking Language* will provide a better and holistic approach to cooking that would overcome the difficulties that recipes face, which we will describe in the next section.

3. Limitation of Recipes

Our challenge is to make a new system of sharing knowledge of cooking that would replace the recipe. A recipe looks somewhat like what is shown in Figure 1. It tells its users the name of the dish they are about to make, ingredients and their amounts that they would need to collect, and the steps they would need to follow. When done exactly as instructed, the cook should end up with a dish somewhat close to that pictured in the photograph.

Figure 1: A typical recipe.

Though recipes seem to be the perfect and only way to scribe out the knowledge about how food is made, the method still faces some challenges. The first is that when many of us cook, we often don't actually use a recipe. Experienced cooks can open the refrigerator to see what's inside, and start to imagine what can be cooked from it. Even while cooking, they use their five senses to capture the condition of the dish, and take necessary acts to drive the dish to a completion. This on-the-spot knowledge is based on experience, and is rarely written down. Though recipes may guide a beginning cook through a series of steps to make a certain dish, it is up to them to make connections with other recipes and to transpose the knowledge to other situations. Below we will highlight some aspects of recipes that cause this to happen in detail. These points of argument are already made in our work in 2014 [2], but we saw the need to recap some arguments since they are important background information for explaining the need for the *Cooking Language*.

3.1 Rigid Contexts

There is one inevitable flaw that all recipes have: they cannot accommodate for each specific circumstance. You forgot to buy butter; you only had two eggs in the refrigerator while the recipe requires three; you want to use up all the milk today before it expires. Recipes often implicitly demand that the kitchen be in a somewhat perfect condition where supplies and ingredients are sufficiently provided. If a chef cannot meet the right conditions, then it is only up to him to overcome these difficulties.

3.2 Unwritten Tacit Knowledge

Another thing that recipes require us: perfection. Situations occur when we put too much of a condiment into the pot, or when we mistake the order which to cook the ingredients. Ways to overcome these mistakes are rarely addressed in the recipe itself. Experienced cooks have knowledge from the past, so usually these situations do not become too much of a problem for them. However, this knowledge from experience is mostly tacit and rarely are they written down. Seen from a beginner, it is these unwritten parts that are making cooking seem hard and mystical for them.

3.3 Possibilities of Variations

When a chef cooks a recipe, very often he makes some alterations to it. The very simplest form of this may be scaling a recipe to make the right amount needed for the night. Advanced variations of the meal can occur at all kinds of levels: using a different kind of meat, adding an extra vegetable, baking the dish instead of frying it, etc. There are an infinite number of variations that a single recipe could have, but ideas for it all depends on the chef's inspirations. These ideas are based on the chef's past experiences of cooking and eating different kinds of foods, and, again, is something that is tacit and unwritten.

3.4 Knowledge Beyond Recipes

One last point of consideration as a limitation of recipes: many of us, when we cook, do not need a recipe. There are many people who can just go shopping, buy ingredients, and cook their favorite dish all without any form of a written recipe. There are others who can open the refrigerator to see what's inside, and then image what can be cooked from it. This kind of cooking often results in a delicious yet nameless dish. It may be the first time that the person cooks the dish, and also the last. The specific ingredients that were available at the time had lead to the one-time-only dish. And of course, a written recipe does not exist for this specific dish.

3.5 The General Problem

These aspects suggest one simple idea: totalitarian order may not be the only answer to good taste. Christopher Alexander, the father of pattern languages, makes a similar argument in his books by criticizing the master plan [4]. Both the master plan in architecture and the recipe in cooking can be said to be representative of the modern industrialized society.

In efforts to optimize production with low costs and less labor, they have lost somewhat an important idea behind houses and food. If people were just taught to read and follow directions on how to cook, the essential principles behind the design process will become lost.

This may be bringing up something more than just a problem in architecture or cooking. Reading and following manuals is something that is done widespread in business and educational contexts. If the mere following of directions is what becomes valued, then we are left with people who do not think for themselves. Efficiency is definitely one important factor in the growing economy, and recipes and manuals will continue to have its importance in many ways. However, we would like to pose another approach to cooking where efficiency is not necessarily the best approach to design and the happiness of living.

Though recipes are important sources for inspiration on what and how to cook, just following its directions would be meaningless. What a good chef has in his mind is not the teaspoons memorized, but is a framework that allows them to cook on the spot. We believe the *Cooking Language*, along with our past pattern works on cooking, will provide such a framework.

4. The Cooking Language

The *Cooking Language* is a method similar to patterns in the sense that it captures relationships that the ingredients inside a dish make with unique names. The *Cooking Language* is composed by a subset of languages that each focus on a certain ingredient e.g. *Egg Language*, *Onion Language*, *Tofu Language*, etc. Its ontology is described in Figure 2 below.

Inside each subset language, there is a collection of *cooking words* for the specific ingredient. Here, the parallel can be made where [Cooking Language] is to [Cooking Words] as [pattern language] is to [patterns]. Each *cooking word* captures an aspect of how the ingredient can be used in a dish, and how it interacts with other ingredients. For example, from the *Egg Language* introduced in this paper, there is a *cooking word* that refers to when eggs are added to a spicy or strongly flavored dish to make its taste milder, and is given the name Taste *Mitigation*. Similarly, the few dozen *cooking words* in the language each capture attributes of eggs within a dish.

The Cooking Language: Applying the Theory of Patterns into Cooking

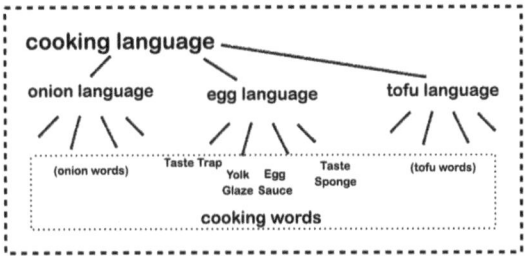

Figure 2: The ontology of the Cooking Language.

Each *cooking word* is written in a rather simple format: it has the *name*, the *context* that the word can be used in, and the *idea* or the actual actions that can be taken to change the state of a dish. Along with this there is a list of sample dishes that use the ingredient in the way it is described in the *cooking word*, an photo of a dish that shows the *cooking word* being used, and an *image illustration* that gives an iconic image of the idea described. A sample page spread from the *Egg Language* we will introduce in the next section can be seen in figure 3 to get an idea how the *Cooking Language* will be like in print. Unlike Alexander's patterns [5], the *cooking word*s are written in a short and simple format since cooking is rather a rapid action, and requires multiple *cooking word*s to be used in a short period of time. Each *cooking word* must be easily understandable and memorable.

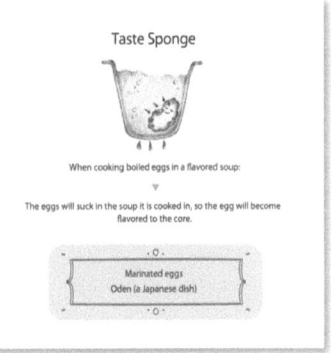

Figure 3: Sample page spread of the Cooking Language book.

241

4.1 Creating the Egg Language

As our first attempt at creating a *Cooking Language*, we have made the *Egg Language*. The *Egg Language* consists of 19 *cooking word*s (or egg words) regarding the use of eggs in cooking. This language was made by analyzing several recipes using eggs by writing out how the egg was used in the recipe, or how it was contributing to the dish, whether taste-wise or function-wise, on index cards. The few dozen index cards were then organized and categorized by similarity using the KJ Method (also known as the Affinity Diagram), a method somewhat similar to the Grounded Theory. This resulted in 19 functions that eggs serve dishes. Each of these 19 categories were described in the *cooking word* format, and then was given a name, an illustration, and a picture to go along with it. A similar process can be taken for any particular food item to create a language for the item.

4.2 The Egg Language

Figure 4 shows the list of the 19 *egg words* from the *Egg Language*. In addition, Table 1 lists the description of all 19 *egg words* in an abstract.

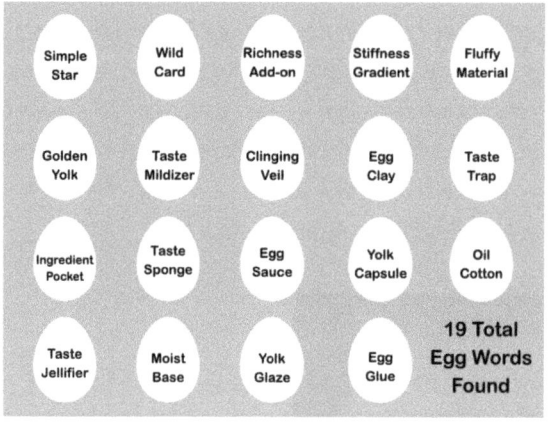

Figure 4: Sample page spread of the Cooking Language book.

Name	Explanation	Sample Dishes
Simple Star	Eggs can become a simple but tasty main plate by itself.	Scrambled eggs, Boiled eggs, Sunny-side up, etc.
Wild Card Ingredient	Eggs go along well with any other ingredient.	Omelets, soups, etc.

Richness Addition	Eggs add richness to the taste of a dish.	Carbonara sauce
Solidity Gradient	The stiffness of an egg can be controlled based on the cooking time.	Boiled eggs of different stiffness
Fluffy Material	Eggs can be used as an ingredient with a fluffy texture	Scrambled eggs
Golden Yolk	The golden color of the yolk adds a visual specialty to the dish.	Sunny-side up
Taste Mitigation	By adding an egg, spicy or strong tastes can be made mild.	Sun Du Bu (a spicy Korean chili soup where raw eggs are added to make it less spicy)
Clinging Veil	Eggs add a veil with a soft texture to a larger ingredient.	Tonkatsu Bowl (a Japanese dish where pork cutlets are cooked with eggs)
Egg Clay	Since eggs start as a liquid and then solidify, it can be molded into any shape.	Omelets, scrambled eggs, etc.
Taste Trap	A liquid condiment can be mixed into the egg before it is cooked and hardened.	Puddings (milk, vanilla, etc. are trapped inside the egg)
Ingredient Pocket	Small pieces of meats and vegetables can be mixed into the egg to be cooked together. The resulting dish will hold in the ingredients inside the cooked egg.	Omelets with other ingredients inside
Taste Sponge	When boiled eggs are cooked in a soup, some of the taste from the soup gets sucked into the egg.	Boiled eggs cooked in soup
Egg Sauce	Eggs can be used as a sauce for bread, pasta, etc.	Mayonnaise
Yolk Capsule	Eggs can be cooked so that the outside is hardened but the inside yolk is still a liquid.	Poached eggs
Oil Cotton	Eggs suck in oil to make the surface browned and crunchy when cooked.	Omelets
Taste Jellifier	Eggs can be used to set liquids to a soft solid.	Puddings
Moist Cake	Eggs add the soft and moist texture to pastries	Cakes
Glazing Yolk	By painting a layer of yolk on top of pastries, it adds a glazing effect when baked.	Pies
Egg Glue	Eggs can be used as a "glue" that holds several ingredients together	Meat patties

Table 1: List of the 19 egg words from the Egg Language

5. Using the Cooking Language

There are several ways that the Cooking Language can be used in. Its uses are listed in the subsections below. Note that rather than just the *Egg Language*, the Cooking Language will have the best outcome when there are multiple languages that for several different food items.

5.1 Source of Ideas

By having the *cooking word*s in mind, a person will be able to cook in a more creative and dynamic matter. For example, if I open the refrigerator to find some eggs and bell peppers, I can combine *cooking word*s from the *Egg language* and the *Bell Pepper Language* to imagine what I can cook from what's available.

5.2 Guideline for Making Kitchen Decisions

During the actual cooking process too, the *cooking word*s will become a source for ideas to add an extra ingredient. For example, I could be cooking a totally different dish that usually doesn't use eggs, but if I feel like the taste is too bold, I can get the idea "oh I can add an egg to this dish as a *Taste Mitigation* to adjust its taste." Likewise the *cooking word*s will become a source for help to prevent or solve any problems that come up during cooking.

5.3 Decoding Recipes and Understanding Completed Dishes

In addition to this, the *cooking word*s will also become a tool to understand recipes and dishes by other people. When a person with the *Cooking Language* in mind reads a recipe, she would be able to recognize some *cooking word*s used in the recipe. This would help her understand the recipe better by realizing why a step or an ingredient exists in the recipe. Based on this, she would become able to make some alterations based on her needs. Also, when a person with who knows the *Cooking Language* eats a dish that someone else has made for her, she will be able to recognize some *cooking word*s existent in the dish. In other words, she would become able to understand why the dish tastes good. By understanding the dish better, she would be able to learn from it and use the same techniques when she cooks a similar dish in the future.

6. Referring Back to Alexander

Up to this point, we have made our discussions on the Cooking Language based on Alexander's method of pattern languages. Before we end the paper, we would also like to take a look at Alexander's other important concept: the theory of *Wholeness* and *centers*.

6.1 The Idea of Wholeness and Centers

Alexander described his ideas of *Wholeness* and centers in his later work *The Nature of Order* [7]. According to the book *Wholeness* is a "system of centers enforcing one another through connection and overlap," where centers are defined as "a physical system that occupies space with a specially marked coherence." Alexander says that centers exist chiefly in relation to the Wholeness. This *Wholeness* is what Alexander used to call the *Quality Without a Name* (QWAN) that is existent among architecture that gives humans a comfortable feeling. Though Alexander had concluded that the QWAN couldn't be directly captured and scribed out, physical patterns of objects that occur when the quality exists can be. By cutting these elements out as patterns, a collection of patterns that are interrelated as a language can be made. By practicing and applying the patterns properly, the quality can be approached again.

6.2 Application to Cooking

Like pattern languages and the fundamental properties by Alexander, the Cooking Language is a method to approach some quality - in this case, a dish that tastes good. Hence, in the context of cooking, we can interpret the *Wholeness* as the dish and the centers as the ingredients, where the ingredients exist chiefly in relation to the dish. This is visualized in Figure 5 with the case of beef stew. Here we can see the ingredients defining the dish, while the dish is defining the roles of the ingredients.

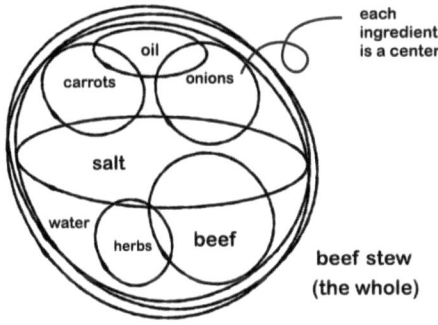

Figure 5: The relationship between the dish (the whole) and the ingredients (the centers)

6.3 A Different Definition of the Cooking Language

Extending on the parallel between patterns and *cooking words*, we can provide a different approach to understanding the Cooking Language. In the context of *Wholeness* and *centers*,

Alexander redefines *patterns* as "rules for creating a new living center to enforce the Whole." Applying the parallel we made in 6.1, we can re-read for our new definition of *cooking words*: *rules for creating a new living center (of ingredients) to enforce the Whole of the dish.*

7. Future Work

The application of the concept of *Wholeness* and *centers* brings up a potential for some future work. We would like to finish off by elaborating on these possibilities for future work.

7.1 Possibility for Cooking Properties

In the *Nature of Order*, Christopher Alexander also defines an idea called *Properties*, which are "structural features that are recurrent among things with a Wholeness that show how centers enforce one another." He lists the *15 Fundamental Properties* that he has found in the Architectural world. Making the parallel again, we come to a new concept which we can call the *Cooking Properties* with the definition: *structural features that are recurrent among delicious dishes that show how ingredients enforce one another*.

As we can see the simplest form of future fork for this study as making more sublanguages of Cooking Languages (the *Onion Language, Tofu Language, Soy Sauce Language*, etc.), the idea of *Cooking Properties* gives us an insight for even further work. When several sublanguages start to exist, we should start to see structural similarities among the cooking words in the different sublanguages (described in Figure 6). We can abstract these similar *cooking word*s to get our *Cooking Properties*.

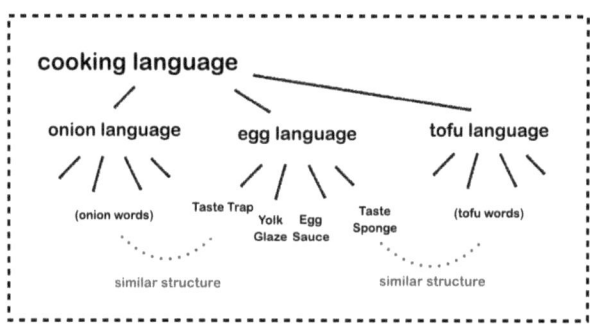

Figure 6: Recurrent structures can be found among different cooking sublanguages.

7.2 Exploring Cultural Aspects

When creating the Egg Language, all of the recipes that we have referenced were Japanese recipes. Hence, many of the *egg words* we have found were also cultural and characteristic of the Japanese cuisine. We saw a similar phenomenon when we have created the *Generative Cooking Patterns* where in many cases we run into patterns that do not have a significant problem section. This is because cooking is highly dependent on culture, and cultural traditions in many cases result from historical backgrounds that do not necessarily have a scientific reasoning. What people say is delicious differ from culture to culture, and people cook in some ways „because it tastes good." Thus, we can say that the Egg Language presented in this paper is an *"Egg Language* for the Japanese Culture." This isn't necessarily a bad thing. As described in 7.1, we have the potential for a *Cooking Properties*. If the *cooking word*s are cultural, then the properties must have strong cultural aspects too. There fore we can create *Cooking Properties* for the Japanese cuisine, Italian cuisine, Indonesian cuisine, German cuisine, etc.. These rather abstract descriptions of features of a particular cuisine will provide a whole new set of language for understanding the culinary of a certain culture. These cultural *Cooking Properties* have many possibilities in teaching cooking and for people who are visiting and joining a new culture.

8. Conclusion

This paper introduced the method of the Cooking Language, along with its first prototype the *Egg Language*. This is a new system of knowledge sharing that could possibly replace the role of recipes by resolving its problems. In the course of its creation and by taking a parallel between Alexander's theories about Architecture and cooking, we saw many possibilities for future work that could potentially change the way people look at cooking. Our inquiry on cooking and patterns continues with our future work to come.

9. Acknowledgements

Our greatest of appreciation goes to Nanako Kono, our fourth project member who had a central role in creating the Egg Language. We would also like to express our gratitude to Midori Moniwa for providing us with the photos used in the Egg Language. Thank you.

10.References

[1] Pollan, M., Cooked: A Natural History of Transformation, Penguin Books; Reprint edition, 2014.

[2] Isaku, T., Iba, T., Towards a Pattern Language for Cooking: A Generative Approach to Cooking, 19th European Conference on Pattern Languages of Programs, 2014.

[3] Isaku, T., Iba, T., Creative CoCooking Patterns: A Pattern Language for Creative Collaborative Cooking, 20th European Conference on Pattern Languages of Programs, 2015.

[4] Alexander, C., Silverstein, M., Angel, S., Ishikawa, S., Abrams, D., The Oregon Experiment, Oxford University Press, 1975

[5] Alexander, C., A Pattern Language: Towns, Buildings, Construction, Oxford University Press, 1977.

[6] Kwakita, J., Hassou Hou, Chuko-Shinsho,1967

[7] Alexander, C. (2002). The Nature of Order: An Essay of the Art of Building and the Nature of the Universe, Book 1: The Phenomenon of Life. Berkeley, California: The Center for Environmental Structure

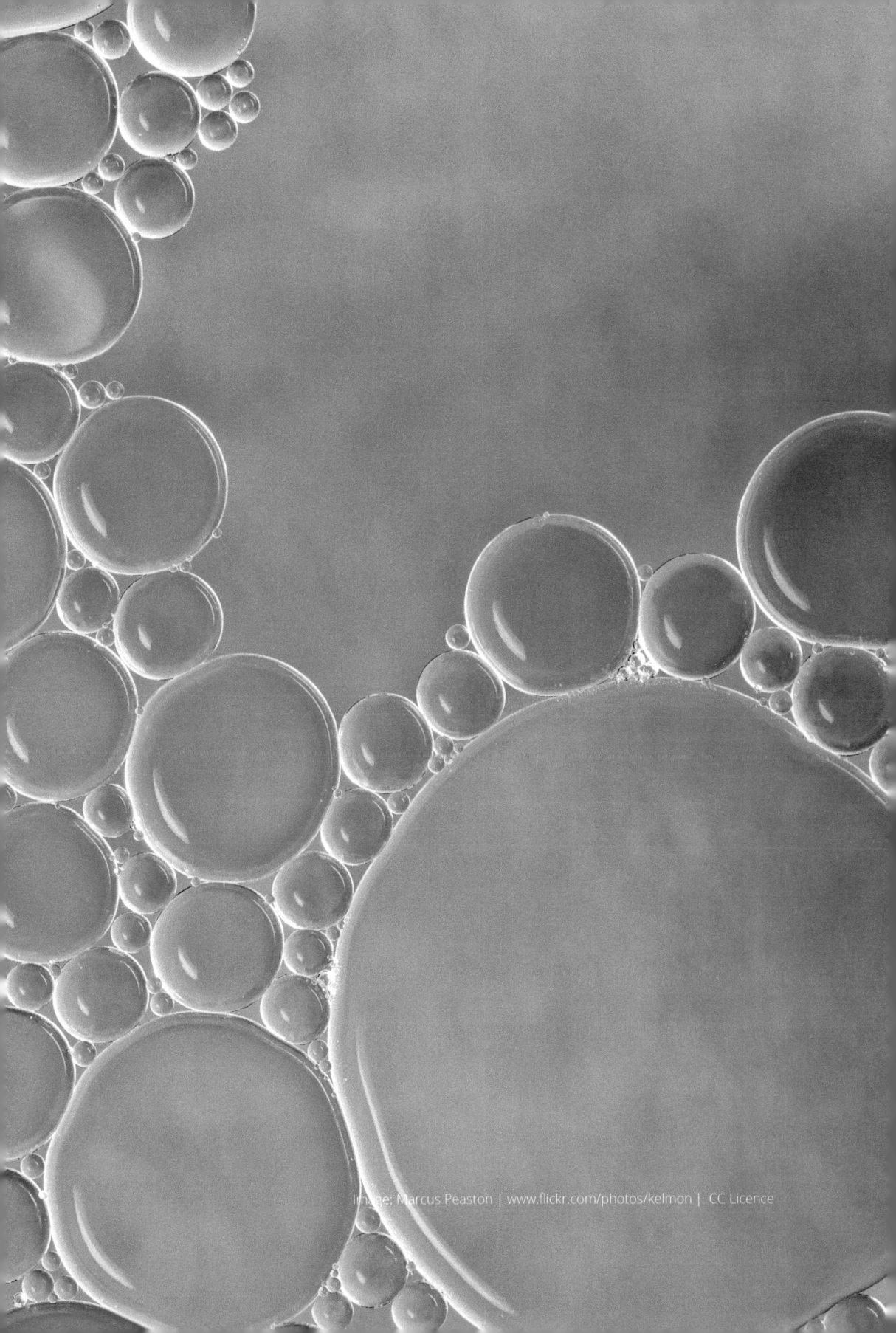
Image: Marcus Peaston | www.flickr.com/photos/kelmon | CC Licence

Fostering Changemakers with Change Making Patterns: A Conceptual Framework for Social Change and Its Educational Applications

Nakamura, Sumire
Keio Research Institute at SFC, Japan
susie002007@gmail.com

Takashi, Iba
Keio University, Japan
iba@sfc.keio.ac.jp

The purpose of this paper is to show the theoretical relation between potential attributes of changemakers and Alexander's (2002a) concept of liveliness with pedagogical approaches. First, we propose a conceptual framework of the skill sets of changemakers who embody social entrepreneurship, highlighting their awareness on intrinsic feelings, empathetic attitude, and social complexity in solving societal issues. Then we present Change Making Patterns (Shimomukai & Nakamura with Iba, 2014) as a pedagogical tool and Change Making Patterns Workbook as an approach for its practical usage (Nakamura, Shimomukai, Isaku, & Iba, 2014). These methods were applied in order to nurture such skill sets among university students through experiential learning (Kolb, 1999). Results have found that the applications has subtly amplified the participants' consciousness of their inner feelings, other people's thoughts, and social interdependency. Future work includes further defining a conceptual framework for social change and educational approaches to instill this foundation among youth.

Pattern Language; Patterns Application; Education; Social Entrepreneurship; Experiential Learning;

1. Introduction

In the 21st century, as existing institutional structures and organizations are faced with modern society's shift in technology, business, and economics, we are endangered with an increasing number of ecological and social challenges. To counteract this situation, individuals who have recognized the values of making a difference through business emerge as social entrepreneurs and take responsibility on the reinforcement of such societal issues. They solve social issues by implementing, monitoring, and evaluating the effectiveness of the selected intervention with their business model.

However, today's increasing development in technology has transformed the world into a more fast-paced society, in which traditional and hierarchical structures are being decentralized. Opportunities emerge, bringing in innovative ideas or strategies and inviting a wide range of actors to participate in a more progressive movement for creating social value. To supplement the missing forces with the impact of social change, growing amounts of social issues require not only certain people such as "social entrepreneurs" to tackle a variety of issues, but also each individual to have a social entrepreneurial mindset to acquire "social entrepreneurship" in order to make a better world (Bornstein, & Davis, 2010). In order to make social change a practice that is inclusive and accessible to any individual, research and ongoing institutions have started to focus on the mechanism between social entrepreneurship and specific cognitive, behavioral, and affective skills, examining the definition and characteristics of social entrepreneurship (Martin, & Osberg, 2007). For example, progressive institution that has established a network of leading social entrepreneurs, has launched an initiative to create a world committed and equipped to ensuring that every child masters empathy. They believe that empathy plays a crucial role in innovation, changemaking, and solving entrenched systemic problems ("Ashoka's Empathy Initiative," n.d., para.1). Acknowledging the broader feeling of empathy, scholars have attempted to explore how it may be responsible for encouraging social entrepreneurship (Miller, 2012).

Yet, there is still relatively little attention to the tools that teach such skill sets of social entrepreneurship (Shimomukai, & Iba, 2012). Faced with emerging social issues, we need to experiment and further investigate the methods and educational approaches to nurture changemakers who embody the skills and characteristics for creating solutions against social issues that predominate our society.

This paper suggests a conceptual way of perceiving the changemaking skill sets and pedagogical approaches to foster such attitude that equips degree of life. We present the theoretical view of changemaking by looking into the internal motivation, altruistic attitude, and the global view for creating social value. As a tool to cultivate these skill sets, Change Making Patterns, a pattern language created based on the tacit knowledge of social entrepreneurs, was applied in a study tour where participants learn the wisdom of changemaking through practical experiences. The objective, program content, and results of the study tour are elaborated along with the process and workshop activity examples.

2. Conceptual Framework Introduction for Social Change

This chapter examines three domain of qualities on how social entrepreneurs become lively in modern days to tackle societal issues in relation to emotional and cognitive attributes. Noting Alexander's (2002a) theoretical steps in defining buildings with life, we organize three essential skills for developing the consciousness on self, others, and outer world that are personified by social entrepreneurs and necessary to foster engaged changemakers who are prepared to create social values.

2.1 Self Awareness

Since society is being continuously re-created, for good or ill, by its members, this fact will strike some as a burdensome responsibility, but it will appoint others to greatness as agents for change (Gardner, 1964). These individuals enter the journey of social change from working on themselves, and observing why they need to change the society is essential in creating a lasting force to propel actions. Identifying and looking closely to one's motivation and past experiences that ignite their actions, changemakers can be authentic to oneself. This can also be said to identifying one's motivation for change. Once the individual has a keen understanding of himself, he will be best equipped to identify the relatable social issues that would provide him with a great sense of fulfillment to work toward solving, and be well matched to his unique talents and personality (Vasan, & Przybylo, 2013). In addition, changemakers score high on the quality of "inner locus of control," locating power within, rather than outside, themselves (Bornstein, & Davis, 2010). This implies that agents who practice social entrepreneurship entail high degrees of self-awareness about their emotions and have great certainty about their motivation whenever encountering a social issue. Alexander (2002a) strengthens these statements by pointing out that the degree of life is interconnected with human feelings and it is the increased amount that gives human the sense of value (p. 308). Thus, changemakers are aware of their great feelings when attached with a social issue, to the extent that they inevitably generate thoughts and actions for constructing a solution.

2.2 Empathy

Though ever daunting and tough, changemakers' mindset to transform their emotions into power for a better world ignites their liveliness when trying to reach their highest-held values of acting on social good. Social entrepreneurship is one of the practices on altruism, where individuals who desire to be involved in the social progress movement are those who become alive by meeting their needs to achieve and to create a better world (Martin, & Osberg, 2007). Change agents see the struggles of their targeted group, thus take initiative in its alleviation even with limited resources and faced with the status quo. The comprehension of one's struggles is part of showing empathy, understanding other's feelings and thoughts. Not only will this skill help them facilitate their motivation on the good cause, but also attract support on their projects. Alexander (2002a) notes that, human feelings is mostly the same from person to person, in every person (p. 4). When these feelings are shared, coined as empathy, this will enable individuals to understand other's feelings. And as human share the same feelings, human can naturally develop empathy. Therefore, changemakers enhance their liveliness when feeling for their targeted group, identifying its inequality or unjust, and trying to create any solution that benefits it.

2.3 Social Interdependency

Social entrepreneurs are also individuals who see social problems consisted of components of larger but less visible structures that affect each other, especially in an intertwined world. Acknowledging that social issues cannot be solved with a single-dimension perspective, changemakers take a step back and observe with various viewpoints on the social issue they are dealing with. Rather than seeing the social issue in a unilateral perspective, they observe the complex interconnected relationship of cause and effect and define the most effective approach in solving the issue. In this scope of understanding both the interdependence and individual elements, changemakers develop awareness of the interdependencies between their actions and possible outcomes. Change agents understand the system in which they operate and the consequences after they take actions. They are prepared to face the counter-intuitive results after taking action. This awareness of social interdependency, and contemplating on the actions as part of the larger system, matches with Alexander's (2002a) viewpoint that we cannot see the connection unless we are conscious and willing that what we make is indistinguishable and inseparable from its surroundings (p. 233). With this regard, when this attribute of acknowledging the interconnection of society and the course of actions is obtained, change agents can feel the liveliness in themselves.

2.4 Three Domains for Social Change

Having a high level of self-awareness of oneself, seeing things from other people's perspectives, and perceiving the social interdependency of actions and consequences, are all required aspects to become designers with life who can create effective solutions to societal issues. These three skills fit to Triple Focus: focusing on the inner state, tuning in to others, and understanding the larger world (Goleman, & Senge, 2014). In respect of this idea, each inner tool that is introduced to survive today's world, can be represented with each domain accordingly; inner focus being self-awareness, other focus being empathetic to others, and outer focus to see the dynamics of the social issue. Tuning into ourselves require inner work, the deep reflection on our beliefs and values during the struggles of combating societal issues. This promotes the awareness of the emotions and thoughts that connect to the purposes for taking actions for social good. The second focus is working towards others, cultivating the sense of compassion and care for others. Not only understanding and feeling about them, but also having the willingness to extend your range of helpful acts. This attention invites others to the margins of a warm atmosphere and building a culture of helping each other. The third focus is systems awareness with the habits of identifying the circular nature of complex cause and effect relationships. This framework of thinking could be explained as a discipline that encapsulates attuned thinkers to the interrelationships among nature, other people, emotions, and thoughts, and themselves (Senge, et al., 2012). Echoing this remark, the three skill sets of changemaking is in alignment with the skills of triple focus - focusing on their inner state, tuning in to others, and understanding the larger world. When social catalysts are aware of the overlapping needs from self, others, and society, they can identify the relationship between their own fulfillment and their target's or society's fulfillment that generates wholeness within all three sides. Alexander (2002a) states:

As a maker of buildings, I simply have the task of making something which creates this happiness in all of us. The nature of the wholeness is such that, when it makes this happiness in me, it also makes it in anyone else who comes in touch with it. (p. 308)

This can also be employed for change agents acting as designers whose happiness is to make a difference in society, ultimately being the happiness of the people involved in their project. Changemakers benefit not only from satisfying their self-interests but also from meeting the demands of others and society.

3. Change Making Patterns

What are the tools to spread this conceptual framework that most social entrepreneurs posses in pedagogical circumstances? In effort to suggest an idea for this underlying question, Change Making Patterns was created based on pattern language, so that the essence and wisdom of social entrepreneurship can be shared among future agents to create their ideal change. The 31 patterns show how "changemakers" identify social issues and create or implement solutions and then scale the solutions to alleviate the issues (Shimomukai, & Iba, 2012). We present an overview of the patterns by organizing them with the conceptual framework for social change.

3.1 Creation Process

In order to encompass more young forces into social change, the hidden wisdom of changemakers were needed to be articulated in a sharable way. We have adopted the pattern language method, which Christopher Alexander, an architect, proposed in order to describe the tacit knowledge of local acts and create global order (Alexander, et al., 1977). A pattern language is composed by a number of elements called patterns. Each pattern is written in a set of a format which consists of a name, a context, a problem which occurs consecutively in a certain context, a force as a premise that causes the problem, a solution, and a action of the pattern. We have mined the patterns first through interviews with Japanese social entrepreneurs, who were role models of creating solutions to social issues in various domains (Shimomukai, & Iba, 2012). After clustering the elements of the extracted tacit knowledge, 31 patterns were formed. Though the initial version of the patterns were called Social Entrepreneurship Patterns, we have revised its name to Change Making Patterns, so that we prevent readers to associate the patterns with business model learning materials and involve a wider range of interested individuals.

3.2 Classification with the Conceptual Framework

Since Change Making Patterns were created from the wisdom of leading social entrepreneurs, they account for the characteristics and skill sets for future change agents to follow the experts' lead. Based on our examination of the conceptual framework for social change, Figure 1 illustrates the patterns, which are organized in three domains: self-awareness, empathy, and social interdependency. Each pattern description was closely observed in order to place it under the three categories. This overall structure of Change Making Patterns can help the readers identify each pattern's role in enhancing the skills needed for changemaking.

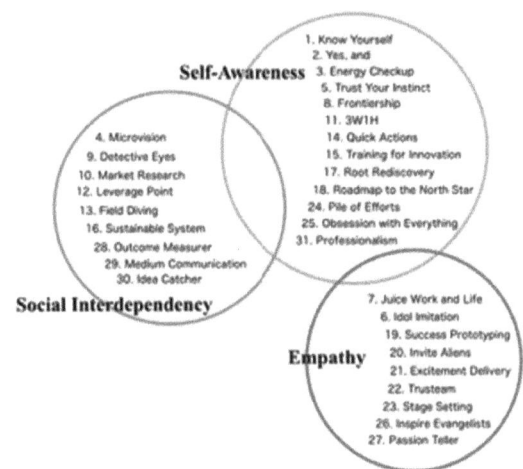

Figure 1: Overall Structure of Change Making Patterns.

4. Application to Workbooks and Workshops

Though the set of Change Making Patterns exhibit and share the wisdom of changemaking, many readers had limitations on the practical application to their daily lives. The patterns became a reading material rather a tool for encouraging the readers to take action step by step, and actually embody the skills. In order to cultivate the changemaking skills from experiential learning (Kolb, 1999), we extended the pattern language into action-forwarding structure for the readers, which is Change Making Patterns Workbook, a notebook to deepen the readers' understanding on the pattern description, associated with a sequences of workshops in a study tour to the Philippines (Nakamura, Shimomukai, Isaku, & Iba, 2014).

The remaining of the section will report on the content and format of Change Making Patterns Workbook, and workshop examples that were conducted in the study tour. Additionally, we introduce the objectives and itinerary of the study tour program, along with an analysis of results gained from pattern workbook-based workshops.

4.1 Change Making Patterns Workbook

Change Making Patterns Workbook was created to intensify future change agent's experience with Change Making Patterns (Nakamura, Shimomukai, Isaku, & Iba, 2014). While the readers were exposed to the literature of social entrepreneurship, we thought the need to create a more useful and encouraging notebook where anyone can apply the learnings to their day to day lives and start their own changemaking project. Therefore, Change Making Patterns Workbook was created as a new approach for a practical use of Change Making Patterns, which included 31 independent activities made accordingly to the pattern description to deepen the readers' understanding of the pattern. As Figure 2 shows, the pattern content is on the left page, and on the right, we included WORK as activities where a problem statement is presented to the readers to answer by themselves in their scope of interests. On the bottom of the right page, CHECKPOINT was added, which is an explanation of a life story from changemakers who exemplify the pattern in their project or business. These stories were excerpted from the interviews during the mining process of the patterns.

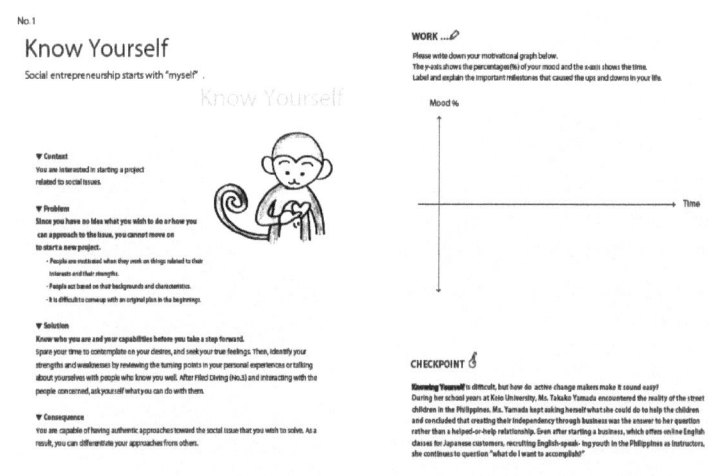

Figure 2: Layout of the pages of Change Making Patterns Workbook. The pattern description is on the left page. The right page contains WORK and CHECKPOINT.

4.2 Philippines Study Tour

The workbook was effective where readers go through a thought process of their own social project but limited the readers' actions once they have insights from their workbook. With this regard, in February, 2014, we conducted a study tour in the Philippines using Change Making Patterns Workbook. During the program, the participants were guided through the workbook-workshop cycle using Change Making Patterns Workbook. We conducted a line of workshops in the program to test the effectiveness of the practical usage of the workbook (Nakamura, Shimomukai, Isaku, & Iba, (2014). Aiming to foster social entrepreneurship with hands-on experience among the participants, the program content was designed, aligning the activities in Change Making Patterns Workbook. Each day, the participants learned the content of the patterns through collaborative workshops and a set of discussions.

In the following section, we will trace the program by highlighting the objective of the overall study tour and workshops that constitute the program. The workshops were designed centered to the corresponding activities illustrated in the workbook pages based on the itinerary. With the help of a facilitator, the participants filled in the sections together and shared the results with one another.

4.2.1 Objective and Workshop Details

The objective of the study tour was to help participants learn about social entrepreneurship and to start their own personal project through hands-on experience using Change Making Patterns Workbook. Conducted in Cebu City and Manila City in the Philippines, the study tour offered the participants the basic knowledge and theory of social entrepreneurship. The program also conducted joint workshops with Filipino students and a Japanese changemaker who had been actively involved in creating social change in the area. Eight students from S.A.L., a Japanese student group in Keio University, aiming to enhance awareness on international issues, also participated. The program was facilitated by one of the authors and invited a local social entrepreneur for mentorship, and the students had an opportunity to study closely how social entrepreneurs creatively solves social issues in Cebu. They were to learn the efforts and the real challenges of creating a difference in the community and find their own way to act on problems in their community. Through interactive workshops, dialogues, fieldwork, and group work using Change Making Patterns Workbook, the study tour aimed to inspire the Japanese students and Filipino youth to create an action plan for their project.

The program was conducted for 10 consecutive days - 7 days in Cebu City and 3 days in Manila City. Figure 3 shows the itinerary of the study tour in the Philippines. It includes some patterns from each category of the conceptual framework aiming to infuse the participants with self-awareness that drives inner focus, empathy for tuning into others, and seeing the whole picture of social issue with outer focus. Workshops were conducted based on this itinerary that were oriented with the activities in the workbook. In the next section, we provide examples of the workshops, together with the pattern description and activities.

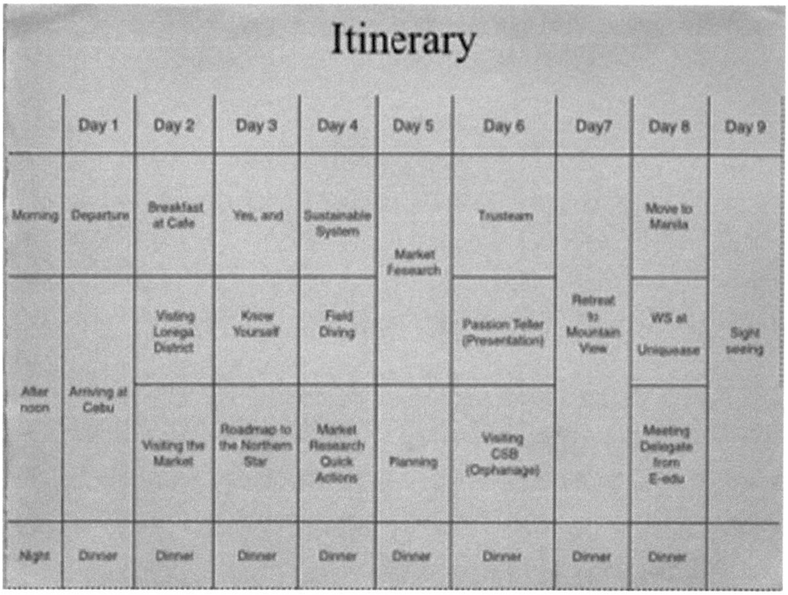

Itinerary

	Day 1	Day 2	Day 3	Day 4	Day 5	Day 6	Day7	Day 8	Day 9
Morning	Departure	Breakfast at Cafe	Yes, and	Sustainable System	Market Fesearch	Trusteam	Retreat to Mountain View	Move to Manila	Sight seeing
After noon	Arriving at Cebu	Visiting Lorega District	Know Yourself	Field Diving		Passion Teller (Presentation)		WS at Uniqueease	
		Visiting the Market	Roadmap to the Northern Star	Market Research Quick Actions	Planning	Visiting CSB (Orphanage)		Meeting Delegate from E-edu	
Night	Dinner	Dinner	Dinner	Dinner	Dinner	Dinner	Dinner	Dinner	

Figure 3: Study tour itinerary, which shows the activities in Change Making Patterns Workbook.

4.2.2 Example Actives from Workshops

Know Yourself

Pattern Description: Know who you are and your capabilities before you take a step forward.
Work: Draw a timeline of events in your life.

This workshop was held early in the program as an icebreaker. The goal was for the participants to know themselves and each other better for the days to come. As we can see in Figure 4, each student wrote a motivational graph outlining their life story, reflecting on the ups and downs of their past experiences. In attempt to disclose their life events to other members, they were put into groups of 4 or 5 to share their life stories in dialogues. Followed by narrative storytelling, not only did the students became aware of their feelings and thoughts toward their life events, but also obtained additional discoveries on themselves through other participants' eyes. Encouraging the students to sharing their past experiences, the workshop played a role in building an intimate atmosphere, influencing them to create a sense of belonging to the group for later workshops.

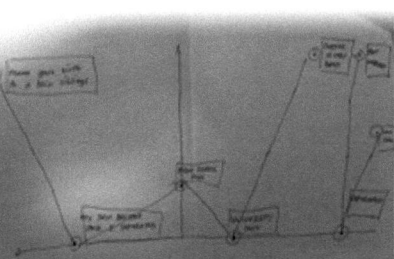

Figure 4: Know Yourself: Student reflecting on their life history (left) and a motivational graph written by one of the participants (right).

Market Research

Pattern Description: Research the background of the issue.
Work: Use various research methodologies to find out the background of the issue.

This activity helped the participants learn about the market on which their changemaking project is conducted. As different ideas for their project emerged in the previous workshops, the students were divided into two teams. One team decided to create a bar business in order to provide career opportunities for youth who are in underserved situations. As in Figure 5, the pattern activity lead the team to obtain the data so that they can learn about the background of opening a bar business through fieldwork, getting some numbers and reliable information. Members went out to identify numbers of the average alcohol expenses and the number of potential customers. However, as members conducted interviews to people on the street, they found out that most of people don't go to bars especially because they are busy with work and parenting. Another insight was that most of the young people go out at night at a certain time period. This navigated the team to reconsider their next step after encountering unexpected facts aside from their initial strategy, and ushered them to grasp the background of their target market.

Figure 5: Market Research: Students looking for useful resources for their changemaking project.

Passion Teller

Pattern Description: Express your experience with the social issue, addressing what you have felt and seen.
Work: Tell your challenge, the things you have seen, and your vision as a story so more people empathize with your project.

We concluded the study tour with a presentation of the social business model that the students have created in front of an audience of students and a local social entrepreneur. In Figure 6, Passion Teller was applied to this workshop so that the students can express their experiences throughout the activities in order to infuse the audience with empathy. Each team presented their motivation towards their changemaking project, the findings they have discovered through various types of research, and expectations after the actual implementation. This activity brought up several inquires, gaining the attention and interests of the audience. Additional remarks were made by the teams on their hardships of overcoming the language barrier among the group members, excitement for gathering resources through fieldwork in attempt to try new things that they would have never do in their normal lives, and the sense of unity within each team.

Figure 6: Passion Teller: Students presenting their social business plan to the audience.

4.2.3 Results

Shown in Figure 7, the accumulation of intensive workshop activities propelled the teams to create preliminary models of a social business. Both of the changemaking projects were reviewed each day during the study tour and have went through many trial and errors after conducing several activities based on Change Making Patterns Workbook. Carefully learning the pattern content one after another, each group successfully shaped their seeds of changemaking project: Waku Mama Bar, a small business that offers job opportunities for local youth for their school tuition, and T-shirt printing service, an ongoing business to flourish women entrepreneurship. Each project included the concept, organizational structure, advertisement of their project, and calculation of money flow stemming from survey facts in their targeted market.

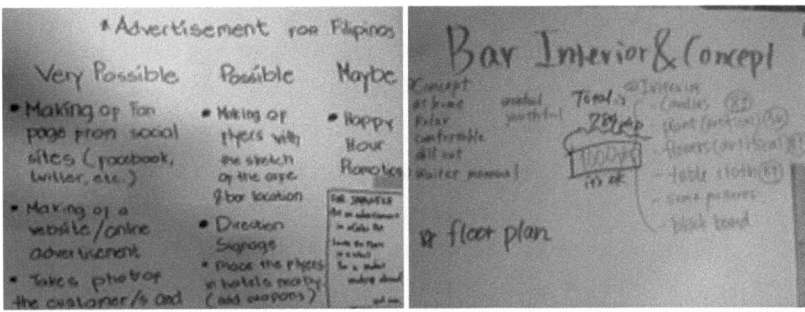

Figure 7: Advertisement plan for T-shirt printing service (left) and interior and concept plan for Waku Mama Bar (right).

At the end of the study tour, each Japanese student created his/her own action plan using Change Making Patterns. Since the objective of the study tour was to learn social entrepreneurship and create their own personal project, the students freely showed their personal thoughts and findings on their overall experience. The pattern names were used directly in the action plan in hopes to integrate the pattern content and knowledge into their daily lives. Below are some of the participants's voices from the submitted action plans, where pattern names are described in bold. These action plans were collected in Japanese, and then translated into English by the authors. We present the participants' comments along with the analysis on the three domain of skills of changemaking.

> *Having some difficulties in expressing my opinion and showing initiative in discussions with the Filipino youth, I realized that I needed to change my passive attitude by improving my English skills and enable myself to speak out to others. In particular, as I will brush up my English level through Skype sessions with students at Brown University, I need to be more aware of having a well-balanced life, using my* **Energy Boost** *and studying English regularly through* **Pile of Efforts**.

This comment shows the substantive increase in the student's awareness of self, and finding points for improvement. The student explains how he confronted a barrier in self-expression and performing leadership in terms of discussions with his team mates. He not only did a self-reflection on his frustrations over failures, but also brought out a perspective for improvements in his communication abilities that he can work on for personal growth. We can see here that he developed his perceptions on his feelings and thoughts as one of the three skills for social change.

To be honest, since I don't have a clear vision of my future pursuits, I would like to listen to one's stories and thoughts, finding out more about my possibilities. Taking the stories and information in careful consideration, I would like to show a **Yes, and** *attitude to others, going beyond grasping their ideas, developing my ideas on them.*

As the student realized for further actions on attentive listening, the program has helped her to cultivate a need for an empathetic attitude so that she could benefit from the insights and findings. She has realized the need to acquire more information and ideas to form her ideal future vision. Though beginning with a self-serving cause for acquiring knowledge, she then continues to express her decision of extending her empathetic attitude to collaboration, by building up on ideas from others. In short, this student was able to develop a behavior of attuning to others, another skill set to reaching the position as changemakers.

After coming back to Japan, I hope to set up a **Trusteam** *using social networking services to keep exchanging our ideas for the T-shirt Printing service and Waku Mama Bar Project. Reflecting on the experiences in the Philippines, I would like to take actions as an* **Idea Catcher** *and have a broader and wider view towards the world.*

This student created a retrospective on her thorough experience of the program, envisioning goals for her team's changemaking project. She elaborates on her future goals of being an Idea Catcher, being aware of surroundings and collect useful facts for projects. What's more, the student expresses interest in obtaining a wider view of the world while gathering knowledge. This implies that she felt the need to understand both the elements that constitute her surroundings and the society that she perceives as a whole.

These action plans do not prove entirely the specific effects of the combination of Change Making Patterns Workbook and workshops, since the program did not cover the entire set of Change Making Patterns. However, with subtle volume differences of three skill sets, the total experience of the study tour has leveraged the student's motivation to develop a wider consciousness of either their feelings, others' thoughts, and society. These results have found that the use of Change Making Patterns Workbook and supplementary workshops has relatively facilitated the participants' awareness towards self, others, and the larger picture of society.

5. Conclusion and Discussion

We have presented a theoretical structure for social change as three dimensions of changemaking skills, which are self-awareness, empathy, and social interdependency. When change agents have a thorough understanding of themselves, their self-awareness enable them to see their inner drives, greatest strengths, personal pitfalls, and values, which help them feel life. To rephrase, individuals who try to start their changemaking project should know who they are in terms of their behaviors, motivations, strengths and weaknesses when encountering social issues, and re-exam the purpose of their actions. However, in order to prevent an oppressive and dominant authority that would exploit other people, one should also understand if his purpose for action is meeting the demands of the people behind the social issue. Changemakers equip attributes such as empathy in pursuit of establishing an approach to alleviate their target groups' suffering. To restate, individuals who try to serve their targeted group should understand the demand and the underlying needs by attaining the same level of viewpoint. This task requires tuning out to others - being able to understand another person's reality and relating to him. Yet, these two channels are not enough to really let social change happen or apply the solution to resolve social issues. Leading changemakers apply their skills to grasp the whole society and its components through examining the interrelations of the elements that are precipitating social issues. Such consciousness of social interdependency is the third framework to follow in order to create systemic change. This third focus of seeing the outer world and understanding the larger picture of society is also required for future changemakers. With such conceptual framework for social change, we suggested Change Making Patterns as a potential tool to capture these three skill sets in a tangible manner, where it can be shared among learners who are prone to take part in creating changes against social issues. To assure that the readers can learn and embody the pattern content in their lives, it was applied in educational settings, in the form of Change Making Patterns Workbook, which included activities and examples to which the readers can refer in their own context. In hopes of encouraging the readers' actions, the workbook was used in a study tour to the Philippines, aiming to foster social entrepreneurship among university student participants with direct experiences through workshops. Throughout the week-long program, the activities in the workbook were deployed in the workshops, participants learning some patterns each day.

As a result, participants oriented themselves into two groups, each completing the study tour by creating a preliminary social business plan: Waku Mama Cafe, a bar business aiming to offer job opportunities for local youths and T-shirt printing service, a business to foster women entrepreneurship in the community. Observing some of the comments from the Japanese participants, we can infer that the workbook and workshops helped the students to develop their need to enhance the changemaking skill sets. The students were able to gain positive attitudes towards making social changes, by working on activities in the workbook and reflecting on them after taking actions during fieldworks. However, since this is the initial step to cultivate changemaking skills among learners, there is still a need for further empirical research on a range of subjects. For example, we should develop a more satisfying conceptual framework for societal change, examining the certain skill sets, which changemakers acquire and encapsulate in tackling societal issues. Future work includes educational approaches that prompts the process of changemaking that attains a degree of life, while learners enlarge the awareness on their feelings, others, and the complexity of society. Moreover, practical usage of Change Making Patterns should be explored to cultivate the liveliness of learners when they act on their purpose as social responsible citizens. This margin is the opportunity that should be taken advantaged of to foster changemakers who take socially conscious choices and action.

6. Acknowledgements

To begin with, we would like to appreciate Eri Shimomukai for inviting us to pursue this research, which we have explored for the entire school years. Heartfelt appreciation goes to all the participants of the Change Making Study Tour in Philippines for their enthusiasm and energy they have provided us to make actions for a better future. Additionally, personal appreciation also goes for Ms. Yamada and her partner Mr. Morizumi and the Waku Work Family and staff for providing support and inspiration in Cebu. We would also like to express our deepest gratitude to the members at Iba, who have always been very generous and accepting with my situation and blunders. Our deep appreciation also goes to friends who have always believed in and provided us with mental support from every corner of the world. Last but not least, we would like to acknowledge my families for their endless and unconditional support, which have instilled us with the motivation to keep striving through difficulties. We hope to pay it forward onto our future generations so that we can advance the stream of social change by nurturing changemakers who are aware of the heart of themselves, others, and society.

7. References

Alexander, C., Ishikawa, S., & Silverstein, M. (1977). A Pattern Language: Towns, Buildings, Construction. New York NY: Oxford University Press.

Alexander, C. (1979). The Timeless Way of Building, Chapter 6. New York, NY: Oxford University Press.

Alexander, C. (2002a). The Nature of Order: An Essay of the Art of Building and the Nature of the Universe, Book 1: The Phenomenon of Life. Berkeley, California: The Center for Environmental Structure.

Alexander, C. (2002b). The Nature of Order: An Essay of the Art of Building and the Nature of the Universe, Book 2: The Process of Creating Life. Berkeley, California: The Center for Environmental Structure.

Ashoka's Empathy Initiative. (n.d.). In About the Initiative. Retrieved from http:// empathy.ashoka.org/about-initiative

Bornstein, D., & Davis, S. (2010). Social Entrepreneurship: What Everyone Needs to Know. New York, NY: Oxford University Press.

Bornstein, D. (2004). How to Change the World: Social Entrepreneurs and the Power of New Ideas. New York, NY: Oxford University Press.

Brock, D., Steiner, S., & Kim, M. (2008). Social entrepreneurship education: is it achieving the desired aims? United States Association for Small Business and Entrepreneurship (USASBE) Conference Proceedings.

Gardner, W. J. (1964). Self Renewal: The Individual and the Innovative Society. New York, NY: Harper & Row.

Goleman, D. & Senge, P. (2014). The Triple Focus: A New Approach for Education (1st ed.). Florence, MA: More Than Sound.

Kolb, D. (1999). Experiential Learning Theory: Previous Research and New Directions, NJ: Lawrence Erlbaum.

Martin, R. & Osberg, S. (2007). Social Entrepreneurship: The Case for Definition. Stanford Social Innovation Review, Vol. 5, No.2, Retrieved from http://www.ssireview.org/ articles/entry/social_entrepreneurship_the_case_for_definition/

Miller, L. T., et al. (2012). Venturing for others with heart and head: how compassion encourages social entrepreneurship. Academy of Management Review. Vol. 37, No.4, 616-640. Retrieved from http://amr.aom.org/content/37/4/616

Nakamura, S., Shimomukai, E., Isaku, T. & Iba, T. (2014). Change Making Patterns Workbook: A Workbook Approach to Pattern Applications, in the 21st Conference on Pattern Languages of Programs (PLoP2014).

Nakamura, S. & Iba, T. (2015). Collaborative Social Change with Change Making Patterns Workbook, in the Collaborative Innovation Networks Conference 2015 (COINs2015).

Senge, P., et al. (2012). Schools That Learn: A Fifth Discipline Fieldbook for Educators, Parents, and Everyone Who Cares About Education. New York, NY: Crown Business, an imprint of the Crown Publishing Group, a division of Random House, Inc.

Shimomukai, E. & Iba, T. (2012). Social Entrepreneurship Patterns: A Pattern Language for Change Making on Social Issues, in the 17th European Conference on Pattern Languages of Programs (EuroPLoP 2012).

Shimomukai, E., Nakamura, S., & Iba, T. (2012). Change Making Patterns: A Pattern Language for Fostering Social Entrepreneurship, in the 19th Conference on Pattern Languages of Programs (PLoP 2012).

Shimomukai, E, & Nakamura, S. with Iba, T. (2015). Change Making Patterns: A Pattern Language for Fostering Social Entrepreneurship. Kanagawa, Japan: CreativeShift Lab.

Vasan, N. & Przybylo, J. (2013). Do Good Well. San Francisco, California: Jossey-Bass. A Wiley Imprint.

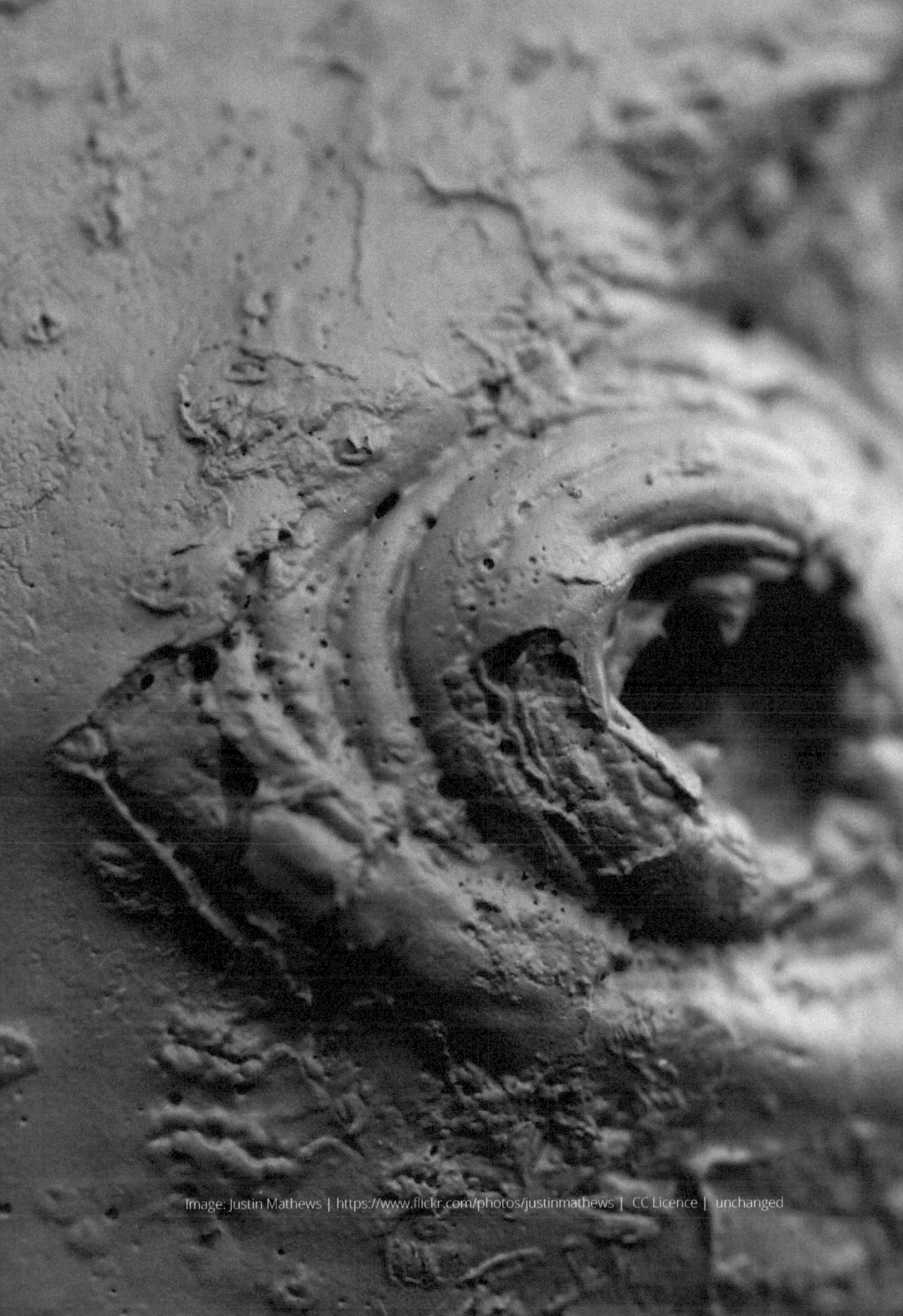

Survival Pattern Language:
A Wayfinding Escape Pattern Language for Surviving an Earthquake with an Accompanying Tsunami

Neis, Hajo
Portland Urban Architecture Research Lab, USA
Hajoneis@uoregon.ed

Wright, Perrin
Portland Urban Architecture Research Lab, USA
perringwright@gmail.com

The Portland Urban Architecture Research Laboratory (PUARL) presents, 'Survival Pattern Language: A Wayfinding Escape Pattern Language for Surviving an Earthquake with an Accompanying Tsunami.' This particular language was created in order to provide coastal communities with a new tool for assessing their current tsunami readiness programs, and to propose changes to improve tsunami evacuation wayfinding, which is what will help evacuees get 'Up and Out' of the inundation zone to safety on higher ground. Not limited to physical signage, the language is composed of a variety of strategies that aims to establish a robust wayfinding chain that enhances Tsunami Readiness through preparation, evacuation, and response.

Earthquake, Tsunami, Evacuation, Wayfinding, Survival Pattern Language

> "The future belongs to those who prepare for it."
>
> Ralph Waldo Emerson (Stein, 2008)

Figure 1: Famous Landmark Haystack Rock, in the City of Cannon Beach, OR

1. Emergency Management on the Oregon Coast

1.1 History of Tsunami Formations

The Japanese word 'Tsunami', (Tsu-Harbour : Nami-Wave) is considered a 'Seismic Sea Wave', which is a series of ocean waves activated by seismic disturbances such as earthquakes, volcanic eruptions, landslides, and even meteorites (NOAA Tsunami Website, n.d.). Location and magnitude of a disturbance determines the force of the wave, while the topography of the coastline and ocean floor will impact the size and speed of the wave as it approaches a shore (FEMA Tsunamis, n.d.). In the deep ocean, tsunami waves can reach speeds up to 500 - 1,000km/hr. However, as they approach the shore, the wave speed decreases and water depth is reduced, causing a concentration of energy upon impact. A wave that reaches just over a meter in height in the ocean, can reach tens of meters high at the coast (IOC Tsunami Glossary, 2013).

The Pacific Ocean is known for its active tectonic plates where slippage along convergent and divergent plate boundaries cause a range of seismic sea wave types. A distant, or 'Tele-Tsunami,' is caused from a source over 1,000km from the coast, with a minimum of 3 hour travel time (IOC Tsunami Glossary, 2013). Although these waves are generally less destructive (Dogami Tsunami Clearinghouse, n.d.), without the proper warning systems in place, there are only a few known signs that indicate the oncoming wave. On December 26th, 2004 the 9.3 magnitude 'Sumatra-Andaman' Earthquake in the Indonesian Ocean caused an ocean-wide distant tsunami that killed approximately 230,000 people. It is often considered the most tragic natural disaster, triggering one of the largest international relief efforts in modern day history, and motivating governments to improve tsunami warning systems and evacuation plans across the globe. (IOC Tsunami Glossary, 2013).

Figure 2: Oncoming Tsunami impact from the 2004 'Sumatra-Andaman' Earthquake in the Indonesian Ocean region.

Unlike distant tsunamis, local tsunamis originate from a source within 1,000km to the coast, and have travel times of under 1 hour. The process of subduction causes oceanic plates to shift under their adjacent continental plates. A common source of local tsunamis, these subduction zones exist close to land masses and are responsible for over 90% of tsunami related casualties (IOC Tsunami Glossary, 2013). Approximately one-third of the recorded large tsunamis have impacted the islands of Japan, (NPR History of Tsunami, 2011), whose people have ingrained a culture of preparation far more robust than any place faced with this threat. On March 11th, 2011, the 9.0 magnitude Tohoku earthquake created waves that reached heights of 40.5m (133ft) and traveled up to 6mi inland. The earthquake shifted the main island of Japan 2.4m to the east, and supposedly shifted the earth between 4-10in on its axis (Wikipedia, 2011 Tohoku, 2015). Even with the cultural tsunami resilience in place, the death toll and destruction reached extraordinary levels.

Figure 3: Oncoming Tsunami impact from the 2011 Tohoku Earthquake in Japan

1.2 Oregon Coast Tsunami Preparation

Contrary to their neighbors across the sea, relatively newer communities along the North American coast have less experience with this type of Earthquake / Tsunami double disaster. The Cascadia Subduction zone is a convergent plate boundary separating the Juan de Fuca and North American plates. This 620 mile long fault line runs parallel to the Pacific Coast from northern California to Vancouver BC (Wikipedia, Cascadia S. Zone, 2015). Major magnitude 8.0 - 9.0 earthquake events are separated by centuries of relative inactivity, that cause the first of many raging tsunami waves to strike the coast within 15-30 minutes (CREW, 2013). Over its 10,000 year rupture history, the average recurrence of major earthquakes strike approximately every 234 years. The last major event occurred Jan, 1700, just over 315 years ago (OPB, 2015). A recent New York Times article about the Cascadia Subduction Zone, stated that the worse-case scenario earthquake would lead to the worst natural disaster in the history of the United States (Schulz, 2015).

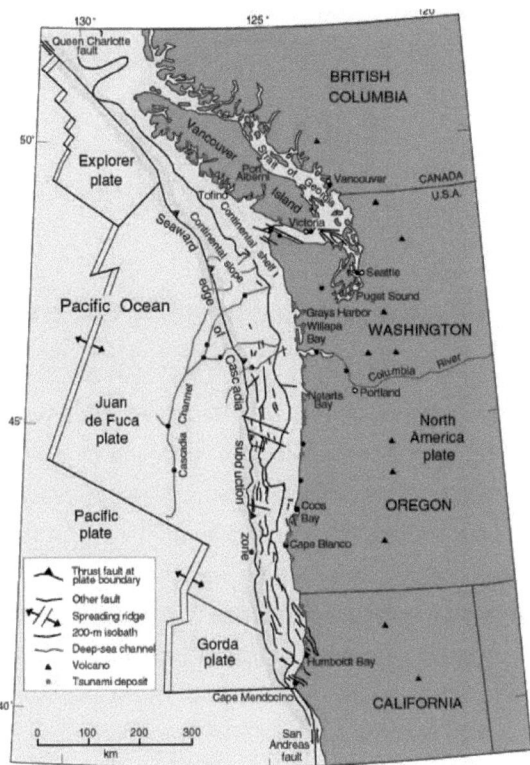

Figure 4: Diagram of the Cascadia Subduction Zone where the Juan de Fuca Plate is slipping under the North American Plate

The global broadcasting of the 2011 Tohoku earthquake caused many US coastal cities to be evacuated. While no waves ever reached the coastline, that experience forced many communities and individuals to acknowledge the threat that has been so often ignored. Since then, the State of Oregon has been spearheading the Tsunami Ready movement and organizations at all levels have been diligently working on understanding the disaster, implementing effective evacuation routes, and establishing Tsunami-Readiness programs (NWS, TsunamiReady, 2015). The Oregon Office of Emergency Management (OEM Tsunami Information, n.d.), and the National Oceanic and Atmospheric Administration (NOAA Tsunami Website, n.d.), recognized the need to implement a robust tsunami evacuation system that addresses the human factor, and provides evacuees the best chance to find their way along those routes to safe ground.

Figure 5: Emblem of the Oregon Military Department, Office of Emergency Management

The Portland Urban Architecture Research Lab (PUARL Website, n.d.), part of the University of Oregon's Portland Architecture and Urban Design Program was hired by these organizations in order to complement the scientific modeling of evacuation routes, through creative planning and design of wayfinding systems. Although research was conducted on a variety of locations on the Oregon Coast and in other parts of the world threatened by tsunami inundation, the city of Cannon Beach was chosen as the specific case study site due to their leadership in tsunami preparedness. Through a series of site visits, the team was able to observe an existing system in order to identify, evaluate, and test key issues that could prevent effective evacuation wayfinding. The public works director along with the Community Emergency Response Team (CERT) were part of an ongoing discussion that provided valuable city and community planning information and resources. Through the pattern language method, the team was able to observe existing conditions, find common problems, and organize strategic solutions. This model was developed into the beginnings of a Survival Language; initiating a new approach for achieving a comprehensive tsunami evacuation wayfinding system.

Figure 6: Charrette workshop in Astoria, the northern most city on the Oregon Coast

1.3 Wayfinding & Signage

In his book, 'Wayfinding Behavior: Cognitive Mapping and Other Spatial Processes,' Reginald Golledge defines wayfinding as, "the process of determining and following a path or route between an origin and a destination. It is a purposive, directed and motivated activity."

A travel plan is the initial action of defining a route, which is a path made up of a sequential series of segments and turns. The legibility, or ease in which these routes can be followed, relies upon the directive cues and external references, which dictate the rate at which the path and its surrounding environment can be learned. The repeated following of routes, supports the ability to establish cognitive maps, where the mind breaks down the route into one-dimensional linked segments that rely upon physical elements that help identify location along the mental map. A more identifiable destination allows the mind to better imagine the relationship of distance and direction from different moments along route.

If a route has never been followed, regardless of route legibility, the spatial recognition of the environment does not exist. However, without effective physical elements that influence legibility, the more difficult it is to establish cognitive maps of the environment. Essentially, the wayfinding process requires multiple types of informational input that rely on one another. The ability of users to create a mental map of an environment, relies on the repeated following of the route, that supports the recognition of physical elements along route, which eventually provide feedback on current location along the mental map. (Golledge 1999)

Wayfinding relies heavily upon information graphics in the form of signs to provide route legibility. The book Signage Design Manual, written by Edo Smitshuijzen, details the process of designing a signage project from start to finish, highlighting important considerations along the way. The book illustrates that an effective signage system's design and implementation into the built environment relies upon a wider variety of factors including purpose, design, placement, upkeep, and systems. A signage system is much more than just a set of signposts and symbols. It contributes a unique character to its surroundings and has the potential to enhance any built environment. Visual design concept is a theme that should be used to link different sign types together. Consideration of different sign types, their purpose, their placement, and their relationship to one another is as important as the individual design of the signs themselves. (Smitshuijzen 2007)

Figure 7 / 8: These two signs were designed as part of a tsunami evacuation sign suite for the second Up & Out Report. They are very similar to existing signs, with slight changes made for design and information clarity.

Figure 7 (left): PUARL redesign of Oregon Coast 'Tsunami Hazard Zone' sign.

Figure 8 (right): PUARL redesign of Oregon Coast 'Tsunami Evacuation Route' sign.

1.4 Tsunami Readiness Wayfinding

The existing tsunami evacuation wayfinding system is primarily thought about in terms of signage, which is composed of 3 fundamental sign types. Each of these signs can be found in section 2.3.1 of this paper.

The first sign is considered a Tsunami Evacuation Map that includes hazard zones and evacuation routes for the entire city. These signs can be found scattered around downtown areas and beach access points, and have been made into a physical brochure that can be also be accessed online. The maps include three colors (orange, yellow, and green) that indicate the inundation level of a distant tsunami, a local tsunami, and safe ground. They include small arrows that point out the general route for evacuation towards an encircled A, representing the assembly point. These signs also include symbols that represent civic landmarks as reference points along the routes.

Tsunami Evacuation Route signs, reflect the routes indicated on the maps, directing evacuees along primary streets to designated assembly areas. The design and placement protocols differ in each city, but are commonly circular blue and white signs that include a wave with the words "Tsunami Evacuation Route" and are paired with an arrow below that indicate direction. Current Federal Regulations state that circular shaped signs are meant to include prohibitive or preventative directives, leading some cities, like Cannon Beach, to update to a rectangular sign, with a printed circle and an arrow below. These updated signs are reflective for night evacuation.

At the end of the route, evacuees might find an Assembly Area sign placed along the side of a road. Each city utilizes a different design, while some cities do not provide these signs. They are commonly the same blue color, and include the words "Assembly Area" with a family holding hands. Assembly Areas are often placed beyond the safety zone threshold, but do not specifically suggest safety, or provide any instructive information for how to assemble. Each city is responsible for establishing a plan for post-disaster campsites, but most designated assembly areas do not seem to be capable of supporting hundreds of people for up to 3-10 days, indicating that those plans are likely take place in a nearby location.

The evacuation maps are meant to teach people what they are supposed to do when the event occurs. The route signs are meant to guide evacuees to safety before tsunami inundation. The assembly signs are meant to indicate where people are supposed to gather. In effect, these signs are represent the three stage of a Tsunami Evacuation Wayfinding system: Before - Preparation, During – Evacuation, and After - Response.

1.5 Tsunami Evacuation Wayfinding:

When considering the process of tsunami evacuation wayfinding, it is important to consider some of the different factors that would impact the functionality of the signage system. A 9.0+ magnitude earthquake would cause intense shaking for up to 5-8 minutes. Many building structures would be destroyed, roads compromised, bridges fallen, and hills liquefied. In the summer months there could be an increase in population of up to 300% causing confusion of who or what to follow. If the event occurs at night or during a storm the signs could be impossible to locate. Sirens and panic will certainly compromise decision making, and a variety of other unforeseeable obstacles will prevent timely evacuation.

Figure 9: This humorous sign was photographed in a Cannon Beach Neighborhood.

Most tourists are vastly unaware of the threat, and like most people in new places, have limited ability to place themselves in relation to high ground. This means that a majority of people that are located closest to the beach and farthest away from safety, will be expected to gather themselves from the destruction of the earthquake, travel multiple miles along routes, that may or may not be functional, to an unknown destination. It is imperative, that the majority of people located in these areas are not having to experience these routes for the first time during the event. Tsunami Evacuation Maps need to be designed and located in a place that encourages passer-byes to study them. They need to include more detailed information allow users to figure out their own personal escape route, and the steps that they should take in case of an event. Hotels and vacation rentals should be required to provide these resources and business staff should be trained to explain evacuation protocol in greater detail. Preparation is perhaps the most important stage, because it is the foundation for successful evacuation and response.

Figure 10: This image shows a primary entrance to the beach in Cannon Beach where there is a Tsunami Evacuation Map.

Even with the above improvements, it can be expected that many people will still be following the evacuation route for the first time, even if they are generally aware of the route. With so few minutes to travel such a significant distance, route legibility may be the deciding factor between life and death. The evacuation route signs need to clearly indicate pedestrian evacuation, and can provide additional information such as distance markers that will detail how much farther needs to be traveled. Once one sign is passed, the next one should be visible. There needs to be a clear system to indicate turns, versus continuation, as well as methods for preventing unwanted turns. If the event occurs at night or during a storm, there needs to be other sources of blue lights that can be seen. Furthermore, if the earthquake destroys or turns signs, there needs to be redundant forms of signage that will continue to guide evacuees. This may come in the form of evacuation leaders, who are trained business staff, prepared to help guide evacuees if the signage is fails. Evacuation cannot rely solely on 2d route signs, but needs to incorporate other strategies for guiding people efficiently, while being able to withstand the destructive forces caused by the earthquake.

At the end of the evacuation route, there is no indication when safety is reached. The assembly area sign, placed alongside a road, is the only indication of safety, and provides no information for what to do next. Some areas have well thought out plans, with resources stored in a container or safe house. However, if for whatever reason no one that knows the plan survives, evacuees will be left to make their own decisions. Many of these areas are surrounded by houses or campgrounds, which can effectively support the campsites. However, experts are saying that with the widespread destruction caused inland and on the coast, these sites will have to be self-sufficient for up to 3-10 days. Possibly supporting hundreds of people with shelter and resources for that time requires a tremendous amount of planning and organization. Each site in each city will be different based off qualities of the surrounding area, but need to have a well thought out plan that is capable of providing the information on where to find the stored resources and how to set up shelter.

1.6   Tsunami Readiness Wayfinding:

It is imperative that tsunami evacuation wayfinding is not limited to 2d signs that are generally ignored by visitors and residents alike. Cognitive mapping of evacuation routes to designated assembly points, especially from high risk locations, is necessary for timely evacuation. Redundant forms of direction need to continue to guide people if the 2d signs fail due to unexpected shocks or a night evacuation. Highly organized assembly sites require methods of directing evacuees, erecting shelters, and providing resources. It isn't fair to say that every route in every city will fail in its current state; but it is widely accepted, even in the most TsunamiReady cities, that existing wayfinding systems need to be improved.

The wide variety of problems may seem unrelated, and easier to solve through isolated solutions. It is true that any and all improvements will likely make for incremental progress. However, the ability to survive a disaster of this magnitude cannot be achieved through a series of individual efforts. It took many hours of observation and evaluation to come to this conclusion, but it influenced the PUARL team to expand the project's definition and expectation of tsunami evacuation wayfinding. This requires a comprehensive system in the form of a sequential chain that encourages preparation, assures evacuation, and organizes response. The Wayfinding Chain, attempts to categorize isolated problems that occur before, during, and after a tsunami event, in order to suggest a network of integrated solutions which can evolve into a chain of elements that establish a system of Tsunami Readiness Wayfinding.

2. A Survival Pattern Language

2.1 A New Type of Language

In order to develop a comprehensive tsunami evacuation wayfinding system, the PUARL team utilized the Pattern Language method. The PUARL works in the tradition of pattern language through research & development, with a close connection to its origins at the Center for Environmental Structure (CES) in Berkeley. But unlike most architecture and urban pattern languages, which are intended for improving the quality of a built environment, the purpose of the survival pattern language is to reduce the loss of life in the event of natural disaster.

This new field for pattern language development was inspired by Iba Laboratory. Based out of Keio University in Tokyo, and led by active pattern language practitioner Dr. Takashi Iba, Iba Laboratory was responsible for a *'Survival Language: A Pattern Language for Surviving Earthquakes'*. This pattern language was developed in order to better prepare individuals for the variety of obstacles that stand in their way of survival during a catastrophic earthquake (Furukawazono, Seshimo, Muramatsu, & Iba 2013).

This inspired the PUARL to develop a language for surviving tsunamis. Although survival languages address a different type of design problem, the pattern language approach stays the same. The language can be considered a written "Design Knowledge" based upon the ability to find and solve problems within a particular domain. The language consists of Patterns, which represent a repeated problem that occurs in that domain, and proposes an effective solution. Patterns address a variety of problem types and scales. Together these individual patterns evolve into a pattern language, which represents the comprehensive "Design Knowledge" for that particular domain. If used effectively, it is a strategy for designers to tackle larger problems, through a series of smaller integrated solutions (Alexander, Ishikawa, & Silverstein, 1977).

This particular Survival Language is the first step towards establishing a written "Design Knowledge" for the domain of surviving an earthquake with an accompanying tsunami.

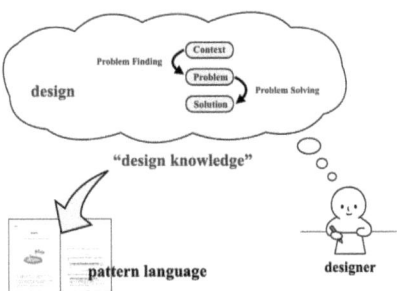

Figure 11: This diagram created by Iba Laboratory illustrates the how Design Knowledge and Pattern Language work together.

2.2 Survival Language Parameters

A Survival Pattern Language for earthquakes and accompanying tsunamis was created in order to provide coastal communities with a new tool for assessing their current tsunami readiness, and to propose changes to improve their wayfinding chain. Problems consist of issues that would prevent successful wayfinding; solutions are methods that any city can use to improve wayfinding conditions. Together, these individual wayfinding patterns can evolve into a survival language that provides a framework for individual wayfinding strategies to be integrated into a robust and comprehensive wayfinding chain.

A successful wayfinding system encourages preparation, assures evacuation, and supports response. Therefore, the survival language incorporates three pattern chapters dedicated to the before, during, and after stages of a disastrous event. Each chapter provides a series of patterns that address a different aspect of the wayfinding system. **Preparedness patterns** work to improve infrastructure that raise awareness. **Evacuation patterns** focus on developing the clarity of evacuation routes. **Response patterns** aim to guide assembly, organization, and utilization of campsites. It is important to note that this language was written for cities as its primary users. Each pattern was therefore evaluated, developed, and proposed to be addressed by larger tsunami planning organizations. While all of these solutions would have to be implemented by a city before the event, patterns are written for the problem's moment of impact. For example, maps are studied before an event, route signs are followed during an event, and assembly areas are filled after the event.

The current survival language consists of 24 individual patterns, numbered and divided into Preparedness, Evacuation, and Response chapters. The pattern titles are used to describe the topic, including a problem and a solution statement, followed by a contextual discussion that considers the issues and opportunities that apply to that specific pattern. Side bars are used as applied concepts that include precedent studies, site testing, creative ideas, and design proposals to demonstrate how these patterns are implemented as projects. Each pattern includes a list of other related patterns that demonstrate how different elements can begin to work together to become a more robust and comprehensive wayfinding system.

2.3 Pattern Chapters: Before, During, & After

2.3.1 Before - Preparation Stage

The Preparedness Patterns chapter includes patterns that should be enacted prior to the disastrous event. These patterns focus on raising awareness through education and on creating community resilience networks that will support survival during and after the event. Successful evacuation and response hinge on effective planning actions, making preparation the most vital stage of tsunami readiness programs. Although this stage is commonly ignored in most disaster situation by regular civilians, disaster survivors commonly speak about how important it would have been for them to have been prepared.

Preparation Patterns

1. | Multi-Purpose Infrastructure
2. | Recognizable Wayfinding Chain
3. | Information Station
4. | Know What Zone
5. | Public-Private Partnership
6. | Mapping your Neighborhood
7. | Relocate to High ground
8. | Route Safety

A SURVIVAL LANGUAGE: TSUNAMI EVACUATION WAYFINDING

Evacuation Symbol: The Wave

Tsunami Evac. Map Sign

Tsunami Evac. Route Sign

Tsunami Assembly Area Sign

Prepare 2 RECOGNIZABLE WAYFINDING CHAIN

People are not aware of the many aspects of a tsunami evacuation system and the connections between them.

Most evacuation wayfinding systems incorporate the use of signs and maps to help people identify their route before an event, follow their route during an event, and assemble after an event. These signs and maps, as well as the public literature that is provided online or at visitors centers, are often proposed at different times, and are not always recognizable as a coherent series of parts. This makes it difficult for people to easily recognize what elements they are supposed to utilize at what times, especially in a highly stressful situation.

Although Oregon designed a tsunami evacuation logo that is now used internationally by coastal communities, the color, shape, and size of the symbol do not always translate throughout different signs. Tsunami evacuation maps often use three shades of color to differentiate the different hazard zones. These colors are found nowhere on tsunami evacuation or assembly area signs. Furthermore, pedestrian signs are often placed under evacuation signs to indicate that these routes are for pedestrians only. However, the color shade and placement with other types of street signs often makes it difficult to identify whether these signs are tsunami related. These type of confusing typology changes make the system less streamlined and intuitive for users.

BEFORE

14

PREPAREDNESS PATTERNS

Prepare 2

THEREFORE: **Design a consistent wayfinding chain that functions as a system. Establish recognizable and streamlined relationships between each element of the system.**

When reassessing and developing tsunami evacuation wayfinding systems, consider ways to help users find commonalities between different wayfinding elements. If updated physical installations to the current system of maps and signs (awareness kiosks, signposts, lighting, assembly areas, and cache sites) are going to be implemented, they should be designed in unison as a recognizable system both in form and function. If people can both actively and subconsciously connect wayfinding elements that address preparation, evacuation, and response, the transition between each phase becomes more seamless.

Consider using the same material, shape, configuration, lighting, or color when designing different elements of the system. Evacuation related information on maps, signs, printed material, websites and apps should have consistent branding, in order to make the system recognizable. Consistency of both 2D and 3D forms should make maps and signs come to life throughout the urban fabric of downtown areas and along evacuation routes. These types of moves can be used to create a brand that a city can advertise to residents, tourists, and other coastal communities that they are ready for the threat of a tsunami.

Evacuation Wayfinding Chain

MAPS → SIGNS → MAIN ROUTES → SAFETY THRESHOLDS → ASSEMBLY AREA → TRIAGE → CACHE SITE

Related Patterns

Preparedness Patterns
1, 3, 4, 6
Evacuation Patterns
9, 10, 11, 13, 14, 15
Response Patterns
18, 22, 23, 24

BEFORE

15

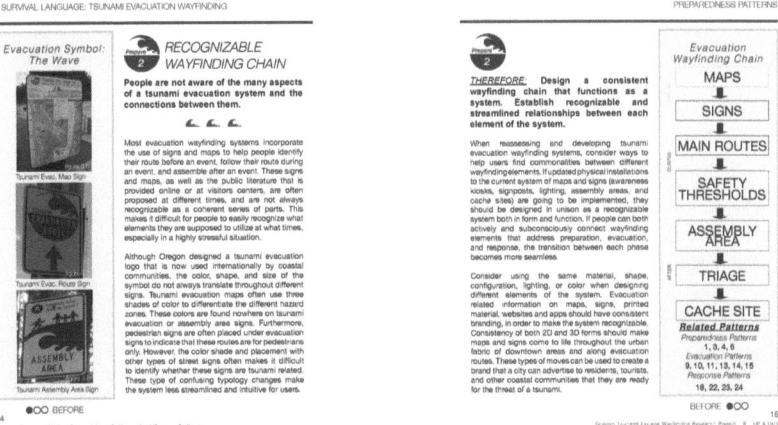

Figure 12 (left): Prepare 2 Recognizable Wayfinding Chain page illustrating the problem statement and discussion.

Figure 13 (right): Prepare 2 Recognizable Wayfinding Chain page illustrating the solution statement and discussion.

Prepare 2: Recognizable Wayfinding Chain

People are not aware of the many aspects of a tsunami evacuation system and the connections between them.

THEREFORE: *Design a consistent wayfinding chain that functions as a system. Establish recognizable and streamlined relationships between each element of the system.*

2.3.2 During - Evacuation Stage

The Evacuation Patterns chapter includes patterns that take effect during the disastrous event. Evacuation is the moment when preparation efforts are put into practice; it is when people have to find their way up and out to high ground. There is an approximated 15-30 minute evacuation window depending on location, making the effectiveness of the wayfinding system, dictate the rate of survival. These patterns focus on creating an intuitive wayfinding system that relies on the clarity of signs and routes to evacuate inundation areas before the incoming tsunami arrives. This system should be robust and redundant, capable of withstanding the many destructive forces and mental shocks that would prevent timely evacuation.

Evacuation Patterns

9. | My Personal Escape Route

10. | Intuitive Signs

11. | The Space Between

12. | Distance Matters

13. | Primary Route Clarity

14. | Other Forms of Signage

15. | Lights at Night

16. | Follow the Leader

17. | Alternative Evacuation

A SURVIVAL LANGUAGE: TSUNAMI EVACUATION WAYFINDING

Nikishi, Japan Evacuation Tower

figure 3.35

"An impressive five-story, 22-m-tall reinforced concrete structure resembling a lighthouse. Founded on a 4-m-deep layer of sand and gravel, the tower is supported on concrete piles extending 6 m below grade. It was designed to withstand the impact of a 10-ton ship at a velocity of 10 m/sec. For day-to-day use, it features public restrooms, a meeting room, firefighting equipment storage space, and 70 square meters of refuge space for evacuees."

www.asme.org

figure 3.36

Evacuate 17

ALTERNATIVE EVACUATION

Timely evacuation may not be possible in some areas that are too far away or geographically blocked from safe ground.

It is estimated that after a large local earthquake, there is approximately a 15-21 minute time window in which to evacuate. Most evacuation routes have been studied and tested to allow enough time to reach high ground if people stay calm and move quickly. However, almost every city has certain routes where evacuation is less realistic.

This may be because of the extreme distances that people would need to travel, requiring them to run at a pace that they are either not trained, or capable of doing. Even if the time allotted would allow for people to evacuate at a brisk pace, the studies rarely account for delayed reaction or confusion. These routes obviously require incline, but some have such a steep incline that elderly or disabled people will not be able to climb them. If large buildings surround routes, the earthquake might cause them to fall over into the road, making them impassable. Other barriers that might prevent evacuation could include bridge collapse or liquefaction of roads.

Many different types of failures are possible and likely to occur during an earthquake. If certain areas in a city exist where high ground can not be reached in time, the people in those areas are given little to no chance of surviving the tsunami.

DURING

38

EVACUATION PATTERNS

Evacuate 17

THEREFORE: **Build alternative methods of vertical evacuation for people who are unable to reach high ground otherwise.**

If it is decided that certain vulnerable populations have little to no chance of survival, consider implementing man made structures that will provide these groups with an alternative evacuation simple, yet well engineered tsunami evacuation towers, which have to be able to withstand the effects of a major earthquake, and be built tall enough to rise above an oncoming wave. They also have to account for holding the estimated number of people that are located in those high risk areas.

These towers can be used as prominent buildings for a variety of purposes. City hall and first responder departments might inhabit them everyday, to assure their survival during an event. The tower could become a tsunami preparedness center for learning and research that monitors sea level change and supports community awareness. Other ideas include mixed use buildings that include traveler accommodations and ground floor retail to support the tourist economy of the town.

A berm that acts as a public park could support evacuation as well by slowing the wave, to provide people with extra time along their evacuation route. More natural forms of vertical evacuation include precedents from India where people found refuge in climbing palm trees.

Occupiable Berm

A berm is either a natural or artificial embankment that is meant to slow the surge of the wave through steering or blocking the water. If shaped like the bow of a ship, a constructed wall could guide the water around an important area to protect such as a tsunami evacuation tower or a pedestrian bridge, giving people a longer time to get to high ground and safety before the oncoming wave.

figure 3.37

Instead of implementing giant seawalls that obstruct view of the ocean, find ways to integrate elevated slopes into public parks for gathering, public events, and tsunami awareness. By including elevated lookouts, berms can provide new views of the ocean and great places to watch sunsets.

Related Patterns

Preparedness Patterns

1, 5, 7, 8

Evacuation Patterns

15, 16

Response Patterns

18, 20, 21, 23

DURING

39

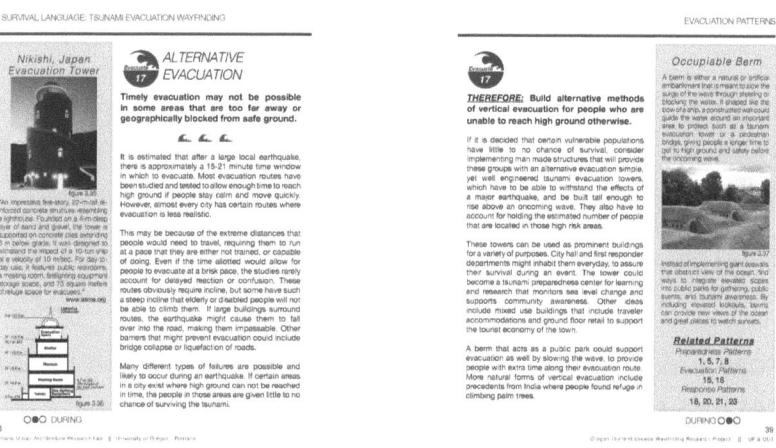

Figure 14 (left): Evacuate 17 Alternative Evacuation page illustrating the problem statement and discussion.

Figure 15 (right): Evacuate 17 Alternative Evacuation page illustrating the solution statement and discussion.

Evacuate 17: Alternative Evacuation

Timely evacuation may not be possible in some areas that are too far away or geographically blocked from safe ground.

THEREFORE: *Build alternative methods of vertical evacuation for people who are unable to reach high ground otherwise.*

2.3.3 After - Response Stage

The Response Patterns chapter includes patterns that will be needed after a disastrous event.

This phase begins the minute that the inundation threshold between danger and safety is reached. The instructive wayfinding strategies that occur after this pivotal moment will dictate the ability to continue to survive. These patterns focus on effective organization of campsites that will be able to support the immediate needs of survivors while also considering the long term needs of the group. Each of these patterns require a dedicated city planning effort that is continuously maintained, as well as the buy in from the surrounding residents that are willing to support their community.

Response Patterns

18. | Safety Zone Threshold
19. | Assembly Area Essentials
20. | 'How-To-Guide'
21. | Triage and Registration
22. | Campsites
    22.1. | Assembly Area Campsite
    22.2. | Safe House Campsite
    22.3. | Cache Site Campsite
23. | Sense of Place
24. | Multi-Purpose Cache Site

PURPLSOC: Designing Lively Scenarios in Various Fields

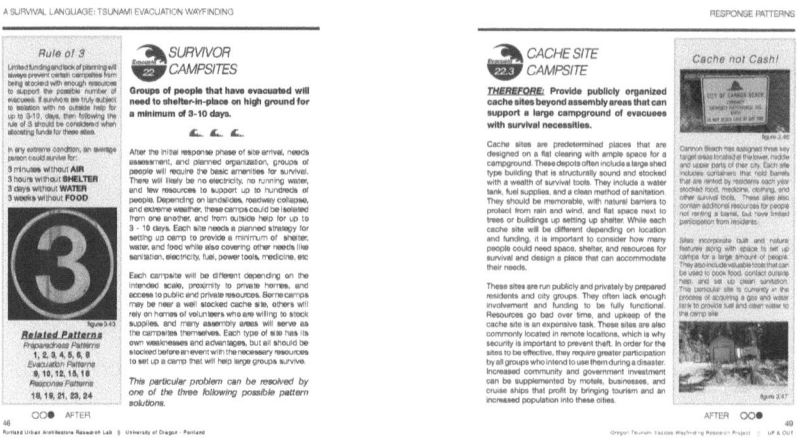

Figure 16 (left): Respond 22 Campsites page illustrating the problem statement and discussion.

Figure 17 (right): Respond 22.3 Cache Site Campsite page illustrating the solution statement and discussion for this particular solution.

Respond 22: Campsites

Groups of people that have evacuated will need to shelter-in-place on high ground for a minimum of 3-10 days.

Respond 22.3: Cache Site Campsite

THEREFORE: *Provide publicly organized cache sites beyond assembly areas that can support a large campground of evacuees with survival necessities.*

2.4 Using the Survival Language

Although problems and solutions are objective elements of disaster situations, patterns can be applied to many coastal community contexts, with a multitude of different design solutions. Each pattern can be exercised through the context of a city's existing wayfinding system based on the specific application needed for that city. The pattern context provides a discussion of the universal principles under which the pattern exists, while the side bars provide some insight on how that pattern could or has been applied to a particular site context. Each of these individual patterns can turn into unique projects that have the ability to upgrade its respective condition for any tsunami evacuation wayfinding system.

The survival language is broken up into 3 chapters: Preparedness, Evacuation, and Response. Chapters are written sequentially to reflect how the wayfinding system exists as a chain of elements that moves people up and out in the event of a tsunami. Each of these patterns can stand alone as individual projects that will incrementally improve tsunami evacuation wayfinding. However, choosing patterns that establish a sequence of solutions for problems that occur before, during, and after the event, allows for a robust system that considers the wide range of issues that each stage presents to coastal communities.

Although patterns can be chosen individually and/or sequentially, they are strengthened when they begin to work together. A resilient system is capable of adapting to chaotic and uncontrollable situations because of the interdependent nature of its structural organization. If unanticipated shocks cause one wayfinding element to fail, than the other members exist for reinforcement. Consequently, a successful pattern language is a sequence of individual patterns that are designed as a complex network of interdependent parts. The related patterns section references the elements that directly impact each other. When the appropriate relationships between the sequential patterns are developed in sync, the network extends beyond identifiable connections to integrate seemingly unrelated patterns into a resilient system.

A survival language should be used by cities as a tool to create a robust wayfinding system, by developing a site-specific project language, which solves critical problems through effective design and implementation. It is important to not rely on the individual patterns as written, but rather to establish new patterns, sequences, and relationships that strengthen a city's specific context. Instead of becoming discouraged by the extensive issues that exist when planning for tsunami readiness, this resource can help make smaller incremental changes within the context of the wayfinding system as a whole. Overtime, with a consistent effort, a community can realize a comprehensive survival language that will make them Tsunami Ready.

Figure 18: This sign is at the entrance of an adjacent business to one of the Emergency Response Sites.

2.5 PUARL Work

The PUARL completed the survival language as part of a larger Up & Out: Oregon Tsunami Wayfinding Research Project. The team was asked to complete a second Up & Out report for the cities of Seaside and Warrenton, where Project Languages were developed for each city.

These two reports can be found on the PUARL website at:

http://puarl.uoregon.edu/

As well as on OEM's website at:

http://www.oregon.gov/omd/oem/pages/plans_train/tsunamis.aspx

3. References

Alexander, C. (2004). The nature of order : An essay on the art of building and the nature of the universe (Vols. 1-4). Berkeley, CA: Center for Environmental Structure; and New York: Oxford University Press.

Alexander C., Neis, H. J., Anninou, A., & King, I. (1987) A new theory of urban design. New York: Oxford University Press.

Alexander C., Ishikawa S., & Silverstein M., et. al. (1977) A Pattern Language: Towns, Buildings, Construction. New York: Oxford University Press.

Calori C. (2007). Signage and wayfinding design: A complete guide to creating environmental graphic design systems. Hoboken, NJ: John Wiley.

Lyle J. (1994). Regenerative design for sustainable development. New York: John Wiley.

Lynch K (1960). The image of the city. Cambridge, MA.: MIT Press.

Golledge R. (1999). Wayfinding behavior: Cognitive mapping and other spatial processes. Baltimore, MD: Johns Hopkins University Press.

McLendo C., & Blackistone M. (1982). Signage: Graphic communications in the built world. New York: McGraw-Hill.

Neis H. J., Brown G., Gurr J. M., & Schmidt J. A., eds. (2012) Generative process, patterns, and the urban challenge. Portland, OR: PUARL Press.

Neis H. J. & Brown G., eds. (2010) Current challenges for patterns, pattern languages, and sustainability. Portland, OR: PUARL Press.

Sloterdijk P. (2014) Die Schrecklichen Kinder der Neuzeit. Suhrkamp, Berlin: Suhrkamp Verlag GmbH

Smitshuijzen E. (2007). Signage design manual. Baden: Lars Muller.

Stark W. (2012) Tacit knowledge and innovation patterns for communities and social systems. Referenced From: Neis H. J., Brown G., Gurr J. M., & Schmidt J. A., eds. (2012) Generative process, patterns, and the urban challenge (89-95). Portland, OR: PUARL Press.

Stein M. (2008). When technology fails: A manual for self-reliance, sustainability, and surviving the long emergency (Rev. and expanded. ed.). White River Junction, VT: Chelsea Green Pub.

Tschumi B. (1994). Architecture and disjunction (pp. 152-168). Cambridge, Mass.: MIT Press.

Uebele A. (2007). Signage systems & information graphics: A professional sourcebook. New York: Thames & Hudson.

3.1 Journals & Online Publications

CREW, Cascadia Region Earthquake Workgroup, Dr. Nourse, K.. Updated Edition (2013) Cascadia Subduction Zone Earthquakes: A Magnitude 9.0 Earthquake Scenario. Retrieved April 16, 2015 from URL: http://crew.org/sites/default/files/cascadia_subduction_scenario_2013.pdf

Folke C., Carpenter S. R., Walker B., Scheffer M., Chapin T., & Rockström J. (2010). Resilience thinking: integrating resilience, adaptability and transformability. Ecology and Society 15(4): 20. Retrieved June, 2014 from URL: http://www.ecologyandsociety.org/vol15/iss4/art20/

Furukawazono, T., Seshimo S., Muramatsu, D., Iba, T. (2013). Survival Language: A Pattern Language for Surviving Earthquakes. PLoP ,13 Proceedings of the 20th Conference on Pattern Languages of Programs. Monticello, Illinois: The Hillside Group. Retrieved June, 2014 from URL: http://www.hillside.net/plop/2013/papers/Group6/plop13_preprint_28.pdf

IOC, Intergovernmental Oceanographic Commission. Revised Edition (2013). Tsunami Glossary, 2013. Paris, UNESCO. IOC Technical Series, 85. (IOC/2008/TS/85rev). Retrieved April 15, 2015 from URL: http://itic.ioc-unesco.org/images/stories/about_tsunamis/tsunami_glossary/tsunami_glossary_en_2013_web.pdf

Meadows, D. (1997). Leverage Points: Places to Intervene in a System. Sustainability Institute. Retrieved June, 2014 from URL: http://www.donellameadows.org/wp-content/ userfiles/Leverage_Points.pdf

Priest G., Watzig R., & Madin I. (n.d.) Open-File Report O-15-XX: Local Tsunami Evacuation Analysis of Seaside and Gearhart, Clatsop County, Oregon. Newport & Portland, OR: DOGAMI, State of Oregon Department of Geology & Mineral Industries.

Portland Urban Architecture Research Lab (2014) Up & Out I. Oregon Tsunami Wayfinding Research Project: Final Project Report and Guidance Document. Retrieved from URL: http://puarl.uoregon.edu/upandout2.pdf

Portland Urban Architecture Research Lab (2015) Up & Out II. Oregon Tsunami Wayfinding Research Project: A Study in Seaside and Warrenton. Retrieved from URL: http://puarl.uoregon.edu/upandout2.pdf

Schulz, K. (2015). The Really Big One. The New York Times. Retrieved August 12, 2015 from URL: http://www.newyorker.com/magazine/2015/07/20/the-really-big-one

3.2 Websites

DOGAMI, State of Oregon Department of Geology & Mineral Industries (n.d.). Oregon Tsunami Clearinghouse: Resource Library. Retrieved April 15, 2015 from URL: http://www.oregongeology.org/tsuclearinghouse/faq-tsunami.htm

DOGAMI, State of Oregon Department of Geology & Mineral Industries (n.d.). Oregon Tsunami Clearinghouse: Evacuation Brochures. Retrieved April 15, 2015 from URL: http://www.oregongeology.org/tsuclearinghouse/pubs-evacbro.htm

FEMA, Federal Emergency Management Agency (n.d.). FEMA Tsunamis. Retrieved April 15, 2015, from URL: http://m.fema.gov/tsunamis

History of Geology, Bressan, D. (2011, March 17). Historic Tsunamis in Japan. Retrieved April 15, 2015, from URL: http://historyofgeology.fieldofscience.com/2011/03

NOAA, National Oceanic and Atmospheric Administration (n.d.). NOAA Tsunami Website. Retrieved April 17, 2015, from URL: http://www.tsunami.noaa.gov/

NPR, National Public Radio, Simmons-Duffin, S. (2011, March 18). History Of Tsunami: The Word And The Wave. Retrieved April 16, 2015 from URL: http://www.npr.org/2011/03/18/134600508

NWS, National Weather Service (last modified May 26, 2015) TsunamiReady. Retrieved April 15, 2015 from URL: http://www.tsunamiready.noaa.gov/

OPB, Oregon Public Broadcasting, Spitz, T. (2015, January 26). Jan.26, 1700: How Scientists Know When the Last Big Earthquake Happened Here. Retrieved April 17 from URL: http://www.opb.org/news/series/unprepared/jan-26-1700-how-scientists-know-when-the-last-big-earthquake-happened-here/

OEM, Oregon Office of Emergency Management (n.d.). Tsunami Information. Retrieved April 16, 2015 from URL: http://www.oregon.gov/OMD/OEM/Pages/plans_train/tsunamis.aspx

PUARL, Portland Urban Architecture Research Laboratory (n.d.) PUARL Website. Retrieved June 20, 2015 from URL: http://puarl.uoregon.edu/

Wikipedia, Free Encyclopedia (last modified June 22, 2015). 2011 Tōhoku Earthquake and Tsunami. Retrieved April 15, 2015 from URL: https://en.wikipedia.org/wiki/2011_Tohoku_earthquake_and_tsunami

Wikipedia, Free Encyclopedia (last modified June 1, 2015).Cascadia Subduction Zone. Retrieved April 15, 2015 from URL: https://en.wikipedia.org/wiki/Cascadia_subduction_zone

3.3   Images

Figure 1: PUARL team photograph

Figure 2: Taylor, A. (2014, December 26). Ten Years Since the 2004 Indian Ocean Tsunami. Retrieved August 23, 2015, from URL: http://www.theatlantic.com/photo/2014/12/ten-years-since-the-2004-indian-ocean-tsunami/

Figure 3: Japan earthquake and tsunami: Before and after the cleanup. (2013, March 7). Retrieved Augest 23, 2015, from URL: http://www.latimes.com/world/la-fg-japan-tsunami-before-after-slider-htmlstory.html

Figure 4: Gagnon, K. (n.d.). Cascadia Subduction Zone and Seismic Worries. Retrieved August 23, 2015, from URL: http://www.standeyo.com/NEWS/06_Earth_Changes/061022.Cascadia.Zone.html

Figure 5: OEM, Oregon Office of Emergency Management (n.d.). Tsunami Information. Retrieved August 23, 2015 from URL: http://www.oregon.gov/OMD/OEM/Pages/plans_train/tsunamis.aspx

Figure 6: PUARL team photograph

Figure 7-8: Portland Urban Architecture Research Lab (2015) Up & Out II. Oregon Tsunami Wayfinding Research Project: A Study in Seaside and Warrenton. Retrieved from URL: http://puarl.uoregon.edu/upandout2.pdf

Figure 9: PUARL team photograph

Figure 10: PUARL team photograph

Figure 11: Iba Laboratory Publication

Figure 12-17: PUARL (2014) Up & Out I. Oregon Tsunami Wayfinding Research Project: Final Project Report and Guidance Document. Retrieved from URL: http://puarl.uoregon.edu/upandout2.pdf

Figure 18: PUARL team photograph

Image: Liz | www.flickr.com/photos/erislove | CC Licence | unchanged

The Production of Cities: Christopher Alexander and the problem of "System A" at large scale

Porta, Sergio
University of Strathclyde, United Kingdom
sergio.porta@strath.ac.uk

Rofè, Yodan
Ben-Gurion University of the Negev, Israel
yrofe@bgu.ac.il

Vidoli, Mariapia
University of Strathclyde, United Kingdom
maria.vidoli@strath.ac.uk

This paper sets out to respond to the question of whether, and how, can Alexander's System A of generating beauty and life in the world be implemented at the large scale. We show that the generation of beauty in cities is a question of time not scale, and that it is a product of morphological evolution, typified by what we call: informal participation. The mechanistic system codified and developed in the last 70 years for building the environment (System B) is not able to accommodate informal participation, and thus incapable of creating beauty or life. It is not planning per se that is the problem, but knowing what needs and can be planned, and what needs to be allowed to evolve. Thus, planning's role can be redefined as creating the structures, both physical and regulatory that will allow informal participation to occur freely and create life, beauty and wholeness in the built environment.

Urban design; grid, building process; urban morphology; built environment

1. Christopher Alexander and the large scale: re-framing the conflict between System A and System B

Alexander's last book "*Battle*" (Alexander, Neis, & Moore-Alexander, 2012) describes how vital establishing a human system of construction is, as opposed to the current system dominated by image, power and money; Alexander names the former "System A" and the latter "System B". In the last chapter of the book, he leaps from the description of one complex project, the new Eishin campus in Tokyo, Japan, which he and the book's co-authors designed and built, to a vision of rebuilding a civilization. There is a gap, however, between the singular project, serving one client, for a single purpose, and the coordination and accommodation of multiple agents striving for different and often conflicting purposes, typical of urban design. That this gap exists and is felt as an issue by the authors themselves, is confirmed by one of them, Hajo Neis: he describes how Chapter 24, entitled *"Large scale building production: Unification of the Human System and the Physical System"*, was ultimately cancelled before publication (Neis, 2014). This anecdote, as the authors confirmed in person, highlights how the problem of System A at large scale was felt by Alexander to be still unresolved, and not ready to be included in the book at the date of "Battle"'s publication in 2012.

This problem is of importance to us for three reasons: first, because Alexander's approach has shown a remarkable amount of success when applied at the small/medium scale, and bringing it up to the urban level would considerably expand its benefit; second, because his insistence on fine-grained community-driven and direct construction appears particularly aligned with the predominantly poor and informal character of urbanization in the Global South, which is where the fight for a sustainable future will be won or lost over the next two generations (Alexander, 2004; U.N.DESA, 2014); finally, because his profound attachment to the evolutionary principles of life in all aspects of building makes his life-long investigation increasingly central in the current debate on a new science of cities and city-planning (Mike Batty & Marshall, 2009). In order to approach the problem, in this paper we set out to explore the following: what is it exactly that prevents System A to be as explanatory and helpful at the large scale as it is in the small scale?

We start in Section 2 by reframing the question within an evolutionary understanding of urban form, by observing the way life occurs in small vs. large-scale, homogeneous vs. heterogeneous, and short vs. long-time building processes. In Section 3 we explore System A at work as a *beauty generating* system of production more than anything else; this leads us to conclude that the problem, which emerged as a scale issue, is rather in essence a time issue, in fact much more a long-term than a large-scale problem. We then go back to Alexander, in Section 4, reviewing his own attempts at defining the problem of System A at large scale, in the light of our new focus on time. In the Conclusions (Section 6) we sum up our findings and clarify that in order for System A to be viable at the large scale, and therefore capable of meeting the challenge of the mainstream, it must necessarily develop a closer comprehension of the specific dynamics involved when beauty emerges *in the long term*.

2. Cities as products of cultural evolution: towards a discipline of the post-design

At first glance, the problem of scale seems to relate to the difference between small and large "projects". That appears to come down to three essential dichotomies: small vs. large-scale, homogeneous vs. heterogeneous and shorter vs. longer projects. However, we should resist the temptation to link up too tightly the project's size, *per-se*, with its profound nature, for example its *complexity*. In other words, smaller projects are not necessarily simpler than larger projects. It is the architecture of the internal relationships between the components of a phenomenon that tells us about its complexity, not its sheer size. Weaver (Weaver, 1948), later quoted by J. Jacobs (Jacobs, 1992, c.1961, p. 429), notoriously distinguished in nature three types of phenomenon: simple, complex/disorganized, and complex/organized. According to this distinction, processes of construction at the urban scale are a problem of organized complexity, as they typically involve human systems of decision makers, environmental systems of spatially defined features and cultural systems of technology, language, images and habits, all of them entailing non-random patterns of mutual relationships between their internal components as well as between themselves as wholes. Projects that operate at the small scale of the building or the aggregate of buildings and those at the large scale of the neighbourhood/city are certainly different in size, but it is the number of actors and systems of control involved along with their fundamental mutual relationships that tells about their grade of complexity.

One thing that we can see very clearly at the large scale, however, and tends to remain hidden at the small scale, is that change in cities does not happen only "by-design" through centralized "projects". In other words, dynamics of continuous modification of the built environment out of any central overarching control are normally clearly visible in the way the urban fabric changes at large scale (J. W. R. Whitehand, 1998; J. W. R. Whitehand, Gu, Conzen, & Whitehand, 2014). In such processes, the elements of the systems involved, human, regulatory, even cultural, typically change in a predominantly uncoordinated way, in a dynamic that is characterized by patterns of emergence and self-organization rather than central control and implementation. Far from being occasional, this type of change is ubiquitous in cities; it is the product of an *evolutionary* process which makes urban systems similar, analogous in fact, to ecological systems at the structural level (Holling & Goldberg, 1971). On what basis then should we talk of evolution in cities in the context of the present discussion on System A at large scale?

Much like beautiful cities, other products of human culture such as marvellous tales that make our life more significant, majestic dreams which embed the essence of our feelings for things like death, birth, youth, courage and fear as a collectivity of human beings, incredibly intelligent skills that allow us to acknowledge each other, light a fire, fly in the air like birds at unbelievable speed or make others understand the most subtle nuances of our moods and thoughts, have never been designed as such by anybody. Though somebody at some point may have designed some of the intermediate steps that brought these things to their current configuration, overall they are what they are because they have *evolved*, and indeed they continue to do so. Obviously, when using the word "evolution" in the context of a study on urbanism we must be aware that we are practicing an analogy, that of the city as a living organism or as an ecological system, which is seemingly as old as the human thought on cities and design (Geddes, 1915; Marshall, 2008; Steadman, 2008). However, while biologic evolution increasingly seems to offer a fertile ground for the interpretation of phenomena that go well beyond the boundaries of life sciences, including cultural phenomena such as the human language (Pagel, 2009), a truly evolutionary approach to cities, as opposed to a conventional biomorphic or at best developmental, is still to be regarded as a matter of pioneering research (Batty & Marshall, in print; Dibble et al., in print).

For the sake of this paper and the problem of System A at large scale, it will suffice to highlight that acknowledging the evolutionary nature of urban change means two things:

1. If we are to decipher why buildings and cities are what they look like today, we need to utilize a *structural* approach. That is: acknowledging that there is something in what we see that is permanent and ubiquitous – "patterns" of change, or the *structure* – around which endless diversity occurs by means of unforeseeable uncertainty. That is the way life takes shape on our planet from an evolutionary perspective, as well as the way other non-living realities work, like chemical or cultural. If city form is a cultural product, which in all evidence is the case, we need to understand how it evolves as such: an entire new branch of urban science has to be established and develop starting in the area of *urban morphology*.

2. We should, all of us, architects, planners, urban scholars, practitioners, make a big leap from a culture that is mostly preoccupied with the design phase (and the designer/

author) to that of the *post-design*. Despite our widespread and undisputed obsession for the design phase, what happens to the urban realm after construction is much more important to us than what happens before it. If we design and plan cities under this new perspective, everything takes a different shape and seemingly established priorities get rapidly subverted: for example, the importance of what we do in the design phase is measured against the consequences that it generates in the post-design rather than *per-se*, like if "there was no tomorrow". In a nutshell, we find ourselves in a new territory: *designing for change*. This territory requires a whole set of different understandings and tools, or, in fact, a *different discipline*.

Most processes of change are of an evolutionary nature, and although they are more evident at the large scale, they regularly occur at all scales (Brand, 1995; Moudon, 1986; J. Whitehand, W R, 1979), interspersed as they are by designed projects. It seems that pre-planned, designed interventions are always followed by evolutionary change, which is made up of many, if smaller scale, designed projects. So our attempt to understand what makes the large scale of development particularly hostile to System A seems to reach a dead end, as there is nothing really, in the large scale per se, that seems to make a real difference in the nature of the processes of urban change involved, be them centralized (projects) or emerging (evolution) (Fig.1). However, with the new focus on *time* that is central to the evolutionary approach mentioned above, we can capture two fundamental principles in urban change that would otherwise get lost: firstly, by definition project change predominantly occurs in the design phase, while evolution in the post-design; secondly, project change occurs over a much shorter amount of time than evolution. By "much shorter" we mean substantially shorter, in a way that involves an entirely different time-scale. If we compare the two types of change with the duration of a human generation, say about 25 years, we can assume that Project change certainly works at a sub-generational time-scale, whilst evolutionary change at a super-generational[1].

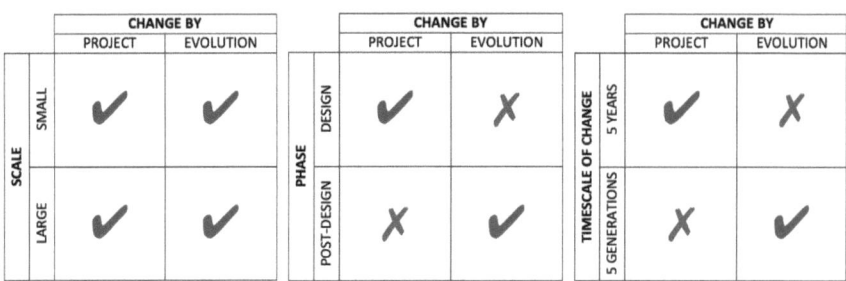

Figure 1: Left: spatial scale does not characterize either of the two different forms of urban change (project and evolution), which equally occur at small and large scale. Middle: time, on the contrary,

---
1   What we mean here by "time frame" is the generative time that it takes to decide, design and build the project, not necessarily its functional/structural/financial life-span, which may typically be much longer.

effectively distinguishes the type of change: projects occur in the design phase only, while evolution in post-design only. Right: analogously, projects normally work over a sub-generational (five years) time-scale only, while evolution over a super-generational (five generations) only. Source: authors.

These two observations, as we will see in the rest of the paper, are of enormous importance, and key to resolve the problem of System A at large scale. Their importance comes through when we analyse System A as essentially a system of *beauty generation*. Under this light, the question is not only who generates beauty and how, but also and primarily: *when is beauty generated?*

3. West Dean, Piazza Santo Stefano and Athole Gardens: the problem of building beauty

Our cities are very often, in all evidence, amazingly beautiful. Endlessly different manifestations of profoundly rewarding historical urban environments are before our eyes everywhere in old cities, and they emerge sometimes, often at smaller scale, certainly less frequently, in recent urban developments. We introduced this obvious observation in a personal conversation with Alexander, emphasizing the role that self-organization plays in generating beauty when large scale and heterogeneity are involved in the long term. We also dropped the word "evolution" by proposing that diversity and beauty emerges at the large scale, that of cities, in ways that may be entirely different from those that occur at the small scale. We argued that we don't work for building something immediately beautiful, but something that may become beautiful, everything going well, in five generations. After a few seconds of silence, Alexander replied: "*No, I can do that in five years*". To demonstrate that, the day after we were accompanied to visit the West Dean College visitors centre, built in 1994-95 near Chichester, West Sussex, UK, for the Edward James Foundation by Alexander and colleagues of the Center for Environmental Structure (CES). There we could test with our eyes the appropriateness of his claim: yes, that timeless quality, the one that makes you sit and breath in peaceful respect and joy, the "quality without a name" (Alexander, 1979), or "wholeness", or "beauty", or simply "life" (Fig.2), was there in tangible, startling abundance. And it is true: he did that in five years.

Figure 2: Christopher Alexander's "quality without a name" as a Wholeness/Life/Beauty circle. This diagram is our interpretation of part of hand-drawn sketch entitled "Chris' learning curve", created by Maggie Moore Alexander in 2014 and graciously donated to us. We use it here under her kind permission.

We were brought, on that occasion, before two apparently opposing realities: on the one hand, Alexander could actually generate beauty in five years (West Dean); on the other hand, the world is full of urban places which clearly exhibit the same quality without Alexander's design, nor indeed anybody else's. If we are to approach the problem of why System A has not become mainstream, we need to understand whether, and in what sense, Alexander himself was essential to creating beauty in West Dean, and how, on the other hand, the same beauty comes across without Alexander, or any other particular creator, in many other cases that we can observe in the world, and does that *as a rule*.

We propose that in order to resolve this apparent contradiction, in line with the evolutionary orientation that we have assumed, we need to focus primarily on the element of time: it took five years to generate West Dean; however, it took centuries to generate the same beauty in Piazza Santo Stefano in Bologna, for example, or Athole Gardens in Glasgow's west-end (Fig.3). To advance in this direction we need to elucidate the nature of the processes that were at work at West Dean, as compared to those that shaped our historical cities to a similar level of beauty, but in a much longer amount of time.

Figure 3:

Above: West Dean Visitors Centre, Chichester, UK. Designed and constructed by Christopher Alexander and CES in a few years. Middle: Piazza Santo Stefano, Bologna, IT. Evolved in about two millennia from a bifurcation along the street that connects Bologna with Tuscany. Bottom: Athole Gardens, Glasgow, UK. Master planned in the second half of the XIXth Century. Beauty is clearly generated in all these three cases. Source: authors.

3.1 The West Dean's way: building beauty in five years

In a System A approach to design and building, the most important thing is the content of life that is brought into the process. The way it happens may take different forms, but it is always and mainly about bringing life into the practical everyday sequence of actions that constitutes the building process in all its phases. There are three ways by which life can be poured into the shaping of a place: *observation*, *interaction*, and *co-action*.

Observation. In "A Pattern Language" (Alexander, Ishikawa, & Silverstein, 1977) life is first of all observed at work. Here recurrent patterns of life expression are identified, recorded and linked up to both higher and lower scale spatial configurations. The observation of how life occurs in the built environment is expected to inform our action of building. Such observed manifestations of life in the land, insofar they are recurrent and reasonably ubiquitous, are "patterns"; they are, essentially, constituent parts of the structure of a place, in that they reveal simultaneously the nature of the land and that of the people who use and live in it. Importantly, as much as patterns are observed recurrent life/environment structures in the land, they cannot be turned into abstract formulations generated only through intellectual speculation. It is the process of pattern recognition that really counts. That has to be a living process, in order to bring life into the patterns themselves. Observation must happen by immersion into the occurrence of life in the land. Patterns emerge, for every project, from the physical, emotional and intellectual immersion of designers and the whole community of inhabitants and builders into a shared process of both speculative and emotional inquiry. This way of exploring patterns evidently requires skills that are normally alien to architectural education, very close to those typical of anthropology, sociology or even ethology.

Interaction. In later formulations, however, Alexander himself has developed a more radically interactive orientation to the process of pattern recognition (Sergio Porta, Russell, Romice, & Vidoli, 2014). According to this approach, life must be carved out from the community of inhabitants and builders by a sensible operation of depth reaching that must be undertaken at the personal level through one-to-one or one-to-few interaction. The ground for that is the acknowledgement that people in our professionalized society grow-up along a path of increasing detachment from their own profound and authentic feelings and desires, such that as adults they do not live in that authentic part of themselves any longer, and they would normally be scared to do so. In Alexander's own words, "*It's immensely hard to help people tell you what they want. Even in the simple practical issue of a building, its entrance, its rooms, its gardens… people cannot easily formulate their vision or their desire*" (Alexander et al., 2012, p. 115). Why then is getting there so important in a building process? Essentially, because that is the place where people share their foundations as human beings. Once interactively solicited at that level, and only at that level, people's desires, feelings and visions are surprisingly alike, and one's vision is, more or less, everybody's vision. There, at that level, is where personal feelings and dreams cease to be (individual, idiosyncratic) *opinions*, and start becoming (shared, objective) *realities*. This way to reach patterns is again only accessible through an intensively human, life-generating process, a form of interview/interaction that requires a set of skills and attitudes that are in fact close to psychotherapy (and, again, completely ignored in current architectural education). It is worth noting how all this resonates with the Jungian notion of the collective unconscious, as well as with experiential approaches to counselling.

Co-action. Life, finally, can be brought into the process of building by the sheer act of building together, or *co-action*. By that, we mean primarily the actual process of making that involves directly the hands of all participants into the practical fact of constructing. Even though co-action predominantly operates in the construction phase, to the extent that its meaning is expanded to the wider notion of "acting together" it may permeate in different forms the whole building process[2]. That enables a wide, extremely subtle and complex set of situations that occur both within and beyond the actual making of things, and are shared by all those who work and build, including for example discussing, trusting, arguing, celebrating, dancing, drinking, playing and respecting. Skills that are crucially relevant to co-action may be very practical at times, but they are by no means limited to technical abilities: they cover for example the ability to listen and speak, visualize ideas in quick sketches or gestures, cook, dance and play, have fun with others, suffer and endure challenges with others, support others under pressure in a generous and competent way; much of these skills are in fact related, at a higher level, to *small-group dynamics*, and are normally very marginally touched, if at all, in conventional architectural education.

Crucially, co-action implies the elimination of the barriers that separate, in conventional decision-making, those who take decisions from each other, places where decisions are taken from each other, and the moments in time when those decisions are taken from each other. Carpenters and inhabitants, architects and electric engineers, planning officers and plumbers, financial advisors and sash-window supplier, in a System A perspective are expected to make decisions together in the same moment and in the same place: *the building yard*. Co-action in fact fundamentally implies direct hands-on construction, though that may be pursued along sometimes significantly different forms. It is this particular aspect of co-action, much more than anything related to observation and interaction, which creates the strongest conflict between System A and System B: co-action challenges the heart of the

---
2   *The three modes of bringing life into the building process, observation, interaction and co-action, which are here illustrated separately for the sake of clarity, never occur in complete separation in real building processes*

established timeframe, culture and overall environment of conventional decision-making throughout the whole building process and that, of course, means challenging the extant forms of power. System A is, in this respect, essentially one single solid process of power transfer from established to new subjects, times and places of decision. As such, System A is inherently subversive of System B's conventional practices; in this respect, Alexander walks on the same ground of other giants, along the line that leads from Koenigsberger and Turner's "radical development" of the 1970s (Boano & Talocci, 2014; Turner, 1977; Windsor Liscombe, 2006), to the current "self-build", "right-to-buy" and "right-to-build" agendas in the UK (Parvin, Saxby, Cerulli, & Schneider, 2011; Wilson, 2013), through various streams of informal, DIY or tactical urbanism (Finn, 2014; Lydon & Garcia, 2015; Sawhney, de Klerk, & Malhotra, 2015).

If we look at the stream of experiences of progressive planning, participatory or community design that have come up in the last half century or so, we see that elements of observation and interaction have made their way into conventional planning and even, in cases like the Congress of New Urbanism "design charrette," or the Prince's Foundation for Building Communities "Enquiry-by-Design" (McGlynn & Murrain, 1994), they have become themselves mainstream in some particularly advanced areas of the planning world-system. However, the same cannot be said for co-action, which has always been practiced in "protected reserves" of the system, mainly academic, or in fact in geographic areas characterized by weak if not essentially absent planning systems, like informal settlements. Alexander himself, his personal career and his intensive and continuous practice as a builder, notwithstanding his extraordinary gifts of leadership and scientific penetration, has not escaped this fate. His is a story of a permanent conflict with System B particularly because of the co-action element of the process. A conflict which System B has, as of now, certainly won. All attempts that have been made to shorten the distance between System A and System B have always come, sooner or later, to the point where either a compromise had to be reached to significantly reduce the co-action element, if not actually exclude it from the process, or to stop the process altogether. If the opposition between System A and System B is a battle, co-action is certainly the battlefield.

After a life on the battlefield, Alexander is very clear on not just accepting, but even defending the idea that the conflict between the two Systems is irreconcilable not just in practice, but in *nature*. System B is the established intricate network of powers that System A's co-action *wants to subvert*. If that is the case the only ground on which System A can operate is one where System B is, in some way, "paused". That effectively means creating an "ecological niche" for System A to survive in a System B dominated world. However, System B is by its same nature pervasive and capillary, it permeates all areas of the building system and it controls all channels that need to be utilized in a process of construction. Pausing it is not easy by any means. It includes managing differently, for example, the whole planning authorization process, countering design regulations at least to some degree, and changing the way suppliers and professionals work. It is about challenging preconceptions and established assumptions first of all in the mind of those involved in the process, which are all very likely to be System B-orientated, if not by anything else just because System B is the normal way of doing things.

In all evidence, pausing System B in a project at the building scale is difficult, often extremely difficult, but what about pausing it in a project at the neighbourhood scale, or that of a masterplan? In this latter case it has to be deemed nearly impossible, as the number of parties involved is normally much higher, and, crucially, because their size is much larger (Akbar, 1988). In current urban-scale decision-making, "parties" mostly means large organizations, be they governmental, non-governmental or private sector. Changing the way people think, feel and operate is hard enough, but doing the same to large organizations is ways more difficult, requires different practices and, crucially, a completely different timeframe, which is incompatible with a five-year perspective. We observe, in fact, that System B has been paused to some extent in many instances in the last half century, allowing for System A to operate and demonstrate its undisputable value, West Dean being one of these cases. But we also observe that the same thing has never occurred at a large scale: no one single example of successful System A-driven large scale project is on record apart from the Eishin Campus in Japan. The Eishin project, the story of which is the subject of "Battle", probably sets the upper limit of what a System A project can achieve in a System B dominated context.

In summary, if we want to deliver a large scale project through a System A human process in a System B dominated world, seeking some form of sub-optimal compromise between System A and System B is not the way forward because such compromise is impossible *in nature* (because of the co-action discriminant). Analogously, pausing System B in a project at the urban scale is not the way forward because it is just impossible *in practice*: System B is much more "effective" than System A in getting the job done in a large-scale project, provided that it is in fact a *project*, i.e. it is centrally managed and engineered to be confined to a sub-generational timeframe. That may not generate beauty, in fact it inhibits life altogether and creates places that are anti-human as a rule, but does nevertheless generate outcomes that are reasonably predictable and profitable for the industry, the technical and legal bureaucracies and the financial investors that created System B. The only way to put System A to work at large scale, and give it a chance to be mainstream, necessarily involves re-conceptualizing our understanding of the way beauty emerges *in the long-term, as well* as how System A works in that, super-generational, temporal perspective. In short, we need to shift our focus from a System A at *large (space) scale* to a System A at *long (time) scale*.

3.2 Our cities' way: building beauty in five generations

If it is evidently true, as recalled at the beginning of this chapter, that our old cities are very often beautiful in the most profound sense of the word and nevertheless none appear to be the products of the organized System A process of development that we have seen at work at West Dean. Not at first glance at least. Beauty in the ordinary parts of our historical cities is very rarely the direct outcome of a "design" (neither one of the product nor of the process), or indeed of the coordinated efforts of any group of builders (neither a community nor a company), or the investigation of anybody's self; nor did their generation in time normally include the on-purpose production of patterns whatsoever. In the history of beautiful urban places we never find the radical forms of co-action described above, with ordinary people building together in the building yard, testing materials and making decisions in due course. Nevertheless, as we experience marvellous ordinary places such as Piazza Santo Stefano in Bologna or the Athole Gardens in Glasgow, we feel ourselves pervaded by the same sense of deep joy, quietness and harmony that we experienced at West Dean; certainly though we can find in those places beautiful patterns that have nevertheless *emerged*. Quite clearly, a remarkable amount of life had filtered into the making of these places over a long period of time in ways that are hard to define in the first place, but certainly are not the same that generated West Dean or the Eishin Campus over a much shorter amount of time. Therefore the question is: if life was not brought into the generating processes of so many of our best urban places by a consciously designed System A sequence, what was it exactly that eventually did that? What different ways life took to penetrate the generative process at that scale, and by that we mean primarily at that *time* scale?

If we observe the way our beautiful cities have come to their current configuration in time, we can easily distinguish recursive spatial patterns at work in the most different environmental, cultural, social and economic contexts. For example, we notice that cities have always emerged around central places, higher centrality tends to go with higher density, higher density is linked to a movement-based agglomeration economy, the plot is the smallest unit of change, dynamics of plot merger and split tend to follow local and global economic cycles, building types are effectively linked to the geometric character of plots, blocks tend to respond in different ways to the different centrality of their four (or three) street-fronts, and this whole ubiquitous complex and organic mechanism of city building is based on two basic principles: 1) plots are relatively small and are developed independently from each other, such that control is distributed, and exerted on any individual adjacent plot by different parties (Habraken & Teicher, 2000); 2) centrality emerges in the street network at a reasonably human scale (main streets crossing each other at about 400 meters or less) (S. Porta, Romice, Maxwell, Russell, & Baird, 2014).

This structure may emerge "spontaneously" or develop from an initial planning determination or, in most cases, by a certain grade of mix of the two. What is important here is that "spontaneous" modifications of the environment are the way life takes place in cities, tend to occur both with and without a planned initial state of development, and are the force that builds beauty in cities. We name this force *informal participation*, i.e. the combination of all the complex and uncoordinated efforts that human beings put into the modification of the environment for their own direct spiritual or practical benefit. In this sense, the way the "initial state" of the evolutionary process is determined, whether through authoritarian top-down planning, coordinated community-action or bottom-up fine-grained initiatives, is not really important, as long as it does not inhibit the full expression of informal participation. The urban fabric of Piazza Santo Stefano, actually a bifurcation along the ancient road from Bologna to Tuscany, has never been planned as a whole, and has evolved to its current state since at least the Vth century A.D., while Athole Gardens was a market-driven planned development designed from the top down without any form of community participation. Again, from an evolutionary perspective the *design phase is not the point*. As long as it produces a *structure* which is fit to solidly bear and foster change in time, the design phase has delivered its task: it is society at large, through continuous informal participation occurring over the following centuries, that brings life into the process and therefore beauty into existence.

3.3 Manufacturing in the mystery of nascence

At a first glance, Alexander's "*I can do that in five years*" sounds like a narcissistic statement, but it is not: clearly that "I" had no personal connotation in the most obvious sense of the word. It actually identified, with Alexander's person, the life-enhancing process of construction that he later named "System A", as applied in West Dean. Moreover, and most importantly, he drove our attention away from a simplistic consideration of the opposition between the small and the large scale. The organized complexity that Weaver was alluding to may apply to human building endeavors largely independently from their size. It would be irremediably ingenuous, simplistic in fact, to underestimate the endless levels of inner conflicts and the incredible variety of themes and matters that even one individual human being has to tackle when putting his hands into even the smallest process of making, if s/he does that *authentically*. When we understood that, we finally captured the hidden level of truth that Alexander's words brought to light for us: the reason why only System A could deliver beauty at West Dean is not that West Dean is smaller in scale, and therefore less complex than building a block or a quarter: it is that *West Dean had to be built in five years*. The West Dean process, pretty much as those in Mexicali, Oregon, San Josè, or indeed all other built works of Alexander, and even the complex of dozens buildings erected in the Eishin Campus, are all ultimately the application of a System A protocol applied to a centralized, *sub-generational* project, one that in fact operates mostly in the design phase (Fig.4).

		Centralized (PROJECT)	Self-organized (EVOLUTION)
CHANGE	PROJECT / DESIGN / 5 YEARS	System **B**	System **A**
	EVOLUTIONARY / POST-DESIGN / 5 GENERATIONS	**X**	**?**

Figure 4: System B is a process of construction that seeks the elimination of uncertainty for maximizing security of investment in the short term; its nature is mechanistic-centralized. Its time-scale is the five years, i.e. the sub-generational. System A is a process of construction that seeks the expansion of life and is, therefore, based on unpredictability; its nature is evolutionary and its time-scale is the five-generations, i.e. the super-generational. However, as a protocol for action System A has been expressed so far in a project form only, and as a consequence in a five years timescale only. The formation of a suitable System A protocol that expresses itself in the five generations timescale will also naturally fit the large scale of development.

This is, in fact, the profound nature of Alexander's life-long effort: he has penetrated like few others in history the subtle phenomena of building, being and living as one whole; he has profoundly understood the deep form of beauty generating processes in Nature as well as in construction, as processes that, step by step, expand and enhance the forms of life on the land over a long, definitely super-generational timescale; he then has moved on to conceive, test and validate a protocol of action, System A, that allows to generate beauty through a truly evolutionary process, but — remarkably — *over the tightly compressed, definitely sub-generational timescale of a project.*

What we have in front of us at West Dean is a tangible manifestation of the success of his endeavor: a nearly super-human achievement that emerges from a *radical compression of time*, where beauty/wholeness/life that should otherwise have taken centuries to evolve, could be created in five years, ending up in the same genuine, crystalline, dynamic perfection. Effectively, he created an artifact that reached the quiet harmony of pure life in a timescale, that of developmental morphogenesis, which is normally only accessible to living organisms during the mystery of nascence.

By doing that, Alexander "invaded" the camp of System B: his focus on the design phase, the sub-generational timescale, the project setting, are all features that are home to System B. Altogether, they constitute the environment that tireless efforts of innumerable committed and talented people created with System B over decades: public officers, management engineers, urban planners, artists, finance and law professionals, scholars in all fields of the built environment, have collaborated to the formation of the impressive endeavour that Alexander termed System B, with the only scope of taming the process of construction and steering it to their own benefit. System B is incapable of dealing with the super generational term and cannot cope with the post design phase: both are too risky, unpredictable and resistant to centralized control and management. All that which allows life to emerge in places through time, especially informal participation, the primary and by far the most important beauty generator in cities, is intolerable to System B. That is why System B since its full explication beginning after WWII has dramatically failed to create beauty on Earth in a way that has never been paralleled in the past, a failure that reaches its peak everywhere the long term is involved. System B is incompatible with anything else than the design phase. That is where its obsession for the "iconic" and "artistic" comes from: an attitude that excludes any possibility for the user to act on the environment and change it as s/he sees fit in the post design, and does that in *principle*.

If what identifies System A in all circumstances is its ability to generate beauty in places, it goes without saying that in all cases where beauty comes about through the self organized expression of a multitude of uncoordinated factors and actors, there we witness System A in action. It is that "version" of System A, the one that only emerges over a super generational timescale, which we need to translate into a protocol for action. This System A though, as all evolutionary processes of urban change, occurs in the post design phase only. Hence the objective of the design phase, and with it our role as urban designers, must be radically reconsidered: rather than struggling to build beauty ourselves, we should aim at setting in place the right structure for beauty to emerge over many generations after the completion of our project. Such understanding positions us firmly in an ecological urbanism perspective as unsuccessfully advocated since the early 1970s: *"The suggestions for change are analogous to ecological control schemes and basically state that the system can cure itself if given a chance. The chance is provided if our interventions give credence to the basic complexity and resilience of our urban systems. [...]. The idea is to let the system do it, while our interventions are aimed at juggling internal system parameters without simplifying the interactions of parameters and components"* (Holling & Goldberg, 1971, p. 229). The evolutionary perspective that we have assumed in this paper entails the entire reconfiguration of our role: *from beauty builders, we have now become structure enhancers*.

Identifying that structure, what it should include and especially what it should not, what needs to be the matter of urban planning and design (the former) and what especially should not (the latter), is the subject of a much needed "new science of cities and city planning", and indeed the foundation of System A at large scale. What is this structure exactly? What are its components, how do they come together and support each other, what are the rules that we must establish so that informal participation can flourish over that structure and continue flourishing in time? Apart from Alexander since the 1960s, all that has been explored in the past by scholars in urban morphology as well as a new wave of quantitative studies ranging from spatial analysis to the physics of networks (Barthelemy, 2011; Michael Batty, 2007; Michael Batty & Longley, 1994; Bettencourt, Lobo, & Youn, 2013; Boccaletti, Latora, Moreno, Chavez, & Hwang, 2006; Sergio Porta, Latora, & Strano, 2010). This programme of research in urbanism is primarily a life science, and as such it needs to cross the boundaries with the established disciplines of life. By looking at the dynamics of beauty generation in processes of evolutionary change, we have identified *informal participation* as a *primary evolutionary force*, like mutation in the evolution of life , while other important forces such as space centrality and building density are equally part of the structure of urban change (Sergio Porta & Romice, 2014).[3]

When action takes place in the long term and evolutionary change comes to the stage, this reframed notion of System A at large scale is the only positive option available. Moreover, as an evolutionary process in nature, System A is a natural fit for that scenario: *that is System A's home*. The challenge in front of us, when talking of large scale "design", is that of fully embracing the super-generational time scale of beauty generation. For the sake of clarity,

---

[3] Even though analyzing the ethical implications of an evolutionary approach to cities goes beyond the scope of this paper, it needs to be clarified that with "informal participation" we want to capture the essential, fundamental energy that moves human beings in making their environment fit directly their own individual needs and that of those towards which they hold a direct individual responsibility, first of all their closest relatives. This must be distinguished from change imposed to the environment by large private or public organizations for reasons of corporate gain (be it private/speculative or public/regulative), i.e. a gain that goes directly to their organization and only indirectly to their officers and employees as persons along the chain of command.

that does not mean that a design in the System A at large scale perspective could only be delivered in generations; it means that in order to truly express System A, a large scale design must set in place a structure which supports and enhances urban change by informal participation, which *then* will occur over the coming generations. In essence: a System A design at large scale is a design protocol for a truly evolutionary post-design phase. In order to do that, we first need to get back to Alexander, and review his work on the large scale under this new perspective.

3.4 Building beauty at large scale: a review of Christopher Alexander's work and ideas at the urban scale

Indeed, throughout his career, Alexander has struggled to define how beauty could emerge at the large scale, distinguishing between "generated" as opposed to "fabricated" structure (Alexander, 2003, pp. 182-185). In this section we look first at his indications with regards to how shall we build beauty at the neighbourhood and city scale in the first place. That comes across mainly in: a) the "Summary of the Language" section of the introduction to "A Pattern Language" (Alexander et al., 1977, pp. xviii-xxxiv) and within this framework, the master plan for the University of Oregon's Eugene campus (Alexander, Silverstein, Angel, Ishikawa, & Abrams, 1975); b) "A New theory of Urban Design" (Alexander et al., 1987); c) "The Masterplan and Process for Harbour Peak" (Alexander, Schmidt, & Buchanan, 2005) and d) Chapter 3 of "Battle" (Alexander et al., 2012, pp. 49, 58-60). Also, we discuss smaller scale examples of planning in his work as presented in e) "The Production of Houses" (Mexicali) (Alexander, Davis, Martinez, & Corner, 1985). Finally, we discuss f) three parts of "Nature of Order": Chapter 15 of Book 2, up to section 6 (Alexander, 2003, pp. 202-220), Chapter 9 of Book 3 (Alexander, 2005, pp. 283-310) and Chapter 15 of Book 3, up to section 6 (Alexander, 2005, pp. 334-351).

The driving question here is: to what extent are Alexander's planning principles oriented to creating beauty within the short term perspective of the design action (five years time scale) as opposed to *after* it, in the successive continuous process of evolutionary change (five generations time scale)? No doubt, Alexander understands fully the evolutionary principles of life; he integrates these principles in everything he talks about, from the "unfolding" nature of design and building to patterns. However, if we focus on the time span of the *action* that he proposes, it seems to be still confined by a project's timeframe, the five years sub generational perspective. That is obviously true of his works at the small scale of the building, where System A manages to compress the inherently super generational timescale of beauty generation into the sub generational timeframe of a project. But is it true for his larger scale works?

Talking of larger designs for multiple buildings urban areas or complex facilities like educational campuses, for Alexander the unfolding structure of beauty must come out from each individual project helping to create a larger whole that is unknowable in advance. That is the proposal of "A Pattern language", where it is recommended that the „Towns" patterns are built up from small scale individual project interventions. That is the uniqueness of the University of Oregon's "master plan without a master plan", where the initiative of user groups is supposed to be the driving force of the evolution of the campus. While there is an overall vision of the whole of the campus, it is given by the patterns as an abstract list and by the diagnosis map of the state of the environment: there is no physical master plan. This view of planning is brought full circle in „A New Theory", where the experiment is to create such wholeness, step by step, from individual building projects, under the guidance of a „planning commission" made up of Alexander himself and his fellow instructors, able to judge and guide the evolving wholeness. A process, that by Alexander's own admission, was not fully successful (ibid. pp. 235-249). The structure that was developing was too loose, too idiosyncratic, lacking the simple order of streets and plots that is typical of an American city like San Francisco, and strangely enough completely at odds with the surrounding area.

Perhaps even more important though than Alexander's insistence of building large scale structures, neighbourhoods, towns, cities and even regions, from small scale projects, is his insistence on the project being always connected to a human group, be it a land owner/developer, an association of people or a community building its own neighbourhood. This is the principle of *interaction* discussed above, and is obviously a prerequisite of any *co-action*. That, and his inherent suspicion of large impersonal (System B) organizations and governments with their bureaucracy, abstract rules and regulations, which do not allow for personal adaptation or exception to the rule where the land needs it, is perhaps the origin of his anti-masterplan stance. This criticism of master planning is not unique to Alexander, it is shared by critics of planning such as Jane Jacobs, and others in the 1960's who saw in comprehensive master planning a form of "physical determinism", representing the power of the elite. Martin argues that the opposition to conventional planning came forth in the early 1960s from a "city as living organism" standpoint, which privileges "spontaneous growth" against mechanistic top-down planning, and includes as main figures in this camp Jane Jacobs and Alexander himself (Martin, 1972). The same decade saw the beginning of planning as advocacy (Davidoff, 1965), and the rise in power of neighbourhoods which insisted on participatory planning. Under these waves of criticism, planning lost much of its previous assurance in its ability to rationally prepare a city for the future using scientific methods, and became much more preoccupied with process, communication, and politics.

The Production of Cities: Christopher Alexander and the problem of "System A" at large scale

Lost in the shuffle, by all critics of modern comprehensive city planning, are the many historical cases which clearly demonstrate the ability of a master plan to structure the growth of a city, as well as allow enough flexibility and autonomy to different subjects in the city to adapt the plans to their needs in such a way that creates beautiful, living structures; Manhattan, Amsterdam, Barcelona, Paris: the examples are innumerable, everywhere, varied and at different scales. Often, these were speculative developments created for financial profit, and under all forms of government, and yet today they clearly exhibit the substrate canvas that has allowed immense beauty and life to emerge in time by the self organized efforts of individuals, groups and organizations, what we called above "informal participation". Indeed, the street and plot structure of a city often outlives its particular foundational circumstances, and outlasts most social and political upheavals. It allows and expresses much more fundamental structures of urban life that go beyond culture, society or politics. That is, in fact, Martin's argument in "The Grid as a Generator" mentioned above, in defense of griddy or however geometrically shaped places proposed as structures for change rather than rigid blueprints of envisioned final states.

Martin addresses this point in open juxtaposition to Alexander's advocacy for complexity in cities as proposed a few years earlier in his notorious "A city is not a Tree" (Alexander, 1965). In all evidence, however, Alexander has fully acknowledged the emergence of very complex living realities over geometrically rigid spatial structures since his very early years. In particular, that comes through quite neatly in "A City is not a Tree", where a list of "natural" cities includes numerous griddy layouts like Manhattan, Liverpool and Kyoto, while conversely curvilinear and seemingly "organically designed" cities like Columbia and Greenbelt in Maryland are labelled as "artificial". This point returns many times in his further works: for example in "A New Theory" at some point a grid street layout is imposed quite forcefully over part of the project site in an otherwise loosely defined step-by-step design process (Alexander, 1987). But it is in "Nature of Order" that the "brutal" imposition of a formal geometric structure over the complex reality of the land is thoroughly addressed and proposed as a fundamental passage of any beauty-generating design process, seemingly at any scale (Alexander, 2003, pp. 401-412); here Alexander reiterates as a general rule that at some point there needs to be a focus on the structural geometrical order of the building itself, ignoring for a while all other considerations of program, land and context (ibid. 408). The same principle applies at the larger scale of the town in the Masterplan for Harbour Peak at Brookings, in Oregon, delivered in its draft form to local public authorities in 2005. In essence, this draft proposal expresses thoroughly the attempt on the one hand to exert control on the overall structure of the future settlement (natural reserves; streets and public spaces; built fabric location, density, rough position and alignment, landmark public buildings) while relaxing such control progressively as decision-making goes down to the scale of neighbourhoods, plots and buildings. That was expected to enable the generation of "*a multitude of processes, acting individually, yet geared towards the evolution of a coherent whole*" (Alexander et al., 2005, p. 12). The small scale of such individual processes comes increasingly to the stage from the neighbourhood level down, but requires a certain level of control from the neighbourhood level up in order to preserve and enhance the structure of the whole.

In the same way, when the problem is the foundation of a new city, the extension of a city to allow for rapid growth, the reconstruction of cities after natural or human made disaster, or the re-organization of cities which have outgrown their movement channels, as has happened again and again in the last two hundred years of accelerated urbanization, there is a need to think of the city as a whole, to provide it with its basic street structure, which will probably last for the duration of its history, to divide the land according to some socially acceptable rule, and to safeguard important natural and symbolic resources. This is essentially what master plans have done throughout urban history. In particular, the „long" 19th century — to paraphrase Hobsbawm (Hobsbawm, 2010), lasting in this case almost until the middle of the 20th century, has left us a legacy of planning for growth that has created urban textures of lasting value, able to adapt to change and to allow for the emergence of beauty and life. In contrast, the legacy of 20th century planning has left us an overly prescriptive and essentially anti-urban and anti-street planning legacy. That is a system tending to create closed and isolated neighbourhoods and projects, to zone uses separately from each other, to separate through from local movement, to limit density and to over-supply public open space, often, in order to pre-determine the economic level of the inhabitants, preferring few large projects (either public or private) to many small and individual ones; and in recent years, in response to criticism of the physical planning of the post-war period, and under the pressure from neo-liberal doctrines to abdicate planning completely (Koolhaas, 1995), to abandon any attempt at a holistic vision of the city and the well-being of its citizens, and to allow large private projects to determine public plans.

So the issue is not between master planning and organic growth; it is about *the appropriate amount of planning* in the appropriate time, at the appropriate scale, to hit just the right balance between structural control and super-structural self-organization. In their overall trajectory of evolution cities are certainly capable of organic growth while at some point needing planning interventions on a large scale, or they may go across periods where parts of them need to be planned at a single moment. Organic growth continues un-abated after more planning intensive periods, or even in parallel with them, working to change and adapt spaces over time. The appropriate amount of planning is one that is enough to create structure and protect essential public resources, but leaves as much freedom to individuals and groups to build and create their own spaces and bring life into the evolution of the city. The existence of the structure of the larger whole is necessary to allow the beginning of the process of unfolding of the smaller structures, and those in turn of the further smaller structures, in a process that is continuous in time and space and is absolutely essential to achieve the quality of a truly "generated" structure: *"that is the secret of the whole thing"* (Alexander, 2003, p. 195). But part of this secret is that the sequential nature of the process is respected so that structures at different levels are shaped autonomously on the basis of those already completed. Any attempt to "skip" this step-by-step form of action and determine structures at many different levels in one shot results in inhibiting the system's capacity to generate beauty by, in fact, overruling the process. In this perspective, planners should consider what they should not plan with equal attention, if not even more, than that they normally devote to what they should.

Thus, System A at large scale is not an anti-planning agenda: rather, it is about *planning less, and better*: difficult as it is, this is a problem of a pure *disciplinary* nature, not one of a larger reorganization of society across its various aspects, social, political, or economic. That leaves us in a quite comfortable, if not overoptimistic, position: System A at large scale *can* be made mainstream.[4]

4. Conclusion. Invitation for a reformed Master Planning practice: towards a System A at large scale

The evolutionary framework that we have outlined so far answers the question: when is beauty generated? At the large scale, in the long term, it is only generated after the design phase by a process of continuous adaptation, essentially enabled by the dynamics of *informal participation*. In order for it to occur in a way that enhances life, urban evolution requires the establishment of a structure that is both spatial and regulatory: *such structure* is the responsibility of planners and the planning system.

Both Piazza Santo Stefano in Bologna and Athole Gardens in Glasgow are examples of evolutionary developments that have reached beauty in a super-generational time frame. Bologna used to be a colonial military camp built by the Romans in 189 BC. Since then,

---
[4] A similar proposal is made by Shlomo Angel for planning for the future growth of cities in the Global South in this century (Angel, 2012). He advocates the creation of a grid of main streets that will carry major infrastructure and public transportation, and conserve those open space resources necessary for insuring water supplies and environmental health. He makes the point that since political and economic resources for safeguarding these public spaces are lacking – planners should not be maximal but minimal in determining the public infrastructure.

the historical core of the city developed in what is now considered an example of dense, compact and diverse medieval urban fabric, now the thriving home of the Alma Mater, the oldest university of the world, as well as innumerable commercial, residential and cultural facilities. Piazza Santo Stefano grew at the bifurcation of the ancient road from Bologna to Arezzo and Tuscany, along the same route that led to one of the two original axis of the ancient Roman camp. Not part of the first grid, the Piazza is therefore more appropriately a street junction, gracefully surrounded by palaces, ordinary housing and beautifully adorned porticoes all around. On one edge of the square, some seven different places of worship have been layered on top of each other since the V Century AD, by altering the previous.

Glasgow was not much more than a village until the mid of the XVIII Century AD. One century later it reached over one million inhabitants and was the second city of the British Empire after London, with a booming economy based on shipyards, industry and trade around the fluvial harbour on the river Clyde. Nowadays, Glasgow has abandoned the industrial economy and made its way into the post-industrial, with a flourishing tertiary economic base mainly relying on culture, education, tourism and the professions. All these changes have taken place between two city centres: the Merchant City, home of administration and commerce offices, theatres and clubs, and the West End, where respectable middle to upper class residential estates are graciously mixed with services, urban parks and retail. Both the Merchant City and the West End of Glasgow have been planned on a rigid grid system of Victorian streets and blocks which were destined to be completely demolished in the immediate post-war period to be replaced by a Corbusian scheme of highways and high-rises, laid out by municipal planners: the so-called "Bruce Plan". After the Bruce Plan was fortunately abandoned in the late 1970s, not before seriously damaging entire parts of the city, the two centres have continued to serve the city, the region and the nation up to our days, across countless adaptations and developments. Athole Gardens is a residential development in the West End, planned and realized in the 1860s for the industrious middle class of the times around a beautiful residential pocket park. It is now a quiet, beloved part of the lively district around Byres Road, the main street and certainly one of the most popular commercial strips in town.

Evolution has taken place in Piazza Santo Stefano and the Athole Gardens starting off in different ways and changing differently along different historical cycles. Life has flourished gloriously over both the rigid grids of the original military camp in Bologna and the Victorian planning schemes in Glasgow, making these two places among the most beautiful and successful on Earth. The diversity of these environments is simply inconceivable by a single human mind; nevertheless everything continues to change and adapt over a *structure* that remains mostly in place, which actually favours and disciplines the occurrence of endless variations in time. Most significantly, by no means are these two stories exceptions; in fact they are the rule: once backed up by reasonably accurate and simple planning structures, both spatial and regulatory, evolution occurs spontaneously by the uncountable and completely self-organized contributions of all, what we have called *informal participation*. Hundreds of cities in Europe and Africa have grown from the initial seeds of Roman camps, or from other grid layouts that are in fact typical of all cities of foundation, anywhere at any time in history (Fig.5a,b).

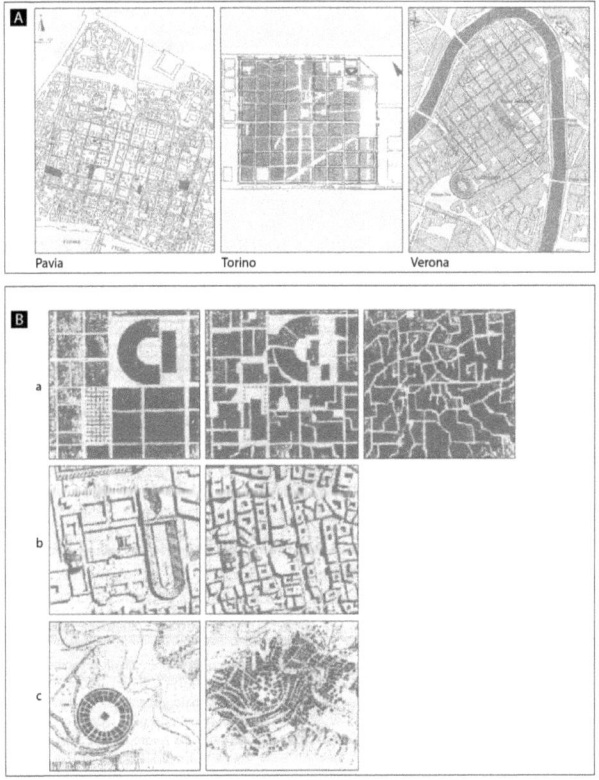

Figure 5: **Panel A**. *Rigidly griddy military camps of the classic roman age have been cradle to hundreds of cities that are now regarded as jewels of urban living. Here we see Pavia (left), Turin (middle) and Verona (right), in Italy. Source (Conventi, 2004):* **Panel B**. *Urban evolution at work on previously rigid geometries. (A) From left to right: the progressive transformation of an ancient roman grid into an Arabic layout; (B) Campo Marzio, in Rome, Italy, in the classic roman age and nowadays; (C) Baghdad (Iraq), in the VIII and the IX Century. Source: (Donato & Lucchi Basili, 1996).*

As Martin points out, in cities of foundation *"the best use of land meant an orderly use, hence the grid plan. In siting it and building it estimates had to be made about its future, about its trade, its population, and the size and number of its building plots. This contributes a highly artificial procedure. But it is of course by no means uncommon. Indeed it is the method by which towns have been created in any rapidly developing or colonial situation."* (Martin, 1972, p. 8).

Evolution does not apply only to grids. It applies to all planned cities, in all cultures and climates, it is the way cities develop as long as their site and location are fortuitous (Vance 1990), enough time is given for them to develop and flourish, and — critically important — no rules are set in place to specifically prevent it by inhibiting informal participation. What Alexander terms "System B", or the conventional planning system which is dominant in the most "advanced" areas of the Global North of the Planet, is in fact, essentially, a gigantic and capillary set of organizations, powers, rules and procedures specifically aimed at countering and inhibiting informal participation in any possible form. Not by chance, processes of formal participation began to develop after WWII, exactly in step with the historical crisis of all the traditional forms of informal participation, when professionalization, bureaucratization and, later on, globalization, begun to take control of mainstream building production. And not by chance, the *modus operandi* of System B at the large scale is essentially the same that it exerts at the small scale, the mechanistic and centralized one that is typical of the short term project. System B cannot cope with evolution, by nature. It cannot deal with the risks of uncertainties that are inherent in the long term evolution fuelled by informal participation. It must occupy all spaces of action, all moments of decision, it must control everyone and everything.

What created both Piazza Santo Stefano and Athole Gardens is in all evidence a different process. It is, essentially, a System A at large scale. If we are to recreate beauty in cities, we need to understand and re-enable the *underlining principles* which drove those processes, which were *both evolutionary and planned*, to generate beauty in our future cities at a large scale and in the long term. That quality, the quality without a name, does not come by design, it comes in the post design; however, the way we lay out the design is crucial to enable evolution in the post design; it is entirely our responsibility as scholars, professionals, decision-makers, stakeholders and lay citizens, to make sure that the right conditions are set in place for that to occur, first of all by distinguishing large scale speculative deployment of common resources from the right-to-buy and the right-to-build of the ordinary people. Without this fundamental distinction, informal participation gets banned by-law from our world, together with change and ultimately with beauty, while — as we can easily see on the ground — speculation and exploitation flourishes as never before. In a mechanistic environment, the biggest, the most powerful, the most insatiable, is undoubtedly the fittest.

5. References

Akbar, J. (1988). Crisis in the Built Environment: the case of the Muslim City: Concept media.

Alexander, C. (1965). A city is not a tree. Paper presented at the Architectural Forum.

Alexander, C. (1979). The timeless way of building. New York: Oxford University Press.

Alexander, C. (2003). The nature of order: an essay on the art of building and the nature of the universe. Book 2: The process of creating life. Berkeley, CA: Center for Environmental Structure.

Alexander, C. (2004). Sustainability and morphogenesis: The birth of a living world. Paper presented at the Schumacher Lecture, Bristol, UK.

Alexander, C. (2005). The nature of order: an essay on the art of building and the nature of the universe. Book 3: A vision of a living world. Berkeley, CA: Center for Environmental Structure.

Alexander, C., Silverstein, M., Angel, S., Ishikawa, S., & Abrams, D. (1975). The Oregon experiment. New York: Oxford University Press.

Alexander, C., Ishikawa, S., & Silverstein, M. (1977). A pattern language : towns, buildings, construction. New York: Oxford University Press.

Alexander, C., Davis, H., Martinez, J., & Corner, D. (1985). The production of houses. New York: Oxford University Press.

Alexander, C., Neis, H., Anninou, A., & Fiskdahl-King, I. (1987). A New theory of urban design. New York: Oxford University Press.

Alexander, C., Schmidt, R., & Buchanan, B. (2005). The Masterplan and Process for Harbour Peak. A Model Creation Process for the 21st - Century Cities Retrieved from Berkeley:

Alexander, C., Neis, H., & Moore-Alexander, M. (2012). The battle for the life and beauty of the earth : a struggle between two world-systems. New York: Oxford University Press.

Angel, S. (2012). Planet of cities: Lincoln Institute of Land Policy Cambridge, MA.

Barthelemy, M. (2011). Spatial Networks. Physics Reports, 499(1-3), 1-101.

Batty, M. (2007). Cities and complexity: understanding cities with cellular automata, agent-based models, and fractals: The MIT press.

Batty, M., & Longley, P. A. (1994). Fractal cities: a geometry of form and function: Academic Press.

Batty, M., & Marshall, S. (2009). The Evolution of Cities: Geddes, Abercrombie, and the New Physicalism. Town Planning Review, 79(Centenary Edition). doi:10.3828/tpr.2009.12

Batty, M., & Marshall, S. (in print). Thinking Organic, Acting Civic: the Paradox of Planning for Cities in Evolution. Environment and Planning B: Planning and Design, tbc(tbc), tbc.

Bettencourt, L., Lobo, J., & Youn, H. (2013). The hypothesis of urban scaling: formalization, implications and challenges. arXiv preprint arXiv:1301.5919.

Boano, C., & Talocci, G. (2014). The politics of Play in Urban Design: Agamben's profanation as a recalibrating approach to urban design research. Bitácora Urbano-Territorial, 1(24), 17.

Boccaletti, S., Latora, V., Moreno, Y., Chavez, M., & Hwang, D. U. (2006). Complex networks: Structure and dynamics. Physics Reports, 424(Issues 4–5), 175–308. doi:10.1016/j.physrep.2005.10.009

Brand, S. (1995). How buildings learn: What happens after they're built: Penguin.

Conventi, M. (2004). Città romane di fondazione: L'Erma di Bretschneider.

Davidoff, P. (1965). Advocacy and pluralism in planning. Journal of the american Institute of Planners, 31(4), 331-338.

Dibble, J., Prelorendjos, A., Romice, O., Zanella, M., Strano, E., Pagel, M., & Porta, S. (in print). Urban Morphometrics: Towards a Science of Urban Evolution. Paper presented at the ISUF International Seminar of Urban Form, Rome, IT. http://arxiv.org/abs/1506.04875

Donato, F., & Lucchi Basili, L. (1996). L'ordine nascosto dell'organizzazione urbana. Franco Angeli Editore, Milano.

Finn, D. (2014). DIY urbanism: implications for cities. Journal of Urbanism: International Research on Placemaking and Urban Sustainability, 7(4), 381-398.

Geddes, P. (1915). Cities in evolution. An introduction to the Town Planning Movement and to the Study of Civics: Williams.

Habraken, N. J., & Teicher, J. (2000). The structure of the ordinary: form and control in the built environment: MIT press.

Hobsbawm, E. (2010). Age of Empire: 1875-1914: Hachette UK.

Holling, C. S., & Goldberg, M. A. (1971). Ecology and planning. Journal of the american Institute of Planners, 37(4), 221-230.

Jacobs, J. (1992, c.1961). The death and life of great American cities. New York: Random House LLC.

Koolhaas, R. (1995). Whatever happened to urbanism? Design Quarterly, 28-31.

Lydon, M., & Garcia, A. (2015). A Tactical Urbanism How-To: Springer.

Marshall, S. (2008). Cities Design and Evolution: Routledge.

Martin, L. (1972). The Grid as a Generator. In L. Martin & L. March (Eds.), Urban Space and Structures (pp. 6-27). Cambridge: University Press.

McGlynn, S., & Murrain, P. (1994). The politics of urban design. Planning Practice and Research, 9(3), 311-319.

Moudon, A. V. (1986). Built for change: neighborhood architecture in San Francisco: Mit Press.

Neis, H. J. (Producer). (2014, 27/03/2015). Battle for the Life and Beauty of the Earth -- Urban Architecture and Urban Design. [Public Conference] Retrieved from https://www.youtube.com/watch?v=tuc8klUHWEQ

Pagel, M. (2009). Human language as a culturally transmitted replicator. Nature Reviews Genetics, 10(6), 405-415.

Parvin, A., Saxby, D., Cerulli, C., & Schneider, T. (2011). A Right To Build-the next mass-house-building industry. Architecture 00.

Porta, S., Latora, V., & Strano, E. (2010). Networks in urban design. Six years of research in multiple centrality assessment. In E. Estrada, M. Fox, D. J. Higham, & G. L. Oppo (Eds.), Network Science: Complexity in Nature and Technology (pp. 107-129). London: Springer.

Porta, S., & Romice, O. (2014). Plot-Based Urbanism Towards Time Consciousness in Place Making. In C. S. Mäckler, Wolfgang (Ed.), New Civic Art (pp. 82-111). Sulgen, CH: Verlag Niggli.

Porta, S., Romice, O., Maxwell, J. A., Russell, P., & Baird, D. (2014). Alterations in scale: Patterns of change in main street networks across time and space. Urban Studies, 51(16), 3383-3400. doi:10.1177/0042098013519833

Porta, S., Russell, P., Romice, O., & Vidoli, M. (2014). Construction and Therapy: an Integrated Approach to Design Build. In T. Cavanagh, U. Hartig, & S. Palleroni (Eds.), Working Out: Thinking While Building (pp. 98-108). Halifax, NS: ACSA Press.

Sawhney, N., de Klerk, C., & Malhotra, S. (2015). Civic engagement through DIY urbanism and collective networked action. Planning Practice & Research, 30(3), 337-354.

Steadman, P. (2008). The Evolution of Designs: Biological analogy in architecture and the applied arts: Routledge.

Turner, J. F. (1977). Housing by people: Towards autonomy in building environments: Pantheon Books New York.

U.N.DESA. (2014). World Urbanization Prospects: The 2014 Revision, Highlights. Retrieved from http://esa.un.org/unpd/wup/Highlights/WUP2014-Highlights.pdf.

Weaver, W. (1948). Science and Complexity American Scientist, 36, 536-544.

Whitehand, J., W R. (1979). The study of variations in the building fabric of town centres: procedural problems and preliminary findings in southern Scotland. Transactions of the Institute of British Geographers, 559-575.

Whitehand, J. W. R. (1998). Continuity and Discontinuity in the Urban Landscape: A Geographer's View. In P. Attilio (Ed.), Rethinking XIXth Century City (pp. 121-129). Cambridge, Mass: The Aga Khan Program for Islamic Architecture.

Whitehand, J. W. R., Gu, K., Conzen, M. P., & Whitehand, S. (2014). The Typological Process and the Morphological Period: A Cross-Cultural Assessment. Environment and Planning B: Planning and Design, 41(3), 512-533. doi:10.1068/b39097

Wilson, W. (2013). Stimulating housing supply-Government initiatives: House of Commons Library Note. London: HoC.

Windsor Liscombe, R. (2006). Independence: Otto Koenigsberger and modernist urban resettlement in India. Planning perspectives, 21(2), 157-178.

Image: THOR | www.flickr.com/photos/geishaboy500 | CC Licence

Combining systems A and B: Creating a Pattern Language for the Unrecognized Bedouin Villages in the Negev, Israel

Rosner-Manor, Ya'ara
Ben-Gurion University of the Negev, Israel
yaara.rosner@gmail.com

Rofè, Yodan
Ben-Gurion University of the Negev, Israel
yrofe@bgu.ac.il

In his last book (Alexander 2012) Alexander distinguishes between two different systems of thinking. He notes that „in System A, creation and production are organic in character, and are governed by human judgments that emanate from the underlying wholeness of situations, conditions, and surroundings" (p.49). System B, on the other hand, is „concerned with efficiency, with money, with power and control [and] production is thought of as mechanical" (p. 11). In the book Alexander refers to the clash between these two systems, the dominance of system B in our world, and the urgent need to balance between them before it is too late. In this paper we would like to contend that the relationship between these two systems can be understood as complementary, and not necessarily as a contradiction. We contend that both systems exist in traditional as well as modern cultures and that they can and should be balanced. We demonstrate this through the case of the unrecognized Bedouin villages that are located in the Negev drylands of Israel.

Unrecognized Bedouin Villages; Informal settlement, Urban codes; Local Pattern Language

1. Introduction

Christopher Alexander's last book (2012) is called *The Battle for the Life and Beauty of the Earth: A Struggle between Two World-Systems*. Alexander defines these systems as follows:

System A – is „concerned with the well-being of the land, its integrity, the well-being of the people and plants and animals that inhabit the land" (p.11). „In System A, creation and production are organic in character, and are governed by human judgments that emanate from the underlying wholeness of situations, conditions and surroundings. This is the primary driving force of every action and every decision" (p.49).

System B – is „concerned with efficiency, with money, with power and control" (p. 11). In System B, the production is thought of as mechanical. What matters in system B are regulations, procedures, categories, money, efficiency and profit. The production process is rarely context-sensitive. Wholeness is left out.

We would like to examine Alexander's argument by looking at one test case - the unrecognized Bedouin settlements in the Negev - as a clear example of SYSTEM A, in relation to the Israeli planning system, which is a clear and even extreme example of SYSTEM B. Looking at the two together allows us compare the way the two systems operate in those areas where Bedouins currently live in unrecognized villages, but where plans for formal, recognized settlements are being drawn up, and see how each system functions and in relation to the communities that live there.

In the first part of the paper we will present the unrecognized Bedouin settlements and briefly establish the degree to which they answer the definition of SYSTEM A. We will also discuss another interesting phenomenon - the way the unrecognized Bedouin villages combine SYSTEM A + SYSTEM B. Their layout is built according to a spatial code that embodies a set of laws and rules, and represents the general interests of the Bedouin society and the power devices in it. In contrast, while the Israeli planning system can be generally considered a clear example of system B, it does also include elements of flexibility, and the ability to adjust locally to the specific site and the people living in it.

In the second part of the paper we will present the gaps between the two systems on a regional scale as well as on a more detailed local scale. We will analyze which of the gaps represent a contradiction and cause an essential conflict between the two systems, and which may cause the two to differ but allow them to continue to exist in parallel.

The third part of the paper shows devices for „combined life": how parts from the two systems can exist side by side, or may contain each other in a way that enables their mutual co-existence, and maybe even a mutual support and empowerment.

In the fourth and last part of the article we would like to propose an alternative direction. This will be the formulation of a third system – SYSTEM C – a system that brings together elements from the Urban Codes of both systems, the Bedouin system and Israeli law, to create a new code. This new code constitutes an infrastructure for decision making that allows the community to be involved in continuing to shape its space, but also acknowledges and responds to the established guidelines as representing the general public interest.

2. Background – the Unrecognized Bedouin Villages

The Bedouins are nomadic people of Arab descent, who arrived in the Negev, primarily from Saudi Arabia, in several waves of immigration that began in the seventh century (El-Aref, 1930; Ben-David, 2004). Over the past few centuries, the Bedouins have begun a slow and gradual transition from their traditional existence as a nomadic society based on the herding of sheep and camels to a more sedentary, semi-nomadic way of life, based on pasture and agriculture (Ben-David, 1982, 2004; Yiftachel, 2013).

In 1948, following the declaration of the state of Israel and the ensuing war that broke out between the Jewish and Arab populations of Palestine, and with the surrounding Arab nations, most of the Arab residents of the area fled or were banished, including most of the Negev Bedouins. Throughout the 1950s, an intensive project of Jewish settlement and development was carried out in Israel's peripheral regions, including the Negev desert. As part of this project, some of the remaining Negev Bedouins were removed from their ancestral territories and relocated to a specific limited area northeast of the city of Be'er Sheva. Other Bedouins were forced to relinquish lands they had used for pasture or agriculture, and which were now put to other uses (Yehudakin, 2007; Yiftachel, 2013; Atzmon, 2013).

The state did not recognize the Bedouins' historical claims to their lands, declaring them officially to be state property (Noah, 2009). The spontaneous Bedouin settlements - both the preexisting ones, which turned gradually from tent-based camps to permanent villages comprising tents, lean-tos and sheet metal cabins, and the new settlements generated by the Bedouins' changing circumstances - are all considered illegal by state authorities. As an alternative, the state built planned towns for the Bedouins, which attracted some of the landless population among them. These towns, however, are beset by economic and social problems, and are not an attractive choice for the remaining population in the unrecognized settlements (Shmueli & Khamaisi 2011, Yehudakin 2007).

Approximately 120,000 of the Bedouins in the Negev reside in more than a hundred settlements that are not recognized by the state (Atzmon 2013). As a result, they are not included in the state's planning and development systems. Many of them are not connected to basic infrastructure and do not receive a proper level of basic civic services (Shmueli & Khamaisi, 2011). Over the past few years, following several government decisions and proclamations, (government decisions no. 3707 and 3708), a gradual process of recognition and regularization of these settlements has begun. As of 2013, 14 previously unrecognized settlements, each including a few groups of families, have been, or are in the process of being, formally recognized and regulated. With recognition, the government has also begun proceedings for the planning and development of the settlements. The plans drawn up for them will serve as the basis for building permits that will enable the development of public services for these villages and the legal construction of their residents' houses.

An assessment of these planning processes, however, indicates that the plans for the Bedouin settlements are unsuited, in most cases, to the current structure of the village, and that they tend to impose western values and planning concepts on what remains an essentially traditional Arab society (Falah, 1983, Fenster, 1999, 1993, Marx & Meir, 2005, Meir, 2003, Shmueli & Khamaisi, 2011). Most of the new plans that have been laid out for the villages in the past few years do not see the value in the existing construction and layout. The implementation of these plans will require the village to be dismantled and entirely rebuilt. Such a process would be so expensive as to be virtually unachievable for the local population, which is at the bottom rung of Israel's socio-economic ladder. Moreover, it will destroy the delicate socio-spatial structure, built over time, which is upheld and encapsulated by the villages as they are now. This is described in the following section (Figure 1).

Figure 1: Unrecognized villages - a typical site (aerophoto by Eli Atzmon)

3. The Unrecognized Bedouin settlements as an example of System A

In Alexander's definition of System A (quoted above), "**creation and production are organic in character**, and are governed by human judgments that emanate from the underlying **wholeness** of situations, conditions, and surroundings. This is the primary driving force of every action, and of every decision" (p. 49). According to Alexander, the main purpose of creating places should be "to provide opportunities and contexts which intensely support and enhance life-giving human situations" (p. 7). To this end, he suggests drawing upon the characteristics of System A to make some major changes to the existing systems that are used to create places.

In the next pages we describe the unrecognized Bedouin settlements in light of the following principles, which are the basis for Alexander's proposal for an alternative approach to planning:

1. The process of creating places is an ongoing, dynamic process
2. Organizations will provide a level of deep involvement in decision making by all concerned
3. The management of money should be controlled via non-profit organizations
4. The land provides the context for every building
5. The fragility of human beings and eco-systems should be respected and protected

The spatial-social Bedouin layout is, of course, a complex one. Here we attempt to "decompose" the system and to "catalog" it according to Alexander's definitions. In reality, things are interwoven with each other in an un-dissolvable way.

3.1 The process of creating places as an ongoing, dynamic process

In previous research (Rosner, Rofè, Abu-Rabia-Queider, 2013), we showed that the Unrecognized settlements are actually a structure-preserving transformation of the spatial deployment that has characterized Bedouin encampments for hundreds of years. The desert was divided into living-areas – territories – between big coalitions of the tribes or "stems." These huge living-areas were further sub-divided, in a series of complex agreements, between the sub-groups that constituted the stem. (Ben-David, 1982; El-Aref, 1930). According to Bedouin law, every man must make his encampment, graze his herd, cultivate land and use water resources only in the region assigned to his family, or with the permission of the owners of the land. Hence, the allocation of space reflects a series of internal agreements and the inter-community divisions (Yehudakin, 2007; Havakuk 1986).

The process of land division is a dynamic process, changing frequently according to changes in climate and precipitation, power-relations between the tribes, inter-tribe economy and other parameters. In other words, the space is created in a slow and gradual process of negotiations, agreements and wars that has evolved continuously over hundreds of years.

The location of the encampment, its size and its shape also respond to the changing conditions. The encampments are usually positioned in a way that suits the conditions of the soil and the climate, but their shape and size change according to the geo-political conditions. In a time of war or tension, many families will group in one area and will create an encampment that makes a wall – exterior circles of tents protecting internal space, where the property, the wives and the children will be located. In times of peace and calm, the families will spread over broad areas and be located in a way that facilitates adjustment to climate and access to water resources and grazing areas.

In the unrecognized settlements of today, it is still possible to identify the systematic base of land division and encampment location. Moreover, the living areas are divided clearly according to natural signs. In most cases, the border line will pass on the watershed line or along a stream. As we were told by Muhamad El-Hawashlla: „A stake or rope can be moved, but nature is eternal. We mark by the signs that nature gave us and so refrain from conflict and war in the future." Today, houses are still located according to the internal divisions in the community and in such a way that protects private and sensitive areas. Along the main road, the „Shig" structures – the meeting rooms for men, the mosque and public and trade structures – are assigned to men and to the public sphere, while the shared kitchen is the center of life for women and children. Animals and property are located in parts that are farther from access road, in the protected and internal parts of the settlement (Rosner, Rofè, & Abu-Rabia-Queder. 2013, Yiftachel, Baruch, Abu-Samur, Shir, & Ben-Arie, 2012).

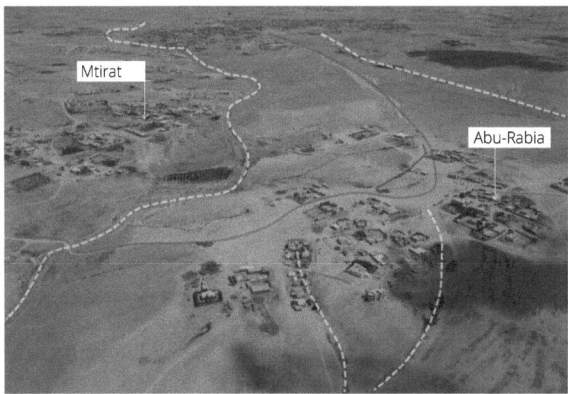

Figure 2: The stream is a natural border separating the Abu-Rabia and Mtirat lands. The watershed lines separate between different groups in Abu-Rabia

In the last hundred years, a process of acceleration has occurred in the creation of Bedouin space (Sofer 2010, Atzmon 2013). Fast population growth, external pressures, and especially the intensive development that followed the establishment of Israel have given rise to an interesting process, in which decisions are taken faster and Bedouin space is changing at an accelerating rate, while retaining the same internal legal structure that has governed space creation for hundreds of years.

The process of decision making in the settlement (see below) always relates to one particular concrete and essential question. It takes place one step at a time – a new house for the couple that is going to marry next month, new herding areas for the shared herd that we plan to buy, a new drain because the old drain collapsed in the last flood, and so on – while always following the spatial Bedouin code, known to the locals as ‚common knowledge'. Thus, the process of creating the settlement and the whole space is actually composed of two complementary processes. On one hand, the whole space and all the decisions made for it, on every scale, operate according to a limited series of accepted **laws** (regulations and procedures) that are known to all community members as ‚common knowledge'. On the other hand, the day-to-day decisions are made **gradually and in accordance with changing needs** - a dynamic and organic process of creating places.

3.2 Organizations will provide a level of deep involvement in decision making by all concerned

Bedouin space is understood mainly as a common space. It does not include public areas, in the Western-modern meaning of the word. Every point in space is assigned to a certain group, and this is according to a complicated set of agreements that define the levels of affiliation.

From the point of view of the traditional Bedouin tenant, all living space is assigned to the coalition of the tribes, and within it the areas that are available to him for herding and cultivating and the water resources allowed and forbidden for use (etc.) are very clear. These areas are, in most cases, common to the extended family, to the tribe or to the stem – all according to the agreements that exist at that time. The living domain of the extended family is also not private – it is common to brothers, their wives and their children.

All decisions, at all scales, are made by the co-partners to the land or by their direct representatives. In cases in which a large-scale decision is made, in which many co-partners are involved (dozens or hundreds), the decision will be made by delegation. In most cases, the delegate will arrive at the meeting accompanied by additional representatives of the sub-groups of the different families, of which the community is constituted and to which the discussed decision has direct relevance. In other words – the community is very highly involved in the decision making at any given moment.

According to Bedouin tradition, in order to make an essential change in common space, it is necessary to achieve a wide agreement. In order to reach such agreements, sometimes months of discussion are necessary. In many cases, a big and significant move will fail because one of the co-partners continues to oppose it, and his brothers and cousins are unable to convince him to change his mind.

This aspect of community participation, however, needs qualification, since more than 50% of the population – the women – are not formal partners in the communal decision making process. In many cases, a husband will consult his wife privately, but the Bedouin public sphere, even in 21th century, is almost completely male. Women may offer opinions regarding issues like child education and family health, and they are often invited to do so; but because the property is in the hands of men, decisions about property, including land and changes in space, will be made, formally at least, only by men.

In summary, the level of involvement of the parties concerned is indeed high. Yet, because Bedouin society (as was explained to the writer by the tenants more than once) „is not equal and not democratic", the term „concerned" relates to men only. And it means that a significant part of the population is not a formal party to decision making (Figure 3).

Figure 3: Residents (men only) consulting about options for planning at the village Qasr-A-Sir

3.3 The management of money should be controlled via non-profit organizations

In a position paper from 2000, Du Plessis refers to the traditional outlook as one that sees the world as an organism in which the whole is more than its endless parts, and perceives humankind as part of that whole (Du Plessis, 2000). Du Plessis' describes societies that are focused on the general-social profit and survival of the community rather than on the advancement and wellbeing of individuals. In them, social status is achieved by contribution to the success of the whole group.

Du Plessis, very much like Alexander, separates between the modern mechanistic society and the systemic society that characterizes the developing world in general and tribal societies in particular. Mechanistic society is individualistic, rational, hierarchical, one that grasps social conduct as linear and goal oriented. In contrast, the systemic society **is process-oriented**, constantly changing, communal and **participatory**. It is intuitive, working by feedback and **based on networks**. In the systemic society, the development model is based on concepts like the right to use the land and manage the responsible household, while the land remains in shared ownership and wealth is measured in terms of social systems that supply safety and levels of satisfaction and contention – immeasurable terms.

Bedouin society is a society in transition (Atzmon 2013that has been undergoing extreme social changes over the past few decades. These changes derive in part from external pressure (like compulsory education or the prohibition to build in open spaces), and in part from the very exposure to modern Western culture. Nevertheless, the affiliation of the individual to the extended family and the shared responsibility that comes with it, are still very significant and dominant components in the Bedouin social layout.

Indeed, in many cases the social status of an individual is determined by their promotion of the interests of the group – beginning with the extended family, continuing with helping families who are blood relations or friends, and culminating in the representation of the wider community in general issues. In this sense, it is possible to relate to each extended family as a „non-profit organization". The land is not conceived as having only a real estate value, but as the origin of life, in the broad meaning of the term. The issue of the financial profit constitutes, in most cases, only one of the considerations - and not necessarily the central one – that determine development and guide other decisions that concern spatial changes. This does not mean, however, that the economic value of the land is not known and understood by the leaders of the extended families. Land trade among the Bedouins themselves, as well as between the Bedouins and the state, is as frequent today as it was in the past.

3.4 The land will provide the context of every building

Just as the Bedouin spatial-social layout is the consequence of thousands of nomadic years in the desert, the rules that guide the decision making are completely adapted to the natural conditions of the historical living areas of the Bedouins – the deserts of the middle east.

Summer was the season for migration, when the Bedouins go out to search for water and grazing areas. The permanent encampment was, originally, a winter encampment (Havekuk. 1986, Ben-David. 2004), so the location of the encampments was always in areas protected from floods and from the strong winter winds. The Bedouin villages today preserve, in many ways, the historic location formation. The settlement will usually be located on moderate slopes, in areas that are outside the flooded areas, and in many cases on slopes facing south-east, which are the slopes that are more protected from winds in the region (Figure 4).

Figure 4: GIS analysis showing the location of houses on shallow protected slopes away from flood plains

The internal structure of the settlement also reflects the natural layout. The roads will be located, almost always, along watershed lines, and create a movement network that represents the topographic structure. The roads usually also constitute the border line between the different communities, and as such mark the borders of the territory. In other words, the layout of the land property is indicated by topography.

Since the road is public (hence – male), the public structures – the „Shig,"' which is the meeting place for men and the central hospitality structure, the mosque, and the trade areas - will be located along it (Figure 5). The inner parts of the settlement – that are assigned to women and children – will be located on the slope and toward the stream. These include the kitchen, which is the cooking area where the women meet to weave and to cook, the orchard and the livestock enclosures (Figure 6).

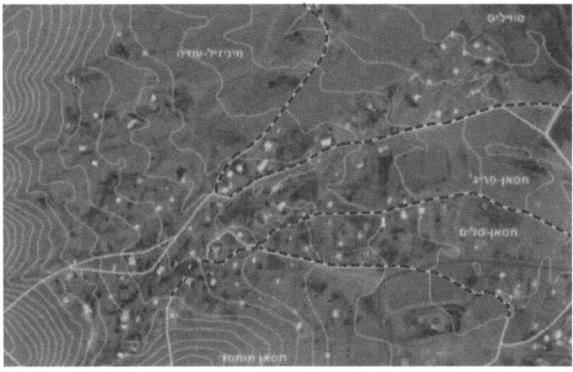

Figure 4: Roads are located along watershed lines and divide the village into sub-units that are related to sub-communities (Mapping – Arch. Eli Elan, 2012)

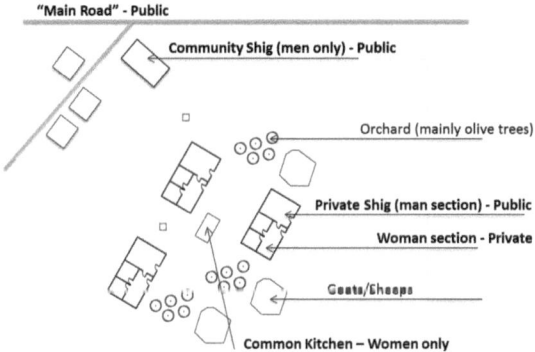

Figure 5: A typical village (mapped by the author, based on the village El-Gora'an, 2015). The common Shig (related to the men) is located along the main road, the common kitchen (related to the women) is located at the protected center of the village)

The agriculture is concentrated in the stream beds and their surroundings, which are usually common plantations. The stream is terraced, which slows the flood waters in a way that prevents erosion and enables better irrigation. There is minimum disruption of flow from the drainage basin, including the living areas, to the stream.

The structure of the house reflects the structure of the tent in its adjustment to the natural conditions. The tent was a long structure, the long axis of which usually lay Northeast-Southwest so it was possible to lift the sheets and enjoy the afternoon breeze to ventilate the tent, as well as the natural warming sunlight in the morning.

In conclusion –the village's components – and as a result the whole space – are built with a high level of fitness to the natural conditions, and with almost no need for interference with the land in the form of massive earthworks, broad scale drainage, etc. It should be noted that because the houses today are being built of concrete, some of the patterns that have been described here are being blurred and are subject to external influences, like the surrounding Israeli modern building, or the Arab buildings in settlements in Israel and in the West Bank.

3.5 The fragility of human beings and eco-systems should be respected and protected

The issue of **sensitivity and fragility** is perhaps the most important subject, and it directly concerns matters of **power and dominance**. Because Bedouin society – and with it Bedouin law – are the product of thousands of years of nomadic existence in desert environments, they reflect **a delicate system of checks and balances** between man and environment. Bedouin law, including its spatial expression, includes references to endless possible situations of interpersonal relationships, and of relations between humans and their surroundings, both as individuals and as communities. In other words, the Bedouin spatial-social layout expresses an elaborate management mechanism of complex relations between man and environment, which includes mechanisms of flexibility and response to geo-political and climate changes, including extreme changes.

This elaborate management mechanism is also very fragile and sensitive. The tension between SYSTEM A and SYSTEM B is revealed at its most extreme in relation to this fragility and sensitivity. During the 67 years of the state of Israel's existence, there were several attempts to create an adjustment between the Bedouin's traditional law and the Israeli planning and developing layout.

One of the most interesting examples of these attempts is the planning process of the town of Rahat – the largest Bedouin town in Israel, which was planned during the early 1970s and established in 1976. In the background documents for the plan, the planners describe the Bedouin society in the Negev, with reference to their social structure, the traditional law layout, sub-communities, characteristic occupations, and so on. Clearly, planning was based on extensive, in-depth research. The planners also addressed the social segmentation of the sub-communities and the internal relationships between them.

The plan outlined for Rahat and the detailed models for development tried to respond to the unique world view of the Bedouins, they recognizing the uniqueness of the community and its needs. Figure 7 shows some diagrams from the plan documents. The master plan assigned land to groups and tribes that have blood relations or alignments and agreements and deals between them, with an effort to achieve the best fit between the social structure (as it was in 1976) and the proposition of the plan.

The urban plan also tried to address internal divisions. The town, which is built on hills, is divided into sub-neighborhoods according to the communal sub-divisions. Even the detailed development planning refers to the extended family structure and to the need for flexibility, allowing for family growth and for the traditional structure of shared living spaces.

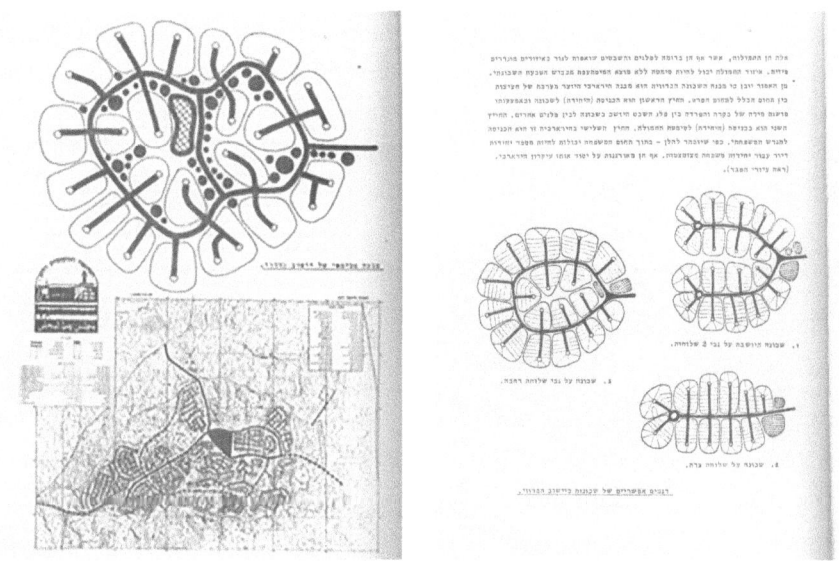

Figure 6: The Master Plan for ‚Rahat' and its schematic ideas: on the left – the urban scheme, on the right – the schemes for different types of neighborhoods as presented by the planners (early 1970s)

But something went wrong along the way. The Rahat of today (2015), and like it the other Bedouin towns, is not able to provide an appropriate social answer (Fenster, 1999). The towns are failed economically (Meir, 2003, Abu-Bader, 2010), in them there are violent confrontations much more severe than those that exist in the unrecognized settlements. In general, they do not embody any of the unique qualities toward which Alexander is directing. Something of that fragile quality faded in the process of moving to a planned town. The planned Bedouin towns constitute a warning sign in the sense of „the road to hell is paved with good intentions". The difficult and complicated question of how to embrace the possibility of development, while retaining and reinforcing the existing qualities of traditional Bedouin life, still remains.

3.6 In conclusion

The Bedouin settlements are a self-organized system and show characteristics associated with SYSTEM A as defined by Alexander. This is a system that is based on a slow pace of decision making, undertaken by community members and with direct representation at every scale. This is a space that is created gradually through endless decisions and changes made on a small scale, all operating according to a series of clear rules that are known to all of the community members as common knowledge.

In light of the failure of past attempts to settle the Bedouins in planned towns, we would like here to suggest alternative approach for the development and creation of spaces. In the following pages we will present the gaps between the two systems, both on the regional scale and the detailed scale, and seek to understand which of the gaps constitute sources of contradiction and conflict and which represent elements that are really different from each other but can nevertheless coexist in peace.

4. The Unrecognized Bedouin Villages and the Israeli Planning System – Gaps & Conflicts

We would now like to map the gaps between the Bedouin and the Israeli planning and building systems. It is important to note, however, that **not every gap is necessarily a conflict**. The question we must address is, which of the existing gaps is conflictual and which is simply a difference but is not a conflict, thus allowing the two systems to exist together? We would like to claim that the Bedouin layout and the Israeli-modern layout have a lot in common. Continuing to rely on Alexander's definitions, we need to formulate the claim as follows:

Both systems are „concerned with the well-being of the land, its integrity, the well-being of the people and plants and animals that inhabit the land [and are] governed by human judgment" (p. 11). Both also have characteristics associated with system B. They are „concerned with efficiency, with money, with power and control" and **they both** include „regulations, procedures, categories" (p. 11).

But while power and control in Bedouin society are decentralized and distributed amongst people and communities, decision making in the Israeli planning system is centralized and hierarchical, with most of the power residing in the hands of the national government. The traditional Bedouin process of decision making is characterized by direct representation at all scales. In contrast, the Israeli bureaucracy includes almost no processes of mutual decision making, and the decisions are made by committees that primarily represent the different ministries.

Table 1 below presents the similarities and the differences between the systems:

Test Case:	
The Unrecognized Bedouin Villages and the Israeli planning system	
System A	System B
The Unrecognized Bedouin Villages	The Israeli – Modern Planning for the Bedouin Community
Bedouin Traditional Spatial Code	**Modern-Western Master Planning**
Rules & regulations	
Concerned with the well-being of the land, of the people and plants	
Context-sensitive (protecting nature & environment)	
Governed by human judgment	
• **Process** - organic in character - concrete step by step decision making • **Power and control** - are decentralized to people and communities • **Representation** - direct representation at all scales	• **Process** - mechanical and efficient - future goal oriented • **Power and control** - centralized by the state • **Representation** - committees – represent the government

Table 1: Comparison between the Bedouin system of spatial development and the Israeli planning and development system

Both systems are based on a series of rules and laws

The Israeli layout is based on the Israeli Planning and Building Law and other relevant laws. It is supposed to reflect the wide public interest, with its regional and national aspects, as interpreted mostly by government ministries, agencies and commissions, with some influence from the local authorities as well. The Bedouin layout is based on the Bedouin law that defines the rules for the division of land, and through which space provides solutions to concrete problems – as presented above. Bedouin law is also concerned with the **wide interests of the community and a long-term vision**. The main goal of Bedouin law is to achieve fair and sustainable balance between people and their environment, and between the groups that constitute the community itself. It should be noted that Bedouin traditional law is very strict, and in cases of conflict between personal interest and the group's interest, an action that contradicts the opinion of the group or violates the law can cost a person his life, or result in confiscation of his goods or the exile of himself and his family.

Both systems are concerned with the wellbeing of humans, the environment and animals – whether through regulations for protecting the environment or through common knowledge and common practices that maintain a balance between man and environment and protect the sustainability of water resources and grazing areas. Both have the potential, at least in theory, to adjust to topography and to natural conditions.

It is clear that the two systems are dictated by human discretion – after all, human beings are those who make decisions in both cases. Moreover, with the development of technology, the Bedouins are also using the modern devices that are at their disposal, so that the use of modern technologies in road construction, water and sewage plumbing etc., no longer constitutes an essential difference. However, despite these similarities, the systems are obviously also very different in the following ways:

4.1 The regional scale: creating the space according to a long-term master plan compared to creating the space through a series of short-term decisions

The two maps below present two pictures of the same region (Figure 8).The map on the left presents a mapping of land uses. The purple spots in the map are the Bedouin settlements, and it can be seen that they are located along the cultivated creeks. The rest of the area is hardly developed, except the recognized town Arara (in orange), some roads and one quarry (in grey).

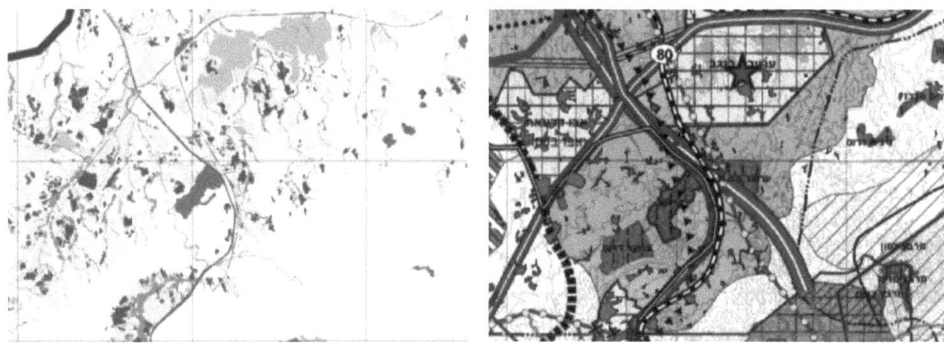

Figure 7: Comparison between the actual land use (left; mapping by Yaara Rosner-Manor and Mor Kertes) and the District Outline Plan 4/14/23 approved in 2008 (right)

The map on the right presents the same segment from the district outline plan. The red spots, which represent the settlements, were added by us. As you can see, the plan does not recognize the existing settlements, and most areas in which they are located are intended as open spaces of different kinds. On the other hand, additional gatherings of settlements are indeed defined in the area intended for rural-suburban settling (color yellow on the map). We will present the detailed planning in these areas below, and we will see that there too no adjustment is made between the existing situation and the planning. We can also see that there are wide swaths of land for infrastructure planned in this region, including wide national roads and railways, as well as quarries and power and gas lines.

In effect, the two maps represent two conceptions with essential differences between them in their relation to space. According to the Western modern conception, the planning teams define the future regional picture (using a regional outline plan), which must then be gradually implemented. According to the Bedouin world view, there is no need and no ability to define a future world picture. The decisions are taken one at a time based on their merit, with reference to the need they address and to Bedouin traditional law. In this mechanism it is hard to promote general massive and expensive interests like regional infrastructure or large-scale economic investments, but it may well be more sensitive to local conditions and more accurate in its response to real needs.

Now that the differences between the systems are clear, we would like to examine them and ask: to what extent do they conflict? Is it possible for both layouts to exist one beside the other, or one inside the other, without disturbance? Might such a coexistence be beneficial?

4.1.1 Infrastructure layout

In Figure 9 below, with the help of GIS software, we isolated the infrastructure layout from all the other land uses of the plan and overlaid this layer with the layer of the unrecognized settlements. The overlaying of this data reveals that about 10-20% of the settlements' residents would have to be moved in order for the plans to be implemented as they are now drawn. A projection in which external constraints cause a change of location and mobility of population to the extent of 10-20% is not extreme, and is, relatively speaking, a minor conflict. Such a change has already occurred in Bedouin history, due to circumstances like the invasion of the region by foreign tribes, periods of drought, etc. We can assume that the Bedouin community would be able to deal, this time too, with a crisis on such scale.

It should be noted that even today every evacuation of population, including evacuation from the unrecognized settlements, includes a mechanism of financial compensation and in some cases also compensation of land. This combination of precedent and compensation means that the infrastructure layout does not constitute an insurmountable barrier to the integration of the two systems.

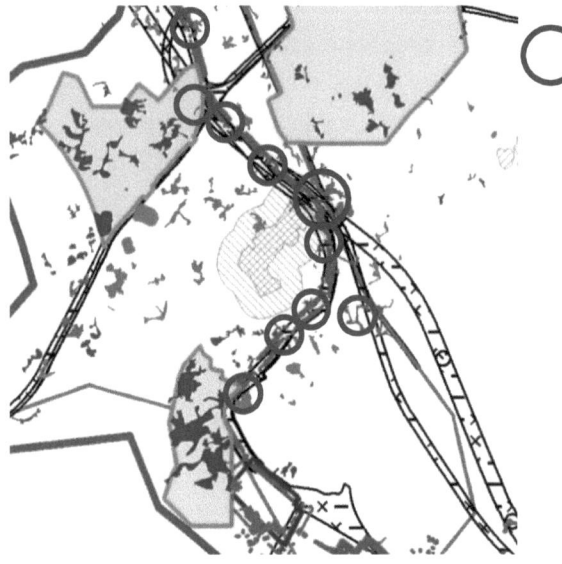

Groups that will have to relocate their village to allow for the passage of infrastructure

Figure 8: GIS mapping - Planned infrastructures and the existing villages (Ari Cohen, Liora Hemi and Yaara Rosner-Manor)

4.1.2 Land-uses

The district outline plan contains a long list of land uses. In a second analysis intended to highlight the conflict areas, we chose to divide the land uses proposed by the plan into three kinds (Figure 10):

1. Land-uses that allow residential use and do so - for the time being – without regard to shape or density (colored black in figure 10)
2. Land-uses that forbid residential uses (colored white).
3. Land-uses that allow residential use under certain conditions – not damaging to the environment, protection of underground water reservoirs (colored grey).

This analysis produces a much more conflicted picture. It shows that 30% of the population lives in areas that are forbidden for residential use (the white areas). If we add to these the areas allowed for residential use under limiting conditions, we arrive at 40-50% of the population. If all these people will indeed be forced to evacuate, these are numbers that create an essential conflict, at a much larger scale than what the Bedouin community would be able to handle with its traditional tools.

4.1.3 Land-uses

The district outline plan contains a long list of land uses. In a second analysis intended to highlight the conflict areas, we chose to divide the land uses proposed by the plan into three kinds (Figure 10):

1. Land-uses that allow residential use and do so - for the time being – without regard to shape or density (colored black in figure 10)

2. Land-uses that forbid residential uses (colored white).

3. Land-uses that allow residential use under certain conditions – not damaging to the environment, protection of underground water reservoirs (colored grey).

This analysis produces a much more conflicted picture. It shows that 30% of the population lives in areas that are forbidden for residential use (the white areas). If we add to these the areas allowed for residential use under limiting conditions, we arrive at 40-50% of the population. If all these people will indeed be forced to evacuate, these are numbers that create an essential conflict, at a much larger scale than what the Bedouin community would be able to handle with its traditional tools.

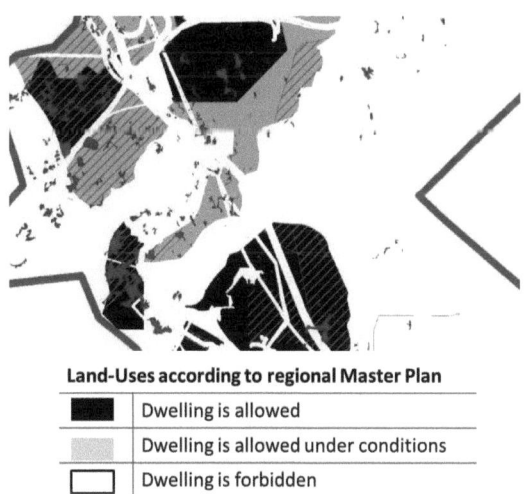

Figure 9: Analysis of conflict between the existing distribution of settlement and the land use designations of the District Outline Plan (Architect Ari Cohen)

From the above discussion we can draw three conclusions:

» Though about 50-70% of cases show a gap between the planned situation and the existing situation, there is no essential conflict between the Israeli modern planning and the traditional Bedouin layout.

» Since the main conflicts concern land use designations and criteria for recognizing the settlements, the state should, by making the criteria more flexible, be able to minimize the amount of population that will be forced to move.

» In cases where there is no other possibility, the state will need to create mechanisms that allow for resettlement, which should – as much as possible - adhere to the way of living and the layout determined by the accepted rules of the Bedouin population.

The search for a planning method that will enable the dynamic existence of the organic layout on the one hand, and accommodate the Planning and Building Law on the other – in other words a method that combines Systems A + B - is the challenge before us. This will be discussed in more detail in the last chapter.

4.2 Local scale – creating a space according to arguments of efficiency and maximal density in relation to spontaneous development

One of the barriers to implementing the plans is their lack-of-fit with the traditional way of living and with Bedouin law.

In Figure 11 below, we show one of the unrecognized settlements, located south of the town Kseife (Mtirat family). In the space where the family is living, there is a detailed plan that does not fit the location of existing homes and the current uses of the land. Instead, the plan represents standard planning, in which the main basis for land division is access efficiency and development costs.

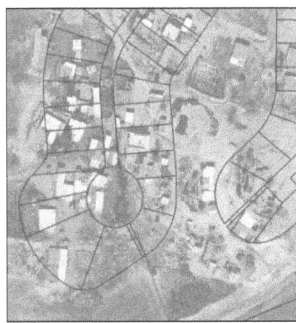

Figure 10: Detailed plan for neighborhoods 15 and 16 in Kseife, in relation to the existing constructions and to ownerships claim (in purple). The existing planning does not accommodate the traditional law and this is one of the barriers to implementation.

While the unrecognized settlement is built according to the traditional principles (as discussed above), this plan, built according to principles of efficiency and regularity, does not allow the community to actualize the way of living it desires. Hence, the Bedouin communities refuse, in many cases, to move into the planned areas that are offered to them. They are then defined as „troublemakers" by the administration, and as a result are under continual threat of demolition for every new building they construct.

5. Combining System A & System B – Few examples

In the pages above, we saw the contradictions and conflicts that exist between the two systems: the Israeli-modern planning and development system vs. the decision making and space creating system in the unrecognized Bedouin settlements. As can be seen – there are several essential conflicts between the two systems, which are one of the major reasons for the fact that today, in 2015, more than 100,000 Bedouin citizens still live in unrecognized settlements.

During the last few years, the state of Israel is changing its approach, and new ideas of planning that is adjusted to community needs have found expression and are being promoted by the state through professional planning teams. It is possible to see, in the work of those planning teams, an attempt to create an alternative method – SYSTEM C – one that follows the Israeli Planning and Building Law but accommodates the Bedouin law as well.

In the following sections we present some examples of the bridging that is being attempted.

5.1 Modern plans that contain the non-regular fabric and enable the continuity of communal functioning, while adjusting to the Israeli planning and building law

In some cases, in which an existing settlement was recognized, it was decided to leave the existing structures in their place and create a modern plan that contains the settlement as it is, as part of the new planning. Since these plans are recent, there is no follow-up yet of their implications for development, for construction in the settlement, or for the functioning of the community living there. However, these plans are an example of the flexibility that is possible within the modern system, in a way that contains the traditional layout.

Figure 12 below is an example of a detailed plan, drawn up by arch. Eli Ilan, for a new neighborhood in the settlement of Kasser A-Sir. As you can see, the architect is making a great effort to preserve the existing structures and also to allow the continued functioning of the settlement, partly relinquishing values like efficiency of layout and infrastructure in favor of keeping the communal structures and the continuation of the settlement's functioning.

Figure 11: Detailed planning of a new neighborhood – allows continuation of the settlement and the community and keeps the traditional structure (Arch. Eli Ilan)

5.2 Plans for resettlement of residents who are forced to evacuate their current place that are based on the Bedouin traditional law and on a process of participatory planning

As discussed above, at least 10% of the residents of the unrecognized Bedouin settlements, and perhaps many more, will have to relocate their communities. We would like to present here the work of a planning team's attempt to create a plan that, despite the discontinuity of settlement, responds to the residents' needs and follows Bedouin law as well as the Israeli planning and developing law – SYSTEM C.

Figure 13 shows a plan for a new neighborhood in the settlement of Abu-Krinaat (Arch' Ari Cohen). The neighborhood is planned for several dozen families that will be forced to evacuate their land for the benefit of a new industrial area. In a process that took several months, the residents – with the help of the planners – defined the program for the plan and the future physical outline in a way that accounts for both the rules accepted by the community and the Israeli planning and development laws. The participatory process is a first stage, which may ultimately facilitate the success of the future settlement.

The plan is currently under review, both with the residents and with the planning committees, and therefore we cannot yet present the final product. But at this stage it is possible to see that in accordance to the request of the tenants, the creeks were kept as natural and agricultural spaces, the residential areas define separate familial compounds and allow for buildings with common family yards that have one façade that is public-commercial along the main road or around the common creek and the open public spaces in it. The public structures that are assigned to women and children, like an occupational center for women and nursery schools, as well as a playground, soccer field, and an area in which it is possible to establish a tent for weddings and funerals, are located in the internal part of the neighborhood, in a way that allows free mobility for women and children.

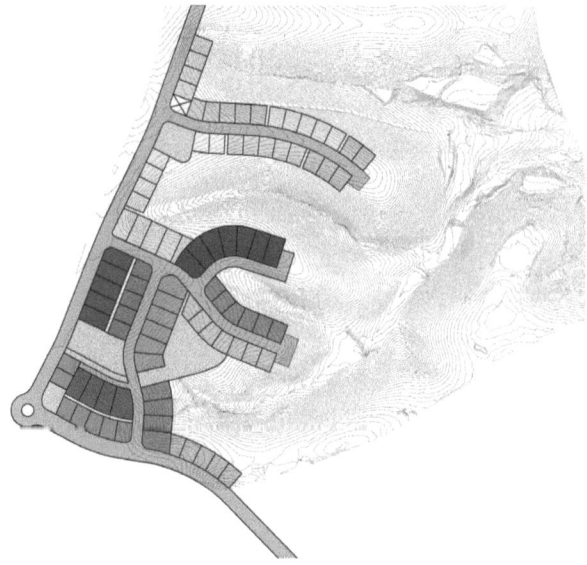

Figure 12: Detailed planning of a new neighborhood – keeps the traditional structure and follows the Israeli law of planning and the acceptable density. The colors represent internal subdivisions to sub-groups (Arch. Ari Cohen)

6. Summary

The relationship between the unrecognized Bedouin settlements and the Israeli planning and development system is a distinct test case of the problematic intersection between System A and System B. In this paper we presented the Bedouin spatial code, on which the spatial-social patterns are based, and the conflicts created between this code and the Israeli-modern system of planning and development. As was presented here, in some cases the difference between the systems is not necessarily conflictual, while in other cases there is a conflict. In many cases, the conflict is so extreme that it creates a complete system paralysis, which is preventing the regularization of more than 100,000 tenants of the unrecognized settlements.

We contend that the two systems – both Bedouin and Israeli – are based on a series of rules, laws and regulations, and that both contain values such as efficiency, economy and use of modern technologies. Also, both systems contain mechanisms the goal of which is the protection and integration of the natural environment and finding a balance between man and environment and between different interest groups. According to this, it is possible and worthwhile to try to create a common ground, as wide as possible, that will be a new system – SYSTEM C. This new system will represent, as much as possible, both the principles of the Bedouin spatial deployment and the principles on which the Israeli planning and building law is based. Making such a new system possible will require an essential change - a change in the process of creating places.

The first necessary change is a change in the mechanism of decision making. As was presented in the examples here, some attempts at are already being made to engage in participatory planning, which integrates the residents in the process of planning and leads architects to make significant efforts to adjust their planning to the community's needs. On the whole, however, tenants today are not part of the decision making mechanism itself and are not represented directly in the planning committees. Also, the attempts made by the State of Israel to accelerate the process have, in many cases, created internal conflicts between the residents themselves, or have not allowed for any participation on their part.

We believe that the two systems – both the traditional system and the modern system – can and must be flexible, in order to bridge the conflicts that exist. The Bedouin traditional layout can find this flexibility in the tools that have enabled the Bedouins to overcome crises and extreme changes in the past, and the modern layout must do so by creating alternative or unique regulation.

We also believe, that the combination between System A & System B is unavoidable, and that at the end of the day it will prove to have been beneficial for all. In contrast to Alexander's view, we believe that direct conflict between the two systems in many cases has the effect of paralyzing both, and does not allow any evolution. It is therefore necessary to try and create as much common ground as possible, as well as an alternative layout – SYSTEM C – that integrates between the processes of creating places in a way that is both effective and economic, that is ordered and receptive to regulation, but also specific, compatible with place and open to the unique expression of individuals and communities. Or, as Alexander defined it in his previous books (1979): a way that makes places that allow the existence of „the quality without a name".

7. References

Alexander, C. (1979). The Timeless Way of Building. New York: Oxford University Press

Alexander, C. with Neis, H. and Moore Alexander, M. (2012). The Battle for Life and Beauty of the Earth: the struggle between two world systems. Oxford and New York: Oxford University Press.

Atzmon, A. (2013). The policy of settling the Bedouins. The Negev - Starategic challenge for Israel (pp. 50-65). Cener Daniel Abraham S. for Strategic Dialogue. The Academic College Netania.

Ben-David, Y. (1982). Stages in the Development of Spontaneous Bedouin Settlement in the Negev. Jerusalem: Hebrew University. (in Hebrew).

Ben-David, Y. (2004). The Bedouins in Israel - Land and Social Aspects. Institute of Research of land Policy and land Uses. K.K.L. pp.- 18

El Aref, A. (1930). The Bedouin Tribes in the Beer-Sheva District. Tel-Aviv: Bustenay (in Hebrew).

Du Plessis, C. (2000). The Mythology of Sustainable Development and its Place in the Developing World – A Think Piece. Proceedings: Strategies for a Sustainable Built Environment, Pretoria, South Africa. CSIR Building and Construction Technology

Falah, G. (1983). The development of the 'planned Bedouin settlement'. Israel 1964–1982: evaluation and characteristics (pp. 311-32).. Geoforum, 14(3),

Fenster, T. (1999). Space for gender. Environment and Planning D: Society and Space. Volume 17. (pp 227-246).

Havakuk, Y. (1986). From the House of Hair to the House of Stone. Jerusalem: Maarachot Press, Ministry of Defense, Government of Israel (in Hebrew).

Marx, E., Meir, A. (2005). Land, towns and planning: The Negev Bedouin and the State of Israel. In Geography Research Forum 25,(pp. 43-61) (In Hebrew).

Meir, A. (2003). From planning advocacy to independent planning: The Negev Bedouin on the path to democratization in planning. Negev Center for Regional Development, Ben-Gurion University of the Negev, Beer-Sheva.

Rosner, Y. (2013). The Unrecognized Bedouin Villages - Internal Spatial Order as a Basis for Future Development. MA Thesis, Beer sheva. Ben-Gurion University of the Negev (in Hebrew)

Rosner, Y., Rofe, Y., Abu-Rabia-Queder, S. (2013). The Unrecognized Bedouin Villages – Internal Spatial Order as a Basis for Development. Correia, M., Carlos, G., Rocha, S., (eds).(pp 531-537). Vernacular Heritage and Earthen Architecture..

Shmueli, D. F., Khamaisi, R. (2011). Bedouin Communities in the Negev. Journal of the American Planning Association. 77: 2, (pp 109-125).

Yehudakin S. (2007). The Unrecognized Villages: Recognition & Equal Rights. Jerusalem: Bimkom, The Arab Center For Alternative Planning, The Regional Council For The Unrecognized Villages Of The Negev.

Yiftachel, O. (2008). Studying Naqab/Negev Bedouins – Toward a colonial paradigm? HAGAR: Studies in Culture, Polity and Identities, 8 (2), (pp.83-108).

Yiftachel, Baruch, Abu-Samur, Shir, & Ben-Arie, (2012). Master Plan for Recognition the Unrecognized Bedouin Villages in the Negev. Jerusalem: Bimkom – Planners for Planning Rights, The Regional Council for the Unrecognized Villages in the Negev.

Patterns that Emotionally Engage

The Application of Storytelling for the Implementation of Pattern Languages

Sickinger, Richard
Danube University Krems, Austria
richard.sickinger@donau-uni.ac.at

Problem:
A pattern language defines the key problems in a field (e.g. architecture) and offers the one best solution for each of these problems. The challenge: Even though pattern languages offer highly effective solutions, many of these solutions are not being put into practice, they are not being applied in daily life.

Findings:
I demonstrate that the utilization of a key attribute of all patterns, combined with a storytelling method, leads to an emotional engagement and a high rate of implementation of patterns.

Conclusions:
Pattern languages which define the key problems in a field and offer the one best solution for each of these problems are not enough for a broad reception of the pattern approach. Patterns and whole pattern languages must be designed in such a way so that people are emotionally engaged and apply them due to intrinsic motivation.

Pattern; Pattern Language, application; motivation; pedagogy;

1. Enabling people to create coherence

For Christopher Alexander the key to to social change in general and to a community that is alive and whole in particular, is a culture that is „made by all people in society" - specialists and laymen - and thereby „these people share a common pattern language" (Alexander, et al., 1977). The more each pattern of the pattern language is implemented and the people in the community participate and contribute to the building of a society which is alive and whole, the more they share a common language, identifying and feeling part of this community and experiencing it as theirs. The conceptual foundation for a coherent, holistic society is laid.

Christopher Alexander's lecture at the OOPSLA Conference in 1996 underlines this approach. He states "So, it (a pattern) is a really useful vehicle of communication. ... However, that is not all that pattern languages are supposed to do. The pattern language that we began creating in the 1970s had other essential features. First, it has a moral component. Second, it has the aim of creating coherence, morphological coherence in the things which are made with it. And third, it is generative: it allows people to create coherence, morally sound objects, and encourages and enables this process because of its emphasis on the coherence of the created whole." (Alexander, 1999)

For Alexander, enabling people to create coherence, to have them develop their solutions based on the core of the solution found in each pattern, to have them identify with the pattern language and experience it as their own language, or even develop their own pattern language, is a key to the success of pattern languages and the formation of a new quality of society which is alive and whole.

This plan did not advance accordingly. In a "Commentary for Readers of The Nature Of Order, Book 2" Alexander states his objective "to move towards a world in which all the people of the world, together, make the world beautiful." But instead: "Architects believed that, as they were, ultimately, they could absorb the content of the patterns and put that to work in buildings and communities - and that they would be able to do this without harm to the paradigm that keeps architecture going, without harm to the paradigms of professional planning, or construction, or banking, or architectural education. In short, the patterns, nice little ideas, could be eaten, crunched up and digested, and then become part of the great machine of architecture, without really changing it." (Alexander, n.d.)

2. The problem: pattern languages are not being put into practice

A pattern language defines the key problems in a field and offers the one best solution for each of these problems. Even though many of these solutions are highly effective, observations made in the pattern language communities show that many pattern languages are not being put into practice. They have not become established in daily life. Douglas Schuler raises the important question: „What can be done to make the pattern content more accessible? What kind of outreach would be useful in getting the word out with the patterns? What kind of training would help people use the patterns?" (Schuler, 2008)

Knowledge is not enough, knowledge must be accessed and applied. Connecting knowledge with action is one of the challenges of our century. Even more so with the knowledge imparted by the pattern language approach. To assure that patterns are put into practice, it is necessary that they can be easily accessed, easily understood and willingly used by both specialists as laymen. The given structure of a pattern offers important elements for reaching this goal: A meaningful and highly descriptive name of the solution, an illustrative and emblematic picture and the identifiable iterative format help to access a pattern. But these elements do not provide per se the intrinsic motivation needed to implement a pattern.

I will demonstrate how a key attribute of all patterns, a solution which can be used „a million times over, without ever doing it the same way twice" (Alexander, et al., 1977) can be applied in a manner which enables a new quality of motivation for implementing a pattern.

3. A new approach

Alexander states as an important aspect of a pattern the following: „a pattern describes a problem which occurs over and over again in our environment, and then describes the core of the solution to that problem, in such a way that you can use this solution a million times over, without ever doing it the same way twice." (Alexander, et al., 1977)

This means that the core of the solution is defined in such a manner that e.g. the designer of a building is given the freedom to solve the problem by himself, in his own way, by adapting it to his preferences, and the local conditions at the place where he is designing it. By limiting the core of the solution to *"what* is to be done" the pattern enables the designer to experience himself as a free agent by giving him the freedom to decide *"how* it is to be done." This makes a pattern authoritarian in principle but democratic in the implementation and gives the designer the experience of being a co-worker and partner in the execution of the pattern.

Now let us turn this approach around and let us accentuate the concrete implementation of the solution, the "how it was done", first: this gives us a story documenting how the designer put the solution into practice. He would tell us about his problem, how he effectuated the pattern, how he detailed the solution and the advantages the solution bought him. Imagine we would collect a number of these implementations, from different designers, giving us a collection of short stories documenting different ways a solution can be implemented. Of course these stories would not be boring treatises but suspenseful narratives: e.g. how difficult it was to find a solution. And all these stories would accentuate and reinforce the core of the solution, making it attractive and emotionally appealing.

Each pattern would be linked to a corresponding collection of present-day stories, with each story proving how valuable and practicable the pattern is. The impact of the stories is to emotionally engage designers and to enable them to implement the patterns due to intrinsic motivation.

4. A model case-study for this new approach

A model case-study for this new approach is an Austrian magazine which applies the method to motivate readers to put family-affirming patterns into practice. The Austrian magazine "Familie als Berufung" ("Family A Vocation") is a quarterly periodical, written for families by married couples. The magazine sets a focus on the practical implementation of family life based on the pedagogy of Josef Kentenich, a pedagogue, educator and priest, with the objective of creating coherence in personal and social life.

Each issue of the magazine consists of three or four topics, dealing with select, current challenges (problems) of family life, which are of relevance to the readers. Each topic consists of two basic elements: firstly, a pattern - in the form of a structured article, but not the problem-solution format of Alexander - describing a problem which occurs over and over again in family life, and then describing the core of the solution to that problem. Secondly, a collection of short stories - five to ten true life events - relating actual experiences in using the solution, described by the pattern, in different ways.

The collection of short stories has a two-fold impact. Firstly, the short stories result in making the solution, proposed by the pattern, attractive to the reader. The reader experiences the power of the solution due to the quantity and variety of different possible applications documented in the short stories. The detailed story-telling also conveys the viability of the solution – the solution is not just a theory but can really be applied. The number of stories allow for a wider access to the solution. Each story addresses different readers, the diversity of the stories enables a better fit of the solution to a wide range of readers.

Secondly they let the reader emotionally connect with the solution which is important for identifying with a solution. The reader connects with the families in the stories, the willingness to accept the solution is given. The reader gets involved with the story and can identify with the solution. Through reading the different stories of a solution, the solution grows on the reader.

The altogether effect of the stories is that the intrinsic motivation of the reader to apply the solution is activated and consequently the probability of putting the pattern into practice is increased.

5. The efficacy of the approach

To measure the efficacy of this approach, a cross-sectional telephone survey of 115 subscribers (4.3% of total) was taken. The survey results revealed the following: 87% of the readers of the magazine felt connected with other readers of the magazine. 72,2% of the readers have implemented a pattern in their daily life. 64,3% of the readers have imparted a select pattern to non-readers of the magazine (Leibrecht, n.d.).

6. Conclusion

The survey indicates a large willingness of the readers of the magazine "Familie als Berufung" to engage with, implement and impart the solutions documented in the magazine. This demonstrates that the utilization of a key attribute of all patterns: that the core of the solution can be applied in many different ways, combined with a storytelling method, leads to an emotional engagement and a high rate of implementation of patterns. This is a possible answer for the important question how pattern content can be made more accessible.

7. References

Alexander, Christopher; Ishikawa, Sara; Silverstein, Murray (1977): A pattern language. New York: Oxford University Press, p.x.

Alexander, C. (1999). The Origins of Pattern Theory: The Future of the Theory, and the Generation of a Living World. IEEE Software, 16(5), 71–82. doi:10.1109/52.795104. Lecture at the 1996 ACM Conference on Object-Oriented Programs, Systems, Languages and Applications (OOPSLA)

Alexander, C. (n.d.). A Commentary for Readers of The Nature Of Order, Book 2

Schuler, D. (2008). Liberating voices. Cambridge, Mass.: MIT Press, pp.542

Leibrecht, Susanne. (n.d.) „Familie als Berufung" Survey.

The PURPLSOC Conference 2015